Yechiam Weitz

THE MAN WHO WAS MURDERED
The Life, Trial and Death of Israel Kasztner

Yechiam Weitz

THE MAN WHO WAS
MURDERED TWICE

The Life, Trial and Death of Israel Kasztner

Translated from the Hebrew by Chaya Naor

Yad Vashem ★ Jerusalem
The International Institute for Holocaust Research

Yechiam Weitz
Ha'Ish SheNirtzach Pa'amayim

Language Editor: Ora Cummings
Production Editor: Gayle Green

P.O. Box 3477, Jerusalem 91034, Israel
publications.marketing@yadvashem.org.il
First published in Hebrew by Keter Publishing House, Ltd., 1995

ISBN 978-965-308-390-5

Typesetting: Judith Sternberg
Produced by: Offset Natan Shlomo Press, Jerusalem

Printed in Israel 2011

To the memory of my beloved friends
Shmuel Almog (1926–2008)
and David Bankier (1947–2010)

Contents

Acknowledgements

Many people assisted me in preparing this book for publication in English: Chaya Naor who devotedly translated the manuscript; Dr. Sarah Bender who assisted me in finding a worthy publisher; Professor Dan Michman who helped me update the English version; Professor Judy Baumel-Schwartz who always agreed to help me with questions pertaining to the English language; Dr. Bella Gutterman, the Director of the International Institute for Holocaust Research; the staff of the Yad Vashem Publications Department who always agreed to help me with anything having to do with the book; and to the book's editors, Ora Cummings and Gayle Green, who turned the manuscript into flowing, readable prose. My deepest appreciation to the Reuven Hecht Foundation, headed by Professor Yoav Gelber, and the Littauer Foundation, for their financial assistance in the translation. My thanks to them all!

Foreword

Israel "Rezső" Kasztner was buried on Sunday, March 17, 1957. At one o'clock in the afternoon his coffin was placed in the square in front of Hadassah hospital on Tel Aviv's Mazeh Street, where it was soon surrounded by thousands of mourners. Alongside leaders of the ruling party and its Knesset representatives—Knesset Speaker, Joseph Sprinzak; Histadrut Secretary, Pinhas Lavon; Secretary of Mapai, Giora Josephtal and others—were delegations from several kibbutzim—Ma'agan, Kfar Hachoresh and Kfar Hamaccabi—whose members had been the only ones to stand by Kasztner in his most bitter hours. Several of the major heroes of the drama that had gripped the country for nearly three years were also there—Attorney General Haim Cohn, Hanzi Brand and Yoel Palgi. Survivors of the rescue train came to pay their last respects to the man to whom they owed their lives. The crowd of mourners was surrounded by a tight circle of security personnel, most of them in plainclothes. In the wake of the assassination, and since some of the dead man's friends had received threatening letters, the police were taking no chances. Members of Kasztner's family stood in stunned silence next to his coffin—his 80-year-old mother, his two brothers, his widow and his only child, 11-year-old Suzi. The thousands of mourners listened dolefully to the Jewish funeral prayer, *Tziduk Hadin*, against a background of Suzi's muffled weeping. Her mother, who barely managed to contain her own grief, tried unsuccessfully to calm the child. Kasztner's mother, too, pressed her granddaughter to be quiet.

Even on his final journey, things did not go smoothly for Kasztner. It was the day of the Purim festival and no eulogies were delivered; and when the funeral procession made its way solemnly up Mazeh Street to the Bilu synagogue, the black burial society hearse carrying the coffin got a flat tire and the coffin had to be transferred to one of the mourners' buses.

At the synagogue, one of Kasztner's brothers recited the *Kaddish*, in a tear-choked voice. From the synagogue, the funeral procession continued to the Nahalat Yitzhak cemetery. Brief farewell speeches were made in the square at the entrance to the cemetery; the first to speak was Josephtal, who said that Kasztner's life and death symbolized all the tragedies of the Jewish people in the last generation. He was almost overcome with emotion when he said, "You tried to rescue others, but were yourself a victim of an assassin. We bid you farewell, our tormented comrade." One after the other, his close friends parted from Kasztner with promises and praise of a kind they had never expressed to him in his lifetime. "Not only were you innocent of any crime, you were one of the greatest men of the Jewish people," said Alexander Rosenfeld of the Association of Hungarian Immigrants, who ended his speech with the vow: "We shall not rest nor shall we remain silent until your name has been cleared." The journalist Yosef Yambur, a close friend of many years, said that all his life Kasztner had been a dedicated, loyal Zionist, a man of integrity; "we shall not rest until his name is completely cleared." "Kasztner's death sentence was pronounced from the witness benches," David Herman shouted, also vowing to carry on the struggle "until the day when there is justice in Israel and your name shines with everlasting radiance," he said, amidst loud weeping.

Eugen Kolb, director of the Tel Aviv Museum, spoke on behalf of the survivors of the rescue train—that same train in relation to which the judge had ruled that Kasztner "sold his soul to the devil." "A verdict of jungle justice," he termed the way in which Kasztner's life had ended, and in the name of the survivors of the train, who throughout the trial had refused to come out openly in defense of the deceased, he stated: "You have fallen for our sakes, and all of us, whom you saved, owe it to you to clear your memory, not to forget your family, to see to it that they lack nothing, and to tell the history of the rescue as we know it."

The body of one of the most tragic figures in the history of the Jews was lowered into the open grave. With his own hands, Kasztner had rescued more Jews than any other Jew before or after him. Because of what he had achieved and the way he had achieved it, an Israeli court passed judgment on him; and he was murdered shortly afterwards.

After the funeral, the thousands of mourners stepped out into the street, which was filled with crowds of people joyously celebrating the Purim holiday, streaming into the town center to watch the annual Purim parade. "Everything written by the solemn steps of the mourners was effaced by the joyous steps of the merrymakers," wrote the author Moshe Shamir, after witnessing the gruesome encounter of mourners and revelers. "An hour or two later, the entire city was awash with the noise of the [Purim] procession, the laughter and the fancy-dress costumes; and the funeral, with its expressions of grief and sorrow, was swallowed up, and the people never even knew it had taken place, there in their midst."[1]

1 On this matter see: "Kasztner's Funeral under Police Guard," *Yedioth Ahronoth*, March 17, 1957; Dr. Kasztner's Funeral—at Noon," *Ma'ariv*, March 17, 1957; "Dr. Kasztner is Brought to His Final Resting Place," *Davar*, March 18, 1957; "Yesterday Dr. Kasztner's Funeral was Held," *Kol Ha'am*, March 18, 1957; Moshe Shamir, "The People did not Know," *Al HaMishmar*, March 22, 1957; Hanzi and Joel Brand, *Satan and the Soul* (Tel Aviv: Ladori Press, 1960), pp. 205–206; Personal interviews with Alexander Barzel, Kfar Hachoresh, February 13, 1992 and Pesach Rudik, Tel Aviv, May 14, 1992.

Introduction

❝ I was born in Cluj in Transylvania; I am an attorney and a journalist." With these words Israel Kasztner began his lengthy testimony in the Jerusalem District Court. Cluj is the unofficial capital of the province of Transylvania, a region that has continuously passed from hand to hand over the years. Between the two world wars it was a part of Romania, in 1940 it was annexed to Hungary and, since 1945, it has once again been under Romanian rule. Cluj, with its large and flourishing Jewish community (numbering 10,000 at the end of World War I), constituted an important center of Zionist activity.

Israel (Rudolf) Kasztner was born in Cluj in April 1906. He studied at the local *gymnasium* and later at the city's faculty of law. As a student he joined the editorial staff of the Zionist newspaper *Új Kelet*, for which he worked intermittently throughout his life. In 1922, still a high school student, Kasztner joined the Zionist youth movement, Barisia, and soon became one of its most active members.[1] From 1930–1932, a shift took place in the Transylvanian Zionist movement, and the older, conservative leadership was replaced by a younger membership with pioneering, left-wing Socialist tendencies. Aged 26 by then and ten years older than the younger members, who were dubbed the "fledglings of Barisia," Kasztner became a leader in the movement. One of these "fledglings" was Emil Nussbacher, who later changed his name to Yoel Palgi. Kasztner, commonly known as "Rezsö," made a strong and indelible impression on his younger charges in the movement, many of whom later immigrated to Israel, where they founded Kibbutz Ma'agan, on the shore of the Sea of Galilee. One of these, Rivka Bar-Yosef, later commented on Kasztner's penchant for attaching himself to people in high positions in order to solicit their support. According to Bar-Yosef, Kasztner was the "lobbyist" for the Zionist movement in Transylvania, and had close relations with Romanian politicians on all levels, a status that granted him a special, respected position in the Zionist movement and boosted his ego. On the other hand, it sometimes caused problems, especially because of his tendency to glibness; he wasn't

---

1   Hillel Danzig, "The Zionist Movement in Transylvania," *Encyclopedia of Jewish Communities in Romania*, vol. 2 (Hebrew) (Jerusalem: Yad Vashem, 1980), p. 39.

always precise in the things he said and often made promises he couldn't keep. Bar-Yosef asserts that his glibness earned Kasztner quite a few enemies, for in spite of his obvious sharp wit and shrewdness, he was sometimes too smart for his own good and was never reluctant to hurt someone's feelings for the sake of a good pun or a droll quip. He was rarely willing to pass up the chance to make a biting remark and this turned people against him.

According to the journalist David Giladi, Kasztner's devotion to the Zionist cause created the impression that:

> [...] he would develop into a leader with a strong personality, who would one day set the tone among the country's 150,000 Jews. Public activity was Kasztner's lifeblood and he appeared on every stage where people were speaking about the Jewish national revival. And people listened to him because he spoke forcefully and his arguments were astute.

The fact is that "fate spoiled Rezsö early on, dealing him a plethora of premature successes that went to his head and caused many of his contemporaries to see him as overbearing and turn many who had been fond of him into his enemies." [2] Still, Kasztner never made a profession of his public activity nor did he base his livelihood on public funds. He earned his living and his fame from his work as a journalist, particularly for the political reportage in which he specialized.

In 1937, Kasztner married Elizabeth (Bodiya) Fischer, daughter of a wealthy, highly respected family in Cluj. Immediately after the marriage, he was assigned a discrete task—to bring an end to the relationship, which the family opposed, between Bodiya's younger sister, Vitza, and her ardent suitor, Emil Nussbacher (Yoel Palgi). Kasztner successfully accomplished this task, but Yoel, who called Vitza "the love of his life," was broken-hearted. As for Vitza, she immigrated to Palestine soon afterwards and met and married Pesach Rudik.

However, Kasztner was unable to enjoy the benefits of his alliance with one of the most highly respected Jewish families in Transylvania for very long. In 1940, his life took a dramatic turn, when Transylvania was divided between Romania and Hungary, and 164,000 of Transylvania's 200,000 Jews found themselves in the part annexed to Hungary. Most of them were pleased

---

2 David Giladi, "When Kasztner Was the Same Age as His Assassins," *Ma'ariv*, March 8, 1957; Rivka Bar-Yosef, personal interview, Jerusalem, September 3, 1992; Zvi Herman, personal interview, Haifa, July 3, 1992.

by this development, because they felt a strong link to the Hungarian culture and language, but their optimism was not borne out by the coming events. Soon after the Hungarian military administration entered Transylvania, a series of anti-Jewish laws were enacted. The Zionist movement also suffered at the hands of the new regime. When the Hungarians entered Cluj, they ordered all the institutions of the national Zionist organization in Transylvania to cease their activities, and also closed down the *Új Kelet* newspaper. Now deprived of their jobs, some of the paper's journalists packed up and moved to Budapest. Among these was Israel Kasztner.

In Budapest, Kasztner found himself in a situation he had managed to avoid in Cluj. He was now a "professional Zionist," making a living from his Zionist activity, a position that did not earn him much esteem among the local Jews. In June 1940, the Ministry of the Interior dissolved all the Zionist organizations in the country, except those in the capital, where the small Zionist movement in Budapest, headed by Ottó Komoly, was the only one in Hungary permitted to operate. While Komoly represented the organization in its contacts with the government or outside agencies, Kasztner was the dominant figure in it. The faction within the organization that he belonged

Israel Kasztner (on the left) talking with Ottó Komoly, 1944
Yad Vashem Photo Archive (YVPA), 1869/1014c

Elizabeth (Bodiya) Kasztner
Courtesy of Suzi Kasztner-Michaeli

to was the Ihud Haolami,[3] whose main activity was to provide aid to Jewish refugees fleeing Poland and Slovakia to relatively safe Hungary.

In the spring of 1942, masses of refugees from Slovakia poured into Hungary and the small Zionist movement there had to bear the almost single-handed burden of helping them. One of its first measures was to set up a new body called "The Aid and Rescue Committee," known simply as "the Committee." Ottó Komoly chaired the committee, but in fact three men ran it: Joel Brand, Israel Kasztner and Samuel Springman. None of the three was Hungarian. Moshe Schweiger, who had come to Hungary from Yugoslavia, joined them. His main task was to settle any differences among the three heads of the committee.

Relations between the two centers of power in the Budapest Zionist movement—the Aid and Rescue Committee and the Palestine Office,[4] were tense and antagonistic. The two had to deal with the crucial problems facing the Jewish community—immigration and refugees. Moshe Krausz, a member

---

3   Literally, the 'world union,' the name by which the Mapai party and its representative in the World Zionist Organization was known in the Diaspora.

4   The office representing the World Zionist Organization (WZO). On the basis of various criteria, its aim was to organize immigration and to allocate immigration certificates, which the Jewish Agency received from the British Mandate government. Every capital city in Europe had such an office.

of the Mizrachi Movement, headed the Palestine Office and held the key to the immigration permits, which, since they enabled Jews to immigrate to Palestine and, even more important, to get out of Europe, grew more valuable by the day. But Krausz, disliked by almost everyone, ran the office as if it were his own private "god-given" property, and was constantly at odds with the pioneering youth movements and the refugees. His relations, even with representatives of Hashomer Hatza'ir, major partners in the coalition that managed the office, were also contentious.[5]

The Committee's relations with the pioneering youth movements were different from those with the Palestine Office. Although its relations with Hashomer Hatza'ir were cool, probably because the movement was on the board of the Palestine Office, the Committee got on much better with the other youth movements. In fact, the Committee's connection with the youth movements was its main source of power and formed the basis for its public recognition. This connection also helped the Committee to forge contacts with the Palestine Delegation in Istanbul, another important source of power, in light of the funds it provided.[6]

Kasztner's activity on the Committee allowed free rein to his tendency to play the role of a public figure, a wheeler-dealer. Brand, whose attitude towards Kasztner was deeply ambivalent, noted how eager he was for honorary positions, however insignificant: "He loved to be elected president or vice-president of any organization, he lusted for honor and tribute [...]; to a certain extent, he had the character of an English lord. He loved to be in the presence of intellectuals and important persons."[7] And whereas Brand, in his work for the Committee, would come into daily contact with "the common people, refugees, smugglers and rank-and-file members," Kasztner was the Committee's "foreign minister." Nonetheless, when Brand nearly collapsed under his heavy workload and its attendant tension, Kasztner was ready to step in and take over so that Brand could take a two-week vacation. "Rezsö Kasztner did not hesitate to take on my difficult work, he stopped his own work, which no one else could do, and began dealing with mine," Brand wrote.

Shortly after the German occupation, the Committee was confronted by a whirl of events that swept it into one of the most fascinating and

---

5 Avihu Ronen, *The Battle for Life—The Shomer Hatzair in Hungary 1944* (Hebrew) (Givat Havivah: Yad Yaari, 1993), pp. 64–66.
6 Ibid., p. 65.
7 Brand, *Satan and the Soul* (Hebrew) (Tel Aviv: Ladori, 1960), p. 31.

Joel Brand
YVPA, 8777/1

heartrending dramas of the twentieth century. At a meeting immediately after the occupation, it estimated that, unless something was done at once, the fate of Hungarian Jewry would be no better than that of their Polish counterparts. The possibility of resisting the Germans by force was immediately rejected, not only because of the ridiculously small number of weapons collected—about 150 pistols, 40 hand grenades and three rifles—but also because of the feeling that in 1944 Budapest the situation was not as desperate as it had been in Warsaw the previous year. Perhaps some Jews could still be saved. The members of the Committee thought the only real alternative left to them was to find an SS officer with whom they could negotiate a ransom payment:

> The decision to try to save Hungarian Jewry by negotiating with the SS was based on assumptions that seemed very logical at the time. In the first stage of the occupation, when the Hungarian authorities absolutely refused to agree to any contact with representatives of the Jews, claiming that the Jewish question was under German authority, the leaders of the Committee concluded that the only chance of rescuing Jews was through direct contact with those who held the real power in the country.[8]

The first meeting with an SS officer took place on April 5; representing the Committee were Brand and Kasztner and they met with SS Officer Dieter

8   Randolph L. Braham and Netanel Katzburg, *The History of the Holocaust—Hungary* (Hebrew) (Jerusalem: Yad Vashem, 1991), p. 339.

Wisliceny and others. The Committee members raised several demands, of which the first was a German commitment that the Jews would not be ghettoized or deported and that those holding immigration permits would be allowed to leave the country. In return for complying with these demands, Wisliceny asked for two million dollars, a tenth of which was to be paid immediately, as a sign of good faith on the part of the Zionists and to prove that they had liquid assets at their disposal.

Towards the end of April, the negotiations took a surprising turn. Eichmann invited Brand to come to see him and offered him a deal: the 'sale' of all the Jews of Hungary, about a million in number, for 10,000 trucks loaded with goods, which he promised would not be used in the war against the West, but only against the Soviet Union. To implement the deal, later known as the "goods for blood" deal, Eichmann was prepared to allow Brand to leave the country in order to set up contacts with the leaders of world Jewry and representatives of the Allies.

In mid-May, Brand left Budapest on his way to Istanbul, accompanied by a man called Bandi Grosz, a small-time crook who was a double, or even a triple, agent for several masters: the Hungarian counterintelligence, the German military intelligence service and others. As far as the Germans were concerned, Grosz, not Brand, was the key figure in the mission; he was supposed to discuss with the West not the fate of the Jews but the future of the Third Reich. This incredible story shows how distorted is the border between reality and hard facts and a world made up entirely of imagination and delusion.[9]

After Brand arrived in Istanbul and told his amazing story to the members of the Palestine delegation, one of them left immediately for Palestine to report on it to the leaders of the Yishuv. With Ben-Gurion's support, Moshe Shertok (who later changed his name to Sharett), head of the Jewish Agency's Political Department, tried to obtain a visa to Turkey where he would meet with Brand. But the Turks, who were not anxious to have negotiations about the fate of Hungarian Jewry take place in their country, refused to grant Sharett a visa, and threatened to send Brand back to Hungary, which, for him would have been tantamount to a death sentence. He had left his wife and children in Budapest as hostages of the Gestapo, and was committed to the rescue mission he had volunteered to carry out. He also realized that he would be murdered as soon as he returned to the area under German control. He finally decided not to return to Budapest. When it transpired that

---

9 About Grosz's mission see: Shlomo Aronson, *Hitler, the Allies, and the Jews* (Cambridge: Cambridge University Press, 2004), pp. 248–261.

Brand could not remain in Turkey and could not return to Hungary unless he had a firm proposal or at least something that demonstrated a desire for negotiations, the members of the delegation decided to bring him to Palestine. At first, the Turks refused to allow him to travel, and he was finally allowed to leave only after the American ambassador in Ankara personally intervened on his behalf. On June 5, accompanied by delegation member Ehud Avriel, Brand arrived in Aleppo on the Turkish-Syrian border, where the British authorities arrested him. Unable to obtain a visa to Turkey, Moshe Sharett awaited Brand's arrival, but was only allowed to see him after four days. Brand was then transferred to Egypt, where he remained in jail until October, when he was allowed to enter Palestine.

In the meantime, the Western powers got word of Brand's mission. The American ambassador in Ankara reported to Washington and the British High Commissioner, Sir Harold MacMichael, who learned about it from Sharett, informed London. Sharett left for London to discuss the matter with Chaim Weizmann and representatives of the British government. The British and the Americans took a dim view of the German offer, suspecting that it was no more than a German attempt to sabotage the West's alliance with the Soviet Union. Nonetheless, they did not totally dismiss it. The Soviet Union, however, after learning about the offer from the Western allies, reacted swiftly by rejecting it out of hand, claiming that "it is neither worthwhile nor desirable to conduct any talks whatsoever with the German government on the said issue." Although the Americans still wavered after hearing the Soviets' position, in the end the West, too, adopted it. The BBC reported on the offer on July 19 in a news broadcast and the next day the story was printed in all the British newspapers, all of whom called it a "monstrous proposal," no less than a despicable attempt to blackmail the Allies and sow dissent among them. Thus, Brand's mission was brought to a halt. Yehuda Bauer wrote about the Western powers' attitude to Brand's mission and their concern vis-à-vis its repercussions:

> If large numbers of Jews had been released—let us say only the first 10,000 or more promised by Eichmann in return for the agreement in principle by the Western Allies—the result would be, in effect, the stopping of some, if not all, military activity, especially in the air, as these people were being gathered and then transported through central Europe. Such a ceasefire may well [have been] one aspect of Himmler's plan.[10]

10 Yehuda Bauer, *Jews for Sale? Nazi-Jewish Negotiations, 1933–1945* (New Haven and London: Yale University Press, 1994), p. 170.

While the allies were wrestling with the issue and Brand himself was languishing in an Egyptian jail, the extermination of Jews in Hungary went ahead at a horrendous pace. This, despite the fact that before Brand left on his mission, Eichmann had promised to halt the deportation of Jews, and to "put on ice" those who had already arrived in Auschwitz.

Brand, who had been expected back in Budapest within two weeks, had disappeared, as if the ground had opened up and swallowed him whole, leaving the members of the Committee in an embarrassing situation. Kasztner and Hanzi Brand, who in her husband's absence had become a key figure both in the Committee's activities and in Kasztner's life, had to try to explain to Eichmann the complications that were delaying Brand's return, and to persuade him to continue with the negotiations regardless. Then there was the Hungarian front; the police, who were very interested in obtaining information about Brand's mission and about the valuables given to the Germans, arrested several members of the Committee, including Kasztner and Hanzi Brand, and tortured them in order to extract information from them.

The Committee members were released on June 2, following six days of interrogation, as a result of SS intervention. Before and after his arrest, intensive, almost daily, negotiations were conducted between Kasztner and Eichmann.

To withstand the almost intolerable tension involved in talks with the devil incarnate, Kasztner had to have enormous courage as well as the ability to persuasively hide his true feelings. The talks, held in the shadow of the annihilation of Jews, focused on an attempt to convince Eichmann to make a gesture of goodwill, which, Kasztner argued, would persuade the Allies that his intentions were serious. In view of the failure of Brand's mission, it was clearly impossible to stop the deportations, and it was best to concentrate on a more feasible objective—to save at least some of Hungary's Jews. The basis for this negotiation was a proposal raised on April 21 by Hermann Krumey, one of Eichmann's top aides, according to which, 600 Jews living in Hungary who held immigration permits to Palestine could leave Hungary for any neutral country or territory under Allied control, except Palestine. Eichmann repeated the offer exactly one month later. The fact that he himself approved this deal had far-reaching connotations—a crack was opened, albeit a tiny, fragile one, in the final solution.[11] Now began one of the weirdest, most highly charged

---

11 Randolph Braham, *The Politics of Genocide—The Holocaust in Hungary* (New York: Columbia University Press, 1981), p. 952.

chapters in the history of Jewish rescue during the Holocaust—the story of the train—that some called the "rescue train" and others called the "VIP train."

Negotiations regarding the train continued throughout June, until its departure on the last day of that month. Eichmann took one more step on June 3 by allowing all the Jews in the provinces who held immigration permits to come to Budapest. He also promised, although this may have been meant as a trap for Kasztner, that he would allow him to bring a special group from Cluj, and 388 persons, mostly Zionists, did arrive from there on June 10, led by Yoske Fischer, chairman of the Jewish Council, who was also Kasztner's father-in-law. The removal of these Jews from Cluj was a highly charged affair, since Jews were already being deported from there; the first transport left Cluj on May 29 and the sixth and last one, on June 13. Kasztner visited Cluj during May, and the question of what he said or did not say on this visit later aroused an acrimonious controversy.

Along with the group from Cluj, the 600 permit holders were housed in a special camp on Budapest's Columbus Street, which was guarded by the SS and was, ironically, one of the safest places for Jews in the very midst of the extermination.

Kasztner conducted the financial aspect of the negotiations mainly with SS Colonel Kurt Becher, whose official job was to supply horses and equipment to the Waffen SS units. In addition, he played a key role in the German takeover of the largest industrial conglomerate in Hungary, the Manfred-Weiss plants. In exchange for the majority shares in this enterprise, the SS undertook to allow 47 Jews from the families that owned the industry to leave for Portugal, and to take large sums of money with them.

The list of passengers for the rescue train constantly grew while the negotiations were underway, from the initial 600, who were added on the basis of their immigrant permits, to 700, when another 100 were added against the payment of money. Kasztner and the other members of the Committee were under colossal pressure. In the prevailing atmosphere of anxiety, hysteria and uncertainty, rumors of the train spread throughout Budapest like wildfire and, as the date of its departure approached, thousands of Jews pounded on the door of the Committee's office, offering all their property for the right to be included on it.

The train left at 1 a.m. on the night between June 30 and July 1, escorted by scores of guards from the SS and the Hungarian gendarmerie. The negotiations over it had been conducted at considerable risk and with a great deal of uncertainty; no one knew for sure whether it was not another Nazi deception and that instead of arriving in a neutral country, the passengers

**Jews that arrived from Hungary on a train
organized by Israel Kasztner, Switzerland, 1944.**
YVPA, 4613/1060

would end up in Auschwitz. But after a ten-day journey, the train arrived at Bergen-Belsen, where the passengers were placed in a separate wing. The first group of 318 persons left for neutral Switzerland on August 21; all the others left on December 3.

Who were the passengers and how were they selected? Eugen Kolb described the group as being quite varied:

> About three-quarters were from Hungary, the rest from Transylvania, in particular from Cluj. There were Zionists, members of non-religious, anti-religious and religious Zionist youth groups, adult Zionists, non-Zionists and anti-Zionists, wealthy men and Satmar Chasidim—a kind of cross-section of Hungarian and Transylvanian Jewry.[12]

There were three main groups. The first comprised Zionists and members of the pioneering youth movements and included some of the main leaders of the Zionist movement in Hungary and their families. Quite a few of Kasztner's

12 Eugen Kolb, "Bergen-Belsen Diary," *Yalkut Moreshet* 57 (Hebrew) (May, 1994), pp. 120–121.

relatives—his wife, father- and mother-in-law, and ten other close relatives—were on the train. The second group consisted of the 388 from Cluj, as well as rabbis, some of them outspoken anti-Zionists, writers, journalists, artists and scientists. The third group was made up of wealthy Jews who financed a large portion of the ransom paid to the SS. It was their money that made it possible to hand over to the SS three suitcases full of gold, diamonds, and other valuables, a precondition for the train's departure. The task of selecting the passengers was not assigned to one man; each group chose its people separately.

With the departure of the train, the Zionist movement in Hungary was left without leaders. Only Ottó Komoly, Israel Kasztner and several other members of the Committee remained. Hanzi Brand, too, who was supposed to leave on the train with her two children, stayed behind in Budapest. But the Zionist leaders were not the only ones to leave. Philipp von Freudiger, a leader of the Orthodox community, suddenly escaped to Romania with his family and some of his friends, striking a devastating blow to the Budapest Jewish community.

Not everyone had accepted Kasztner's reasoning, according to which, the major, if not the only, way to rescue Jews involved negotiations with the Germans. Other routes were explored; contacts were established with the Hungarians and with foreign consulates in Budapest, particularly those of neutral countries. Krausz was the man who followed this line. Like other leaders in the community, he had been arrested when the occupation began, but was released a few days later as a result of the Committee's intervention and found refuge in the Swiss Consulate in Budapest. The close ties he established with the Consul played a large part in the success of his rescue effort, which was based on a decision by the Hungarian government, taken under heavy international pressure, to halt the deportations and to permit the emigration of 7,800 Jews, 7,000 of them under Swiss protection. Krausz and his associates interpreted the decision very broadly, claiming it referred to 7,000 families, or about 40,000 people. Since the Consulate was unable to house so many people, Krausz was given a nearby building, which enjoyed extraterritorial status. The building was referred to as the "glass house," since it was made almost entirely of glass.

It was in the "glass house" that Krausz began compiling lists of those who would be leaving. Thousands of Jews, hoping to leave Hungary by this route, besieged the building after the departure of Kasztner's train; the possibility of escaping the country now seemed less of a fantasy. The certificates that were granted said that the holder's name "appears on a collective passport to Palestine and thus until his journey he is under the protection of the Swiss

Consulate." The certificates were printed on official Consulate forms and bore its stamp, but bore no photographs and the Hungarians agreed to exempt their holders from forced labor. At the end of August, when it was clear that there would be no emigration, these certificates accorded their holders a preferred status and a modicum of security. Under the protection of the Swiss Consulate, the glass house became a center for rescue activity, including the production and distribution of false documents and the transfer of Jews to neighboring countries.

The tension between Kasztner and Krausz, which had existed even before, increased during the occupation while relations deteriorated between Krausz and members of the pioneering youth movements. Even though they used the glass house a great deal, they did not agree with the way he was running things, and never forgave him for having hastened to save his own skin in the first days of the occupation.

One of the most difficult, perhaps the hardest and most highly charged, episodes that Kasztner had to deal with during those horrific days involved the three parachutists from Palestine—Hannah Szenes, Yoel Palgi and Peretz Goldstein—who arrived in occupied Hungary. The three, all natives of Hungary or Transylvania, parachuted into Yugoslavia and crossed on foot into Hungary. But their heroic mission failed even before it began. Szenes was arrested the minute she crossed the border, while Palgi and Goldstein, who crossed on June 19, were under surveillance as soon as they stepped on Hungarian soil. Since they were cut off from any source of information for two months, during which they stayed with the partisans, they knew nothing of what had happened to the Hungarian Jews in the meantime. In Hungary, they learned that all the Jews had already been deported, and they feared that no Jews now remained in the country. Only after they reached Budapest did they see Jews in the streets wearing the yellow Star of David badge.[13]

In Budapest, the three parachutists discovered that they were being followed and, not knowing what to do, turned to Kasztner, the only person through whom they could contact the activists of the Jewish pioneer youth movements. This put him in a grave predicament because it was just one week before the rescue train was scheduled to depart. Palgi described their dramatic meeting. After waiting for hours at the door to Kasztner's office and using a fictitious name, he was called in to see Kasztner, his childhood friend, who didn't recognize him. Palgi asked to speak to him alone, and when the

---

13 Asher Cohen, *The Halutz Resistance in Hungary 1942-1944* (New York: City University of New York Press, 1986), pp. 119-121.

door closed behind them, he asked: "Israel, don't you know me?" Kasztner hesitated and then grew pale, his eyes opened wide and he said in a shocked voice: "Yoel, Yoel, are you insane? How did you get here?"[14]

From this meeting, the two parachutists learned about events in Hungary since the occupation. Later, they also discovered that their Hungarian contacts who had helped them cross the border had betrayed them, as they had earlier betrayed Hannah Szenes. It soon became clear that the two young parachutists who had come to Hungary to carry out a lofty mission at great risk to their own lives, had become a burden to the pioneering movements and the Committee and were jeopardizing the rescue train.

Kasztner came up with a daring idea. Since the parachutists were being watched and there was no chance of Brand returning from Istanbul, he proposed that Palgi report to the Gestapo claiming to be a representative of the Jewish Agency. Under the prevailing circumstances, the idea was not totally absurd—the delegation in Istanbul had been thinking of sending Menachem Bader, the Hashomer Hatza'ir representative in the delegation, to negotiate with Eichmann, but had abandoned the idea in the face of British opposition. But the two parachutists had neglected to inform Kasztner that they were in fact officers in His Majesty's armed forces, nor had they mentioned Hannah Szenes, who was already in the hands of the Hungarians. According to Asher Cohen, Kasztner broached the idea because he was entirely engrossed in arrangements for the rescue train, "and was so worried that the whole thing would fall through, that his thinking was probably not entirely coolheaded or logical."[15]

Surprisingly, Palgi accepted Kasztner's suggestion. His decision involved "more than just courage; it was almost a willingness to sacrifice himself for the sake of the train's passengers."[16] Palgi emerged unharmed from his first meeting with the SS, but was arrested later by the Hungarians and kept in various prisons until November. Goldstein was the only parachutist still at liberty. He hid in the 'Columbus camp' with his parents, who were supposed to be leaving on the train. Kasztner claimed that the Germans knew Goldstein was hiding in the camp and had issued an ultimatum: either he turned himself in, or all the passengers scheduled to leave on the train would be transported to Auschwitz. In a conversation between the two men, the details of which are

---

14 Palgi, *A Great Wind a-Coming* (Hebrew) (Tel Aviv: Am-Oved, 1977, second edition), p. 90.
15 Cohen, *The Pioneering Underground*, p. 54.
16 Ibid.

unknown, Kasztner presented Goldstein with a dreadful dilemma. Goldstein turned himself in to save the lives of 1,685 passengers, including his father and mother.

At first Palgi and Goldstein were held in a Budapest jail; from there they were taken to Pecs from time to time to be interrogated by the Hungarians and the Germans in an attempt to learn their code. Despite being subjected to terrible torture, they refused to disclose their secret. In November 1944 they were sent by train to a forced labor camp in Germany. Palgi managed to escape from the train, while Goldstein subsequently perished in the camp. On November 7, Hannah Szenes was executed by a firing squad in Budapest, the city of her birth.

> The mission of the two parachutists from *Eretz Yisrael* [...] had in fact failed and lives had been lost. Nonetheless, in those tragic days, when we were standing orphaned [and] alone, we found this mission to be of enormous symbolic significance and it will never be forgotten in the annals of the Jewish defense and rescue operation.[17]

After the rescue train left, and it was clear there would be no more such trains, Kasztner opened negotiations with Saly Mayer, the representative of the American Joint Distribution Committee in Switzerland.[18]

The first meeting with him, on the bridge at the Swiss-Austrian border and in the presence of Kurt Becher, was held on August 21. This was after the first group of passengers on the rescue train had been transferred from Bergen-Belsen to Switzerland and Himmler had issued an order that the Jews of Budapest were not to be deported for extermination. Kasztner left for Switzerland on October 27, 1944 in order to conduct the negotiations; a few days later he arrived in Nazi Germany. He never returned to Hungary.

Towards the end of the war, Kasztner was engaged in trying to save any Jews still alive in concentration camps, going from camp to camp, dressed in an SS uniform and accompanied by Kurt Becher, who early in 1945 had been appointed by Himmler as "the Reich's special representative in all the concentration camps." On April 10, Kasztner arrived in Bergen-Belsen. Approaching one of the prisoners, a Dutch Jew by the name of Yosef

---

17   Rafi Benshalom, *We Struggled for Life* (Jerusalem: Gefen Publishing House, 2001), p. 102.
18   Yehuda Bauer, "Negotiations between Saly Mayer and Representatives of the SS from 1944–45," in Yisrael Gutman and Efraim Zuroff, eds., *Rescue Attempts During the Holocaust* (Jerusalem: Yad Vashem, 1977), pp. 5–45.

Melkman, he asked if he knew Nathan Schwalb, the Halutz representative in Switzerland. When Melkman said he did, Kasztner told him: "I promise you that you will all be sent to a good place."[19] At the time, Kasztner was with SS officers from morning 'til night and, while it is difficult to assess what effect that strange experience had on him, it may provide an explanation for some of the things he did after the war.

Kasztner returned to Switzerland at the end of April 1945, as the war in Europe was coming to an end, thus bringing to a close the period in which he had had to cope daily with impossible situations and the most dreadful trepidation. But this was also a time of decision making, a time when he was responsible for determining the fates of many and a time when he was at the epicenter of an unparalleled historical drama. Benshalom described him as an exceedingly courageous man, the only one who dared enter the 'lions' den.' "But on the other side of his courage was a trait I would not hesitate to define as megalomania. After Horthy's speech in mid-October (regarding Hungary's exit from the war), he was really depressed, fearful that if Hungary joined the Allies, he would be robbed of his chance to carry out his grand historical act."[20]

---

19 From Yosef Melkman's testimony at the Eichmann trial, *Eichmann Trial I*, pp. 465–466.
20 Personal interview with Benshalom, Kibbutz Haogen, January 19, 1992.

CHAPTER ONE

Geneva, 1945–1947

I

Budapest was liberated in stages. On January 1, 1945, the Red Army entered the city's eastern section, Pest, in which the ghetto was located, containing most of the city's remaining Jews. Most of our protagonists had not survived. Ottó Komoly had disappeared at Christmas, taken away by the Arrow Cross for interrogation. "No one ever saw him again; even his place of burial is unknown."[1] Joel Brand was in Palestine—a sad, embittered, broken man, who would be haunted by the stinging failure of his mission until the day he died, twenty years later.

Rudolf Israel Kasztner was in Geneva, where he lived until he immigrated to Palestine in December 1947 and where his only child, Suzi, was born.

He lived frugally but in reasonable comfort in the Sergei, an inexpensive *pension*. He had no money of his own and all his expenses were covered by the Jewish Agency office in Geneva.

Israel Kasztner and his daughter Suzi
Courtesy of Suzi Kasztner-Michaeli

---

1   Emil Feuerstein, "In His Nation's Service," Mordechai Arieli, ed., *Natan Ottó Komoly: A Profile* (Hebrew) (Kfar Glickson: Bet Marton, 1970), p. 11.

Occasionally, he would reflect on the dramatic, intensely eventful life he had left behind and he boasted to Pino Ginzburg, a senior member of Hamossad Lealiyah Bet,[2] who was then in Geneva, about his activities during the German occupation. Ginzburg was particularly put off by Kasztner's descriptions of his social relationships, which had included fraternizing with senior Nazi officers. "I found his behavior repulsive," Ginzburg said—not the relations as such, he explained, but Kasztner's arrogant portrayal of them.[3]

Kasztner's future was unclear. He constantly quarreled with his wife, Bodiya, and their bickering became even more intense once Hanzi Brand arrived in Switzerland, when Kasztner made no secret of their intimate relationship.[4] Both mentally and physically, Kasztner, who had been devastated by the horrific drama of Budapest, was a shadow of his former self. Dr. Max Weisberg, his personal physician since 1941, wrote that the man he found in Switzerland was physically enervated and suffering from deep psychological distress; he had undergone a profound change since the German occupation, before which, thanks to his good health, he had suffered from no more than an occasional cold.[5] Aware of his grave medical condition, Kasztner engaged in scarcely any public activity in Switzerland, devoting most of his time to the "Hungarian affair."

Why didn't Kasztner return to Budapest or immigrate to Palestine immediately? The Budapest option was raised on several occasions. In the fall of 1947, for example, it was suggested that he go to Budapest to persuade the leaders of the regime to support the majority recommendation of UNSCOP, the United Nations Special Committee on Palestine, in favor of partition of Palestine. The Ihud Haolami's[6] emissary to Budapest wrote to the journalist Hillel Danzig that he had recommended for Kasztner to "serve as a diplomatic envoy of the Jewish Agency in Budapest. He is ready to travel to Hungary [and] in my view the suspicions regarding his possible activity are unfounded." In reply, Danzig wrote that the thought Kasztner was "the suitable candidate for this position [...] [But], in light of the suspicions concerning his activity in the

---

2   An agency for the coordination of illegal Jewish immigration to Palestine, established in 1939.
3   Pino Ginzburg, personal interview, Jerusalem, January 28, 1992.
4   Hanzi Brand, personal interview, Tel Aviv, December 1, 1992.
5   From an undated report on Kasztner's state of health written by Dr. Weisberg after Kasztner's death. (The report is among the documents of Suzi Kasztner-Michaeli.) Dr. Weisberg, who was among the survivors on the train, has been a resident of Haifa since his arrival in Palestine in 1945.
6   The Labor Party.

rescue attempts, I propose that he go to Hungary with no official diplomatic title and after some time (if his work arouses no opposition) the Jewish Agency will grant him the necessary authorization."[7] However, nothing came of this proposal, either.

Kasztner had good reason not to return to Budapest. His colleagues in Ihud Haolami were sorry he had left,[8] but reported that the social-democratic press in Hungary was disseminating lies about the rescue train, the worst being the allegation that Kasztner and Brand were British spies.[9]

His reluctance to exercise the Palestine option was similarly bound up with vague fears related to his wartime activity. In November 1945, David Ben-Gurion noted in his diary: "Kasztner, Brand's comrade in Switzerland, thinks he is being accused of having been a collaborator. Pino [Ginzburg] wants his status clarified. He is afraid to come to Palestine. I promised Pino I'd appoint a committee to clarify his status."[10]

After his arrival in Palestine Kasztner himself offered a different explanation. Speaking at a reception in his honor, he said he had not come sooner because he had continued to engage in rescue activity even after the war. In a note, written in imperfect Hebrew, he declared that "after all, for a person who was active his whole life in Zionist affairs, my place has long been in the Land of Israel." Why then had he not immigrated sooner? "The answer I will give [...] is closely connected to the role assigned me during of the war; in other words, with the problems of rescue."[11] This reply attests to the struggle that drove Kasztner, to his dying day, to achieve two conflicting goals. The first was to clear his name of the accusations, in some cases vague, concerning his activity under the German occupation. The second was to gain recognition as a national hero, a status he felt he deserved by virtue of that same activity. He had remained in occupied Europe until the end of the war, even returning there from Switzerland, while many other leaders had abandoned the fray. He was particularly incensed at Philipp von Freudiger, the leader of the Orthodox community in Budapest, who had fled to Bucharest in August 1944.

7   Moshe Walter to Hillel Danzig, Geneva, Labor Archives, IV104/89-217, September 5, 1945.
8   See Béla Dénes to Melech Neustadt on the party's situation in Hungary, Budapest, November 28, 1945, Central Zionist Archives (CZA), S53-9; Dénes was the head of Ihud Haolami in Hungary.
9   Béla Dénes to Ihud Haolami in Tel Aviv, May 27, 1946, Labor Archives, IV104/89-213.
10 Ben-Gurion's Diary, Ben-Gurion Research Center Archives (BGRCA), November 3, 1945.
11 Kasztner-Michaeli, undated.

Kasztner's dual struggle was expressed in the dozens of letters, memoranda, and reports he sent from Geneva. In December 1945 he wrote to Eliahu Dobkin, head of the Jewish Agency's Immigration Department, accusing him of starting a whispering campaign against him in the inner circles of the World Zionist Organization (WZO) and Mapai Party. The rumors involved the circumstances in which Yoel Palgi had been handed over to the Germans. In the campaign that was being waged against him and his partners in the 'sacred' work of saving lives, he wrote, it was especially painful for him to discover that Dobkin, of all people, lacked the courage to make his suspicions public. He insisted that Dobkin immediately refrain from "methods of a behind-the-scenes game," asserting that he and his colleagues had the right to know exactly what they were being accused of.[12]

Stunned, Dobkin noted in the margins of the letter, "I am amazed at what he says. I have no complaints or suspicions against him." He made the same point in his reply, adding that he had always had the highest esteem for Kasztner's invaluable work and the heavy responsibility it entailed, and that he had said so plainly on more than one occasion. He had heard of the "investigation" Palgi was demanding, but insisted that he [have] absolutely nothing to do with that."[13]

Kasztner was beside himself whenever he felt that anyone was trying to play down, even slightly, his role in rescuing Hungary's Jews. One such incident occurred when Saly Mayer, the representative of the American Joint Distribution Committee (AJDC, or "Joint") in Switzerland, claimed that through his own efforts the lives of 20,000 Jews, including the 1,700 Jews of the rescue train, had been saved. Mayer's daring was lauded at a press conference held in October 1945 by two leading officials of the Joint. They related how Mayer had negotiated for months with Nazi representatives in order to gain time and possibly save the lives of hundreds of thousands of Hungarian Jews. At one point, the two officials said, "Mayer took his life in his hands and entered Nazi Germany in order to pursue the negotiations." It was while these talks were underway, they added, that a rescue train was organized.[14]

---

12 December 22, 1945, CZA, S6-651.
13 Ibid., January 6, 1946.
14 On this press conference, see: *The Jewish Chronicle*, October 19, 1945.

Kasztner flew into a rage when he heard about the press conference and fired off a scathing note to Mayer.[15] He attacked the claims one by one with the obsessive pedantry that characterized his approach to his work in Hungary:

> The truth is that **we organized that transport**, which consisted of Jews from the provinces who were rescued and brought by us to Budapest; Hungarian, Polish, Slovakian, Yugoslavian Jews—refugees who were in the Hungarian capital. It was **thanks to the agreement we concluded with the Germans in Budapest that they were brought here** [to Switzerland] [emphases in the original].

Kasztner was also incensed by what he perceived as Mayer's effrontery. He described him scornfully as a Swiss citizen for whom the hair-raising experience of negotiating with SS officers was as remote as the chilly towns of Berne and Geneva were from occupied, bombarded Budapest.

"I was obliged to return [from Switzerland] to Budapest," he wrote, "to the mercies of the Nazis and the terror of the Arrow Cross. You, a free Swiss citizen, left that task to me." However, his deepest wrath was reserved for his demands that the lost honor of his comrades and friends, both the living and the dead, be restored:

> All of us, who experienced the prisons of the Gestapo, the police, and the counter-espionage service—the degradation of our human dignity and our Jewish pride—in the name of our dead comrades and for the sake of our colleagues' honor, those who were left alive by the vagaries of fate, raise our voices in protest [...] against the bizarre way in which we have been dispossessed of our work, our sacrifice, and our achievements.

Earlier still, in August 1945, Kasztner described his wartime activity in a letter addressed to "Dear Friends."[16] One of its recipients (apparently Dobkin) wrote on it: "Kasztner reports from Switzerland." Kasztner began the letter by referring to his activity on the Relief and Rescue Committee:

> Much has been said about whether there was any point to that activity, above all about its moral justification and political usefulness. I do not believe that the time has come for us to arrive at a final judgment

15 October 29, 1945, CZA, L22-176.
16 August, 1945, CZA, S6-4560.

concerning these issues. The cause we represented in Budapest was first and foremost and above all else: rescue; in other words, saving human lives. That goal was for us, in the first instance, a series of commitments, which we endeavored to fulfill through all our efforts. In general, I can assert confidently that the first thing that should be written about our effort is that in the liberated areas of the west alone, over 200,000 Jews remained alive, and a further ten thousand were freed by the Russians as they advanced.

In the rest of the letter, which resembled a concise draft of the report he would submit a year later, Kasztner went into some detail about the history and activity of his rescue work: from the "excursion" to Romania through the initial contact with the Germans and Brand's mission to Istanbul, to the rescue operations themselves—the Jews sent abroad, the 30,000 Jews who had been sent to Austria rather than Auschwitz, and the rescue train. Then, toward the end of the war, the decline in the number of Jews sent on Eichmann's death marches following the Szálasi revolt, and the fact that the massacre of tens of thousands of Jews, concentrated in the Budapest ghetto, was prevented. Kasztner felt that he was fighting alone, completely unaided by either national or party institutions: "So deeply am I engrossed in this cause that I will continue to bear sole responsibility for the operation even when the Jewish Agency and the *Ihud* no longer involve themselves because of various principles."

II

In March 1944 Moshe Schweiger was arrested and sent to the Mauthausen concentration camp in Austria. He was freed shortly before the camp was liberated and joined Kasztner in Switzerland, where he tried to work with him. As a popular and respected member of Ihud Haolami, Schweiger began to correspond with its leaders in the Yishuv (the Jewish community in British Mandate Palestine), including Joseph Sprinzak, Melech Neustadt, and others. Two of his favorite themes were the committee's activity and Kasztner's personality. Shortly before the press conference on Saly Mayer's activity, Schweiger described Kasztner's work together with the Rescue Committee:

> And now on a special matter: appreciation for the intense and devoted work of comrades who, risking their lives, dedicated themselves to the

rescue activity and showed the utmost restraint despite their revulsion at having to maintain ties with the Nazi beasts. Are only the shots fired by the partisans' pistols dear to our history and not the modest efforts and prolonged political endeavors, which resulted in the rescue of one hundred thousand Jews from Hungary, or perhaps more than that number? For the sake of Jewish history, we must clarify and take note of what men like Kasztner did, through the party, in these dark times.[17]

"We want you to know," the Ihud Haolami secretariat wrote back (in a letter signed "H.S.," probably Haim Shorer, later editor of the daily *Davar*), "that there is no dispute between us concerning [our] appreciation for the enormously dedicated rescue activity on behalf of Jews, such as that of Dr. I. Kasztner and others. **There is no doubt that the nation will grant them the esteem they deserve and that history will join their actions to those of the ghetto rebels and the partisans in depicting a magnificent heroic episode [in the life] of our afflicted people** [emphasis added]."[18]

There was also a political aspect to these events. In May 1947 a Mapai-affiliated journal[19] published an article claiming that there had been "three attempts at organized Jewish resistance" during the war: the Warsaw Ghetto uprising; the activity of Jakob Edelstein, the "Elder of the Jews" in Theresienstadt; and "the instructive and fascinating attempt by the Rescue Committee in Hungary, [which] can be said [to have] been more successful than its predecessors." The article noted that the central figure on this committee, which was composed of "members of our party," was Dr. Kasztner, who argued that in light of Germany's imminent defeat, negotiations should be held with the highest institutions of the SS and, indeed, those negotiations achieved a great deal: not only by gaining time and rescuing Jews, but also by transmitting valuable military information to the West. The article was a part of an attempt by the Mapai party to undermine the Zionist left's monopoly on

---

17 October 22, 1945, CZA, S44-187. This is an incomplete translation of a letter originally written in German (Labor Archives, IV104/127-216): "I worked with him [Kasztner] for a full year. In a period that was extremely difficult, when Brand and Springman were already in Palestine, I was in a concentration camp, and thus he remained entirely alone working on our behalf in Budapest, bearing the full brunt of worry." Melech Neustadt (Noy) was a senior official in the Histadrut.

18 December 30, 1945, Labor Archives, IV104/127-216.

19 "Hungarian Chapters," *Ashmoret—Journal of the Mapai Young Guard* (Hebrew), May 8, 1947.

the heroes of the Warsaw Ghetto uprising and all other Jewish heroism in the Holocaust; like Kasztner, Edelstein was also a member of Mapai.[20]

In one of his letters, Schweiger described Kasztner's depressed frame of mind, which had induced him to fire off his diatribe to Dobkin. Why was it, Schweiger asked, that if a rescue effort was carried out, "which was a departure from the rescue missions we were accustomed to seeing," was it received with a frosty silence? "Why this secrecy on the part of our fellow party members?" Although Kasztner knows he is being accused, he does not know why or for what, because no one is willing to bring things out in the open: "If he did wrong, let him be told so outright. We hear that he is being accused, but we have not yet been able to find out by whom, of what, and in front of whom?"

> He has turned to you. Who else can he turn to? And what was your reaction? Total silence. Is this any way to relate to the moral positions of comrades who worked devotedly in the most difficult situations imaginable during that period? Why are you so ready to relinquish people like him? Are there many [like him] in our camp?[21]

III

Moshe Schweiger was not the only one heaping praise on Kasztner, while implying vague allegations against him. Yoel Palgi did so too, but he took a different approach. It was Palgi who revealed the fate of Hannah Szenes, one of his fellow parachutists into Hungary,[22] although at the end of the war the fate of another, Peretz Goldstein, was still unknown. His death was confirmed only at the end of 1945. Goldstein's parents, who had reached Switzerland on the rescue train, tried to find out what happened to their son and their hope that he was still alive was based on assurances given to them by Kasztner. On February 17, 1945, they wrote to their son Yehezkel on Kibbutz Nitzanim:

---

20 About Edelstein see: Ruth Bondy, *"Elder of the Jews": Jakob Edelstein of Theresienstadt* (New York: Grove Press, 1989).

21 January 11, 1946, Labor Archives, IV104/89-214. Mapai was a moderate, centrist Zionist-Socialist party, founded in 1930. At that time it was the dominant party in the Zionist movement and in the state of Israel.

22 "In Prison and Before Death" (Hebrew), *Mibifnim* (Tishrei, 5706; September, 1945), pp. 198–200; Hannah Szenes, who parachuted into Hungary as part of a rescue mission organized by the Jewish Agency in cooperation with the British, was executed by the Hungarian authorities in November 1944.

"We were with Perko [Peretz] a few hours before we left Budapest. In the meantime, we have met with Rezsö [Kasztner] briefly. He told us that he left Perko in a safe place under some sort of protection."[23] Others also tried to involve Kasztner in the search for Goldstein.[24]

Palgi, though, became a national hero. In the January 1949 elections to the Constituent Assembly (the first Knesset) he was given the twelfth slot on the Mapai list, although he resigned from the Knesset after the elections to serve in the army. Palgi's book, *Behold, A Great Wind Came*, originally published in 1946 by Hakibbutz Hameuchad Press, immediately found its place in the pantheon of heroic literature. A review in *Davar* depicted it as "compelling in its riveting power and boldness as one of the great books, a shining example of 'man's indomitable spirit.'"[25] Palgi had returned from Budapest torn between his illustrious public image and a gnawing feeling that he had failed in his mission and that his glory was undeserved. People who spoke to him described him as distraught. "He came back from there like someone bearing a cross on his back," a childhood friend said.[26] Palgi himself suggested as much in the second edition of his book: "I withdrew into myself, and deep in my heart the feeling grew that I had returned from another planet, that those who sent me there and the community to which I returned would never fully understand."[27]

He wrote warmly about Kasztner: "Leadership, talent, and a Jewish heart merged in this man [...] I found him to be someone who could be relied upon at difficult moments."[28] At the same time, he blamed Kasztner for the failure of his mission and for not providing him with enough help. Palgi was also bitter about the fact that Peretz Goldstein's parents had been included on the rescue train, while his own parents were transported to annihilation in Auschwitz.[29] And, according to Hanzi Brand:

[...] Palgi's poor opinion [of Kasztner] stemmed from his need to find a reasonable excuse for the failure of the parachutists' mission in Hungary

---

23 CZA, S25-8895. On February 23, 1945, Yosef Goldstein, Peretz's father, sent a similarly worded telegram to his daughter Leah in Jerusalem.

24 Ibid. For example, on May 16, 1945, Melech Neustadt wrote to Nathan Schwalb: "Please question Kasztner regarding the fate of Perko Goldstein."

25 K[arol] Zvi, *Davar Hashavua* (Hebrew), December 12, 1946.

26 Amos Manor, personal interview, August 6, 1992.

27 Palgi, p. 243.

28 Palgi, p. 89.

29 Hanzi Brand.

[...] Palgi [was unable] to resist the temptation to single out Kasztner and the Rescue Committee as the ones to blame for the fact that his mission and the mission of the two who were killed accomplished nothing. But Yoel Palgi knew as well as I did that in Hungary, the objective conditions did not exist for the kind of operation he may have wanted to carry out, and that he was not equipped—either psychologically, materially, or militarily—with the means to implement a mission of rescue or revolt. In these circumstances, the parachutists' mission amounted to no more than a pathetic message of regards from the Yishuv to brothers in distress, a handshake to those going to their death. That is perhaps no small thing, but it was no more than that.[30]

The causes and tangible expression of Palgi's dilemma were actually more complex. He had played the "hero game" out of his commitment to the rules of the ritual, as dictated by both the movement and the nation to which he belonged. According to these rules, the myth of the parachutists was inviolable and had to be nurtured even if this ran contrary to one's innermost personal feelings. In the Kasztner trial Palgi addressed this issue in a subdued tone: "[As regards] my mission, I have serious psychological inhibitions, because my comrades fell and I remained alive at the end. This is not easy for me. I am trying to forget that episode."[31]

The disparity between the heroic image and problematic reality of the parachute rescue operation in Hungary were what characterized the entire operation. Attempts to nurture the parachutists' myth, in particular that of Hannah Szenes, began immediately after the war. Over the years, it has been systematically inflated, not least because of the need to glorify the Yishuv's role in the saga of Jewish heroism during the Holocaust.[32] In Hungary, though, the episode left a bitter taste. Immediately after the liberation the leaders of the pioneering youth movements there summed it up thus: "The loss of dear friends is very painful, and the fact that the operation was organized so poorly is very painful too."[33]

---

30 Brand, *Satan and the Soul*, p. 106.
31 From Palgi's testimony on March 18, 1954, Jerusalem District Court Records, pp. 106–107.
32 See, for example: "The Heroism of the Parachutists" (Hebrew), *Al Hahoma*, November 10, 1954 (an article marking the tenth anniversary of the parachutists' mission).
33 Letter from, among others, Zvi Goldfarb and Peretz Révész, to Venia Pomerantz in Istanbul, Budapest, March 1, 1945, CZA, S25-7865. Pomerantz was a member of the Yishuv rescue delegation in Istanbul.

IV

Writing just before his return to Palestine, Palgi asked: "What brought about the miracle that allowed so many Jews to survive the Holocaust in Hungary, as compared to all the other occupied countries?"[34] He was more explicit on this subject in the first edition of his book: "[Kasztner] was active until the closing days of the war and did great things to rescue our brethren. It was he who approached the Americans with a white flag in the name of the commandants of Bergen-Belsen."[35] And it was only thanks to him that the camp was turned over without a battle and with no further murders [and] with the tens of thousands of Jews who survived in it" (p. 382). This passage was deleted from the book's second edition.

Palgi reserved his greatest praise for late 1947, when Kasztner arrived in Palestine. Kasztner, he wrote, was one of the greatest rescuers of Jews during the Holocaust; hundreds of thousands of people do not realize "that for their lives they have to thank this journalist who left his newspaper in order to make history instead of writing about it." Palgi offered an ardent defense of Kasztner's negotiations with the Germans, castigating "the moralists who steered clear of contact with the Germans, and with their lofty morals did not save [even] one Jewish life during the Holocaust."[36] Nonetheless, Palgi also took Kasztner severely to task. His accusations were circulated in whispers and some of them were apparently written up in the report drawn up by Zvi Yehieli based on his talks with Palgi.[37] Kasztner became an object of suspicion. As Kasztner wrote to Dobkin, "People assume that the attitude toward me is related to the affair involving Yoel Nussbacher [Palgi, Y.W.]."[38]

The subject of Kasztner and Palgi's troubled relationship was raised during the 22nd Zionist Congress, which was held in Basel in December

---

34 "On the Affair of the Defense and Rescue of the Halutz in Hungary" (Hebrew), *Mibifnim* (Tishrei 5706; September 1945), pp. 189–196.

35 Actually, Bergen-Belsen was liberated by the British army in April 1945.

36 "On the Arrival of Israel Kasztner" (Hebrew), *Davar*, December 11, 1947.

37 I was unable to locate the report itself but there is proof of its existence. In a letter that Palgi sent to the Attorney General on February 22, 1956, he noted that as he was writing he had in front of him "notes from remarks I made, taken down by Zvi Yehieli in Cairo, in June 1945." Kasztner himself wrote to Melech Neustadt (Labor Archives, IV104/123, November 7, 1945) that when he was in London in the fall of 1945 he commented on the report to Reuven Zaslani (Shiloah) and Yehieli. Reuven Zaslani was a senior official in the Political Department of the Jewish Agency and Zvi Yehieli was a senior member of Hamossad Lealiyah Bet.

38 Kasztner-Michaeli, undated.

1946. It was also discussed in an internal inquiry committee established by the Haganah, apparently at Kasztner's demand. This is at least implied in the second edition of Palgi's book, where he wrote that he had met Moshe Shertok, the head of the Jewish Agency's Political Department, during his stay in Cairo, before returning to Palestine, and demanded that the Haganah investigate the events in Budapest; and that until then, Kasztner should be barred from holding any public office. "And indeed, that demand was accepted. He was denied a position which had been earmarked for him in the World Jewish Congress" (p. 244).

According to Palgi, Kasztner had defended his motives in the inquiry held at the Zionist Congress: "If he had acted wrongly—he said—he would pay for his mistakes, but he was outraged that he had been branded with the mark of Cain" (Ibid.). The judges, whose names Palgi does not cite, were persuaded that Kasztner's only purpose had been to rescue Jews and that everything had been subordinated to that end. "I found it difficult to accept the judgment," Palgi wrote, in concluding his brief description of this obscure episode.

In his testimony in the "Kasztner trial," Palgi mentioned the affair laconically. The committee, he said, which had been established by Shaul Meirov (Avigur), head of Hamossad Lealiyah Bet, included Israel Galili and Moshe Auerbach (Agami)—a member of Kibbutz Kfar Giladi as well as the organization, Meirov—but "the episode was of no importance whatsoever and I can remember nothing about it."[39]

The only written record of the "inquiry" is a letter from Galili to the writer Hanoch Bartov following an article Bartov published in 1982 about the "Kasztner trial."[40] "I read [the article] fervently," Galili began his letter,[41] which was never sent. "It brought to mind matters which had faded over so many years and even stirred in my memory whispers and facts that I had not thought about for a long time." What memories was Galili referring to? During the 22nd Zionist Congress, Joseph Sprinzak, who was effectively the head of Ihud Haolami,[42] had asked him to take on, for half a day, "an absolutely passive role: to listen, only to listen, without having to draw conclusions.

---

39 Jerusalem District Court Record, p. 97. Israel Galili was a leader of Hakibbutz Hameuchad (United Kibbutz Movement) and a senior Haganah commander.

40 "Kasztner, Tamir and the Evil Slander" (Hebrew), *Ma'ariv*, May 27, 1982. The article was written in the wake of two television programs on the subject, directed by Yehuda Kaveh.

41 Kibbutz Na'an, May 28, 1982, United Kibbutz Movement Archives (UKMA), Section 15, Galili Archive, Folder 2, File 6.

42 Later he was the first Speaker of the Knesset.

Sprinzak did not mention the names of the people to whom I was being asked to listen."

Galili's instincts told him that he "was being asked to hear a story that would not bring joy to the human heart." At first he tried to evade the task, "but I could not refuse Sprinzak." Thus, when he opened the door of his hotel room on the appointed morning, he "was embraced by Yoel Palgi, our emissary to Hungary. Yoel, from Kibbutz Ein Gev [in fact he was from Kibbutz Ma'agan] was with someone I did not know. Yoel introduced him as Rezsö Kasztner, one of the leading activists in the rescue of Jews in Hungary." The three sat themselves down in armchairs and Galili heard out his visitors with bated breath. Apart from a few very guarded questions, he said nothing. But what he heard shook him profoundly. "At times I was barely able to sit still," he wrote decades later. "I got up, walked about, I went out to the balcony; **I felt as though I was sitting on burning coals** [emphasis added]."

Galili was highly agitated when the two went on their way, many hours later. "I was unable to return to the normal world," he wrote. He set down his impressions there and then and, reluctant to assume full responsibility, he called in Moshe Agami as his partner to the document. With a huge sense of relief, he handed the document to Sprinzak the following day. As for his conclusions, he wrote that he had considered two alternatives:

> Either we end it like this, or we fall into a deep abyss and are caught up in a powerful vortex, unable or not even entitled to assume the task of passing judgments, since we can have no conception of the horrors that were described to us verbally.

The conclusion of Galili's letter accurately reflects the spirit of the things he wrote in the document he submitted to Sprinzak.[43] Palgi, he noted, said nothing that "could be construed to personally impugn Rezsö or be taken as a personal accusation." However, its main point was that Galili and Agami could not decide whether Kasztner and Hanzi Brand's behavior in the Palgi affair had been "right or wrong." "This is an extremely difficult task," they wrote. "The circumstances were very complicated. To reach an opinion on this matter one would need to have a thorough knowledge of all the complexities and intricacies of that period, and we do not undertake to make that judgment." This affair, they summed up, was connected with the

---

43 The document, which was written in Basel on December 24, 1946, is now in the UKMA, Section 15, Galili Archive, Folder 7, File B.

rescue efforts "that involved, in various forms, negotiations with the Nazis. In general, it has some unfathomable aspects and we are wary of delving into them without having a thorough knowledge of it and without having heard some sort of accusation."

Galili's reluctance to pass judgment did not stem only from the fear of "falling into a deep abyss." In his investigation of the matter, Reuven Zaslani had concluded that it was impossible to explicitly accuse Kasztner of wrongdoing, and Galili was almost certainly aware of that report.[44] Once the Congress was over, Palgi stopped accusing Kasztner—some say at Meirov's insistence.[45] However, the affair would resurface later, this time without the benefit of secrecy, tact, or discretion.

V

Now back in Palestine and in order to avoid having to answer why and how he had abandoned Goldstein and returned alone to Palestine, Palgi circulated a distorted version of the events, according to which, Goldstein had turned himself over to the Germans. He maintained that Kasztner had asked Goldstein to remain in Hungary too, to improve the chances of getting Palgi released from prison. This version does not allude in any way to a connection between Goldstein's decision to turn himself in and the fate of the train and its passengers. In the epilogue to the second edition of his book, Palgi claims that Yehieli ordered him to disseminate this version: "The British must not be told the whole truth about Peretz's arrest. They will not understand [...] They are liable to use it against us" (p. 243).

Palgi also had an ambivalent attitude toward the other protagonists of the drama. In his book, he described Moshe Krausz as a ridiculous coward. "Moshe K. was [...] a puny Jew with a large head, which sat on his neck in complete disproportion to the rest of his body. His large nose supported a pair of spectacles through which he looked at God's world with a piercing, distinctly unpleasant gaze [...] During the period of the deportations and the tough battle to save Jewish lives, the man hid in holes and cracks. However, he reemerged when things improved, full of wondrous plans [...]."[46] On the

---

44 The conclusions (undated) are found in the Israel State Archives (ISA), FO/4373/8. I am most grateful to Professor Yoav Gelber for bringing this document to my attention.
45 Amos Manor.
46 Palgi, *And Behold, a Great Wind Came* (Hebrew) (Tel Aviv: Hakibbutz Hameuchad

other hand, he described Krausz elsewhere as a resourceful person whose initiative and inventiveness had enabled the rescue of tens of thousands, and had served as an example for the rescue work of others, including Raoul Wallenberg.[47]

VI

Moshe Krausz was also obsessively preoccupied with Kasztner's actions. He was bitterly angry with Kasztner, claiming he had been ousted from his job as head of the Palestine Office because the pioneering youth movements had supported Kasztner's position. Krausz's removal had set in motion a chaotic situation, which lasted for months. On May 25, 1945, Haim Barlas, director of the Jewish Agency's Immigration Department, informed Krausz in writing that a new Palestine Office, to be headed by Dr. Alexander (Shimshon) Nathan (Sandor), had been established; Nathan was the unanimous choice of the representatives of all the parties and movements.[48] Deeply offended, Krausz decided to fight back. Having done good work, he felt he was now being punished and instead of being honored he was being pilloried. A few months later, he vented his resentment, "After 11 years of work, including six spent in exerting a successful, superhuman effort; in honor of my unconditional service I am being condemned and pushed aside. I have served my purpose, and they now have no more use for me."[49]

These developments occurred as a result of complaints about Krausz's behavior during the German occupation; also it was the general consensus of the Zionist parties and movements that he was not the right person to run the office.[50] Outright accusations against him appeared in a report prepared a

Publishing House, 1946) p. 297. (This passage is from the chapter entitled "Hungary's Jews," which was deleted in the second edition.)

47 "On the Affair of the Defense and Rescue of the Halutz in Hungary" (Hebrew), *Mibifnim* (Tishrei 5706; September 1945), pp. 193–194.

48 Dr. Shimshon Sandor Nathan, Oral Documentation Division, Institute of Contemporary Jewry, Hebrew University of Jerusalem, Project 4, Testimony 130 [henceforth Nathan]: "It is possible to say that no one was satisfied with Krausz's activity during the Holocaust period, they were more favorable to Kasztner's stand, but at the same time they involved themselves in the assistance project that was organized under Moshe Krausz's management."

49 Krausz's Report to the Jewish Agency Executive, Budapest, March 4, 1946, ISA, Prosecution Exhibit Number 124, Kasztner Files.

50 Rafi Benshalom, telephone conversation, August 25, 1992. Benshalom was a member of the Hashomer Hatza'ir youth movement.

few months later by Rafi Friedel (Benshalom)[51] for a commission of inquiry investigating Krausz's behavior during the occupation. At the time, Benshalom ran the Palestine Office in Prague, a position he held until his immigration to Palestine in 1947 (a year later he returned to Prague to serve as advisor to the Israeli legation and as Ehud Avriel's right-hand man).

Benshalom leveled a series of general accusations at Krausz involving his management of the Palestine Office, along with complaints regarding his specific actions during and prior to the German occupation. The way in which Krausz undemocratically concentrated all the office's powers into his own hands, Benshalom maintained, had serious derogatory effects on immigration to Palestine. Even in normal times no one person could possibly handle all the complex activity involved in organizing immigration; certainly not under the harsh conditions of pre-occupation Budapest. Moreover, according to Benshalom, Krausz was lazy: "His working day lasted no more than six or seven hours."

The combination of Krausz's lethargy and his pathological fear of delegating authority had created a situation of chaos in the office: "Krausz did not handle incoming correspondence with the speed required. There were hundreds of letters in his office from every part of the country that had never even been opened." However, these accusations paled in comparison to his behavior during the occupation: "We saw Krausz for the last time on March 19 [1944, the day on which the Germans entered Budapest, Y.W.] at a meeting of the Jewish National Fund and after that, two or three times more [...], he then disappeared and no one knew where he was. More than seventy people were ready to immigrate to Palestine and expected him to do everything possible to ensure that they would be able to do so. [But] after March 19 Krausz simply did not turn up at the Palestine Office. The result was that on March 19, 1944 [...] seventy immigration certificates were 'frozen' in the Palestine Office and most of their holders subsequently perished during the occupation."

Another allegation made by Benshalom involved the Hannah Szenes affair. For a long time, her mother, Katerina Szenes, had been trying to meet with Krausz with regard to her daughter but he had refused to see her. He later claimed that had not dealt with the parachutists, which [he said] was a political matter, and was amazed that the daughter of Béla Szenes[52] could

---

51 The report is titled "Writ of Prosecution (*Klageschrift*) against Moshe Krausz, the former director of the Palestine Office in Budapest." It was written in Prague on April 14, 1946, and is to be found in the personal archive of Rafi Benshalom, Kibbutz Haogen Archive, 6/221.

52 Hannah Szenes' father was a well-known author in Budapest.

have become involved in such an affair. According to Benshalom, Krausz did not lift a finger to help Szenes, nor did he discuss the subject with anyone else. In short, he asserted, in light of Krausz's behavior during the occupation there was absolutely no justification for renewing his appointment as director of the Palestine Office after the liberation.

Krausz and the Mizrachi Movement[53] appealed the decision, arguing that it was "contrary to the constitution." Krausz even physically prevented the office from functioning properly by refusing to remove his effects and continuing to hold on to the funds and documents.[54] The office's inactivity immediately after the liberation was a serious matter, liable to affect efforts to achieve a swift evacuation of the survivors. "The push for immigration is very great," a report at the time stated. "A considerable number of the survivors—about fifty thousand—are very anxious to immigrate."[55]

Faced with this situation and in order to avert total anarchy in the office's operation, the parties involved finally reached a compromise mediated by Levi Kopelevich (Argov), who was described as "the representative of the Jewish Agency." According to his memorandum of understanding, both Nathan and Krausz would act as directors of the office pending the hearing of the appeal.[56] However, after the compromise, Krausz behaved like Samson shorn of his locks; some of his lost honor may have been restored, but his dominant status as the all-powerful ruler of the Palestine Office was lost to him.

For years, the insult festered in Krausz's mind. Not only had he been pushed aside after the war, but also he was growing increasingly dissatisfied with his life in Israel, where he arrived in 1953. Under these circumstances, his feeling of having been grievously wronged intensified: "The fact that I am forced to this day—two years after coming to Israel—to live with my wife as a subtenant in a furnished room," he wrote, "is the dismal result of the regrettable attitude of the Jewish Agency for Palestine towards me. It has not yet seen fit to pay me the salary due to me since 1944, although I have appealed to it repeatedly in this regard. The resulting circumstances, which have left me totally destitute, have induced me to approach you [the Supreme Committee for Veteran Zionists], as the representatives of the organization I served faithfully for dozens of years, with the modest request for assistance in obtaining the most elementary thing any person—particularly a new

---

53 A religious Zionist movement.
54 Levi Argov, personal interview, Moshav Kidron, March 13, 1992.
55 Sandor Nathan to the Jewish Agency's Immigration Department, October 2, 1945, CZA, S6-1640b.
56 Ibid., the memorandum was signed in Budapest on July 15, 1949.

immigrant with decades of rich Zionist activity behind him—is entitled to expect, namely a roof over his head."[57]

To the commission of inquiry that was investigating his activity Krausz submitted a glowing personal report.[58] The report's main contention was that Kasztner passed up concrete rescue programs for the sake of his negotiations with the Germans; for example, three days before the German occupation, 600 holders of Palestine certificates in Budapest could have left for Constanza, on the Black Sea, and sailed from there to Palestine. Once the occupation began, this plan could only be carried out with the authorities' approval. Kasztner, who had negotiated with the Germans from the first days of the occupation, could have obtained that authorization, Krausz wrote, but "days and weeks went by and Dr. Kasztner still did not get the promised authorization from the Gestapo." In early May, Kasztner was responsible for Brand's trip to Turkey on a mission for the Gestapo, "but its immediate goal was not achieved." Moreover, Krausz noted, the deportation of the Jews from the provinces began on the day after Brand's departure.

"In view of the hopeless situation," Krausz wrote, "I decided to try other means of rescuing Jews." He looked for connections and rescue channels in the Swedish and Swiss consulates in Budapest. In the meantime, Kasztner kept up his fruitless contacts with the Gestapo. "One day followed the next [...] and the Jews of Hungary were deported from the provinces at an ever faster pace." Following the Allied invasion of Normandy in June 1944, Krausz discovered that "the Gestapo, with its empty talk, was only distracting our attention and lulling our vigilance, and [fully] intended to delude us regarding the [fate of the] Jews." Krausz, therefore, decided to wash his hands completely of Kasztner's activity. And because "at a time when the fate of our brethren is so grave, we ought not to gamble everything on one card," he found other avenues of rescue, which did not intersect or interfere with Kasztner's activity.

---

57 Moshe Krausz to the Supreme Committee for Veteran Zionists, June 2, 1955, CZA, S41-27II.

58 The report, which was written in Budapest on March 4, 1946, was addressed to the Jewish Agency in Jerusalem, c/o Haim Barlas, and was headed, "Memorandum on the Operations of the Palestine Office During the Critical Years of the War, 1941–1945" (*Memorandum über die Tagkeit des Palestina-Amets in Budapest in den Kritischen Kriegsjahren*): Prosecution Exhibit 129, Kasztner Folders, ISA. The report was written in German and the author found a Hebrew translation of the first pages, which deal with the period up to the German occupation, in the files of attorney Micha Caspi.

VII

The story did not end with the conclusions of the commission of inquiry, which exonerated Krausz—for lack of proof. These only intensified Krausz's anger and grief. Exactly two months later the curtain went up on the next act of the drama: the 22nd Zionist Congress in Basel in December 1946. This was undoubtedly the most tragic and painful of all Zionist Congresses; it was the first Zionist convocation after the Holocaust and was held in the shadow of that terrible catastrophe. In describing the opening session, Chaim Weizmann, President of the World Zionist Organization, wrote, "It was a dreadful experience to stand before that assembly and to run one's eye along row after row of delegates, finding among them hardly one of the friendly faces that had adorned past Congresses. Polish Jewry was missing; Central and Southeast European Jewry was missing; German Jewry was missing."[59]

At the Congress, the name of Moshe Krausz and the episodes connected with him were raised almost exclusively in backroom committee meetings, the very existence of which was a well-kept secret from the vast majority of the delegates. Publicly, the subject came up during a special ceremony in the plenum in honor of the Swiss Consul Carl Lutz, who was registered in the "Golden Book" of the Jewish National Fund and praised by Weizmann.[60] Sitting in the audience, as reported in *Hatzofeh*, the newspaper of Krausz's movement, was "a modest young man from Budapest thanks to whose initiative sixty thousand Jews were saved from certain death." Only the Swiss gentile, the paper noted, "mentioned his name and his tremendous work." Because he "is not a member of Mapai [or even] a member of the General Zionists [...] the biased Jewish speakers did not mention his name."[61] Kasztner did not even enjoy that much honor; he had no official status at the Congress and was there as the correspondent of a Budapest paper.[62]

During the Congress, Kasztner made public his report on the operation of the Relief and Rescue Committee and his activity during the German occupation. Some reacted enthusiastically, even emotionally. Mordechai Zagagi, an official of the Jewish Agency's Financial Department in Geneva,

---

59 Chaim Weizmann, *Trial and Error* (London: East and West Library, 1950), p. 543.

60 Evening session, December 22, 1946, Stenographic report of the 22nd Zionist Congress, The Jewish Agency Publishing, Jerusalem, pp. 415–416.

61 Donesh [Shabtai Don-Yihyeh], "Respect for the Rescuers of Jews" (Hebrew), *Hatzofeh*, January 5, 1947.

62 CZA, LK11, Box 11, File 19 (unsorted material).

who was handed the report by Chaim Posner,[63] read it with bated breath and described it as a document "that should [...] be read by everyone living in our wretched generation and everyone who cannot forget what happened to our brethren, to elderly Jews, women and children in this calamity that we now call the Holocaust of the Diaspora."[64]

However, the affair that was seen in a dignified light on the rostrum assumed the form of fierce combat elsewhere. One battle scene was a court of honor, established by Ihud Haolami, probably at Kasztner's urging, to discuss Krausz's complaint against him. The court consisted of three members: Aryeh Kubovy (Leon Kubowitzki), chairman; Binyamin Vest; and Dr. Yosef Meir.[65] It held two sessions, but like another forum created during the Congress (Galili's clarification), it reached no decision. Following its two meetings, the court sent a statement to the executive of the Ihud Haolami faction, the true meaning of which could only be grasped by the initiated:

> In accordance with the proposal contained in your letter of December 12, 1946, we assumed the task of holding an investigation regarding the activity of Dr. I. Kasztner. We held two meetings and heard two witnesses, **one of whom, Mr. Nicolaus Kreuss, could be considered a prosecutor** [emphasis added].
>
> However, we realized in the course of our investigation, that there is a great deal of work to be done and that we would be unable to complete it here in Basel. We heard the two witnesses, but did not even manage to finish the first article of the charge (which contains six articles). We would need a few days of intensive work to complete only the testimony of these witnesses and would be unable to hear the defense witnesses at all. Considering the importance of the subject and the accusations involved, we could not permit ourselves to act so superficially by concluding such an investigation within a few hours; superficiality such as this would border on irresponsibility.

63 Chaim Posner was the representative of the Jewish Agency in Geneva.

64 From his letter to Dr. Neumann (apparently Oskar Neumann, a leading member of the Zionist movement in Czechoslovakia) (date blurred), CZA, A204-25.

65 Aryeh Kubovy (1896–1966) was a senior official of the World Jewish Congress and after the establishment of the state was a minister in the Israeli legations in Czechoslovakia and Argentina, and then chairman of the Yad Vashem-Holocaust Memorial Authority. Binyamin Vest (1896–1975) was active in Hapoel Hatza'ir and afterward in Mapai. He was also a member of the Supreme Court of the General Histadrut (Labor Federation) and active in the World Jewish Congress. Yosef Meir was a physician and served as the director-general of the Ministry of Health.

We decided therefore, to discontinue our investigation and to recommend that it be conducted elsewhere, where the judges can devote considerable time to the matter.[66]

Intensive pro-Kasztner lobbying was going on as the court was in session, led by the two youth movements that consistently supported him and opposed his adversary, Krausz. This support took the form of a letter signed by all the representatives of the Labor Zionist parties in Hungary—not only the heads of Mapai and Ihud Haolami but also by Zvi Goldfarb for Ahdut Ha'avoda-Poalei Zion and Rafi Priedel and Alexander (Shuni) Groszmann for Hashomer Hatza'ir.[67] The letter contained the following declaration:

> To the best of our knowledge, Dr. Rudolf Kasztner, in his capacity as head of the Relief and Rescue Committee from 1942–1945, particularly in the critical period of Hungary's occupation by the Germans, carried out his task with complete altruism and with a readiness to sacrifice his life and the lives of his family. Tens of thousands [of people] should be grateful for the work of his rescue enterprise. We are convinced, therefore, that Ihud Haolami as well as the Zionist institutions will commit themselves to expressing their recognition of his great achievements.

The Kasztner issue was also raised during a session of the Ihud convention at the Congress. Yosef Shefer, a leader of Gordonia-Young Maccabi in Hungary and Ottó Komoly's former secretary, tried to persuade the faction to adopt a resolution in support of Kasztner. "As for Dr. R. Kasztner, whose reputation has been tarnished, he has been seeking clarification since London,[68] and his comrades and friends have been making efforts on his behalf. A special commission has been established by the movement, but it turns out that this is a drawn-out affair and that a great deal of material is involved." Shefer then read out the declaration, "which is favorable to him." The convention "indeed took the statement under advisement," but Shefer's motion was rejected by a majority vote; his was the only vote in favor.[69]

---

66 The Ihud court of honor issued a statement according to which discussions on the Kasztner matter were to cease, Basel, December 19, 1946, ISA, Defense Exhibit B, Kasztner Folders.

67 December 22, 1946, Micha Caspi Archives, Prosecution Exhibit 24.

68 The reference is to August-September 1945, when the first postwar Zionist Convention was held. Kasztner was there in order to make his first statement at the Nuremberg trials.

69 Ihud convention in Basel, December 24–26, 1946, Labor Party Archives, Section 3, 46/21.

In spite of the convention's refusal to adopt Shefer's motion, at the closing session Sprinzak read out a fairly ardent statement issued by the Ihud secretariat in support of Kasztner.[70] It pointed out that the secretariat had established a commission at Kasztner's request in order "to examine [...] the rumors being disseminated by his political enemies regarding the rescue operation in which he was engaged in Hungary." The commission, which had been unable to conclude its work due to the "pressing needs of the Congress and the shortage of time," had approached the heads of the Labor Palestine parties in Hungary "who, together with him, had taken part in the rescue operations [...] or had direct knowledge of them." They were unequivocal in declaring that Kasztner had done tremendous work during the war on behalf of the masses of the Jewish people." In the wake of that declaration, the secretariat announced that the investigation, which had been undertaken at Kasztner's request, had concluded and that Kasztner himself "had carried out his mission faithfully and had devoted his life to saving Hungary's Jews." These events made a deep impression on Sprinzak, as he indicated after the Congress, in a letter to his wife, Hannah: "At the time I didn't want to go to Basel," he wrote. "However, after all that happened at the Ihud convention, I do not regret it [...] I have understood and studied several amazing matters regarding our experience in the Diaspora and the meaning of various episodes of our operations."[71]

VIII

At the same time as Krausz filed a complaint against Kasztner, Kasztner himself submitted one against Krausz to the Zionist Organization's court of honor, whose chairman, Dr. Moshe Smoira, later became the first President of Israel's Supreme Court. In his letter of complaint,[72] Kasztner asked for the accusations against him to be investigated and for a decision to be made as to "whether or not I fulfilled my task with integrity." He explained that he was referring to Moshe Krausz's "charges and libels" against his work and against his former colleagues—both living and dead—and asked the court to determine "whether the behavior of those 'so-called defendants' met the minimal standards of Zionist ethics and Zionist discipline." The very fact

---

70 Micha Caspi Archives, Defense Exhibit G.
71 January 11, 1947, Labor Archives, IV104/127-36.
72 December 16, 1946, CZA, A215-42/1.

that accusations had been raised, Kasztner maintained, undermined Zionist discipline and the Zionist agenda. There were many important people currently in Basel, he added (referring to the letter of the pioneering youth movements), who represented the Zionist interest as a whole rather than just a narrow interest and who could testify that the accusations against him were spurious.

The gist of the accusatory claims to which Kasztner was referring had appeared in a work entitled *The Black Book*[73] and was also included in Krausz's memorandum of March 1946. The main points were that the ties between the Rescue Committee and the Gestapo had been totally unnecessary and caused only damage; that Krausz began to work to rescue Jews when it became apparent that the committee, which had pushed him aside, had failed in its rescue operations; and when it also emerged that in November 1944 Kasztner had traveled to Switzerland in the company of a senior SS officer. Kasztner also noted that Krausz had sent a letter in the summer of 1944 to Chaim Posner and Richard Lichtheim[74] in which he accused the committee of collaborating with the Germans and claimed that the people on the "rescue train" had been sent to their deaths. Kasztner concluded his complaint by citing a list of people who could testify to the nature of his work.

What became of the complaint? The only clue is a note in Dr. Smoira's handwriting: "I hereby appoint Mr. Yosef (Franz) Yambur as an investigator in the matter of the accusation brought by Dr. Kasztner against Moshe Krausz before the Zionist court of honor and request him to hear the necessary testimonies and submit the results of his investigation before the court of

---

73 The book was published in Budapest in 1946. Written by the Hungarian journalist Eugen Jenö, inspired and encouraged by Krausz, it deals with the fate of Hungarian Jewry under the German occupation. (An English edition appeared two years later: *The Black Book on Hungarian Jewry*, Zurich: Central European Times Publishing Company Ltd., 1948.) Kasztner's wartime activity is severely criticized in the book. He is accused of managing his affairs despotically, of never reporting, unless forced to do so, to the Jewish leadership on any progress in the negotiations and that even then the impression he gave was that his report was not credible. Fearing someone might cast doubt on his leadership, he insisted on doing everything himself. The result was that the discussions and debates over the fate and future of the Jews were held as though they were in Kasztner's private domain and of his immediate circle. This behavior, Jenö argues, was not accidental. It stemmed from Kasztner's character: undoubtedly he was very talented, but he had tyrannical inclinations and was jealous of everyone he thought overshadowed his achievements. His ambitions were sky-high—he wanted to be the sole rescuer of Hungary's million Jews—but the lack of any managerial or organizational ability made him incapable of carrying out the mission (pp. 261–271).

74 Lichtheim was the director of the Palestine Office in Switzerland.

honor."[75] Yambur was in Basel during the Zionist Congress and from there he proceeded to Hungary as an emissary of Keren Hayesod. Even people who were very close to him knew nothing about his appointment as an investigator in this affair.[76]

The complaint had the same fate as the other two episodes linked to Kasztner during the Congress, that is, the clarification and the investigation referred to by Smoira never took place. A few years later, by which time Smoira was already President of the Supreme Court, an official of the WZO's Department of Organization asked him what should be done about the uncompleted investigation. Smoira suggested laconically that the whole matter be shelved, as it seemed to him to be anachronistic and of no public interest. "I believe the discussion on this subject can be dropped, since so much time has elapsed and we have had no request to renew [it]."[77] Smoira's reply came a little over two years before the appearance of Malkiel Gruenwald's mimeographed bulletin, which would occupy the public in Israel for many years, as well as the institution of which Moshe Smoira was the first President.

IX

Since leaving on his mission, and particularly since his arrest, Joel Brand's feelings of rage and frustration grew progressively stronger. All his attempts to arouse public interest in his own and his mission's fate proved futile; he may as well have banged his head against a brick wall. His issues were far from the mind and heart of the public. Occasionally he encountered a sympathetic reaction, but an opaque curtain of alienation and suspicion began to gradually separate him from the rest of the world. Describing this feeling in his memoirs, he wrote, "Immediately after my release, I went from one office to the next in Tel Aviv and in Jerusalem, hoping to ascertain what was going on in Hungary [...] and, if possible, to return to Budapest. I encountered a friendly attitude and commiseration, but there was no one able or willing to help me. Everyone understood very well what I was saying, but probably found it difficult to understand what I was asking of them. Also, everyone was too busy with important tasks."[78]

75 December 28, 1946, CZA, A215-48. Yambur was a journalist who was born in Kasztner's native town and had known him for many years.
76 Rivka Bar-Yosef; Shlomo Yitzhaki, telephone interviews, February 28, 1992.
77 November 3 and December 6, 1949, CZA, A215-42/5.
78 Brand, *Satan and the Soul*, p. 76.

His efforts to meet personally with the leaders of the Yishuv all failed. "Well-trained secretaries," he remarked bitterly, "would tell me glibly that their bosses, whom I had asked to see, were out and no one knew exactly when they were due to return."[79] In desperation, Brand began to bombard them with memoranda, most of which dealt not with the fate of Hungarian Jewry but with his own personal plight and the functions he was worthy of fulfilling. In his first memorandum,[80] he demanded that a rescue operation be mounted immediately to save the hundreds of thousands of Jews he believed to still be alive in European countries; he also demanded a major role in such an operation. "It will help matters if I am included in every consultation regarding the fate of the Jews in the occupied countries," he argued. When no reply was forthcoming, he sent another memorandum,[81] in which his demands were more explicit: that he be given official recognition as the representative of the survivors of Hungarian Jewry and included in all discussions concerning that community; that all information, including all the telegrams, pertaining to Hungarian Jewry be transmitted to him; and that he be given all necessary assistance.

In his memoirs Brand emphasized the atmosphere of insensitivity and hostility that he encountered. He described meetings with officials of Hamossad Lealiyah Bet, invariably members of Mapai, who warned him that his life would become intolerable if he did not stop pestering them. "Drop the matter, wipe everything that happened out of your mind," they told him, "otherwise you won't even be able to get a job cleaning streets in Tel Aviv."[82]

The impasse was broken in May 1945. Brand sent a sharply worded letter to Shaul Meirov, which led to a decision to send him to Europe. There he had an emotional meeting with Kasztner: "We exchanged a quick look and embraced wordlessly." Brand found Kasztner in a depressed frame of mind. He looked the same, and seemed in even better condition than he had been in Budapest, but his inner light seemed to have gone out. In Hungary he had been a vibrant personality, brimming with ideas, whereas on the railway platform in Geneva, the man Brand encountered was tired and listless, bereft of ambition, "gray not only in his features but also in his thoughts."[83]

Despite their happiness at meeting there was tension, even hostility, between them. In the background, there was Kasztner's contention that if

---

79 Ibid., p. 73.
80 It was sent on November 19, 1944; Ibid., pp. 73–75.
81 December 7, 1944, CZA, S53-1590.
82 Brand, *Satan and the Soul*, p. 76.
83 Ibid., p. 93.

Israel Kasztner in Geneva
Courtesy of Suzi Kasztner-Michaeli

he and not Brand had gone to Istanbul, the mission would have turned out differently; and then there were the rumors Brand had heard from his niece, who lived in Davos, about an intimate relationship between Kasztner and Hanzi. She had tried to provoke his jealousy by telling him that "Rezsö and his wife were very friendly and were always seen together."[84]

In Switzerland, Brand had an emotional reunion with his wife, who arrived from Hungary. But within hours, the initial excitement and joy wore off and a bitter quarrel erupted between them. On their first night together, Hanzi accused him of not having understood what happened in Istanbul. You should have returned to Budapest at any price, she told him in no uncertain terms, even if it was totally opposed to the view of the Jewish Agency delegation. It was absolutely wrong to leave Turkey. His reply—that "in wartime many men are plucked from their families' arms"—did not satisfy her.[85]

84 Ibid., p. 83.
85 Ibid., pp. 90–91.

They also failed to see eye to eye when it came to Kasztner. His criticism was unwarranted, she said, asserting "Kasztner did some tremendous things. If not for him we would all be among the dead." They also quarreled over whether they should immigrate to Palestine or settle somewhere in Europe. Hanzi favored the European option, while Joel, "for the sake of the Zionist past [and] loyalty to the ideals in which we believed," insisted on Palestine. Once back in Palestine, Brand joined Lehi,[86] an organization highly critical of the approach taken by Mapai and the Yishuv leadership of the rescue of European Jewry.[87] By affiliating himself with Lehi he effectively cut himself off from the path he had taken previously.[88] After his death, one writer noted, "it was only natural that after the disappointing contacts with his comrades in Mapai and Haganah, Joel Brand sought and found his way to Lehi."[89]

This, then, was a step that symbolized and to a large extent determined his attitude toward the rescue of Hungarian Jewry during the 1950s, the years of the Kasztner trial, and the 1960s, during the Eichmann trial. His affiliation with this organization provided him with a convenient platform from which to vent radical opinions about the Zionist leadership's stand during the Holocaust.[90]

X

During the first three years following the war, Kasztner was involved several times in the Nuremberg trials. On September 13, 1945, a few months after the war ended, he arrived in London from Geneva and submitted a sworn affidavit on the situation of Hungarian Jewry under German occupation, with special emphasis on the activity of the Rescue Committee. In his report, Kasztner proudly noted that this affidavit, which he gave to an American

---

86 Hebrew acronym for Israel Freedom Fighters, also known as the Stern Gang, extremist underground Zionist organization in Palestine, founded in 1940 by Avraham Stern (codename: Yair) after a split in the right-wing underground Irgun Zva'i Le'umi (IZL), or National Military Organization.

87 Yosef Heller, *The Stern Gang—Ideology, Politics and Terror, 1940–1949* (London: Frank Cass, 1995), pp. 114–116; Israel Eldad, *The First Tithe* (Hebrew) (Tel Aviv: The Veterans of Lehi Press, 2008), pp. 114–120.

88 Brand, *Satan and the Soul*, p. 96.

89 Rashdal, "Joel Brand: Three Missions" (Hebrew), *Etgar*, July 23, 1964. Rashdal was the code name of Yaakov Yardo, who ran the Stern Gang's political activity in France.

90 For example, "Eichmann Slaughtered, Weizmann Mute" (Hebrew), *Etgar*, June 1, 1961.

investigative panel headed by Judge Robert Jackson,[91] was presented to the International Tribunal at Nuremberg on December 13, 1945.[92]

His detailed statement included a chronological account of the main action taken against Hungary's Jews in the course of the German occupation. Kasztner also alluded to his relations with the senior Nazi officers about whom he later testified. He opened his statement by noting that he had managed to escape the fate of Jewish leaders in other countries both because the Germans had not succeeded in completely eradicating Hungary's Jews, but also because:

> SS *Standartenfuehrer* Becher took me under his wing in order to establish an eventual alibi for himself. He was anxious to demonstrate after the fall of 1944 that he disapproved of the deportations and exterminations and endeavored consistently to furnish me with evidence that he had tried to save the Jews. SS *Hauptsturmfuehrer* Wisliceny repeatedly assured me that in his opinion Germany could not win the war. He believed that by keeping me alive and by making some concessions in the campaign against the Jews he might have a defense witness [for such a time as] he and his organization find themselves having to account for their atrocities.

In his testimony to the Jerusalem District Court nine years later, Kasztner described his intervention as follows:

> From Switzerland I went to Nuremberg early in 1947 at the invitation of General Taylor, the Chief Prosecutor in the IMT (International Military Tribunal). I was the prosecution's advisor on matters relating to the annihilation of Jews, I also took part in investigations and searches for Eichmann and a number of his aides who had disappeared. I worked in Nuremberg until August 1947. From Nuremberg I returned to Switzerland in order to immigrate to Palestine.[93]

---

91 See *Kasztner's Truth: Report of the Jewish Rescue Committee in Budapest, 1942–1945*, p. 202 (no citation of place or date); Robert H. Jackson, a justice of the United States Supreme Court, was appointed on May 2, 1945, as the American representative on the commission that interrogated the heads of the Axis Powers.

92 "Testimony of Zionist Activist from Hungary on the Proposal of Adolf Eichmann, the Archenemy, to Sell Hungary's Million Jews for $2 a Head" (Hebrew), *Ha'aretz*, December 14, 1945.

93 From Kasztner's testimony in Jerusalem District Court, February 22, 1954, ISA, District Court Record, Kasztner Folders, pp. 21–22.

These two statements reflect one of the most problematic and bizarre episodes in the entire Kasztner case: publicly, he claimed that he participated in the trial in order to assist in exposing the Nazis' horrific crimes against the Jews, while at the same time he was giving testimony and making statements, which in some cases were beneficial to senior SS officers.

On more than one occasion Kasztner referred to his role in bringing war criminals to justice. Following his arrival in Palestine, in late 1947, several articles appeared in the press that underscored his efforts to that end. One such report stated that he had collected considerable information about Adolf Eichmann "and had asked the occupation authorities in Germany to conduct a trial against him and his aides, even *in absentia*."[94] He did not so much as hint at the other aspect of the evidence he had given.

On August 4, 1947, the day before his departure from Nuremberg, he submitted an affidavit in favor of Kurt Becher.[95] Kasztner claimed that thanks to the negotiations he conducted with Becher, the lives of tens of thousands of Jews were saved between 1944–1945. Although the negotiations had begun on a financial basis, they had produced very good practical results. "There can be no doubt that Becher was one of the few SS leaders who had the courage to take a stand against the extermination program and who made an attempt to save human lives," he declared. Among the rescue operations he cited were: the rescue train, which saved 1,685 Jewish lives; Himmler's October 1944 order to cease the murder of Jews, which was issued due to Becher's intervention, over the strong objections of Eichmann and of Ernst Kaltenbrunner;[96] tens of thousands of Budapest Jews who were saved thanks to Becher's intervention in late 1944 and early 1945, despite the extermination plan of Ferenc Szálasi's puppet government; and his responsibility for the transfer of concentration camp prisoners to the Allies, contrary to demands by radical circles in Himmler's headquarters (who objected to any negotiations with the Jews) for the annihilation of these Jews. Kasztner concluded the affidavit with the following words:

> Since there were personal ties between myself and Becher between June 1944 and mid-April 1945, I wish to point out and emphasize that Becher

---

94 "Jews Among the Gentiles in Europe (A Conversation with Dr. Israel Kasztner)" (Hebrew), *Davar*, December 26, 1947.

95 Micha Caspi Archives, German version, Defense Exhibit C.

96 On the order, see Livia Rotkirchen, "The Final Solution in its Final Stage," *Yad Vashem Studies*, vol. 8 (1971), pp. 27–28; Ernst Kaltenbrunner headed the RSHA, the Reich Security Main Office of the SS, from 1943–1945.

did everything he could, given his ability and position, to save innocent lives from the blind murderous rampage of the Nazi leadership. For this reason, I never for a minute doubted his good intentions, even if the form and basis for our negotiations were of an objectionable character. In my opinion, Becher deserves the fullest possible consideration when his matter comes up before the Allied or German authorities.

Kasztner signed this deposition in the presence of the notary public, Benno H. Zelke—a seemingly trivial detail that in later years would turn out to be critical.

In the summer of 1947, Kasztner suggested to the office of the Chief Prosecutor of War Crimes at Nuremberg that a separate trial be held regarding IVB4, Eichmann's office in the Reich Main Security Office (Reichssicherheitshauptamt, or RSHA), which carried out the "final solution" in practice.[97] Only such a trial could reveal the full scope of the annihilation program, he said, and the facts that would be presented could be used later in the personal trial of Eichmann, who had in the meantime disappeared, and in the trials of his senior aides, who had not yet been arrested. Kasztner went on to list several "potential defendants" (as he put it) who were already in custody. He noted in particular two of Eichmann's assistants, Dieter Wisliceny, who was under arrest in Slovakia—"the Bratislava authorities are eager to extradite him to the United States and would be willing to turn over the documents in their possession"—and Hermann Krumey.

On the face of it, this letter belongs to the public aspect of Kasztner's attitude toward war criminals. But it also contains a passage that can be attributed to another, hidden, facet —an attempt to assist Wisliceny:

> It should be noted that the only one in Eichmann's entire headquarters who can be apprehended is Wisliceny and it is he who can provide a credible and full picture of the annihilation program and those who were involved in its implementation. The authorities in Slovakia will probably execute him—unless he is extradited—and then all the proof he possesses will be lost.[98]

---

97 June 22,1947, Micha Caspi Archives, Prosecution Exhibit 33, Criminal File 124/53.
98 The letter of reply, dated September 17, 1947 (Prosecution Exhibit 34), rejected the idea of holding a special trial focusing on the crimes against the Jews, on the grounds that this matter was discussed extensively in other trials. The letter is silent on the proposal to extradite Wisliceny to the United States.

What prompted Kasztner to make a statement in support of Becher and, altogether, to behave as he did? This question, which became crucial during the "Gruenwald trial," has never received an unambiguous answer; one can only suggest partial and relative explanations. To begin with, there is the megalomaniac explanation. During the German occupation of Hungary, Kasztner held center-stage and determined the fate of tens of thousands of Jews. Once the war was over, he found himself living in a cheap *pension* in Geneva, bereft of influence and power. The situation in Nuremberg thus afforded him the opportunity to re-experience at least a fraction of the power he wielded during the occupation: he was back at center-stage, determining people's fate.

With regard to the reasons that induced Kasztner to go to Nuremberg immediately after immigrating to Palestine, Brand wrote: "In Nuremberg he regained the feeling of power—picking up the phone, a good word, intervention, a written statement—these had been enough to save human lives."[99] There would seem to be no escaping the conclusion that, from Kasztner's point of view, his relations with senior Nazi officers were not only an unavoidable necessity but part of his self-image and sense of belonging to "high society" and to the circle of decision makers. His other testimonies, which we will consider later, support this conclusion.

Almost everyone who knew him or spoke with him mentioned these as his most prominent personality traits. Some even claimed they were his defining features. Moshe Alfan (Pil) described him as "someone with boundless and unrestrained ambition and drive," and said it was his "devious, arrogant character [that] led him to Nuremberg and, a few years later, to the trial in Jerusalem."[100]

The second explanation is what may be called the gentlemanly explanation. According to this version, Kasztner genuinely believed that Becher had a hand in the rescue of thousands of Hungarian Jews and testified on his behalf out of a sense of gratitude and because of the promise, which he had apparently made to Wisliceny toward the end of the war, that he would repay him when he could. Professor Yehuda Bauer maintains that Kasztner testified in favor of Becher and others because of "his misguided perception of gentlemanly decency and because of actions taken by those Nazis at the last

99   Brand, *Satan and the Soul*, p. 110.
100   Personal interview, Tel Aviv, January 23, 1992.

minute to create alibis for themselves when it became obvious that Germany's defeat was imminent."[101]

It is possible that Kasztner really did believe that Becher had assisted in the rescue of Jews and therefore deserved gratitude and a reward. In a letter he sent to the heads of the Jewish Agency in October 1945,[102] Kasztner wrote that Becher's aid had made it possible for the Budapest ghetto to be spared; for the rescue train to be sent to Switzerland; and for a few concentration camps—Mauthausen, Bergen-Belsen, Theresienstadt, and Neuengamme—to be handed over to the Allied forces without the need for hostilities. In order to write as he did to the Jewish Agency leaders, Kasztner must have been convinced that Becher had indeed provided him with concrete assistance in the rescue of Jews.

Yet another explanation—this one offered by Hanzi Brand—for his testimony can be termed *cherchez la femme*. During the war, she maintained, Becher had been friendly with a countess who later became his wife and who grasped before he did that the Nazis would lose the war "and that someone like Kasztner could be of immeasurable service to her beloved." At Nuremberg, the countess said to Kasztner, "I helped you, now you must help me." This request, combined with the fact that "friendly relations suddenly blossomed" between the countess and Kasztner underpinned his testimony, according to Hanzi.[103]

Another explanation involves Moshe Schweiger, who, as we shall see later, was in touch with Becher in April-May 1945, just as the war ended. A memorandum he wrote[104] in the summer of 1945 portrayed Becher in a very positive light as someone whose actions "truly saved many Jews," including the "peace-seeking act" of handing over the concentration camps together with their inhabitants to the Americans. In describing his personal relationship with Becher, he wrote: "During the entire period, Becher behaved courteously toward me. He saw to my wellbeing and my health like a good relative. He treated me as an equal and, during the first days after my life in the concentration camp, that was truly embarrassing."

101 Yehuda Bauer, "The Kasztner Affair: The Historical Truth and the Political Use" (Hebrew), *Ha'aretz*, May 25, 1985.
102 The letter, written in Geneva on October 21, 1945, was addressed to David Ben-Gurion, Moshe Shertok, and Yitzhak Gruenbaum, CZA, L22-176.
103 Brand, *Satan and the Soul*, p. 107; Hanzi Brand.
104 The memorandum was written in Salzburg on August 7, 1945, Micha Caspi Archives, Defense Exhibit 125, Criminal File 124/53.

The favorable opinion rendered by Schweiger, with whom Kasztner maintained close ties, certainly influenced him and was one of the factors that induced him to testify on Becher's behalf. In early November 1945, about two weeks after Schweiger arrived in Geneva, Kasztner wrote: "Thanks to the intervention of Kurt Becher, my German counterpart in the negotiations, Moshe Schweiger, who was terribly weak and ill, received particularly good treatment during the last four weeks he spent at Mauthausen."[105]

This letter contains another key to solving the riddle. Kasztner wrote later that Becher's leaving with Schweiger some of the ransom that he had been given for the train passengers—intending for the valuables to reach Saly Mayer and himself—constituted the fulfillment of a promise Becher had made to him in Budapest. Kasztner added that Becher was arrested after he had entrusted the valuables to Schweiger,[106] and was taken to an American prisoner of war camp:

> Afterward, and particularly of late, negotiations have been conducted in connection with him, and I expect it is our duty to assist him in some way. Moshe Shertok expressed the same opinion in London. Can you advise me on this matter?

According to Amos Manor, Kasztner's megalomania, with which Manor was very familiar, partially explains his affidavit. Manor maintains that the relations that developed between Kasztner and Becher, like any relationship between an agent and his handler, entailed his deep commitment to Becher.[107]

This brings us to the psychological explanation, which involves the principle of cognitive dissonance: the prolonged proximity, which made him dependent on people he abhorred, made Kasztner want to see them in a different light, one that absolved and vindicated them, in order to justify himself in his own eyes and enable him to go on negotiating with them; and more than that, to enable him to live with himself after the war. This explanation sheds light on his efforts to assist not only Becher but others as well. Yet if Kasztner's friends could somehow understand his attempt to help Becher, they were at a loss to comprehend his attempts to intervene on behalf of the others.[108]

---

105 From his letter to Melech Neustadt, November 7, 1945, Labor Archives, IV104/203.
106 Becher, he wrote, had "fallen victim" (*zum Opfer fallen*) to Austrian "freedom fighters" who had detained him. His use of this term indicates his attitude toward him.
107 Manor.
108 In this regard, see Manor.

One such attempt to help involved Hermann Krumey,[109] with whom Kasztner also had personal ties, although he considered him to be a war criminal who should stand trial. During his cross-examination by Tamir in the Jerusalem District Court on June 4, 1954, Kasztner said that Krumey was a Nazi who in various capacities had for years been connected with the annihilation of Jews.[110] Nevertheless, on February 5, 1947, when Krumey was in a prisoner of war camp run by the British in Italy, Kasztner sent him the following letter:

> Very honorable Mr. Krumey!
> I was able to contact your family, but I have not yet received a reply to my letter in which I ask how I can be of help to them. In a comprehensive report that I presented in Basel, I stated clearly and formally the roles played of [sic] those who aided us. I hope the steps that were taken will make it easier for you to regain your freedom and to begin your life on a new basis. As far as conditions permit, I will try to help you in this. Certainly this will not be easy for you to do, but I do not easily forget those who showed us understanding at certain moments. [Original in English].

Kasztner, himself, later tried to furnish an explanation for this letter. In 1956, he wrote to the Attorney General[111] that Krumey had been one of Eichmann's key aides "in concentrating and deporting the Jews of Hungary" and, as such was "a war criminal who must pay the penalty"—despite the fact that on several occasions he had shown readiness to assist the Relief and Rescue Committee, "and the committee had exploited that readiness." He said he had written the letter in an attempt to find the man's exact whereabouts so he could be tried—needless to say, an extremely lame explanation.

In January 1948 about a month after he settled in Palestine, Kasztner appeared at the Nuremberg trials for a third time; this time he spent about three months in Nuremberg. Upon his return, the papers were full of reports about his exploits in denouncing war criminals and bringing them to trial. One article, which appeared immediately after his return, noted that a meeting of the Ihud Haolami secretariat, held on May 10, 1948, had welcomed back

---

109 Krumey, a senior aide to Eichmann, came to Budapest with him to implement the Final Solution in Hungary and took part in the negotiations with Kasztner and the Rescue Committee.

110 On this subject, see Tamir's letter of February 29, 1956, to the Attorney General, Micha Caspi Archives.

111 August 26, 1956, Micha Caspi Archives.

"Dr. I. Kasztner who had been at Nuremberg to testify at the trials of the leaders of the Nazi murderers."[112] He also gave interviews to the press and published articles himself, including one on Eichmann;[113] another, which was very significant and to which we will return later, on the Madagascar Plan;[114] and in a Johannesburg journal, he published documents concerning attempts by the Grand Mufti to destroy Tel Aviv.[115]

However, during his stay in Nuremberg he also involved himself with matters about which he was silent in his articles and interviews. On May 5, 1948, he submitted a sworn affidavit on behalf of Hermann Krumey in which he described Krumey's behavior at a time when he was responsible for a group of about 15,000 Hungarian Jews who were being transferred from Hungary to Austria:[116]

> I wish to state that Krumey performed his tasks displaying remarkable good will towards those whose life or death depended to a great extent upon the way he understood to implement his orders.
> As I spent the last three months of the war in Vienna, I myself was able to convince myself of the above-mentioned facts. I put forward a number of proposals to Krumey aimed to alleviate the plight of this special group, and I was always met with full understanding and sympathy on his part.[117] [Original English of the affidavit.]

Kasztner provided another sworn statement, this one on behalf of SS General Hans Jüttner, concerning the "death march" of Budapest's Jews, which Jüttner witnessed on his way from Vienna to Budapest:[118]

---

112 "In the Ihud Haolami" (Hebrew), *Hapoel Hatza'ir*, May 25, 1948.

113 "The Truth about Eichmann" (Hebrew), *Davar*, June 2, 1948.

114 "Weeks that Ended in a Verdict" (Hebrew), *Molad*, vol. 1, No. 2–3 (May–June 1948), pp. 121–125.

115 "The Mufti's Attempts to Destroy Tel Aviv: First Publication of Three Documents from Nuremberg" (Hebrew), *Barkai*, No. 145 (Tevet 5709; January 1949), pp. 8–9.

116 From the request for a new hearing in the Kasztner trial submitted by attorney Shmuel Tamir to Attorney General Gideon Hausner on July 22, 1962. The Hebrew version is to be found on pp. 21–22 and the English original is attached as appendix IX. It should be noted that this document was discovered only in the 1960s and its existence was unknown during Kasztner's lifetime.

117 *Kasztner's Truth*, pp. 176–178; this, I believe, is the passage to which Kasztner was referring to in his letter to Krumey of February 1947.

118 A photocopy of the English version of the affidavit appears as Appendix XVIII of the request for a new hearing.

On his arrival in Budapest, Jüttner protested to Winkelmann against the conditions under which these deportations were proceeding,[119] asking that they be stopped. This fact was stated to me at the time not only by Becher, but even [sic] by Adolf Eichmann... who commented that Jüttner, by intervening, had overstepped his authority.

Kasztner gave yet another affidavit, perhaps the most puzzling of all, in favor of Wisliceny.[120] Dieter Wisliceny, Eichmann's aide, was active in Bratislava and Budapest and negotiated with Jewish representatives on a lives-for-cash deal. He was executed in Bratislava in February 1948, before Kasztner made his sworn statement. In that statement Kasztner claims that Wisliceny, remembering the Slovakian example,[121] proposed, upon his arrival in Hungary, "to negotiate on preventing the deportation of Hungary's Jews. As a result of these negotiations, the Germans made a number of concessions: 15,000 Hungarian Jews were sent to Austria and 1,700 Jews were permitted to leave for Switzerland" (on the rescue train). This paved the way for additional German concessions regarding the annihilation process, but clearly Wisliceny was "the first SS officer who obtained concessions, however minor, that breached the principle of total annihilation which was then in effect."

Following his return from Nuremberg, Kasztner wrote to Finance Minister Eliezer Kaplan:[122]

> Approximately three months ago, I was invited to testify at the Nuremberg trials. I took the opportunity to speak with Kurt Becher. As is known, Becher was a former SS colonel who served as a liaison officer between Himmler and me during the rescue operations, and has in the interim been released by the occupation authorities thanks to my personal intervention. The conversation centered on the financial matters that are of interest to us.

This letter, as we shall see, was inaccurate, but a few years later it would cause Kasztner irreparable damage.

---

119 General SS Otto Winkelmann was the supreme commander of the SS and the police (Hohre SS und Polizei Führer) in Hungary.
120 It was given on May 5, 1948, CZA, L17-897.
121 The first negotiations between Jewish representatives and SS officers took place in Slovakia in 1942. Wisliceny participated in these negotiations.
122 July 26, 1948, Micha Caspi Archives, Defense Exhibit 22, District Court.

XI

Financial claims that arose primarily from the so-called "Becher treasure," cash and valuables that had been given to the Germans in ransom for the rescue train survivors and had fallen into Becher's hands, hounded Kasztner. On the eve of the liberation, part of the treasure reached Moshe Schweiger by a roundabout route. From there it found its way to American counter-espionage. Thus, from being a prisoner in Mauthausen, the most dreaded of all the concentration camps, Schweiger had become an esteemed protégé of the SS leadership, in charge of a vast treasure. He first put the story into writing in the summer of 1945, shortly after being liberated and before he went to Geneva, where he joined Kasztner.[123] His account was terse and attests to the twilight-like atmosphere of the final days of the "Thousand-Year Reich."

Moshe Schweiger had been arrested in April 1944, shortly after the beginning of the German occupation of Hungary, and sent to Mauthausen in July. By April 1945 he felt his end was near—his strength was ebbing, he was sick, his condition was deteriorating—when suddenly his life changed radically. During the evening roll call on April 20, he was ordered to report to the camp's "political department" and from there to the infirmary—not to perish, as he had expected, but to regain his strength and be rehabilitated. He was allocated a room in a new stone building, complete with hot water and the same food as was served to the camp's staff. Schweiger was stunned and uncomprehending. A week later, he was taken to the office of Commandant Franz Ziereis, where he was introduced to an SS officer he did not know, Kurt Becher. The conversation flowed cordially and he felt himself to be equal among equals, rather than a prisoner terrified of the last of his captors. Finally, Becher whispered in his ear: "Something is now going to happen to you." He was led to Bloc 1, the "bloc of the privileged," given a private room that resembled a suite in a luxury hotel, his worn, torn, and filthy striped pajamas were exchanged for civilian clothing, and he was exempted from participating in the endless roll calls. It was like one giant hallucination.

On May 4, the evening before the Americans entered the camp, Schweiger was transferred to a vessel anchored on the Danube, near the town of Waldsee. Becher awaited him on board, the very epitome of courtesy. He had already tried several times to bring about his release, Becher said, but only now had he succeeded in locating him. And why did an inmate from

123   August 7, 1945, Micha Caspi Archives, Defense Exhibit 125, District Court.

Mauthausen become an honored guest aboard an SS boat? I want you to take something to Kasztner who is in Switzerland, Becher said; I would do it myself, he explained, but the French Army is in control along the Swiss border.

The next day, the day before the surrender, he went with Becher to a hunting lodge outside the town of Bad Ischl, where they stayed about a week. On May 12, Becher and his cohorts were arrested. Before being taken away Becher gave Schweiger a large hoard of valuables—gold, platinum, diamonds—to transfer to Switzerland and to hand over to the Jewish Agency and the Joint; these items never reached their destination.

Following Becher's arrest, Schweiger left the lodge and found a place to stay with a farmer in a nearby village. He had no idea what to do with the treasure for which he was now responsible:[124] "The treasure was under the bed and like some kind of Shylock, I am guarding the gold. I would rarely venture out of the room. I was awaiting the arrival of a responsible Jew to whom I could hand over the treasure and be rid of my difficult and dangerous mission." In the meantime, the military authorities announced that anyone found in the possession of property that had belonged to the SS would be executed. Schweiger was petrified. "Even in Mauthausen, I knew quieter days," he wrote. He decided to approach the headquarters of American counter-espionage at Bad Ischl and leave the valuables with them "in safekeeping for the Jewish Agency and the Joint." In the unit's office (CIC Unit 215) he placed the valuables in the hands of a Jewish officer with the rank of captain.

In October 1945, Schweiger left Austria and moved to Geneva, where he found accommodation in the *pension* where Kasztner was living. In Switzerland he related the entire story to the Jewish Agency. The report he submitted in Geneva differed in some details from his previous one in Salzburg. In contrast to his laconic description at that time, the second report was far more detailed. The main difference between the two concerned the physical transfer of the treasure, which emphasized that he had received the items from Becher without an itemized list and had given them to the Americans "again without an inventory, because I had no knowledge of the worth of the goods." From the officer he had received only a receipt stating that the items had been handed over for safekeeping.[125]

---

124 Moshe Schweiger, "Ransom Payment of Hungarian Jews Kept by a German SS Man" (Hebrew), *Davar*, October 5, 1947.

125 Ibid. The report was incorporated into a joint letter, dated October 21, 1945 and mentioned above, which he and Kasztner sent to Ben-Gurion, Shertok, Gruenbaum, and

In the letters they sent, Kasztner and Schweiger estimated that the valuables were worth about eight million Swiss francs, or $2 million at the time.[126] On other occasions, Kasztner mentioned an even higher figure: "My estimate is that the property has a value of at least 10–15 million Swiss francs, if not more," he wrote to Melech Neustadt.[127]

At first, the Jewish Agency ignored Schweiger's report—"they thought it was too far-fetched"—and only took action after repeated pressure by Schweiger.[128] In February 1946, the Jewish Agency appointed Gideon Ruffer (Raphael), a senior official in the Political Department and later a senior Foreign Ministry ambassador, to investigate the fate of the treasure. Ruffer, who was in Europe as the Jewish Agency's special representative to a conference that was preparing the Nuremberg trials, was instructed to track down the "gold train"—eleven cars filled to the brim with the property of Hungarian Jewry and worth tens or even hundreds of millions of dollars.[129]

When Ben-Gurion was appraised of these developments, he noted in his diary at the beginning of November 1945: "The Nazi money (Moshe Schweiger), how to obtain it. (4 November 1945)" In February 1946, when he was in Frankfurt during his second visit to the displaced persons camps, he met with Ruffer, who gave him a report about the "gold train."[130] In November 1946, Ben-Gurion wrote to Jewish Agency Treasurer Eliezer Kaplan:

We have been told unofficially that the military authorities in Austria prefer to turn over to the IGC both the "gold train" and the 'Becher treasure.' We are continuing to press for the transfer of the "Becher

Pino Ginzburg, CZA, L22-176. The letter was included in the documents submitted in the District Court and marked 142.

126 For example, in the letter to Ben-Gurion and the others cited in note above.
127 November 7, 1945, Labor Archives, IV104, 129.
128 Schweiger, "Ransom Payment of Hungarian Jews Kept by a German SS Man" (Hebrew), *Davar*, October 5, 1947; it should be noted that no figure is mentioned in this article, which was written after the existence of the treasure was exposed, and he notes only that "a few weeks after my immigration to Palestine I was pleased [to learn] that the treasure had been transferred to Switzerland, to the [relevant] institutions."
129 On the train, see the report (unsigned and undated): "*Über die Bericht: Geschichte des beschlagnamanahmten jüdischen Vermogens in der französichen Zone*," CZA, S25-176; Letter of Berl Locker (Member of the Jewish Agency Executive) and Gideon Ruffer to Sandor Nathan, director of the Palestine Office in Budapest, April 18, 1946, CZA, L17-897.
130 Ben-Gurion's Diary, Paris, November 4, 1945, BGRCA; Ibid., Frankfurt, February 1, 1946.

treasure" to the Jewish Agency. This is still a possibility, but no [necessary] steps are yet clear and the outcome is not certain.[131]

In March 1946, Ruffer issued a report on the "Becher funds."[132] In the letter he stated that in June 1944 Kasztner had transferred to Becher valuables worth about eight million Swiss francs in return for the release of the passengers on the rescue train. Ruffer had heard this estimate from Schweiger at a meeting they held in late 1945 or early 1946.[133] Becher himself, who was imprisoned in Nuremberg, was awaiting trial together with the commanders of the Melk concentration camp.[134] It was likely that in his defense he would cite the fact that he had returned the valuables to the Jewish Agency. In early March 1946, Ruffer had visited the headquarters of the U.S. Occupation Forces' counter-espionage section and discovered that no progress had been made in investigating the fate of the valuables. Ruffer added that the Jewish Agency was very interested in getting to the bottom of this matter and that Kasztner and Schweiger were ready to help in any way they could.

Kasztner and Schweiger continued their pressure even after Ruffer had issued his report. In the summer of 1946, the two were still insisting that everything possible should be done to locate the property and demand its return, since this was not enemy loot but "property in safekeeping of Jews who were transported to Poland and had dedicated it to assist and build Jewish Palestine."[135] Subsequently the Jewish Agency appointed David Arian, a senior official of the Financial Department, to deal with the transfer of the property to the Jewish Agency. Arian tracked down the valuables and, in February 1947, arrived in Salzburg together with Ben-Zion Hameiri, the director of the Jewish Agency's Financial Department in Geneva, in order to claim them. However, the contents of the package he was given were worth not $2 million but $55,000 or at most $65,000. Instead of an official, orderly inventory there was only a handwritten, improvised, undated list, which Arian thought Schweiger had written in the presence of an American officer

---

131 David Ben-Gurion, *Toward the End of the Mandate—Memories (June 1946—March 1947)*, Meir Avizohar, ed. (Hebrew) (Tel Aviv: Am Oved, 1993), p. 238. In 1948, Kaplan was appointed first Minister of Finance.

132 "Jewish Funds Deposited by Moshe Schwiger [sic] with CIC Unit 215," Frankfurt, March 6, 1945; Micha Caspi Archives, Prosecution Exhibit 129, District Court.

133 Shalom Rosenfeld, *Criminal File 124* (Hebrew) (Tel Aviv: Karni Press, 1955), pp. 196–197.

134 Melk was an extension of the Mauthausen concentration camp.

135 Haim Barlas to David Baharel, director of the Jewish Agency's Financial Department, Jerusalem, July 25, 1945, Micha Caspi Archives, Defense Exhibit 130.

when he turned over the treasure to the U.S. military authorities.[136] The low figure came as a surprise to the heads of the Joint, who had expected the valuables to be worth at least $800,000, and they sent a series of letters and queries on the subject to Kaplan.[137]

How, then, did several million dollars worth of valuables dwindle to tens of thousands? Arian's reply to that question was that Becher had given Schweiger only a fraction of the valuables:[138]

A comparison with the list, and talks I held in Austria and later in Geneva with all those connected with the matter, such as Yoel Nussbacher [Palgi, Y.W], Dr. Schweiger, Dr. Kasztner, and others do not allow us to believe that Becher gave Schweiger, who subsequently transferred it to the American military authorities, more than what we found [...] In other words, [it is not feasible] that after the items were received [by the Americans], valuables disappeared. It is perfectly clear that Becher transferred to Schweiger only a minuscule fraction of the valuables he received in Hungary from Jews who were interested in obtaining exit permits.

Confronted by Arian's account, which explicitly blamed Becher for the disappearance of most of the treasure, Becher offered his own version. In April 1948, in Nuremberg, he gave a sworn affidavit describing in detail several financial matters in which he had been involved, including the Schweiger affair.[139] Becher stated that shortly before the end of the war he had brought about the release of Kasztner's associate, Moshe Schweiger, from the Mauthausen concentration camp, and had given him gold and other items worth about two million Swiss francs.

In the summer of 1948, immediately after his return from Nuremberg, Kasztner sent a letter to Eliezer Kaplan, now the Finance Minister,[140] in which he effectively accepted Becher's version and tried to protect him by intimating

136 Report of David Arian, March 13, 1947, Defense Exhibit 131, District Court.
137 See, for example, Kaplan's letter to Dr. Walter Butler, of the Joint's legal department, November 23, 1947, Micha Caspi Archives, Defense Exhibit 134, District Court; Kaplan stated that the American officers with whom Arian spoke estimated the valuables to be worth between $60,000 and $80,000, and that they did not understand on what basis the previous high estimates had been cited.
138 Arian Report; Rosenfeld, p. 193.
139 The statement was made on April 12, 1948, just at the time when Kasztner was in Nuremberg, CZA, L17-897.
140 Tel Aviv, July 26, 1948, Prosecution Exhibit 22, District Court.

that the question of the lost valuables should be directed to the officials of the Jewish Agency.[141]

XII

The "Becher treasure" was not the only financial issue that preoccupied Kasztner. He was also troubled by requests from the passengers of the rescue train who had deposited money with him. It had been necessary to apply enormous pressure, both concrete and psychological, to raise the funds necessary to underwrite the train. The occupation was at its height, the deportations were proceeding relentlessly, and uncertainty, particularly with respect to the train, was rampant; the overriding fear was that the Hungarians would get wind of the plan to organize the rescue train and to raise the money for it. In these circumstances the ransom money was collected haphazardly— certainly not in the way such large sums would have been handled under normal conditions; cash was collected in various currencies together with valuables whose exact worth no one knew. Everything was done pell-mell. "The first transport left on June 30, 1944," Shulem Offenbach, the committee's treasurer recalled:[142]

> We collected the valuables at the very last minute, just days before the departure. It was very dangerous in those days to deal with Jewish valuables and therefore, we tried to carry out the collections as quickly as possible. There was no possibility of preparing an account. I evaluated the goods roughly and threw them into a briefcase. The jewelry was immediately forwarded to Swabian Hill [where Eichmann and his staff were located] because we feared a repetition of the Semsey Andor street events.[143]

141 Later in the letter, Kasztner directs Kaplan's attention to additional goods that had been given to Becher, and if "great energy, attention, and caution are exercised in dealing with the matter," it might be possible to locate them. It should be noted that the items to which he referred, and particularly 163,000 Swiss francs that Becher had transferred in November 1944 to SS General Jüttner, were also mentioned in Becher's statement. It is therefore a reasonable assumption that Kasztner was familiar with the statement and that his account was coordinated with Becher.

142 From testimony he gave at the headquarters of the state police in Budapest on July 20, 1946, *The Tragedy of Hungarian Jewry*, Randolph L. Braham, ed. (New York: The City University of New York Press, 1986), pp. 315–320.

143 The reference is to the looting of diamonds and other valuables by the Hungarians

In 1948, Marcel Syphos, a survivor from the train, wrote Posner a detailed letter[144] claiming that in the summer of 1944 he had given the Relief and Rescue Committee the sum of $14,700 in return for a promise that he would be given a receipt in Switzerland that would enable him to reclaim the money. However, even though several years had gone by since then, and despite correspondence with Kasztner on the subject, he had not received the promised document. Kasztner's reply to Posner was not long in arriving.[145] He explained that the committee had needed money on such short notice as a condition for the departure of the rescue train and the whole scheme was hanging by a thread:

> Mr. Syphos is overlooking one small detail, namely that he and his family received their lives [as a gift]. Our primary mission was to save human lives; [it is to this end] that we fought for a whole year, we worked, we took risks and we assumed the terrible responsibility of the Bergen-Belsen group's journey. Under those circumstances, who could undertake technical-legal commitments? Where was the SS, our partner in the contract, when our own lives were so like a game of ping-pong every day? [...] Is Mr. Syphos sorry that he was rescued as a result of our efforts and thereby lost a certain amount [of money] or did he strike—as I believe—a good deal?[146]

Nevertheless, Kasztner was deeply troubled by these matters and constantly pored over the Rescue Committee's financial reports. In October 1945, not long after his arrival in Switzerland, he sent a letter to Jewish Agency senior officials[147] that dealt in part with the funding of the rescue operations. Payment was required in return for Jews who were sent abroad or to Austria, he noted. There was a fixed price: $1,000 for every person sent abroad and $100 for everyone sent to Austria. How was the money obtained? The rescue train was financed mainly with money and valuables from wealthy Jews:

---

following Offenbach's arrest in the apartment of the Brand family on Semsey Andor Street.
144 March 6, 1948, CZA, L17-897.
145 March 12, 1948, CZA.
146 From his letter to Eliezer Kaplan, August 21, 1946, CZA.
147 The letter, which was addressed to Ben-Gurion, Shertok, Gruenbaum, and Pino Ginzburg, was sent on October 22, 1945, CZA, L22-176.

Among [the train passengers] there were 120 whom we added to the journey in return for a large sum [of money] that they paid on top of valuables, gold cigarette cases, watches, diamonds, and objects made of gold and platinum. These together with a pengo [the Hungarian currency] account made up the financial basis for the interim agreement (which enabled the train to set out).

At the end of the section dealing with the financial matters, Kasztner noted that the sum that was transferred to the Germans was not counted. They received money and valuables worth a total of eight million Swiss francs but are claiming that it was less than four million, and "this disagreement has not been resolved."[148]

A financial report submitted in December 1946 to Jewish Agency Treasurer Eliezer Kaplan concerning activities of the Jewish Relief and Rescue Committee,[149] which included a detailed account of the committee's "revenues" and expenditures, was treated as a final report. A few months later Kasztner wrote to Mordechai Zagagi, the official of the Financial Department in Switzerland,[150] expressing his hope that the financial matters would be resolved. He described the course of events that had created the problem and emphasized the intensive efforts he had made to make careful and provident use of the Jewish Agency funds he had received from Istanbul. "Like my colleagues on the Rescue Committee," he concluded, "I believe that this is our last chance to conclude this very melancholy chapter. Perhaps the minimum we can do is to cast political, moral, and legal blame on those who imposed this task on us."

But, despite the hopes and the harsh words, the affair was not over. At the time Kasztner sent his letter to Zagagi, he was involved in another financial dispute, this time with Andreas Biss, a relative of Joel Brand's and a member of the Rescue Committee. Biss, who brought Posner and Barlas into the dispute, demanded 65,000 Swiss francs from Kasztner, who insisted that the money had already been returned. The correspondence between the two, which was occasionally vituperative, continued until the second half of 1947, right up to the time Kasztner left Geneva.[151]

---

148 This letter, which was sent shortly after Schweiger joined Kasztner in Vienna, also has a connection to the "Becher treasure" affair.
149 December 22, 1946, CZA, L17-897.
150 September 20, 1947, CZA.
151 CZA, L17-897.

CHAPTER TWO

1948–1954

I

K asztner arrived in Israel with his family in December 1947 and had a hard time adjusting to his new life. Having arrived penniless, he was obliged to borrow money from his brother-in-law, Pesach Rudik,[1] in order to purchase a musty one-and-a-half room basement apartment on 14 Adam Hacohen Street in Tel Aviv. A group of friends, appalled at the shameful conditions in which he was living, collected enough money to allow him to purchase a two-room apartment for key money on Amsterdam Street. Later, he moved to 6 Immanuel Harussi Street, which is where the assassin's bullet found him.

The plunge from the splendor of Budapest to the tiny basement apartment on Adam Hacohen Street was very distressing, and his despondency was aggravated by the fact that his father-in-law, Yosef (Yoshko) Fisher, who before the war had been a wealthy man in Cluj, was now destitute. But despite all the hardship, Kasztner did not remain anonymous and the fact of his arrival in Israel reverberated throughout the country.

Mishmar, the daily newspaper of the Hashomer Hatza'ir movement, which subsequently changed its name to *Al HaMishmar* and became the *Mapam* (United Workers Party) party paper, printed an article describing Kasztner's meetings with Eichmann.[2] Its author was Mapam member Eugen Kolb, and one of the survivors of the rescue train, who would later become director of the Tel Aviv Museum. "Despite the enormous efforts invested in the operation, the results of the Jewish rescue work have been virtually erased and forgotten, in comparison with the enormous number of victims who were doomed to die," he wrote. "For this reason, we ought to be especially

---

1 Pesach Rudik, personal interview, Tel Aviv, May 14, 1992.
2 Eugen Koleb, "Face to Face with Eichmann—On the Arrival to Israel of Dr. Kasztner, the Man Involved in Rescue" (Hebrew), *Mishmar*, December 19, 1947.

appreciative of the work of men like Dr. Kasztner, who, thanks to his courage and diplomatic skills, succeeded—with the help of Jewish and international forces—in rescuing thousands of Jews from Transylvania, Hungary and Czechoslovakia in the raging storms of war and transferring them to a neutral country. Tens of thousands of deportees, about to be sent to Auschwitz, were transferred to special camps in Austria, where they were allowed to stay until the end of the war. We must credit him and his friends for the fact that the Budapest ghetto was saved, to the extent that it was saved."

Haolam Hazeh[3] (before Uri Avneri became its editor) published an interview with Kasztner in August 1948, describing him as a "bespectacled, slightly built man, of medium height." The interview focused on the rescue of Hungarian Jews. Basing many of his conclusions on Yoel Palgi's article in *Davar*,[4] Dr. Emil Feuerstein wrote:

> Palgi is reliable. He knows what he is writing about. A man who has looked death in the face many times does not engage in idle chatter. He saw Kasztner in action in Budapest during the war. That is where the man became a hero. There is a concept of heroism: a parachutist is dropped behind enemy lines, carries out his mission, is caught, tortured, escapes or is executed. Kasztner's heroism is rarer and of a finer cast: he did not fight against the Nazis with weapons; they would not have been easily vanquished with weapons. He fought against them with the weapon of diplomacy. He is the only Jew who won out against the Nazis, who thrashed them soundly […].

In a letter to Chaim Posner, Kasztner wrote, "I have been very warmly received here. In the press—in *Davar*, two articles and one interview were published and a truly heartwarming article also appeared in *Mishmar*—as well as in the party."[5]

An item about Kasztner's reception at party headquarters appeared in its paper, *Hapoel Hatza'ir*: "Dr. Israel Kasztner, a veteran member of our movement in Hungary, one of the major figures active in efforts to rescue European Jews in the midst of the Holocaust, has arrived in Israel. The

---

3 Dr. Emil Feuerstein, "A Brief Visit with Israel Kasztner" (Hebrew), *Haolam Hazeh* 569 (August 19, 1948).

4 "Upon the Arrival of Israel Kasztner" (Hebrew), *Davar*, December 11, 1947.

5 January 11, 1948, CZA, L17/897.

movement sends its greetings to him upon his arrival [...] to make his home here in our land."[6]

In May 1948, when Kasztner returned to Israel from a brief visit to Europe, a meeting of the Ichud Haolami was held for the purpose of "welcoming [our] movement's activists in Europe, who have settled in Israel, and our emissaries who have returned." This included Kasztner who had "returned from Nuremberg, where he testified at the trials of the chief Nazi murderers."[7]

Kasztner himself wrote an article on the Madagascar Plan of 1940, which was published that same month in the periodical *Molad*:[8]

> There was one brief period, during these horrible years, a breathtaking moment, when you might have assumed that the drama was not moving towards its denouement, and that the decisive forces—the historical trend, the character, the situation of the moment—in their fickle madness were going to give the Jewish people a chance to remain alive [...] the Nazis hesitated for a moment at a time when they thought, after defeating France, that they were the rulers of Europe, and then found it vital to resolve the Jewish question, as they imposed the "new order" on the Continent. That is how the Madagascar Plan was born.

The plan, to deport European Jews to the island of Madagascar, was momentarily considered an option after the occupation of France. In the author's estimation, in September 1940, Germany had already given up its plan to invade Britain and was considering the possibility of attacking the Soviet Union. The very fact that they were weighing this option meant "the fate of Europe's Jews was sealed, almost automatically":

> The attack on the Soviet Union inevitably exposed the political aims of Germany in relation to Communist influence over the peoples of the Soviet Union, who from that point onward would be subject to the laws of the Third Reich and would serve its grandiose ambitions. The Soviet peoples had to be taught discipline. This involved the destruction

---

6   *Hapoel Hatza'ir*, December 23, 1947.
7   The meeting was held on May 10, 1948, and reported in *Hapoel Hatza'ir* on May 27, 1948.
8   "Weeks that Ended in a Verdict" (Hebrew), *Molad*, vol. 1, No. 2-3 (May-June, 1948), pp. 121-125; the periodical's editorial board described him as the man "who became well known for his efforts to rescue the surviving Jews by negotiating directly with the chief murderers."

of Communist influence. And in Nazi doctrine this proposition was organically and inevitably linked with the extermination of the Jews.

So the possibility that the Jews might have any kind of fate, other than extermination, was forestalled. The faint glimmer of light that had flickered was extinguished—this time permanently. But does this mean that Kasztner's belief in 1944 that a light had flickered again in Budapest was totally unfounded?

II

Kasztner was a candidate for Mapai in the January 25, 1949 elections to the Constituent Assembly, which was Israel's First Knesset. Since he was number 59 on the party's slate, he had no real chance of being elected; indeed, in these elections, Mapai won only 46 seats.

It had been Sprinzak's idea to add Kasztner to the slate, but, aware of the problems his name might raise, Sprinzak sought Yosef Yambur's advice. Although, in his opinion, Kasztner was a man of unbridled ambition, Yambur was ready to support his candidacy because of his rescue work. At times like these, he argued, "only people with an emotional makeup like his are capable of such acts."[9]

Kasztner was also a candidate in the elections to the Second Knesset, held in the summer of 1951—this time he was number 53 on the slate. Once again, he was not elected, since Mapai won only 45 mandates.

III

Besides his public activity, Kasztner also obtained a position in the government of the new Jewish state—as spokesman for Dov Joseph, a key figure in Mapai; a stern Canadian Jew, who earned a great deal of respect by serving in the War of Independence as governor of besieged Jerusalem. Joseph served continuously as a minister during the terms of the first and second Knesset, heading a different ministry in each of the first six governments. Kasztner and Joseph's personal secretary, Yosef Harris (Harish), who was several years younger than him, formed Dov Joseph's personal team, wandering with him

---

9 Shlomo Yitzhaky of Kibbutz Evron, telephone interview, February 28, 1992.

from ministry to ministry. In the 1949 and 1950 government yearbooks, Kasztner's name appears as director of public relations in the Ministry of Supply and Rationing; in 1951, as director of public relations in the Ministry of Transportation; in 1952, as director of public relations in the Ministry of Commerce and Industry. In 1953, his name no longer appeared. Until April 1953, the Ministry of Commerce and Industry paid his phone bill, and then it was transferred for payment from his personal account.[10] No real friendship developed between Kasztner and Joseph, beyond the correct relations

**President of the Supreme Court Yitzhak Olshan and Minister of Justice
Dov Josef (right)**
Israel National Photo Collection (INPC), D429-109

between a minister and his spokesman. An introverted, unyielding man, Joseph was never personally close to any of his employees, not even to his personal assistants.[11]

As a senior government official, Kasztner lived a normal life, very far from the dangerous and heady atmosphere of wartime. As spokesman for the

10 On this matter, see the letter by N. Leibel of the southern postal services to Israel Kasztner, dated August 24, 1954, documents of Suzi Kasztner-Michaeli.
11 Yosef Harish, personal interview, Jerusalem, November 18, 1991. Harish was the Attorney General between 1986 and 1993.

Ministry of Supply, he issued press releases under his signature announcing a ration of two eggs and two hundred grams of butter and stating that, in ration stamps, seven olives were equivalent to one egg. Later, towards the end of 1951, when he was the spokesman for the Ministry of Commerce and Industry, the newsprint quota for the weekly, *Haolam Hazeh*, was reduced, and journalists held a sit-down strike outside the Ministry. Kasztner received them amiably in his office. At that time, it never occurred to Uri Avneri that the smiling spokesman would, in a short time, be at the epicenter of a stormy drama.[12]

IV

Another career track that Kasztner turned to was the Hungarian-language press. He obtained a position with the Hungarian daily, *Új Kelet*, whose editor-in-chief was Dr. Arno Marton and Kasztner's position was that of night editor. The paper's influence at that time was considerable—there was a large Hungarian community in the country, many of whom did not speak Hebrew. For them, therefore, the paper provided the main, at times, the only, source of information on events in Israel. Kasztner was also made responsible for Hungarian-language broadcasts for the Voice of Israel (later the Israel Broadcasting Service). Part of this job was connected to the security services and he was a member of a committee that included such people as Shaul Avigur, Isser Harel and heads of the eastern European desk in the Foreign Office—Arieh Levavi and Shmuel Bentzur.[13]

One person who remembered Kasztner well for his work on *Új Kelet* was the journalist Yosef (Tommy) Lapid.[14] Lapid was discharged from his army service in September 1951 and Kasztner hired him to work on the paper shortly afterwards. The two were constantly in touch until Kasztner's assassination in 1957. Kasztner had a cynical sense of humor, Lapid recalled, and a lot of charm, which had its effect on women in particular. About two weeks after Lapid started work, Kasztner said to him: "Now you're already a veteran journalist, experienced enough to go over to the kiosk across the

---

12 Uri Avneri, personal interview, Tel Aviv, June 14, 1992.

13 Minutes of the October 27, 1953 committee meeting refer to various issues connected with broadcasts to eastern European states. For example, the question of whether there was a need for broadcasts in Bulgarian.

14 Yosef Lapid, interview in Tel Aviv, December 7, 1991. Lapid was a senior journalist with *Ma'ariv* and Minister of Justice from 2003 to 2004.

street and buy me cigarettes." According to Lapid, Kasztner was a superb journalist, capable of dictating a flawless article, which needed no editing or corrections. He also remembers that he was ambitious and arrogant, qualities that earned him more than a few enemies.

Kasztner also tried his hand at perpetuating the memory of the Holocaust and not only in his newspaper interviews. After returning from Nuremberg, he wrote to the management of Yad Vashem, which was still in its early stages of organization.[15] In Nuremberg, he wrote, he had encountered embarrassing rivalry between the various Jewish organizations, including the American Joint Distribution Committee and the World Jewish Congress, whereby each one was demanding sole responsibility for the issue of war criminals. He, himself, had met General Telford Taylor, who headed the Council of the War Crimes Office, and reported to him on Yad Vashem's plans. Although Taylor felt that such a concentration of Jewish work in the field would lead to the closure of the War Criminal Office, he promised to help Yad Vashem in every way. This letter appears to emphasize the enlightened aspect of Kasztner's stay in Nuremberg. However, it can also be conceived as part of his desire to avoid becoming anonymous in his new homeland, a "has been" like Yoshko Fisher, the father-in-law he so admired.

V

How did Kasztner adjust to the transition from being a man holding the fates of others in his hand, to being an immigrant struggling to find his place in a new country? Relatively late in life—over forty—he had to begin all over again. One day, in 1949, walking on a Tel Aviv street, he met Yonah Rosen. "How are you?" Rosen asked. Kasztner replied with a stale joke, a vestige from the days of the Hapsburg Empire: "The driver of Maria-Teresa's carriage always marked on a special calendar the days when he had sex with the Empress. One day the calendar was accidentally erased and the furious driver sputtered: 'Damn, now I'll have to start all over again!'[16] That's exactly the situation I'm in," Kasztner said with a wry smile. He was not the only one to feel that if he had come to Israel in a coffin, he would not have had to fight for recognition of his efforts. Zvi Yehieli, a key figure in the Mossad Lealiyah

15 Letter from Tel Aviv, May 12, 1948.
16 Yonah Rosen, interview in Kibbutz Ma'agan, August 28, 1992. Rosen was a young member of "Barisia."

Bet, once said to Hanzi Brand: "If you had arrived in Israel in a box, we would have given you a reception worthy of a heroine."[17]

His in-laws' health deteriorated further and the burden of caring for them fell on the Kasztners and the Rudiks. In April 1952, shortly before the storm connected with his son-in-law began to gather momentum, Yoshko Fisher died. Kasztner's moving eulogy referred not only to the deceased, but to himself as well:

> He has left us silently, not making a sound. The seven years since he came to the Land of Israel that he loved so much and served so faithfully were seven lean years. As it had to Job, fate dealt him blow after blow and put him to the test. Worries, disappointments, serious illnesses, poor living conditions and troubles cruelly encircled him, as if he were being tested once again. Dr. Joseph Fisher accepted his harsh fate with a pure soul, a fine, strong character and human nobility, and he went on living with his head held high, modestly, without rebelling or complaining. He came to terms with his bitter fate and he responded to all the afflictions and agony of the new reality with a smile that expressed his wisdom and understanding, and the gaze of a man of faith who has accepted what destiny has dealt him.[18]

Hanzi Brand had a different view of how well Kasztner had integrated into Israeli life. "When he returned from Germany he was warmly welcomed into the party, and began working in it and for it. The barrier that had come between him and Palgi in Budapest and between him and like-minded friends in Geneva and in Israel, fell as if it had never existed, or at least that's how it seemed. For the first time in his life, in Israel Rezsö was happy." In contrast to his state of mind in Geneva, where she had found him dispirited and despairing, in Israel he was full of hopes and ambitions he believed he could really achieve. It wasn't easy for him to get his name included on the list of Mapai candidates to the First and Second Knessets, but the fact that he was a candidate gave him a lot of satisfaction. "This time he thought he had a chance of reaching a position as high as that of his father-in-law, who had always been a role model for him," Brand wrote.[19]

17 Hanzi Brand.
18 From an article in *Ido*, April 24, 1952; the Hebrew manuscript from documents of Suzi Kasztner-Michaeli.
19 Brand, *Satan and the Soul*, pp. 110–111.

Kasztner rarely spoke about the Hungarian affair during his first years in Israel. According to Rudik, who had become much closer to him, he never mentioned anything connected with the German occupation,[20] although he made no efforts to repress his memories of that time.[21] Although he intended to write a book about the period, daily concerns and his work on the paper, which took up so much of his time and energy, made the project no more than a far-off dream.[22] Upon his return from Nuremberg, a newspaper item stated, "he is now writing a book about the extermination [of the Jews]. Excerpts will appear in *Davar*."[23] But the book was never written and excerpts of it were never published—neither in *Davar*, nor anywhere else.

VI

Even when it seemed that Kasztner had opened a new page in his life and the Hungarian affair had become a past memory, it never really disappeared. The rumor that surrounded him, although hushed, never actually ceased. "All around Rezsö, there was the sound of slander and gossip," Hanzi Brand wrote. "In nearly every conversation about him, someone would say, 'Yes, but...'" She understood why. "And once again we realized the truth of the saying—how hard it is for a man to be a survivor and to carry the burden of gratitude to his rescuers."[24]

VII

The story never died down and remained quite low key until the summer of 1952, when it was revived by a septuagenarian Jerusalemite named Malkiel Gruenwald. Throughout the 1950s and early 1960s, Gruenwald distributed mimeographed newsletters entitled "Letters to my Friends in the Mizrachi"

20 Pesach Rudik.
21 For example, the 1952 *Who's Who in Israel* (English, p. 373) states "Israel Kasztner negotiated with the Nazi authorities in World War II over the fate of Hungarian Jewry. He helped rescue Jews in a number of concentration camps. He appeared as a witness before the International Tribunal in Nuremberg. He was advisor to the American occupation forces in Germany."
22 Rivka Bar-Yosef.
23 "A Conversation with Dr. I. Kasztner Who Has Returned from Germany" (Hebrew), *Davar*, May 18, 1948.
24 Brand, *Satan and the Soul*, p. 112.

(a religious Zionist party). The first newsletter to bring up the Kasztner affair was issue number 15, which was published on July 5, 1952 and contained six densely-filled typewritten pages.[25] Most of the newsletter was devoted to fierce attacks on leading figures in religious Zionism, such as Yitzhak Werfel (Raphael), but one part focused entirely on Minister Dov Joseph. In the newsletter's seventeenth paragraph, between the attack on one of Yitzhak Raphael's relatives and an attack on Knesset Member Moshe Kelmer (of Hapo'el Hamizrachi – a religious Zionist party), Gruenwald wrote about "the new leader," Dr. Israel Kasztner, "who appears in Israel as the new leader of the Hungarian community […] who trails behind Dr. Joseph, accompanying him from ministry to ministry as his press officer."

Most of the accusations hurled at Kasztner in this paragraph related to his need to constantly be in the limelight, which had become evident soon after his arrival in Israel and, even earlier, in Hungary. His activity in Hungary during the German occupation was mentioned only incidentally.

Gruenwald devoted the issue number 17 of his newsletter entirely to Kasztner and several pages dealt with his conduct during the German occupation of Hungary. Gruenwald emphasized the link between Kasztner and Kurt Becher and claimed that Kasztner had come to his friend's defense at Nuremberg because of the huge sums of money he had acquired during that period:

> Why did you save him from the punishment he deserved, death by hanging? [Why] did you fly to Nuremberg to save the life of a war criminal, a mass murderer, a robber! […] My dear friends! I am giving you the answer and the explanation: He wanted to save himself; he wanted to prevent Becher from disclosing to the international tribunal their common "business transactions" and robberies, in order to defend himself and accuse Kasztner! Heaven forbid!

He also wrote about the Bergen-Belsen transport: "He saved no fewer than 52 of his relatives on this transport, the lists for which were prepared by the Council of Hungarian Jews, with the aid of money from foreigners. And hundreds of other Jews, most of whom were converts, bought their salvation from Kasztner by paying millions!" He claimed that Kasztner had threatened members of the Judenrat in Hungary with Nazi revenge "if they would not

---

25 Newsletter No. 17 was attached to the writ of indictment against Gruenwald and can be found in many places, including Rosenfeld, *Criminal Case*, p. 20.

put on that transport some men who were in Kasztner's good graces because he had made so much money from them, while Kasztner left thousands of old-time Zionists, members of Mizrachi and ultra-Orthodox Jews, in the valley of the shadow of death."

Gruenwald summed up by saying: "I hope that Dr. Dov Joseph, who although really very obnoxious, is a man of integrity, will find this proof [presented in the newsletter] sufficient to rid himself of this disgraceful stain and condemn him to oblivion." These words were extremely blunt, even for Gruenwald, whose style had always been far from delicate.[26] Elsewhere he wrote: "Because of his criminal machinations and his collaboration with the Nazis, I regard him as implicated in the murder of my dear brethren." And his "opening" which became one of the consummate symbols of the sorry affair, was:

> The stench of a carcass is grating on my nostrils!
> This will be the finest funeral yet!
> Dr. Rudolf Kasztner must be annihilated!

This newsletter snowballed, and grew into an avalanche. How did a measly newsletter, that was not on the fringe but on the fringe of the fringe of society, incite an affair that rocked the young state to its very foundations? But before addressing this issue, there is another question I'd like to address first, and that is—who was Malkiel Gruenwald?

VIII

Very little reliable information was available about Gruenwald and, being a virtually anonymous figure, he remained quite enigmatic: "The scion of a Viennese family, he immigrated to Palestine from Nazified Vienna, where for many years he had been active in Jewish community affairs and journalistic work for the Mizrachi Movement."[27] He owned a small hotel in the center of Jerusalem, but with "his stormy temperament, he found no satisfaction in the hard work of running the third-rate guest house, which scarcely provided him with a livelihood." Consequently, he devoted much of his time to those

---

26 See, for example, Tom Segev, *The Seventh Million–The Israelis and the Holocaust* (New York: Henry Holt, 1991), pp. 255–256.
27 Rosenfeld, *Criminal Case*, p. 15.

mimeographed bulletins, "in which he waged war against corrupt community figures and holders of public office who, in his view, were not worthy of their high positions." He was also said to be a supporter of the IZL (Irgun Zva'i Le'umi—National Military Organization); his son, fighting in the ranks of that organization, was killed on Mount Zion during the War of Independence and Gruenwald changed the name of his hotel to Har Zion (Mount Zion).[28] When he died in 1968 at the age of 86, the obituaries in the press noted that his daughter, Rina Barzilai, who had been active in the Lehi (offshoot of IZL, dubbed by the British the Stern Gang), had committed suicide at a very young age, leaving him alone and childless. Someone wrote about him that he was born in Vienna, moved to Hungary and "succeeded in immigrating to Israel before the Nazi occupation;" also that he had edited a Mizrachi newspaper in German, that the leaders of the movement had renounced him because of his extreme views and pugnacious style; but that he had continued to bring out the paper, "in it, attacking everything that was generally agreed upon in the community."[29]

Although everything known about the man was fragmentary and tendentious, some information about his character can be gleaned from the newsletters he wrote. For example, Newsletter number 15 dealt mainly with Raphael, who at the time was facing a demand to resign from one of the two positions he held—member of the Jewish Agency Executive and Member of Knesset:

> The world that demands purity and honesty demands his removal from the Jewish Agency and from the Knesset, but certain circles in Hapoel Hamizrachi are offering him an alternative—a choice between the Jewish Agency and the Knesset. In his typically crafty way, he wants to hold on to both of them, for the following reasons: He wants to sit in the Knesset because he is sure that sooner or later, the blister that covers his criminal activities will burst, and he hopes to enjoy immunity, on the assumption that the Mapainiks, who in so far as their corruption is concerned, are no better than he is and will not hand him over easily, because he'll get some help from the connections his father-in-law (Maimon) has in Mapai […] He has to sit on the Jewish Agency Executive because of

28 Segev, *The Seventh Million*, pp. 255–256.
29 For example, *Hatzofeh*, March 8, 1968; "I'm afraid of no one," *Panim el Panim*, March 8, 1968. Many details about him are missing, such as the date of his immigration to Palestine.

his many trips abroad "under the guise of official business," so he can continue conducting his own business and his smuggling and because the cat can't stop hunting for mice. But these black deeds of his will not meet with success, in spite of all the filthy intrigues that helped this "family," within a few years, rise from the mire of debts to the ranks of millionaires. For the good of Mizrachi, an end must be put to this fellow![30]

In his testimony to the police, Gruenwald claimed that everyone was talking about the sizeable property Raphael had acquired: "I knew that Raphael's hands weren't clean—at the Jewish Agency, in the Knesset and in the party. He acquired all these enormous assets by dirty means." Later in his testimony, he said he was proud that he had achieved his objective of causing Raphael's defeat in the internal Hapoel Hamizrachi elections. "In the end Raphael really did lose the elections and Shapira's faction won—thanks to me!"[31] Because of Gruenwald's involvement in "ploys" of this kind, he was suspected of receiving benefits—financial and others. Moreover, there were those who may have felt that his libelous writings were advantageous, because he was prepared to print the kind of things that others could only whisper behind closed doors.

As well as publishing his newsletters, Gruenwald conducted a one-sided correspondence with leaders in the government. Some of these letters bore an unequivocal instruction: "to be filed." Early in 1953, he wrote (in German) to Peretz Bernstein, who, shortly before, had been appointed Minister of Commerce and Industry:

The indolent "political Commissars" of Mapai, the scoundrels of the Secret Service, sit in the Generali building as well as in the Palace Hotel [the two buildings in which the Ministry had its offices]—these men serve only Mapai and criminally engage in its acts of snooping and prying. They are involved in propaganda, incitement and intrigues, but they do no work. They enjoy the highest salary grades, but they

30 In his memoir, *Not Easily Came the Light* (Hebrew) (Jerusalem: Edanim Publishers, 1981), p. 437. Raphael writes that the bill forbidding anyone to hold more than one position was directed against him.
31 In the internal elections that were held in the summer of 1952, Shapira's faction received 40% of the votes while Raphael's got only 25%. The rest of the votes were given mainly to the Lamifneh faction headed by Yosef Burg and Moshe Unna (Raphael, see n. 28, p. 437). Moshe Shapira was the party's leader and senior minister between 1948 and 1958 and again between 1960 and 1970.

sabotage the work [of the Ministry]. They snoop around the Ministry and immediately afterwards report to the party.[32]

As might be expected, Newsletter number 17 did not arouse much attention; the only newspaper that referred to it was *Herut*. Mentioning no names, the young journalist Yoel Marcus noted, "For three years now, many Jews from Hungary have been accusing a man in an official position of testifying on behalf of a Nazi criminal, of dark dealings and fat profits at the expense of saving Jews. Why doesn't [this man] clear his name?" Based on the newsletter, Marcus presented some singularly inaccurate details about the affair. For example, he wrote that, before immigrating to Israel, the person in question had, in 1945, "tried to return to Hungary, but had remained in Vienna when he learned that the Hungarian authorities were seeking him for having been a collaborator." Marcus concluded his article by saying:

> Accusations of this kind that are being whispered against a well-known personality, who has contact with the public, are hardly likely to raise our civil morale. If these rumors [and accusations] are completely baseless, then [surely] this man is in possession of all the facts [necessary] to clear his name—but it's important to know why to this very day he hasn't done so.[33]

Very few people gave any serious thought to Gruenwald's newsletters, which were received by families connected to Mizrachi and who, if they wanted some fun after their Friday evening meal, would take up a suggestion to: "[…] read from Reb Malkiel's newsletters?"[34] Members of these circles regarded the newsletters primarily as slander and saw Gruenwald as odious—party members took exception to his extreme right-wing views, as well as to his personality and his unbridled attacks on the party leaders. Rabbi Yehudah Fishman-Maimon, a leader of Mizrachi and the first Minister of Religious Affairs, despised Gruenwald and vetoed his membership in the party.[35] Nor did journalists take him seriously. "I have come across many Gruenwalds in

32 Letter dated February 19, 1953, CZA, A309-22b.
33 Yoel Marcus, "From a Citizen's Notebook—The Mysterious Journey of an 'Important Man' in the State to Nuremberg" (Hebrew), *Herut*, August 26, 1952; on this, see: Ronny Stauber, "The Controversy in the Political Press Over the Kasztner Trial" (Hebrew), *Zionism*, vol. 13 (1988), pp. 219–246.
34 Professor Yehudah Blum, personal interview, Jerusalem, January 12, 1993.
35 Ibid.; Professor Menaham Zvi Kadari, personal interview, Bar-Ilan University, July 22,

my career," Uri Avneri told me.[36] Nevertheless, the Attorney General's Office decided not to disregard the newsletter, but to institute a libel suit against Gruenwald on behalf of the state. Since Kasztner was a civil servant, any libel against him was tantamount to libel against the state.

It was Haim Cohn who took the decision to put Gruenwald on trial. Throughout the nineteen fifties, Cohn had served as the Attorney General, but during the period in question he was also Minister of Justice and in this capacity, on August 25, 1952, he sent a letter, classified as secret, to the Minister of Commerce and Industry, Dov Joseph. This marked the turning point in the affair:[37]

> Re: Dr. Rudolf Kasztner
> It has been brought to my attention that a publication entitled "Letters to My Friends in the Mizrachi" No. 17, dated August 1, 1952, contained an "article" signed by Malkiel Gruenwald, relating to Dr. Kasztner of your Ministry.
> It is my view that we cannot remain silent about this publication. If there is an iota of truth in the grave accusations that appear against Dr. Kasztner in this article, it is incumbent upon us to investigate them and to draw conclusions; if, as I presume, there is no truth in these accusations, the man printing them should [himself] be put on trial.
> Unless I hear from you otherwise, I shall ask the police to organize an investigation into the matter and shall inform you of the results.

What motivated Cohn to adopt this position? The determining factor as far as he was concerned, was neither the writer nor the vehicle he used, marginal as these were, but rather the gravity of the accusations. Over the years, he repeated this claim many times. In an interview with me,[38] he stated that it was unthinkable that allegations such as those made by Gruenwald, particularly when directed against a senior official in the government service, would not be met with a fitting response. His decision, he asserted, also resulted from the fact that, during those years, he lived under the powerful and profound shock of the Holocaust.

1993; Advocate Yehudah Spiegel, personal interview, Tel Aviv, August 5, 1993. Spiegel was Rabbi Maimon's personal secretary.

36 Uri Avneri, personal interview.
37 ISA, Dov Joseph, personal archive, container 10, file 717.
38 Haim Cohn, personal interview, Jerusalem, March 30, 1992.

Cohn never regretted his decision. In 1985, as he left the Cameri Theatre, visibly moved by the premiere performance of the play *Kasztner* by Motti Lerner, he said: "If today I had to reconsider my decision to place Malkiel Gruenwald on trial, I would do so again." Afterwards he added that if he had not taken that decision, "To this very day, people would believe that Kasztner had collaborated with the Nazis."[39]

Haim Cohn
INPC, D708-117

There were not many who agreed with his position. Rosen, who had been Justice Minister until 1951 and had then taken up the post again at the end of 1952, cautioned him against filing the indictment. It was his belief that Cohn was wrong, that it was not worth reawakening such a painful subject and that it was best to ignore a man of Gruenwald's ilk. When he saw that Cohn was not prepared to accept his view, he said: "If I were you, I wouldn't do it."[40] Then, he sighed and said to him in German, "Do what you cannot leave alone." Still,

---

39 Gabriel Strasman, "Today, Too, I Would Place Gruenwald on Trial" (Hebrew), *Ma'ariv*, July 25, 1985.

40 Ruth Bondy, *Felix—Pinhas Rosen and his Time* (Hebrew) (Tel Aviv: Zmora, Bitan Publishing, 1990), p. 490.

Rosen gave Cohn his full support in the face of all the attacks and invective he had had to endure as a result of the trial—as if he, Rosen, had been the one to initiate it.[41] The State Attorney, Erwin Shimron,[42] and Dov Joseph,[43] the Minister who was Kasztner's boss and himself an experienced attorney, were also opposed to the indictment against Gruenwald. In his memoirs, Joseph wrote that since the indictment did not relate in any way to Kasztner's job in his Ministry, but rather to events that occurred outside the state of Israel and prior to Kasztner's immigration, "It was his personal business to decide whether he wanted to take any action against Gruenwald. "I intimated to him that it might not be worth his while to sue [the man] for libel, considering the way such trials are often conducted in Israel."[44]

Pinhas Rosen
INPC, D709-041

41 Michael Shashar, *Haim Cohen, Supreme Court Judge* (Hebrew) (Jerusalem: Keter Publishing House, 1989).

42 Yechiel Gutman, *The Attorney General Versus the Government* (Hebrew) (Jerusalem: Edanim Publishers, 1981), p. 89. In a conversation with me, Cohn said that most of those whom he consulted advised him not to put Gruenwald on trial because it would be a very problematic legal action. Joseph and Rosen, with whom he was close, warned him against the trial and to reconsider.

43 Ibid.

44 Dov Joseph, *The Dove and the Sword* (Hebrew) (Ramat Gan: Massada Publishing House, 1975), p. 321.

IX

These were the positions taken by Cohn and Joseph; as far as Kasztner's own position was concerned, however, the matter is more complicated. "Kasztner told me in no uncertain terms that he did not want this," Haim Cohn told me. "He wanted to put that entire period out of his mind and erase it from his memory. He did not want to recall it. But I was not interested in Kasztner's personal attitude. I was interested in the matter [...] I was insistent."[45]

Kasztner's widow, Bodiya, expressed a similar attitude. In the only interview she ever gave, on the tenth anniversary of his murder,[46] she claimed that Rezsö did not want the trial but he was faced with a cruel choice—to agree to the indictment against Gruenwald or to resign from his government post. She thought he ought to resign, "but he replied that he has no choice, he has to agree to the institution of the legal proceedings [...]" In reply to the question, who forced him to agree,[47] she said that Cohn wrote to Joseph that if the libel suit against Gruenwald was not filed, Kasztner would be put on trial under the law regarding Nazis and their collaborators. "Just imagine," she said in a blend of amazement and anger, "he wanted to put my husband on trial, under the same law under which Eichmann was sentenced to death."[48]

This version of the facts, which may be regarded as the "official" version, suggests that the filing of the libel suit was an injury to Kasztner, because it was forced upon him completely against his wishes. However, from conversations with many people who knew him well—there are no written testimonies on this issue—a much more complex picture emerges. Kasztner had an ambivalent attitude toward the libel suit, and to a certain extent he had some interest in its being brought. Peretz Révész[49] believes that Kasztner's attitude to the affair was at first one of utter contempt. When they met by chance in the corridors of the Ministry of Commerce and Industry, Kasztner said partly in anger and partly in derision, "After they wrote a whole pile of shit about me in Hungary—so [what if] there's one more pamphlet. I'll [just] throw it away." Later, he changed his mind and decided to attend the trial.

---

45 In a conversation with me, Cohn said that Kasztner had been strongly opposed to the libel suit and agreed only when he was faced with two choices: to agree to having the state submit a suit or to resign and sue Gruenwald himself.

46 Dan Ofri, "My Husband Spoke Only the Truth" (Hebrew), *Yedioth Ahronoth*, March 17, 1967.

47 The wording of the question is misleading. Kasztner did not file the suit nor was he a formal party to the trial. The suit was filed by the state.

48 In my estimation, it is very unlikely that such a threat was made.

49 Peretz Révész, personal interview, Kfar Hamaccabi, March 12, 1992.

Révész takes the view, based on what he learned from his friend Hanzi Brand, that Kasztner was pushed into taking this step by Dezső (David) Herman, who told him: "This is your chance to become a part of history." Brand herself told me that Herman had in fact persuaded Kasztner to support the idea of a trial and even to testify as the first prosecution witness. In her view, this was bad advice. It created a situation in which Gruenwald did not have to prove his accusations, but Kasztner had to prove his innocence.[50]

Amos Manor was a witness on that occasion. At a party in the home of the lawyer Alexander Rosenfeld, a member of Mapai and a leader of the Association of Hungarian Immigrants, Manor met Kasztner and tried to dissuade him from going to the trial—"Nothing good will come of it," he told him. Herman, who overheard their conversation, broke in and said to Kasztner: "This is your opportunity to achieve the status and fame that you deserve." Afterwards, he said something in Hungarian meaning "to immortalize the fame." A strident argument broke out, at the end of which Kasztner accepted Herman's opinion. In Manor's view, Kasztner, at least ten years his senior, found it difficult to take his advice. He had no idea that "that pipsqueak" was the deputy head of Israel's security services. "Kasztner was almost convinced by my arguments," he added, "but Dezső steamrolled him into it."[51]

Others believe that Kasztner himself was interested in seeing the trial take place, regardless of Herman and his pressures. Rivka Bar-Yosef,[52] his wife's cousin, thinks that Kasztner believed the trial would give him the stage he was looking for. "In the family, we talked about the trial restoring to him the status of hero and saint," she told me. Rudik took a similar view.[53] In his estimation, Kasztner was anxious about the opening of the trial, but hoped that during it, his activity on behalf of Hungarian Jewry in its hour of grave adversity would be presented and that at its end, he would become a national hero. That hope tipped the scales in the end, making Kasztner favor the idea of a trial. However, Rudik added, had his father-in-law, Yoshko Fisher, been alive at the time, Kasztner would have taken a different view. Fisher, who was a lawyer and had a great deal of influence on Kasztner, would never have allowed him to go to the trial.

Others explicitly warned him against the trial. One was Zvi Herman, Dezső's brother, who was then a member of the Jewish Agency Executive.[54]

50 Hanzi Brand, personal interview.
51 Amos Manor, personal interview.
52 Rivka Bar-Yosef, personal interview.
53 Pesach Rudik, personal interview.
54 Zvi Herman, personal interview.

Kasztner came to ask his advice and Herman told him emphatically: "Don't go to the trial! Don't react!" He told Kasztner that in the forties, when he himself was active in the organization responsible for illegal immigration into Palestine (Mossad Lealiyah Bet), he had learned there was no point arguing with those people who had remained alive, nor was it possible to contend with their accusations. He also told him of a meeting he had had with a group of survivors from Slovakia who had even hurled accusations at Gizi Fleischmann, who, he said, raising his voice, "was like a saintly angel to us." But all those who felt they had been dealt in injustice during those terrible days could not be dissuaded, nor was it possible to mend the wounds in their heart. Kasztner told him, too, that he had been left no choice; that Joseph had threatened to dismiss him from his job. Angered, Herman retorted that if Joseph were so interested in a trial, he ought to sue Gruenwald himself for the pamphlets he had written against him. There is no way you are going to come out of this affair of yours with your hands clean, he concluded the conversation.

Manor was opposed to the trial, but for different reasons. In 1944, after the German occupation, he was arrested and taken to Auschwitz. On being released, he returned to Budapest, where he began working as a glazier; as nearly all the glass in the city's windows had been shattered. In his work, he came to Cluj (he himself was from nearby Sighet), where he went to visit a childhood friend. His friend was not at home; he had gone to the synagogue to pray and attend a protest rally against the British policy forbidding the immigration of Jews to Palestine. Manor went to look for him in the synagogue where he found a huge crowd. About a thousand people were listening intently to speeches directed not against British policy, but against Israel Kasztner and the rescue train, an affair he knew nothing about. When the speakers were through, he asked his friend what it was all about, and was told about the train and the suspicion that those who got on it were chosen on the basis of favoritism and personal connections.

The rally left a strong impression on Manor, not because of the accusations that had been made during it, but rather because of the intensity of the emotions the affair had evoked. He understood all too well that in connection with such a sensitive, charged issue, things were sure to get out of hand. This feeling was strengthened by the things he witnessed after his immigration to Israel.[55] He met many people who spoke out against Kasztner,

---

55 Manor immigrated to Israel in 1949, spent a brief period at Kibbutz Ma'agan, moved to Tel Aviv and, a short while later, was recruited by the General Security Services (famously

first and foremost among them, Yoel Palgi. He also estimated that there was no chance of a libel suit against Kasztner succeeding in Israel, and that it should therefore be avoided at all costs.

Kasztner was not eager to see a trial take place, perhaps he was even apprehensive about it, but his adventurous spirit and his craving to be in the limelight got the upper hand. He saw the trial as an opportunity to escape the mundane drabness of his job as spokesman for a government ministry and to attain the position he deserved. But it never occurred to him that the limelight that was about to turned on him would be so intense as to burn him to a cinder.

X

Events moved at a snail's pace once the decision had been taken to institute a libel suit against Gruenwald. In October 1952, Gruenwald and Kasztner were interrogated by the police; Kasztner on the 2nd and Gruenwald on the 12th. The police did not attribute much importance to the investigation, and assigned a sergeant, Carmel Levanon, to conduct it, rather than an officer.

At the interrogation, Gruenwald, who introduced himself as a journalist, stated[56] that for scores of years he had been fighting against corrupt politics, particularly in his own party and had always been opposed to politics being turned into a profession that became a person's livelihood. "In Europe, too, I fought against the corruption that had spread throughout the Zionist movement and 'Mizrachi'. My principle was that work in the party should be only voluntary and that no one ought to make a business out of his politics," he said. To emphasize his loyalty to this principle, he told the interrogator: "Never throughout my life, have I received money for writing articles against people [...] and never did I receive any money for keeping quiet. If I saw any injustice in the party, I would fight against the entire party [...] I am convinced that everything I did in my newsletters will purge Mizrachi of the dirt that has adhered to it."

He stated that he had already begun publishing his newsletters in Europe and that he thought they were more effective than writing articles for the

known as the Shabak). In 1952, he was appointed deputy to the head of the GSS, Izi Dorot (Roth), whom he replaced in 1953 (Amos Manor, personal interview).

56 The two interrogations were submitted as exhibits to the Jerusalem District Court. Kasztner's was marked Exhibit 1 for the defense, and Gruenwald's was Exhibit 37 for the prosecution. They were not preserved in the 'Kasztner trial' containers in the State Archives, and I found Gruenwald's in the files of attorney Micha Caspi.

press: "After I found out that you can't write acrimonious articles in official newspapers, I would, at my own expense, print handbills and send them by mail to all kinds of people who had some interest in Mizrachi. Ninety percent were sent to members of Mizrachi, and the rest to people interested in Zionism." When he came to Israel, he began receiving information from people, by word of mouth, by phone, and by mail, about the corruption that had spread through the various parties. "I printed many letters in my newsletters just as I received them from citizens, in their own words [...] but I didn't print them until I had made inquiries to verify [their contents]."

As for his connection to Kasztner, he was asked only at the end of the interrogation, and even then, only briefly. "I know Mr. Kasztner from the Ministry of Commerce and Industry, from meetings of Hungarian immigrants and from letters I received from Hungarian Jewish immigrants," he replied. "I don't know if Kasztner knows me." In his interrogation, he admitted that he had been questioned in the past about things he had written, but the police had decided, "They would intervene only if there was an order from above."

XI

It would be another seven months before the Attorney General filed the indictment, on May 25, 1953. It was a file whose bureaucratic marking later became a kind of symbol: "Criminal case No. 124/53." And a further seven months passed until the trial itself opened in the Jerusalem District Court, on January 1, 1954.

The trial was conducted before a single judge: the President of the Jerusalem District Court, 44-year-old Dr. Benjamin Halevi, a native of a small city in Germany. In 1933, after completing his law studies at the University of Berlin, he immigrated to Israel and spent about a year in agricultural training at Kibbutz Degania Bet. In 1934, he began his clerkship at the law office of Mordecai Eliash, a prominent Jewish attorney during the Mandatory period and Israel's first minister to London. In 1938, he opened his own law office in Jerusalem, and only a few months later, at the age of 28, was chosen to serve as a judge in a Jerusalem Magistrate's Court. He was made a judge in the Jerusalem District Court shortly after the establishment of the state, and several months later, became its president.[57]

---

57 The details are from "Special Author, Dr. Halevi—The Judge in Stormy Trials," (Hebrew) *Ma'ariv*, July 4, 1955.

Halevi received a great deal of publicity in 1953, when he served as president of the special military tribunal that tried the accused members of the Tzrifin Underground. This radical nationalist group favored the establishment of the 'Kingdom of Israel,' to extend from the Mediterranean Sea to the Euphrates River. Its members were accused of acts of violence that were intended to thwart the reparations agreement with Germany and of placing bombs near the embassies of Eastern Bloc countries. In November 1952, they placed a bomb near the building that housed the Czech legation; in January 1953, they tried to set fire to the Soviet ambassador's car; and in February 1953, they laid a bomb near the Soviet Embassy, injuring three of the legation's staff and seriously damaging the building itself. The Soviets reacted by severing diplomatic ties with Israel.

In July 1953, the trial of 15 members of the underground, accused of activity in a terror organization, opened in the Tzrifin camp (from which the group got its name) near Rishon LeZion. Judge Halevi adjudged the trial, after first being inducted into the army and brevetted to the rank of colonel. Two military officers sat in judgment with him. The prosecutor was the Attorney General Haim Cohn and the underground members were defended by a young attorney named Shmuel Tamir-Katznelson. Judgment was handed down on August 23, 1953 and many were astounded by its severity. The accused were sentenced to long terms of imprisonment—one of them, Shimon Bechar, was sentenced to 12 years in prison, and another, Yaacov Heruti, whom the court found had played a key role in the organization, was sentenced to ten years. A month later, after receiving an opinion from the Supreme Justice, Shimon Agranat, Pinhas Lavon, the Acting Minister of Defense, confirmed the verdict.[58]

The entire legal proceeding, the harsh sentences in particular, came under a great deal of criticism. It was most severely censured in the newspapers *Haolam Hazeh* and *Herut*. Trying civilians in a military court, *Haolam Hazeh* claimed, was a bad and dangerous proceeding, whose true purpose was to undermine the authority of the civil courts in general and of the Supreme Court in particular: "[Benjamin Halevi was] the only professional judge prepared to undertake this job, after all his colleagues had refused it as an affront to their dignity. He completely justified the trust placed in him by the

---

58 On this matter, see Segev, *The Seventh Million*, pp. 267–268; "An Underground in Israel" (Hebrew), *Rimon*, March 20, 1957; for a detailed description of the underground's activities, see Isser Harel, *The Truth about Kasztner's Murder—Jewish Terrorism in the State of Israel* (Hebrew) (Jerusalem: Edanim Publishers, 1985), pp. 73–75.

Attorney General. His verdict was even more severe than was demanded by the Attorney General himself."[59]

The weekly argued that Justice Agranat also opined that Halevi had shown a "tendency towards harsh judgment," and the secret report he submitted had recommended that the sentences of the accused be cut in half. The writer of the article also contended that since Halevi had gone too far, it had been decided that he would not chair the judicial group in a further trial to be conducted against two suspects from the underground, but would be replaced by a regular military judge.[60]

In an article in *Herut*, the leader of the Herut Movement, Menahem Begin, asserted that the verdict "clearly demonstrated vindictiveness and the reasons behind it are tainted by hypocrisy and arrogance." Not only "official vindictiveness" but the personal vindictiveness of the judges "whom the accused angered by their 'non-acknowledgment' [of the military court's authority to judge civilians, Y.W.], by words or acts of contempt." However, Begin added, their failure to acknowledge the authority of military officers to judge civilians "is not only the right but also the duty of the accused".

Aside from vindictiveness, Begin also discerned in the verdict what could be defined as "double *chutzpah*": The judges allowed the prosecution, rather than the accused, the benefit of the doubt; "judicial *chutzpah*," he called it. When the judges stated that the actions of the accused were a continuation of acts carried out in the pre-state period, he saw that as a victory for the British general Evelyn Barker, whose "work was done by others, by 'judges' of the state of Israel, who he wanted to choke to death […]."[61]

Halevy's legal career almost came to an end during the final months of 1953. In December, four new judges were appointed to the Supreme Court: two were to take the place of judges who had retired (Simcha Assaf and Menahem Donkelblum) and two were appointed because the number of Supreme Court judges had been increased from seven to nine. Two of the four new judges were Zvi Berinson, former Director-General of the Ministry of Labor, and David Goitein, who, from the establishment of the state, had

---

59 "Man of the Year—Haim Cohn—Authority against the Man" (Hebrew), *Haolam Hazeh*, September 7, 1953. In his memoirs, Justice Olshan wrote that it was he who recommended Ben-Gurion to appoint Halevi to the position, see Yitzhak Olshan, *Deliberations* (Hebrew) (Jerusalem and Tel Aviv: Schocken Publishing House, 1978), p. 317.

60 *Haolam Hazeh*, Ibid.

61 Menachem Begin, "The Tzrifin Trial" (Hebrew), *Herut*, August 27, 1953.
    General Evelyn Barker (1894–1983) was the commander of British Forces in Mandate Palestine (1946–1947).

served as a senior diplomat in the Israeli legations in the United States and South Africa. The other two were district judges: Yoel Zussman of the Tel Aviv District Court and Moshe Landau of the Haifa District Court. As far as Halevi was concerned, this was an intolerable situation. He had served longer than the two district judges selected and, as President of the District Court, had greater seniority. Nonetheless, he had not been a candidate for a position in the Supreme Court.

Infuriated, he decided to take an unusual step. On December 23, 1953, he sent Justice Minister Pinhas Rosen the following letter:[62]

Dear Minister!

In light of your failure to appoint me or even to nominate me for an appointment, despite my 15 consecutive years of devoted service as a judge, to one of the four vacant judicial positions in the Supreme Court, I hereby regretfully submit my resignation as district judge and President of the District Court and ask that you accept it as of the beginning of the coming budgetary year, i.e., April 1, 1954.

Halevi's move was not a secret—a day later *Ha'aretz* ran the complete story, according to which Halevi had informed the Minister of Justice by telephone and that he would be meeting him and, although this was a grave step on his part, he was determined to go ahead. Moreover, many people—judges and friends—had pleaded with him not to resign, and that the committee for appointing judges had unanimously confirmed the appointments to the Supreme Court.[63]

Halevi took another step that was not so widely publicized; he applied to Ben-Gurion, who was then about to retire to Sede Boker,[64] asking him to intervene on his behalf—an extraordinary action by any standard. In his letter to Ben-Gurion[65], he reminded him of their conversation after the Tzrifin Underground trial, in which he "told [you] about my strenuous

---

62 The letter is from Micha Caspi's archive; a copy of the letter was sent to the President of the Supreme Court, Justice Moshe Smoira and to the Director of the Courts, Judge Eisenberg.

63 "Judge Dr. B. Halevi Has Resigned because He did not Receive a Supreme Court Appointment," *Ha'aretz*, December 24, 1953; Judge B. Halevi submitted his resignation to P. Rosen, Ibid., December 27, 1953.

64 Ben-Gurion resigned at the beginning of December 1953 but continued to serve as interim prime minister until the establishment of a government headed by Moshe Sharett, on January 26, 1954.

65 This letter and the other letters on this subject are labeled in the BGRCA as "Correspondence."

efforts within the judicial system to advocate a statist approach to national problems, and how I aspired to champion this approach within the supreme judicial institution, which sets policy for all the judges in the country." Halevi claimed that Ben-Gurion had promised, "to inform the Minister of Justice of the content of our talk."[66]

Further in his letter, Halevi noted with regret that he had been overlooked in the present round of appointments, "However, in view of Dr. Smoira's long, drawn-out illness, there is a possibility and a practical need to appoint an additional judge." At this point he named the members of the Committee for Appointing Judges—so that if Ben-Gurion wished to intervene, he would have no trouble finding out who to speak to. "If you believe, as I do, that there is a great need to reinforce the statist approach of the judges, and that I have the power to push through this trend in the Supreme Court, then I ask that you help me fulfill this task," he concluded.

Ben-Gurion hastened to reply to Halevi and to send a letter to the Minister of Justice in this regard. On December 23, he wrote to Halevi that he was not certain that an additional judge was to be appointed, but "I greatly appreciate your judicial approach and will write my opinion to the Justice Minister—this time as an ordinary citizen and as an old friend of his." To Rosen he wrote (on December 29) that many judges in the Israeli judicial system acted not as judges in the state of Israel but as "judges under the [British] Mandate, revealing a total lack of understanding of statism." One judge "who knows the law and also has a statist attitude" is Halevi. Therefore, although he (Ben-Gurion) does not know whether Halevi is in any way superior to the judges selected to serve on the Supreme Court, "his retirement from the court is a grave blow to the legal system in Israel." Hence, he urged Rosen to do his utmost to get Halevi to reconsider. There was a good chance of this because, "from what I know of the relationship between you, I believe that if you insist on his withdrawing his resignation—he will do as you ask."

Less than a month later, Minister Rosen visited the district court and met with Halevi. A statement was later issued, according to which the latter had consented to continue serving as a judge.[67] He gave his reasons in a letter to Ben-Gurion on January 17, 1954, the very date on which the Gruenwald trial opened. His protest against the policy of appointments to the Supreme Court had remained unchanged, he wrote, but "it is clear to me that my place

---

66 It is possible that this conversation took place when the issue of appointments to the Supreme Court was already under discussion.

67 "Dr. B. Halevi has Retracted his Resignation" (Hebrew), *Ha'aretz*, January 22, 1954.

is in the court system and not outside it and I have been persuaded that I must not abandon a state position because of a temporary disappointment." This strange story concluded with a brief letter from Ben-Gurion dated January 18, 1954 stating how pleased he was that the affair was over, "because your leaving the Israeli judiciary would have been a loss to statism and the cause of great damage." The affair was mentioned again during Halevi's checkered career, when, in late 1969 he exchanged the bench of a Supreme Court judge with a seat in the Knesset on the Herut Movement list. Haifa attorney Yosef Kushnir, who in 1953 was one of the Bar Association's representatives on the Committee for Appointing Judges and later served as a Knesset member for Mapam, recalled it as an arrogant move by a man "who thought the committee had no right to choose one man over another and to judge matters according to its own considerations."[68]

The matter of Halevi's appointment to the Supreme Court also resurfaced in the summer of 1954, in the midst of the Gruenwald trial. Following Smoira's resignation, which he had foreseen, the Appointments Committee convened to select a new supreme justice. Halevi was a candidate this time and, in the belief that his appointment was a sure thing, *Ma'ariv* wrote that the Minister of Justice was about to issue a special order allowing him to remain a judge in the District Court, along with his position in the Supreme Court.[69] *Haolam Hazeh* wrote that "the most likely candidate for the position of the new Supreme Justice is the [man who judged] Gruenwald-Kasztner, Benjamin Halevi."[70] But Halevi was not the only candidate for the position and Alfred Witkon was ultimately selected. This time, Halevi did not repeat his resignation ploy, even though the appointment probably aroused his ire: not only had he been passed over again, but the man chosen was the relieving president of the Jerusalem District Court, namely, his deputy. After the fact, one of the newspapers wrote that his resignation threat about eight months earlier had damaged his case. He was not appointed to the position to avoid the impression that past pressure had led to his appointment at the present time.[71]

Only in 1963 was Halevi appointed to the Supreme Court, after another round of appointments had passed him by. Following the deaths of Justices Cheshin and Goitein, two new judges were appointed to the Supreme

68 "Yosef Kushnir, "It is Becoming to a Former Judge, Too, to be Humble" (Hebrew), *Al HaMishmar*, October 17, 1969.
69 "Halevi is Nominated as a Supreme Court Judge" (Hebrew), *Ma'ariv*, July 27, 1954.
70 "Forecast," *Haolam Hazeh*, July 15, 1954.
71 *Herut*, July 28, 1954.

Court—one of them was Haim Cohn. It is no wonder that one headline read: "For nine years, Justice Halevi has been waiting for his appointment to the Supreme Court."[72]

An unusual problem arose during Halevi's term as President of the District Court following the 1960 capture of Adolf Eichmann. It transpired then that, by law, Eichmann had to be tried in the Jerusalem District Court, and therefore it was up to Halevi to decide on the composition of the tribunal. Since it was Halevi who had stated that Eichmann was the "Satan" to whom Kasztner had sold his soul, Justice Olshan, then President of the Supreme Court felt it was not fitting for him to be one of the judges. He based this view on the custom that if a judge had voiced any opinion whatsoever on a matter that later became the subject of a trial, he ought to disqualify himself from sitting in judgment at that trial.

Olshan called Halevi in for a talk to learn his reaction to this view, which was shared by Justice Minister Rosen. Halevi's response was unwavering: he intended to sit on the tribunal that would judge Eichmann as well as to serve as its president. All of Olshan's efforts to dissuade him were to no avail— Halevi stuck firmly to his decision. Rosen, too, tried to get him to change his mind, but his arguments were futile. Left with no other choice, the Minister decided to pass a law in Knesset stating that if an accused is liable to receive a death sentence, the President of the Supreme Court is authorized to establish a special tribunal, headed by the Supreme Justice with two district court judges serving alongside him.[73]

In the end, Rosen suggested a compromise, to which Olshan agreed. The final version of the law stated that the Supreme Justice would appoint the president of the court and that the president of the district court would appoint the other two judges to serve on the tribunal. This gave Halevi the opening to appoint himself as one of the judges of Adolf Eichmann.

When, in 1969, Halevi resigned his position in the Supreme Court, it was the only time in the history of the state that a judge, moreover one in the highest court of law, left the judge's bench in order to be elected to the Knesset as a member of the Herut Movement, and his move resounded throughout the media. However, his stature was greatly diminished during the twelve years he served in the Knesset. An article about him in the press under the headline, "From a seat in the Supreme Court to the back benches of the Knesset,"[74] reflected this comedown.

---

72 *Ma'ariv*, May 16, 1963.
73 Olshan, *Deliberations*, pp. 315–317.
74 Shlomo Nakdimon, *Yedioth Ahronoth*, March 14, 1975.

Halevi's parliamentary career, too, suffered many twists and turns. In 1974, after adopting a more dovelike position, he left the Herut Movement to become a one-man faction. In 1977 he joined the Dash party (Democratic Movement for Change) and after several splits, he ended up in one of the party's fragments—with Yigael Yadin and Shmuel Tamir. Benjamin Halevi eventually left the political arena in 1981. But, on a cold, blustery Jerusalem winter's day, back in 1954, he began presiding over the trial of criminal case 124/53.

XII

At the trial, Amnon Tel, Assistant Attorney of the Jerusalem District, represented the prosecution. The press archives contain nothing about him, and had he not taken part in this trial, his name would probably have fallen into oblivion. Tel was born in Bucharest in 1903, where he opened a law office in 1935. In 1940 he immigrated to Israel. He learned Hebrew while serving in the British army during World War II and, following his discharge, he passed the bar exams in Israel. He interned with Attorney Pinhas Rabinowitz and secured a job in the State Advocacy office as assistant to State Attorney Erwin Shimron in the early fifties. Afterwards, he moved to the Jerusalem District Advocacy and served as assistant district attorney until his death in 1972.[75]

Those who remember him from the trial have scant praise for his legal skills. One person, known for his predilection for understatement, told me "Tel was a very mediocre lawyer, even in comparison to other lawyers of his level and grade." Someone else simply defined him as "a fourth-class lawyer."[76] However, those who worked with him in the district advocacy have an entirely different recollection of him. Judge Meir Wolinsky, who shared an office with him, recalls that Tel was very dedicated to his work. He invested hours of work in every case assigned to him and went to court as if going into battle— always thoroughly prepared. Yonah Blatman, later the State Attorney, worked in the district advocacy during the sixties. He remembers Tel as a very serious attorney who always did his utmost to keep abreast of current professional literature and judgments. As far as his personality was concerned, there was

---

75 I was given the details by his widow, Lily Tel, in a personal interview, September 27, 1993.
76 Advocate Haim Zadok, personal interview, January 29, 1992; Advocate Yehudah Spiegel, personal interview.

a certain contradiction: he was very intimidating, especially to the young lawyers; on the other hand, however, he was always prepared to help.[77]

In Blatman's view, it was unfair to assign him to the libel suit against Gruenwald, for two reasons: his specialty was civil, not criminal, law; and his Hebrew was poor. His widow says that he had to prepare for every trial not only from the legal standpoint, but also from the linguistic point of view. For Tel, Blatman asserts, the trial was a trauma, and he never spoke about it. Wolinsky also believes that he did not deserve the negative image he was saddled with because of the trial, which apparently plagued him for many years.

Tel was assigned the case by chance. The Jerusalem District Attorney, Ezra Hadaya, was looking for Wolinsky to assign him the libel suit against the eccentric old Jerusalemite, Gruenwald. Since he was out of the office that day, Hadaya gave the case to Tel. No one attributed much importance to the affair; they all thought it was an open and shut case and that it would be over in a matter of days.[78]

Shmuel Tamir-Katznelson
INPC, D709-067

77 Judge Meir Wolinsky, personal interview, September 14, 1993; Advocate Yonah Baltman, personal interview, September 12, 1993.
78 Meir Wolinsky, personal interview.

In contrast to the unknown attorney who represented the prosecution, Gruenwald's defense lawyer was Shmuel Tamir-Katznelson, who was already quite famous. By the end of the trial, he was a very famous man indeed.

Tamir-Katznelson was born in Jerusalem in 1923 to one of the most prominent families in the Yishuv. Politically, the family was polarized; some of its members were right-wingers and Revisionists, while others were at the very heart of the Mapai establishment. One of his uncles, Yosef Katznelson, who was known as the 'black prince', was among the founders of the IZL (Irgun Zva'i Le'umi) underground movement, was sent to Poland in 1938 to organize Revisionist illegal immigration, and died there. Tamir's youngest son bears his name. According to one of the profiles of him that were printed during the trial, largely at his instigation, "his favorite was his uncle, Yosef Katznelson, who brought thousands of illegal immigrants into Palestine together with Abba Ahimeir, Uri Zvi Greenberg, and Yehoshua Heschel Yevin [...] he was Shmuel's only hero."[79]

A memorial book on Yosef Katznelson, published by the Jabotinsky Institute,[80] contains an article by his nephew. The tone is impersonal, the style lofty, but it does show how closely Tamir identified with the uncle he idolized:

> Yosef prepared himself for the role of a leader... As someone preparing for leadership, he did so with unmatched thoroughness. He related to life with profound gravity, despite his unusual sense of humor. Thus, although he did succeed in educating a generation, although he was one of the chief shapers of a political school of thought [...] although he made a key contribution in preparing the ground for the establishment of the state of Israel—despite all these, Yosef Katznelson's greatness lay more in what he was than in what he managed to do in his lifetime.[81]

From his youth, Tamir was associated with the Revisionist movement and, in 1938, aged 15, he joined the IZL. Only a few years later, he became an IZL commander in the Jerusalem district; in 1947 he was deported to the detainees camp in Kenya, where he completed his law studies. In 1948, he returned to Israel, and in the summer of that year, he was among the founders of the Herut

---

79 "The Man Who Tore the Curtain" (Hebrew), *Haolam Hazeh*, September 29, 1954. They were the leaders of the radical right in 1930s Palestine.

80 Yosef Ahimeir, ed., *The Black Prince—Yosef Katznelson and the National Movement in the Thirties* (Hebrew) (Tel Aviv: Jabotinsky Institute in Israel, 1983).

81 "Shmuel Tamir, The Jerusalem Rock," in Ahimeir, *The Black Prince*, p. 19.

Movement. In 1950, along with member of the First Knesset Shmuel Merlin, he led the Lamerchav faction that challenged Begin's leadership. The long relationship between the two men was marked by many ups and downs.[82] In the fall of 1950, after Herut's poor showing in the municipal elections, Tamir lashed out at Begin: "Why does the dictionary contain the word 'resign' if you won't resign?" Tamir's faction was defeated at the Second Herut convention in February 1951 and he left the movement.

Tamir's hostility towards the 'Ben-Gurionist regime' was particularly vehement, even by early 1950s standards. According to *Haolam Hazeh* publisher Uri Avneri, Tamir's hatred for Ben-Gurion, whom he held responsible for his deportation to Kenya, was a dominant motif in his life.[83] The depth of his animosity towards the Mapai governments is obvious from articles he wrote during the early days of the state—the state's elected government is depicted as a foreign, collaborating, treacherous government that seized power from the underground fighters, who really deserved to have it. In 1951, when the debate began concerning reparations from Germany, he wrote:

> So this is the position of the heads of this nation—and of this community—who regarded their brethren as 'human dust,' who were adamantly opposed to rescuing them before the World War by way of a speedy, all-inclusive evacuation [from Europe] and bringing them 'illegally' into Palestine, who abandoned them to their fate during the World War, who suppressed the news of their annihilation, and who fought against the desperate attempt to save them when the great revolt broke out at the end of the war. This is how they stand now, the heads of this nation, voraciously eating the fruits of the revolt they fought against—rulers in the liberated state—and now they want to ensure their deceitful, parasitic rule [by accepting] "reparations" for the extermination—for which they are partly responsible—'reparations' for the flesh and blood of their own people, even if these are reparations for the flesh and blood of their own fathers and mothers.[84]

---

82 On this matter see Yohanan Bader, *The Knesset and I* (Hebrew) (Jerusalem: Edanim Publishing House, 1979), p. 49; Sasson Sofer, *Begin—Anatomy of Leadership* (Oxford: Basil Blackwell, 1988), pp. 80–82. Shmuel Tamir, *Son of this Land* (Hebrew) (Tel Aviv: Zmora, Bitan Publishers, 2002), pp. 196–210. On the relationship between Tamir and Begin, see: Shlomo Nakdimon, "Begin-Tamir: Anatomy of Relations" (Hebrew), *Yedioth Ahronoth*, August 8, 1980.

83 Uri Avneri, personal interview.

84 Shmuel Tamir (Katznelson), "To the Cemetery, Beggars!" (Hebrew), *Herut*, March 16, 1951; "The Great Revolt" is the declaration of IZL's uprising against the British in 1944.

During the fifties, Tamir became one of the best-known lawyers in Israel. He appeared in some high-profile, widely publicized trials. He was the defense attorney for Dov Shilansky, who placed a bomb in the Ministry of Foreign Affairs to protest the ratification of the reparations agreement with Germany; for the accused in the Tzrifin Underground trial, and for *Shurat Hamitnadvim* (Volunteer Service), a movement that originated among Mapai members who saw their mission in its behavior and, even more so, its very essence, in the Diaspora. This pattern of Diaspora-like, or *galuti*[85] behavior explained the Mapai leadership's appeasing behavior towards and collaboration with the British during the Mandate, as well as its defeatist conduct in the War of Independence—when it stopped short of capturing the West Bank and withdrew from the areas it had taken in the Sinai Peninsula. This motif—the struggle of the "sabra," the first generation after the redemption, against the *galuti* leadership—would be most strikingly expressed during the trial of Criminal Case 124/53.

XIII

Tamir was very conscious of the media in general and particularly of how he was portrayed in it. His self-image was reflected in several articles printed in *Haolam Hazeh* during the trial. They emphasized his status as a symbol of the New Hebrew, the native-born 'sabra'.[86] In 1952, the weekly ran a 'mock trial' for Israeli youngsters. In it, Tamir played the role of prosecutor. The caption under his picture read: "The prosecutor, Shmuel Tamir, who in age, belongs to the same category as the defendant [i.e., the older generation], has undertaken the prosecution [...] as befits a first-rate finagler like him. His summation was marked by warmth—the short speech (about ten minutes)

---

85 *Galuti*—the adjectival form of the Hebrew word *galut*, which means exile or Diaspora. It refers to the behavior and mentality typical of the Diaspora Jew and has negative connotations. The term is used to contrast the figure of the Israeli, a new, improved breed of Jew. It conjures up the old, stereotypical image of a Jew, who, in his relations with the landowner or the civil authority, is servile, soft and spineless, who, instead of insisting on his rights or taking a moral stand, tries to reach an accommodation by offering bribes or currying favor.

86 Uri Avneri, personal interview; years later Avneri wrote: "During those years, Shmuel Tamir appeared on the cover of *Haolam Hazeh* many times, and we also chose him as 'Man of the Year.' We wrote thousands of words about him—and he went over nearly all of them before they were printed" ("The Avneri-Tamir Romance," *Yedioth Ahronoth*, October 26, 1980).

was in fact more in the nature of a call to the youth to rise up and take action, than the denunciation of an opponent."[87]

The things printed about him during the Gruenwald trial—as his relationship with the weekly became close—were much more detailed and explicit. One such article appeared in the Rosh Hashanah (New Year, 5715) issue (September 29, 1954), naming Kasztner "Man of the Year." The article[88] took up a whole page, a third of which was devoted to a photograph of Tamir, endowing him with the perfect image of "David" fighting "Goliath"—a symbol of the state's vast, sinister "apparatus of darkness." "It was a battle between unequal forces: Tamir, aided by only three assistants, facing the state's large legal system and its entire investigative apparatus." Without actually saying so, the article strongly suggested that the reason Tamir was defending Gruenwald was to fulfill a dream of his own: "to strike at his old enemy—the state's ruling classes." He was depicted as one-dimensional, as a man who throughout his life had fought for justice against the establishment that was distorting it; his battle in the Gruenwald trial was nothing more than a continuation of the struggle he had conducted as a child at the time of Chaim Arlozoroff's murder and the Stavsky trial; it was "one of the landmarks in Tamir's way of life." At that time, when "stones were flying and windows were shattering," Tamir was about to throw a stone at the building of the *Vaad Leumi* (the National Council). Batsheva, his mother, hastened to take it out of his hand—after all, his Uncle Abraham was in that building:

> This year, Shmuel Tamir lifted the stone again, to throw it at the same window. This time, no one will come to wrest it from his hand. The same people, who twenty years ago sat in the building of the National Council, are still occupying key positions in the government. They were also at the head of the Jewish Agency ten years ago, when the events connected with the Kasztner affair took place.

The article also claimed that Tamir belonged to the radical faction of the IZL and was in fact closer in his views to the Lehi. "He was opposed to [Jews] volunteering for the British army, and emphatically demanded support for the *Lehi* position on the murder of Lord Moyne." Lehi was perceived as a more 'Hebrew' movement than the IZL, and the claim was put forward to

87 *Haolam Hazeh*, October 30, 1952.
88 "The Man Who Tore the Curtain" (Hebrew), *Haolam Hazeh*, September 29, 1954.

stress that any element of 'cooperation' with the British was anathema to Tamir, even though he belonged to IZL.

That is how Tamir was depicted in *Haolam Hazeh* in the mid-fifties. Years after the cooperation between Tamir and Uri Avneri, the weekly's editor, turned into eternal enmity, Avneri lashed out at him during a debate in the Knesset at the end of Tamir's term as Justice Minister: "Mr. Tamir did not [...] serve even one day in the Israel Defense Forces. After he returned to Israel in May 1948, during the following eight months of the war, when all decent young men of his age [he was then 25, Y.W.] were risking their lives night and day on all fronts—he was sitting in his home."[89]

Uri Avneri
INPC, D708-047

Thus, the libel suit brought by the State of Israel against that eccentric old man became the major arena for a struggle to transfer the reins of power to those deserving it: the generation of sabras, the native-born Israelis, under the leadership of Shmuel Tamir-Katznelson—he and none other than he.

89 A debate on the Minister of Justice's report on the activity of his ministry, June 9, 1980, *Knesset Record*, vol. 88, p. 3247.

XIV

This is the place to pose two questions. First, how did a young patrician lawyer get to that wretched old man? And second, why did he do it? Tamir himself related to the first question in a series of interviews he gave to the journalist Yeshayahu Ben Porat shortly after he resigned his position as Justice Minister.[90] He claimed that since he was known as a "lawyer concerned with public affairs," Gruenwald came to him one day with the request to defend him in the libel suit the state had brought against him. Tamir knew it would be a difficult, drawn-out trial and that he would not get a suitable fee ("[Gruenwald] was a pauper, living on a miserable pension [...] he offered me his stamp album, of course I refused it"), but he agreed to undertake the task, after imposing two conditions on Gruenwald. The first was that the trial would not be restricted to the issue of libel, but would become a trial of the Jewish leadership during the Holocaust. The second condition related to the way the trial would be conducted: "I demanded of him not only a formal, but absolute power of attorney, in other words, complete freedom of action concerning my tactics in the trial." Gruenwald agreed to both conditions, the first of which suggests an answer to the question of how the trial swelled to the proportions it did. In the interview, Tamir's reply to the second question was very laconic. When the interviewer implied that he had taken on the job of defending Gruenwald, "because you were convinced from the outset that he was in the right," Tamir made no reply. (He simply said: "Here's the main point. I gave him two conditions.")

Other testimonies present a slightly different picture. According to Attorney Shlomo Zalman Abramov[91] it was he who was largely responsible for setting up the contact between the two. Members of *Shurat Hamitnadvim* (Volunteer Service) contacted him and asked him to recommend a defense lawyer for Gruenwald—and he recommended Tamir, who had impressed him by his opposition to Begin when he had been a member of the Herut Movement. Avneri, however, stated that Reuven ("Romek") Greenberg, a former member of Lehi, an associate of Eldad and Gruenwald's friend, had made the contact between Gruenwald and Tamir. He also played a part in the trial. In a series of articles about him, replete with information about his

---

90 Yeshayahu Ben Porat, "Conversations with Shmuel Tamir" (Hebrew), *Yedioth Ahronoth*, September 19 & 26, 1980.
91 Advocate Shlomo Zalman Abramov, personal interview, Jerusalem, June 3, 1992. Abramov (1908–1977) was Member of Knesset between 1959 and 1977.

dark past, published in *Rimon* in 1957, the claim is made that he was the man responsible for raising money to finance Gruenwald's defense.[92]

As for the question of why Tamir consented to represent Gruenwald—the following picture emerges: Tamir understood the potential offered by the trial and saw the possibility of turning it into a stage from which to attack Ben-Gurion and his rule—in both the forties and the fifties. Shalom Rosenfeld insinuated as much when he wrote: "As soon as Tamir took on the job of defending Malkiel Gruenwald his political instincts immediately told him that here for the first time was the opportunity to raise before a court in Israel—and through it, the public at large—the whole complex tangle of political and moral problems involving the Holocaust and rescue attempts."[93]

Tamir's friends, as well as his rivals, agree that he strove to reach the highest ranks of power in as short a time as possible. Avneri, a bitter adversary, claims that Tamir had a trait that was characteristic of the entire second generation of Israelis—impatience. From his point of view, and he was only thirty at the time, the premiership was a goal to be attained, not in another 20 or 30 years, but tomorrow.[94] I heard a similar view from Abramov, who regarded Tamir as a close friend. He told me that Tamir "engaged in politics with a stopwatch in his hand." He was in a rush, he didn't have the patience to struggle for the things he wanted to achieve. Tamir was certainly aware that a trial of this kind—one so fraught with political significance and intense emotionality—was likely to propel him towards the aims he craved to achieve. That also explains why he didn't take a fee from Gruenwald, although it was going to be a long, complicated trial that would interfere considerably with his legal practice.[95]

Tamir himself, with uncharacteristic righteousness, steadfastly refused to relate to the possibility that he took on the Gruenwald case in order to advance his own career. Reacting to Ben Porat's claim that for lawyers, as for journalists, the desire to expose the truth is "a fundamental drive, or perhaps an aspiration to stand out in society and gain some status in it," Tamir said that for him, the trial was more than a challenge. "Excuse the expression," he said to Ben Porat, "I felt it was a mission, however pompous that may sound."

92 "The Man Who Handed Over His Friends," *Rimon*, May 15, 1957.
93 Rosenfeld, *Criminal Case*, p. 21.
94 Uri Avneri, personal interview.
95 Not only Tamir himself, but others (like Advocate Abramov) had also pointed out that Tamir had represented Gruenwald without taking a fee.

XV

This, then, was the order of battle on the day the trial opened: Halevi in the middle, flanked on both sides by the prosecutor Amnon Tel and the defense lawyer, Shmuel Tamir-Katznelson. Israel Kasztner was neither a plaintiff nor a defendant, only a witness. So he had no official status. Nor did he enjoy any of the rights or protections from which an accused person benefits.

The opening of the trial was barely covered in the press. The only item, on the very eve of the trial's opening, appeared in *Haolam Hazeh*[96] and was devoted mostly to Malkiel Gruenwald, who "has a somewhat unusual hobby. He writes, not love songs [...] his writings [...] contain scathing denunciations of a large number of people." Until now, the news item went on, most of his victims have preferred to keep silent without reacting to his attacks. The first who decided to react was Haim Cohn, "and the charge: the slanderous libel of Dr. Israel Kasztner, a high ranking official in the Ministry of Commerce and Industry, against whom Gruenwald hurled a long series of accusations, spread over more than six densely printed stenciled pages and calling him, among other things '[...] a saboteur of efforts to rescue Hungarian Jewry, etc.' And the 'et cetera' suggests that Gruenwald was guilty of many other accusations that Cohn did not specify, either for lack of space, or for some other reason [...]."

Thus, with a soft whisper, the libel suit brought by the state of Israel against Malkiel ben Menahem Gruenwald, opened.

96 "Justice, Seek out Justice," *Haolam Hazeh*, December 31, 1953.

CHAPTER THREE

A Trial in Jerusalem, 1954 (A)

I

Malkiel Gruenwald's trial opened on a Friday—the first day of January 1954. It was very brief session—the indictment was read and Gruenwald, the accused, pled not guilty. Since he appeared alone, without defense counsel, he asked for a postponement so that he could hire an attorney. Judge Halevi acceded to his request. This was the first postponement.

Two and a half weeks later, on Sunday, January 17, the second session, also a brief one, opened. This time Gruenwald was accompanied by his defense attorney, Shmuel Tamir-Katznelson. The prosecutor, Amnon Tel, who was apparently in a hurry, asked to open the proceedings immediately. He wanted to hear the policemen who had interrogated Gruenwald as well as the first prosecution witness—Shmuel Bentzur. Bentzur, a native of Hungary, was a senior official in the Ministry of Foreign Affairs and was then head of the East European desk. Defense counsel Tamir asked for a further postponement—he had not had time to study the material and properly prepare Gruenwald's defense. The prosecutor adamantly objected to Tamir's request. Once again, Halevi granted the defense's request, but this time very grudgingly. He postponed the opening of the trial for a whole month—until mid-February—and at the same time, fined Gruenwald to the amount of 20 Israeli pounds for his "negligence in preparing his defense."[1]

It was obvious from Tamir's brief statement that he had come to the session unprepared—the accused had contacted him only a few days earlier; although he was just starting out, he intended to seek out primary sources, to order exhibits from abroad and perhaps witnesses too, as well as to obtain the transcripts of the Nuremberg trials—all this in an effort to prove that everything Gruenwald had written was true. Moreover, he pointed out that

---

1   The details are from Appendix A, Rosenfeld, *Criminal Case*, p. 451.

113

"the prosecution has brought a series of witnesses to prove Dr. Kasztner's virtuous character, even though the prosecution is not obliged to prove any such thing." He said this to stress that he, too, was entitled to summon witnesses and in fact to broaden the scope of the trial.[2] However, despite his aggressive demeanor, he admitted that he did not yet have a thread of evidence to prove his case.

On January 18, most of the newspapers reported at length on the second session. *Yedioth Ahronoth* even printed a photograph of Kasztner "testifying at the Nuremberg war crimes tribunal."

The trial reopened a month later, on Thursday, February 18, 1954. There was some coverage—sympathetic to Kasztner—in the press. On the day the trial began, *Yedioth Ahronoth* wrote that "The holocaust of Hungarian Jewry during the war, the rescue efforts and the abuse and slander spread by Malkiel Gruenwald against Dr. Israel Kasztner, formerly director of public relations in the Ministry of Trade and Industry, are now resonating in the Jerusalem District Court, as the President of the Court, Dr. Benjamin Halevi, who had resigned from his position, opens the hearing on the indictment issued against Malkiel Gruenwald for libel." No one knows, the journalist went on to say, "who is providing the considerable sums of money for printing, translating and distributing the newsletters."[3]

The third session opened with the testimony of the prosecution's witnesses. The first to testify was Dr. Israel Kasztner. He took the witness stand against the advice of Hanzi Brand and his friends who had worked with him in the rescue efforts. The press also agreed that Kasztner's testimony was superfluous and that his decision to take the witness stand was a mistake. In its first report on the trial, *Haolam Hazeh* commented that a man suing for libel is not obliged to prove anything, other than the fact that the accused has libeled him. Therefore, from the prosecution's standpoint, Kasztner's testimony was totally unnecessary. But "the prosecution was unable to forego the pleasure of presenting Kasztner, giving him publicity and some glory, and in doing so, dug its own grave."[4]

Kasztner enjoyed a moment of illusory delight—once again he was at center stage, basking in the limelight. His testimony lasted for three weeks—until March 10. Until February 24, he gave his own version of the events and

2   Trial transcript, January 17, 1954, p. 2.
3   "The Holocaust of Hungarian Jewry in the Court in a Libel Suit," *Yedioth Ahronoth*, January 1, 1954.
4   "The Legal Battle: To Life and Death," *Haolam Hazeh*, March 11, 1954.

afterwards was cross-examined by the defense counsel. During his testimony, he had the opportunity to tell the story of the Jewish Rescue Committee and his personal story from his own viewpoint, and he did so with hardly any interference. Time after time, Halevi overruled Tamir's objections. Kasztner testified in Hebrew, a language in which he was not very proficient—rather than in Hungarian or German, in which he was completely fluent. So long as he was giving his testimony, there was nothing to disturb him, but under Tamir's cross-examination, he found it increasingly difficult to remain in control of the situation.[5]

In his testimony, he referred to his contacts with Nazi officers and had favorable things to say about them. Hans Jüttner, he said, had put an end to the "death marches," and Kurt Becher continued to assist in the rescue of Jews in the final stage of the war, although it was clear to him that he would gain no benefit from that.[6] He also took the opportunity to give the "favorable version" of his testimony at Nuremberg. He talked about the sworn affidavit he had given in London in September 1945, as well as his testimony in 1948 at Edmund Veesenmayer's trial. About Gruenwald's insinuation in his newsletter that he had been "a defense witness [for] Becher" and had saved him from death by hanging, he said:

> When I was in Nuremberg the first time [1947] and the second time [1948] I gave no testimony in regard to Becher, neither before the court nor before any of the institutions or offices of the international tribunal. What was written in the article, that I traveled to Nuremberg to give evidence to save Becher—that too is a lie. The German Denazification Court invited me to appear at Becher's denazification trial [...] I did not go. I had no desire to appear there before the Germans; I had had enough of them during the war. On the other hand, I did agree to give a sworn affidavit, in which I stated everything I knew about him."[7]

He referred briefly to the parachutists dropped by the Haganah in a rescue effort. In June 1944, when he was in touch with Yoel Palgi and Peretz Goldstein, he said, "I did not see or know about her [Hannah Szenes'] arrival." Later, in mid-October, he already knew she was in Budapest and had attempted to get

---

5   Yehudah Spiegel, personal interview.
6   Trial transcript, February 22, 1954, p. 19.
7   Ibid., p. 22. Veesenmayer was the German Minister and Reich Plenipotentiary in Hungary.

her and the two others released. An agreement on this matter was reached, but never materialized, because of Szálasi's coup. In a few terse sentences, he described the chain of events leading to Goldstein's arrest: "They threatened to shoot Palgi if Goldstein was not found within 24 hours. We asked permission to contact Peretz, he was hiding somewhere. We described the situation to him and told him it was up to him to decide. If he wanted to run away, we were prepared to take the consequences. He decided to turn himself in."[8]

He also described how the passengers on the train were chosen: 150 places were allocated, he said, to wealthy Jews whose money was meant to finance the cost of the train; he was not involved in the financial aspect or the selection of the candidates for the train; which, he said, was handled by a committee headed by Ottó Komoly, whose members were Hanzi Brand, Shulem Offenbach, Zvi (Arno) Szilágyi of Hashomer Hatza'ir, as well as representatives of the Neologs and the Orthodox. Most of his relatives, more than 100 men and women, were sent to Auschwitz where they perished. "On the transport leaving the country, there were the following members of my family: my mother, my wife, my brother Avraham, my father-in-law Dr. Yosef Fischer. There were no others from my immediate family. There were two or three of my wife's relatives, all from her immediate family."[9] He added that before the war's end, Becher had given Moshe Schweiger a large portion of the monies handed over to the Germans in Budapest. He stated that at the request of the then Minister of Finance, Eliezer Kaplan, he had written to him in mid-1948 about the fate of the "Becher deposit" and had suggested that Komoly take steps to transfer the funds to the government of Israel.[10] As for his own financial situation, he said: "I have no property, I have debts...I didn't make any 'deals.'" An editorial in the press wrote about the impression left by Kasztner's testimony:

> For three days, Kasztner stood, and calmly, soberly and in chronological order, first things first and last things last, told the judge the story of how Hungarian Jewry was lost and about his and his comrades' rescue efforts.
> This story had a broad historical backdrop; it contained some profound political analysis, fascinating descriptions of meetings with leading

8   Ibid., p. 15.
9   Ibid., pp. 11–12.
10 Ibid., p. 24.

figures among the murderers, and many tales of daring, suffering and dedication.

And behind the story, ostensibly there was a man of steel nerves and iron logic, of broad horizons and profound vision.

And the scale tipped—in his favor.[11]

The impression his testimony made even led Halevi to ask the accused whether "in light of [Kasztner's] testimony, he was prepared to retract his claims or some part of them." Tamir's reply was negative, although the end of his reply suggested that his confidence may have been shaken somewhat: "There are some charges that [Gruenwald] will not be able to prove, and he is prepared to admit to the facts in relation to this part."[12]

II

The sense of triumph did not last long. The optimistic mood and complacence dissipated into thin air when Tamir began his cross-examination. He focused on several subjects, including Kasztner's evidence in Becher's favor. Tamir never let go of this point,[13] and Kasztner repeated his own version of the affair time after time:

> Yes. I did give a sworn affidavit at Nuremberg to the notary of the international tribunal and I did so because I did not want to apply to the notary of a German court. But my intention was to tell the truth, not to do anything to either help him or to harm him; it was up to the court to decide whether the result would do him any good or harm.[14]

The high point of this subject, which to a great measure was the high point of the entire trial, took place on February 25, 1954, the second day of the cross-examination. That day, Kasztner was questioned for over three hours and stuck tenaciously to his version of the facts. Again and again, he repeated his claim that it was not his intervention that led to Becher's release in December 1947. Afterwards, with a highly dramatic gesture, Tamir presented the letter

---

11 Rosenfeld, *Criminal Case*, p. 26.
12 Trial transcript, February 23, 1954, p. 24.
13 Ibid., February 25, 1954, p. 30.
14 Ibid., February 25, 1954, p. 32.

Kasztner had sent to Finance Minister Kaplan in July 1948, in which he wrote that "Becher was released thanks to my personal intervention." At this point, the following dialogue took place:

Tamir: Do you admit having written this letter?
Kasztner: Yes.
Tamir: A minute ago you said it was a lie that Becher was released from Nuremberg thanks to your personal intervention. Do you still stick to that statement?
Kasztner: I stand by what I said in this courtroom.

About these dramatic—and decisive—moments in the trial, I have several comments to make:

First, the said document was provided to Tamir by the prosecution— Kasztner's letter to Kaplan was introduced as evidence by the prosecution as its exhibit number 22. It was the letter that Kasztner himself had mentioned in his initial testimony to prove that most of the assets given to Becher had been returned in the end to the Jews. He himself presented the letter to the court.

Second, this slip-up on the part of the prosecution completely changed Halevi's attitude towards Kasztner and the prosecution in general. After the discrepancy in Kasztner's testimony was exposed, the judge shot a hostile glare at him, and that evening Kasztner, perturbed, said to Hanzi Brand: "From now on, he won't believe a word I say."[15]

What caused this snag? One answer is that Tel had advised Kasztner to take that course of action. One evening, Brand said, Kasztner had appeared at her home and told her "he had been instructed not to mention his recommendation to Kurt Becher."[16] Brand, astonished, told him angrily "That is something that cannot be concealed, after all there were black on white documents attesting to the existence of that recommendation. Moreover, a political person who gives such a recommendation is obliged to stand up and explain it." Finally, after many attempts at persuasion, "Rezsö promised to tell the truth, [but] the following day, like a man possessed, he replied with the same lie he had been taught." Another answer blames the prosecution's slipshod conduct of the case, which handed the lion its prey on a silver platter. After all, Kasztner never denied having given an affidavit on Becher's behalf (only on the facts, not in his favor), and had it not been for the boast included in his letter, that particular Pandora's box would never have been opened.

---

15 Brand, *Satan and the Soul*, p. 119.
16 Ibid., pp. 118–119.

Another question is, when was Kasztner telling the truth—in the courtroom or in his letter to Kaplan? This question was made perfectly clear in 1956 before the Magistrate Judge, Moshe Peretz. In either case, it was at this point that the process of Kasztner's demonization began, not only because he was represented as a liar but also as a man who had something to hide in connection with the darkest of all realms.

III

Over the few days during which Kasztner was cross-examined, both his mood and his appearance changed. Hanzi claims that until that moment, he had managed to maintain a hold on himself, but afterwards he completely lost his confidence.[17] The press' attitude to the trial also changed. Until that stage, the newspaper reports were rather bland. Even the daily *Herut* covered Kasztner's direct examination in a matter-of-fact manner:[18] "Tense atmosphere during Dr. Kasztner's cross-examination," read the headline on the first day of the cross-examination, but the following day, on February 26, the headline was: "In his letter to Minister Kaplan, Kasztner admitted: The SS Officer Kurt Becher was released through his intervention." The news item opened by relating what had taken place in the courtroom, but also conveyed the feeling that this trial might yet be a bloody one:

> A dramatic development occurred yesterday in Dr. Kasztner's cross-examination by Malkiel Gruenwald's defense attorney, Shmuel Tamir, who submitted to the court Dr. Kasztner's letter to the late Finance Minister E. Kaplan, in which Dr. Kasztner stated that "The SS officer Kurt Becher was released by the occupation forces in Nuremberg thanks to my personal intervention." An oppressive silence fell upon the courtroom when the document was submitted, and the judge studied it for a long time.

At the end of the cross-examination, Kasztner was tense and exhausted. At one point during the examination, he said he was nervous, felt ill and asked for the examination to be stopped. A doctor was summoned, and Halevi, who

---

17 Hanzi Brand, personal interview.
18 See, for example: "Details on Hitler's Order to Prevent the Extermination of the Jews at the End of the War" (Hebrew), *Herut*, February 23, 1954.

saw how pale and weary the witness was, declared a recess, to allow him to recover and regain his composure.[19] A day later, a special recess was declared for a second time during the proceedings, after Kasztner once again stated he was distraught. When the recess was over, Tel asked Halevi to end the cross-examination, because Tamir's examination was "more than a man can bear."[20] The following day, when the examination ended, Tel felt that the ground had been pulled from under his feet and declared that the Attorney General would do well to announce that the trial be discontinued. To dispel the unbearable tension, Halevi declared a three-day recess in the proceedings. Kasztner walked slowly down the stairs of the courthouse. He was quiet, looking tired and thin, and his hair seemed to have suddenly turned gray.[21]

After Kasztner, other witnesses for the prosecution testified—Professor Benjamin Akzin, Dean of the Hebrew University Law Faculty and Shmuel Bentzur of the Foreign Ministry. The two, who were not directly linked to the affair, were called as part of the prosecution's policy of summoning leading figures whose very appearance on the witness stand would make a favorable impression. There were some who were opposed to this strategy. In a meeting of the Rescue Committee, it had been decided, with Kasztner's consent, "that various people who had worked with him on the rescue efforts, *halutzim* (pioneers) associated with him in Budapest, as well as those whom he had looked after and had helped leave Hungary for Switzerland, would be called as witnesses." Now it turned out that these were not the people who would be called to testify, but rather "well-known people who, although they had not seen any of Kasztner's rescue work and had not even been in Budapest, had impeccable reputations in Israel, so that the judge would believe their hearsay evidence."[22]

Tel called Akzin because of his activity on the War Refugees Committee, but he was also an old-timer in the Revisionist movement and during the war had been active on the Emergency Committee to Save Europe's Jews in the United States, under the leadership of Hillel Kook and Shmuel Merlin, Tamir's associates in founding the opposing faction in the Herut Movement.

---

19 "Dr. Kasztner Requests a Recess in his Testimony," *Yedioth Ahronoth*, March 3, 1954; "The Agency Stifled News about the Extermination in Hungary," *Herut*, March 3, 1954.

20 "Dr. Kasztner Breaks Down under the Pressure of the Prosecutor's Questions," *Herut*, March 4, 1954.

21 The description is taken from: "Prosecutor Agrees to Stop the Trial Against Gruenwald," *Herut*, March 5, 1954; "The Legal Battle: A Fight to the End," *Haolam Hazeh*, March 11, 1954.

22 Brand, *Satan and the Soul*, p. 125.

And, as a matter of fact, in his testimony, Akzin raised some points that were useful to the defense rather than to the prosecution. The Emergency Committee, he claimed, published huge ads in American newspapers about the extermination of Europe's Jews, although compared to the Jewish Agency and the JDC, it had very limited funds. "This is one of the reasons why I cooperated with this body and not with the Agency," he said. He also said that some important people in the Agency and the JDC had attacked the Emergency Committee and its habit of advertising in the media as a means of propaganda: "I was very embittered by the position taken by these prominent figures," he added.[23]

Throughout Akzin's testimony, Tamir asked questions that would help him introduce into the legal proceedings the issue of the Zionist institutions' behavior during the Holocaust. Tel objected to these questions on the grounds that they were irrelevant, but Halevi, who during the early days of the trial had sustained most of Tel's objections, now accepted Tamir's position.

Halevi's leniency towards Tamir in allowing him to expand the scope of the trial without any connection to its declared aims met with harsh criticism. Yitzhak Olshan, who from the summer of 1954 was President of the Supreme Court, later wrote that "Halevi, who, as the single presiding judge was obliged to take a firm stand and to prevent anyone exploiting the court proceedings in order to create an arena for partisan-political bouts [...], gave [the parties] free rein and the testimony of witnesses for the prosecution, including Dr. Kasztner, went on for far too long and without any restraint."[24]

By this stage—less than two weeks into the trial—several things had already changed. First, Tamir openly asserted that the assignment for which he had been retained—to gain Malkiel Gruenwald's acquittal—did not interest him at all and that his true aim was to place Israel Kasztner in the dock, along with the Jewish Agency and Mapai. Second, the man who was formally accused, namely Malkiel Gruenwald, seemed to vanish into the intricately expanded web spun by Tamir, who now ascribed the epithet of "accused" to Kasztner. One day, when Gruenwald did not appear at the trial *Haolam Hazeh* wrote the headline, "Gruenwald has done his bit" and went on to say: "There was no apparent reason for Gruenwald's presence in the courtroom: he has been completely forgotten [...] the affair has now exceeded the limited

23 Trial transcript, March 10, 1954, p. 77.
24 Olshan, *Deliberations*, p. 306.

bounds of the Gruenwald-Kasztner dispute and has become the trial of an entire period."[25]

IV

On March 16, the prosecution summoned Yoel Palgi, a man who had been at the very heart of the affair, to the witness stand. A well-known figure, holding at the time the position of deputy general manager of EL AL (Israel Airlines), Palgi was regarded as a national hero. Several days before he began his testimony, the press ran a glowing profile of him, full of flattering superlatives.[26] For example, Palgi's book, *Into the Inferno*, was described as: "One of the most beautiful books written here in the last ten years. It is an epic of the heroism and supreme sacrifice of our generation, a Jewish and universal document that [leaves the reader] profoundly moved."

From the prosecution's standpoint, calling Palgi to the witness stand seemed like a sure thing. Not only was he a national hero, but his favorable attitude towards Kasztner was well-known and his article in *Davar* on Kasztner's arrival in Israel was also introduced as an exhibit (number 39) by the prosecution. His statements in support of Kasztner and his actions, particularly following Kasztner's own testimony, could not fail to benefit Kasztner and greatly improve his situation: "Palgi's prestige among the people was so great and the mythical aura that always surrounded him was so tangible, that it seemed his testimony would once and for all crush the defense attacks on him."[27] The prosecution was apparently unaware of Palgi's complex and ambivalent attitude to Kasztner.

Palgi testified for three days—from March 16 to 18—and this was also one of the high points of the trial, which had already become a *cause célèbre*. Throughout Palgi's testimony, Judge Halevi, who had already adopted Tamir's position, sustained all his objections and overruled all of Tel's. On the first day of his testimony, Palgi related to Moshe Krausz's dismissal from his job in the Palestine Office in Budapest. Tel wished to expand on this point, and that led to the following dialogue:

---

25 *Haolam Hazeh*, March 18, 1954.
26 D. Diyukanai (David Lazar), "Heads in Israel—Yoel Palgi"; "A Great Wind is Coming to El Al," *Ma'ariv*, March 12, 1954.
27 Immanuel Prat, *The Great Trial—The Kasztner Affair* (Hebrew) (Tel Aviv: Or Publishing, 1955), p. 69.

Tel: What caused the parties to demand Moshe Krausz's dismissal?

Tamir: Objection.

Tel: Krausz is behind this trial. He is the hand and the accused is the knife. Krausz will be a witness for the defense. I want to show something about his character and his attitude.

Tamir: Irrelevant. Not factual. I declare on behalf of the accused that when he wrote the article he did not know Krausz and had never met him.

The judge: I won't allow the question.[28]

Palgi's direct examination lasted an entire day. He ended it with the following words:

> If I am asked whether I think Kasztner was a traitor or a hero, to say he was a traitor I think is sacrilegious. As for his being a hero, I don't know what heroism is. If a man risks his life for someone else, to save someone else's life, that is heroism. As far as I'm concerned, I think that in those days this was an elementary duty of every Jew and I think that Kasztner fulfilled that duty.[29]

Things changed radically when Tamir began his cross-examination. He adopted two tactics in examining Palgi: the first was to point out the discrepancies between what he had said in his testimony and what he had written in his book—in order to destroy his credibility and to prove that he also had something to hide. For example, before crossing the border between Yugoslavia and Hungary, Palgi and Goldstein had left a suitcase containing a transmitter. The suitcase was handed over to a man who was ignorant of its contents; all he had to do was hand it over to someone who would give him a prearranged sign. Realizing he was being followed, Palgi was no longer certain as to what he should do with the transmitter. In his direct examination, he said he had consulted Kasztner about whether to delay the arrival of the transmitter and then told him he was a British officer and that his mission also had a military aspect. Why had he decided to consult Kasztner? "I had already made my decision, but felt I needed to reiterate it and, believing

---

28 Trial transcript, March 17, 1954, p. 98.
29 Ibid., March 16, 1954, p. 97.

Kasztner to be a man of sharp intelligence, I chose him. At the same time, I sent a cable stating that the transmitter should not be brought."[30]

The following day Palgi was subjected to a fierce cross-examination:

Tamir: Did you consult Goldstein before disclosing the existence of the transmitter to Kasztner?

Palgi: No. I told Kasztner about my military mission without asking Goldstein. Things were rapidly deteriorating and I saw no need to stop the meetings in order to ask Peretz' advice.

Tamir: I am telling you that you did not disclose your military duty to Kasztner.

Palgi: If you say I didn't tell him, you are lying!

Tamir: But on page 116 of your book you write, "When all is said and done, for the time being, we shouldn't disclose our military role."[31]

The book lies on this point too, Palgi retorted. **"I wrote a novel; I did not write history** [emphasis added]." In response to the judge's question: "Why did you find it necessary to change the truth in relation to Kasztner and the transmitter?" Palgi replied, "That may be a bad characteristic in a liar; when he doesn't want to tell the truth, he overplays it." These replies stunned everyone at the trial. For a moment, the judge stopped taking notes, laid down his pen and turned an astonished gaze on the witness, who, lowering his head, remained silent.[32] Later, Palgi admitted that in his book he had also written a false account of the circumstances surrounding Goldstein's arrest. "Technically speaking," he said, "[Kasztner] led Goldstein and handed him over to the enemy. That's why I didn't write the true version of Goldstein's arrest, not only to protect him if he remained alive, but also to protect Kasztner and the whole affair."

There were also discrepancies in the accounts of Palgi's meeting with the Gestapo. On June 25, 1944, he reported to the Gestapo and informed them that he had been sent to Budapest by the Jewish Agency to find out whether there was any truth in Joel Brand's fantastic story. At the end of the conversation, he asked the officer he had spoken with for a paper to ensure his safety. On this point, the following exchange took place:

30 Ibid., p. 92.
31 Rosenfeld, *Criminal Case*, p. 130.
32 The description is from Prat, *The Great Trial*, p. 74.

Tamir: You asked [the Gestapo officer] Zeifrat, at the end of your talk, to give you a paper stating you were in the service of the Gestapo!

Palgi: I asked for a paper stating I was under the protection of the Gestapo, not in the service of the Gestapo.

Tamir: And I tell you that on page 131 of your book you wrote explicitly, "in the service of the Gestapo."

Palgi: I may have written that. It's almost the same thing. I asked for the paper, because I needed it.[33]

Tamir, however, did not think that "in the service" and "under the protection" were "almost the same thing"—"I am telling you that you allowed yourself to ask for this paper because you behaved with them in a manner that led them to conclude that you were collaborating with them against the Allies!" he tore into Palgi. "You presented yourself as a man ready to serve the Nazi interests!" The courtroom was in an uproar. The prosecutor broke into Tamir's words, claiming that he was "slandering national heroes" and adamantly demanded that the question not be allowed, but recorded in the transcript so that Tamir would be responsible for it.[34] And Palgi yelled at Tamir, "That's a vicious lie!" After ruling that "what defense counsel is doing is not slandering, rather he is investigating the affair and the court is interested in discovering the truth," Judge Halevi allowed the question.[35]

These exchanges demonstrate how Tamir's two tactics intersected: he was trying to claim that the discrepancies between the versions concealed a monstrous secret—that Yoel Palgi, the parachutist and hero, was in fact a collaborator, like Kasztner, like everyone in Mapai—the party that both he and Kasztner belonged to.

Tamir: Are you a member of Mapai?

Palgi: Yes.

Tamir: You were a Mapai candidate to the Knesset?

Palgi: Yes.

---

33 Rosenfeld, *Criminal Case*, p.133.

34 At that stage, questions were not recorded in the transcript, but this question appears at Tamir's request; he claimed he was capable of proving his assumption (Trial transcript, March 17, 1954, p. 102).

35 "I Appeared as an Emissary of the Agency and Saluted 'Heil Hitler!'," *Herut*, March 18, 1954.

> **Tamir:** And you would not like to see your friend Kasztner's name blemished?
>
> **Palgi:** I would not like to see either his name or his actions blemished.[36]

In another part of the cross-examination, the following exchange took place:

> **Tamir:** Why did you decide [...] to report to the Gestapo?
>
> **Palgi:** I preferred to try to move the wheel that had begun turning in Budapest and continued in Istanbul. That's why I went to the Gestapo.
>
> **Tamir:** Were those your instructions from the Agency?
>
> **Palgi:** My instructions from the Agency were to save Jews.
>
> **Tamir:** Did it ever occur to anyone in Palestine that in order to do so you would report to the Gestapo?
>
> **Palgi:** No.
>
> **Tamir:** Is it true that one of your aims was to call on the Jews to sell their lives at a high price, to fight for their lives?
>
> **Palgi:** That's correct.
>
> **Tamir:** And when you went to the Gestapo you still hoped to organize resistance?[37]

From these words—and others like them—Tamir constructed a clear-cut conclusion: This Mapainik had accepted the approach of the other Mapainik, and instead of encouraging the Jews of Hungary to resist their murderers, he had, in fact, become a collaborator.

> **Tamir:** You were an idealist who left the country to save Jews and to serve in the Allied forces. You risked your life. But when you got there, the situation was so bad, and you were influenced by Kasztner, that under his pressure and the pressure of circumstances, you decided to collaborate with the Gestapo to save your own skin. That's why you stayed alive. And Peretz [Goldstein] and Hannah [Szenes] remained there. **You returned because you accepted Kasztner's approach!**[38] [emphasis added]

36 Ibid.
37 Rosenfeld, *Criminal Case*, p. 132.
38 Ibid., p. 149.

How did Palgi react? Choking back his tears, he turned to Judge Halevi: "Your honor, I request permission not to respond. My reply would insult the dignity of this Court," he pleaded. But Halevi did not accede to his request and ruled: "You will answer the charge, yes or no." An expression of pain contorted the former parachutist's face. Gritting his teeth, he shouted, "No!"[39]

Palgi's testimony did the prosecution no good; in fact, it made its situation more difficult. Instead of making the hoped for impression of a self-confident man who knows how to fight for the truth, Palgi emerged as a broken man, heavily burdened by memories and feelings of guilt. The exchanges between him and Tamir, instead of focusing on arguments or rebuttals, took the form of a humiliating confession. "That's a lie [...]," "Yes, I distorted that [...]," "On this point, I wasn't being accurate [...]," "Here I was deliberately vague [...]" It was a litany of confessions on Palgi's part.[40]

Moreover, Palgi made some statements during his testimony that astounded the spectators at the trial. About going to Gestapo headquarters, he said: "According to my military concepts, if a soldier willingly gives himself up to the enemy, that's treason. From a purely military point of view, I too betrayed my military duty."[41] The following day, this statement became the headline in the daily, *Herut* with the statement: "Palgi admits: I am a liar! From a military standpoint, I am a traitor!"

It is not surprising that in a book about the trial, the chapter devoted to Palgi's testimony is entitled "The Shattered Legend."[42] After his testimony, the prosecution was left with no ammunition. The main weapon in its arsenal had been turned against it.

V

Early in 1956, nearly two years after he testified and several months after Halevi's verdict, in the midst of preparations for the appeal, Palgi wrote a long, revealing, and moving letter to Attorney General Haim Cohn.[43] This letter, unquestionably a rare document, shows how torn and tormented Palgi

---

39 Ibid.
40 Trial transcript, March 18, 1954, p. 108.
41 Rosenfeld, *Criminal Case*, p.135.
42 Prat, *The Great Trial*, p. 69.
43 The letter was written in Tel Aviv on February 22, 1956. It was given to me by Dr. Ilana Kaufman-Palgi, Yoel Palgi's daughter. I am deeply grateful to her.

was following his heroic mission to Hungary and how much his testimony at the Kasztner trial had exacerbated his mental anguish:

> I have known no peace since giving my testimony. I had thought it was my responsibility to find solutions to the motives behind the actions taken at the time. They seemed so flawed to me in their logic when I testified in court, that I began studying and relearning the affair I gave evidence about. I began asking questions, riffling through archives, checking my memory in light of documents written about ten years ago, and comparing them with the court transcripts. To my astonishment, I found that the testimony I gave the court on this affair is incorrect on 13 points. In these, as far as I can tell, the events as they occurred do not correspond with what, from my memory, was reflected in my testimony in court.

The major portion of the letter is devoted to those 13 points—where he lied and why. For example, he said his testimony about going to the Gestapo was "not reliable" and the new version he presented to Cohn represented a rather damning indictment against Kasztner. Kasztner, who believed that Palgi and Goldstein had been arrested by the detectives who were following them, "informed the Gestapo about the arrival of two agents from Palestine who had supposedly come in connection with Brand's mission." This placed Palgi in an intolerable situation, leaving him several options—he could hide, flee to Romania or return to Yugoslavia. But knowing that if at least one of the agents was not found, that would mean "an end to the bluff and to the rescue train," he had no choice but to "swallow the bitter pill and go to the Gestapo, hoping that they were all stupid and would believe his lame story." And why he and not Goldstein? Not because he was the older and more experienced of the two, but because that was the day he had learned that his parents were dead while Peretz's were scheduled to go on the rescue train: "Maybe it sounds a bit complicated, but I thought that no son should sacrifice himself for his parents."

In addition to the details that show how muddled his testimony was, the letter reveals Palgi's twisted relationship with Kasztner, his love-hate feelings for him, his bitter resentment alongside his desire to be fair. In his letter, he leveled harsh criticism against Kasztner, and didn't shrink from words of animosity:

> Among all the horrible tidings I received at this meeting [with Kasztner, a day before he reported to the Gestapo], I was told that my sister and

parents had been sent to an extermination camp. Kasztner said that when the list for the rescue train was being made up, they had already left the ghetto and were on the first train [for extermination]. I knew he was lying. I knew he knew nothing about the fate of my family and it had never occurred to him to find out. On the other hand, I learned that Peretz's parents were among those chosen to be rescued […]
My arrest, Hannah's and Peretz's, the debacle, the physical and mental collapse, hunger, the horror of death all around us, Hannah's death, the horrifying extermination I was witnessing, the information that my family had been killed, all raised my bitterness to a crescendo of blind hatred for this man whom I saw as the source of all evil: he had deserted us, brought catastrophe upon us, abandoned those dear to me […] my hatred was so intense that in Cairo, when I heard that Kasztner was alive, I cried out: What a pity! [It would have been] better if he had perished!

And he tried his utmost to suppress his anger and hatred, to draw a distinction between his inner truth and the historical truth:

At the end of 1945, I wrote my book, *And Behold a Great Wind Came.* I did much soul searching before and while writing the book. My writing compelled me to look at things through the eyes of history and of the Jewish tragedy, to distinguish between an historical right and an historical crime; to discuss revolt and the submission of the Jews, in the case of Budapest; and whether it was right or wrong to save individual Jews in the shadow of the extermination of millions. I discovered that my personal pain over the loss of my family was clouding my pure judgment. What right do I have to feel resentment towards him? I asked myself. Because he didn't save my parents rather than other Jews? If so, do I have any right to cast a stone at him? Or did he have the right to inform the Gestapo of our arrival and to lead Peretz to the Hungarian Gestapo or the Hungarian Gestapo to Peretz, if the choice was our lives or the lives of others? Consumed by doubts, hatred, admiration, guilt, vindictiveness, and love for a friend, I wrestled with myself as I wrote the book.

Palgi continued to torment himself while the commission of inquiry, established by the Zionist Congress, met in 1946, at his demand—"For nights and days I tortured myself, wrestling with my conscience and rummaging through my doubts: How should I behave? Do I have the right to speak ill of him? Isn't it because I am blinded by my personal bitterness that I am making him the scapegoat for my great sense of orphanhood?" The commission's refusal to intervene in the dispute between them did nothing to mollify him. "There are very few people I have respected more than the judges, but I was left with all the anguish; I was burdened by a heavy sense of guilt for having immigrated to Palestine on the eve of the war and leaving my parents to their bitter fate. Kasztner could have saved them. The death of Hannah and Peretz were my failures, for which I held him responsible. And I knew, too, that there were no grounds for these accusations. I knew I was indebted to him: by accusing him I was casting a favorable light on my own weaknesses and by doing so eclipsing the greatness of this man, so full of contradictions and inconsistencies."

Word after word, he revealed the profound ambivalence that had led him to become so confused on the witness stand: "When he came here, I did all I could, perhaps more than I was obliged to, to welcome him and help him get settled. I did that with a clear conscience, but still with some reluctance," and then:

> Strange, weird and wonderful are the means people use to heal psychological wounds: forgetting is one of these. The facts had become blurred in my memory and sometimes things were switched around. Many of the events that occurred during that period became buried inside me, and I was no longer sure if they were real or a dream, or perhaps a legend I had heard. To the question put to me repeatedly by the President of the court, I could only reply: "with regard to my entire mission, from beginning to end, I have many serious psychological blocks, as I said, because my comrades were killed and I remained alive. It's not easy for me, I am trying to forget this whole affair. I saw too much blood, [too many] dead people, [too much] destruction."

Thus Palgi's testimony, which certainly went a long way towards defiling the atmosphere at the trial and tipping the scale against Kasztner, was marked by the duality in his attitude towards him. Although testifying in his favor, deep in his heart Palgi really wanted to incriminate Kasztner.

VI

For about two weeks after Palgi's testimony the court heard other witnesses; until the first week of April, when the court took a two-month recess. One of the most important witnesses to testify during those two weeks was Joel Brand, who was preceded by two other prosecution witnesses, both from the Kibbutz Ha'artzi movement. One of these witnesses was Menachem Bader, a member of Kibbutz Mizra. During the war, Bader (who became a member of the first Knesset after the establishment of the state), represented his kibbutz movement on the Yishuv's 1943 delegation to Istanbul where, in this capacity, he met with Joel Brand. In his testimony, he mentioned his arrival in Istanbul in January 1943; however, his natural focus was on the mission that was intended to be carried out by Brand, who arrived in Istanbul in May 1944.

The proposal Brand had brought with him, he said, stunned him and the other members of the delegation. At first, they thought it might be a devious plot concocted by the Germans with one aim in mind: to prove to the world that the Germans were not the only ones who wanted to see the Jews annihilated. On second thought, however, they considered the possibility that the Germans were aware of their imminent defeat and wanted to establish an alibi for themselves. Beyond that, they were deeply convinced that they were duty bound "to consider any proposal, however diabolical and dubious. We knew that if we didn't act quickly, for the rest of our lives we would be haunted by the dream that we could have saved Jews and that because of us [that dream] had come to naught." They decided to send Venia Pomerantz[44] to Palestine to submit Brand's proposal to the highest levels of the Zionist leadership for their consideration and decision. The extent of the confusion, bewilderment and anxiety that Brand's arrival aroused among the delegation members is reflected in the following words:

> I remember, as if it were today, how we sat there not knowing what to say. Each of us could hear his own heartbeat. As the hands of the clock moved [...] we saw how time was running out, how quickly those two weeks would pass that Brand told us Eichmann was giving him for negotiation with the international Jewish community, a hiatus between the death and the life of a million Jews.[45]

In his testimony, Bader also referred to the reason why Brand had not returned to Budapest and the circumstances under which he had arrived in

---

44 Venia Pomerantz (Zeev Hadari) was a representative of the Kibbutz Hameuchad movement on the Yishuv's rescue committee in Istanbul.

45 Trial transcript, March 24, 1954, p. 127.

Syria, where he had been arrested by British intelligence. He stated that two days after his arrival in Istanbul, the Turkish authorities had cancelled Brand's visa as well as that of Bandi Grosz, who had come with him, and arrested them both with the intention of expelling them. At the time, Moshe Shertok (later Sharett), head of the Agency's political department, was trying to get to Istanbul to meet Brand and to hear for himself about the proposal, but under pressure from the British, the Turks refused him a transit visa. In the meantime, the British agreed to allow Brand to go to Jerusalem to present his proposal to Jewish Agency leaders. Brand was released and most of the committee agreed with him that he should travel to Palestine—Bader was the only one who argued that it was all a trap. In any case, Brand was in a hurry to depart for Palestine when he was arrested by British Intelligence on the Syrian border. He met with Shertok at the place where he was being held under arrest in Aleppo, in the presence of a British Intelligence agent.

In his cross-examination, Tamir tried to prove that the Jewish Agency had turned Brand over to the British, in the belief that it was more important to cooperate and maintain good relations with the British than to rescue Jews. This, then, would be Tamir's main objective in the trial—to place the Agency and the Mapai leadership in the dock, charged with abandoning the Jews of Europe and with the responsibility, albeit indirect, for their extermination.

But Bader was a tough nut to crack. "Menachem Bader made a powerful impression," *Haolam Hazeh* wrote. "He stood in the witness box with unruffled calm, staving off Tamir's frontal attacks with slick, lengthy replies [...]; it was the first time Tamir had come up against a witness who rebuffed all his verbal assaults with such ease and agility." This is how the exchange between the two went:[46]

> **Tamir:** Is there any basis for Brand's accusation that because of the way you handled his proposal, you bear the responsibility for the extermination of tens [if not] hundreds of thousands of Jews?
> [...]
> **Bader:** I don't know if he waited for him to arrive. He waited at the border for a day or two until he was able to cross the border.
> **Tamir:** I am telling you that it was not, as you claim, a Turkish Jew who accompanied Brand to the border; it was Ehud Avriel.

---

46 "M. Bader Completed his Testimony in the Kasztner-Gruenwald Trial," *Al HaMishmar*, March 26, 1954.

Bader: [Avriel] also accompanied him, and he had no reason to conceal the fact.

Tamir: You know that Avriel was with him when he was arrested, but that he himself was not arrested.

Bader: He was not arrested, because he was a Palestinian citizen.

Tamir: I am telling you that Ehud Avriel, Teddy Kollek and Haim Barlas [members of the Yishuv's legation in Istanbul, Y.W.] worked for British Intelligence.

Bader: I can't keep you from saying that […]

Tamir's mention of Sharett was not accidental. His aim was to bring the Prime Minister to the witness stand and cross-examine him relentlessly. For this purpose, during his cross-examination, he made an outrageous claim that caused even Halevi some misgiving, alleging that it was Sharett who turned Brand over to the British. *Haolam Hazeh* described what happened then in the courtroom: "This claim of Tamir's was too strong even for the surprise-filled Gruenwald-Kasztner trial. All those present held their breath, and the judge, Benjamin Halevi, glared at the young attorney, who become pale with excitement. 'What connection is there between these claims and the trial?' [he asked]." Tamir's reply was that his claim "may seem fanciful, provocative and political, but I take full responsibility for it, and I ask the court to display patience until I can bring a witness to prove that it is not my imagination." So, despite Bader's refusal to play the game by Tamir's rules, Tamir managed to introduce the name of Israel's Prime Minister in 1954 into the proceedings of a trial that was dealing with Hungary of a decade earlier.

VII

Joel Brand testified on April 1 and 2. After his testimony and with the agreement of all parties, the trial was postponed at first until April 26, and then to May 13 and, in actual fact, the proceedings were resumed only two months later, on June 1. Brand being called to the witness stand and the shift in focus to his story marked a change in the nature of the trial: since Brand had not been in Budapest from mid-May 1944, his story did not involve Kasztner and the Jewish leadership there, but rather Sharett and the Jewish leadership in Palestine.

The prosecution had not included Brand on its witness list, and for obvious reasons preferred to call his wife, Hanzi, to the stand. Tamir, who

Joel Brand at the Eichmann trial
YVPA, 4613/227

probably knew that Brand wanted to take revenge on both Kasztner and the Yishuv leadership, made every effort to get him to testify. Zeev Hirsch, a member of the Herut Movement and a friend of Brand's, established contact between the two men. Hirsch told Brand that here was his chance to get even with Kasztner for his despicable acts: "I know Tamir very well," he said, "I can introduce you to him. Have a talk with him, the two of you can help each other."[47]

After some hesitation, Brand agreed to meet with Tamir. They met several times, surreptitiously, in out-of-the-way places—on the Herzliya beach, in Tamir's car while driving, or at his parents' home in Jerusalem. They also devised ways to get in touch with each other by phone—afraid their phones might be tapped or that Hanzi might learn about their meetings.[48]

47 Brand, *Satan and the Soul*, p. 120.
48 Yeshayahu Ben Porat, "Conversations with Shmuel Tamir," *Yedioth Ahronoth*, September 19 & 26, 1980.

Brand came to these meetings torn and wavering, while Tamir marshaled all his charm into persuading him to testify. Kasztner, whom he had never heard of until the trial, was of no interest to him at all, he told Brand—"The historical affair is what counts. I want to prove to the world the role played by the Jewish Agency in the catastrophe. I am convinced of their guilt [...] Peace and quiet in the country and control over the Yishuv was more important to them than saving millions. You have to reveal everything you know about this affair."

Brand listened quietly and then warned Tamir that if he were to testify, he would tell everything he knew—"I will praise the work of the Committee and much of Kasztner's activity as well." Therefore, "my testimony is liable to damage the side you are representing." Tamir would not let go. "It's important to me that you testify, even if you praise Kasztner," he replied. Whatever you heard [there], it was only until you left; but Kasztner is a megalomaniac, and his delusions of grandeur pushed him to the moral abyss into which he plunged."

Brand had another argument. They—namely the government and Mapai—"will not allow me to say the things I want to say." He was already beginning to sense strange movements around him. "They won't let me. They just can't allow themselves to. You'll see. They'll find a way to prevent my testimony." Tamir was adamant—he was not a man to back down:

You will testify, Mr. Brand; [and] very soon. I will impose that on them, and we can't play around with time. You have to testify before the recess. You know too much for them. I, too, am apprehensive about your fate— but only until you have had your say. After that, nothing will happen to you. Just as long as you take care of yourself—and your nerves. Don't tell anyone about our conversation. Tomorrow we'll meet again [...] if anyone follows you when you're on your way to see me [...] give them the slip. Be very careful.[49]

It is hard to determine where the facts end and the myth—assiduously nurtured by Tamir—begins, that the establishment did its utmost to muzzle him and intimidate his witnesses. Pressure was brought to bear on Brand— particularly by his wife, who was Kasztner's right hand during the trial. It was she who arranged a meeting between Brand and Tel, where it was agreed that Tel would ask him no questions, if he called on him to testify, but would

49 Brand, *Satan and the Soul*, p. 129–130.

leave the questioning to Tamir. He also recommended that Brand testify in his mother tongue, German and not in English, and that as he testified he should look at the judge, not at Tamir. Brand accepted these conditions.[50]

Those attending the trial knew nothing about these meetings. "Until the very last minute, no one knew if Brand would be called to testify and by whom," Rosenfeld wrote. On March 30, Tamir asserted in the courtroom that Brand "was in physical danger so long so he had not yet testified; and I demand he be given police protection until then, whether he testifies for the prosecution or for the defense." At the session's end, when it was still unclear as to which side Brand would testify, Tamir declared that if the prosecution did not call him, he would.[51] The following day, on March 31, Tamir informed the court that he wanted to start Brand's testimony immediately—"And I want to place on record that efforts are being made to prevent his testimony; to remove him from the country. Also, his life is in danger—to the best of my knowledge, during the last few days, all his papers have been stolen from him."[52]

To Tel's question as to why all this was being done, Tamir replied that "the reference is to Moshe Sharett having handed Brand over to the British and there is obviously someone interested in preventing his testimony on this matter;" and added jeeringly, "I'm not afraid of you, [or] of your 'Rezsös.'"[53] In compliance with Tel's explicit demand, this sentence was recorded in the transcript. Tamir's words made headlines in the daily *Herut*: "Tamir demands police protection for Joel Brand, the man sent on a rescue mission" (March 31), and "Tamir: The prosecution fears Brand will reveal how he was handed over to the British by Moshe Sharett" (April 1). Brand himself was surprised by the huge newspaper headlines, claiming that his life was in danger. Although he wasn't totally at ease, he did not feel that there was any threat to his life. "Nowadays, I wonder what would have happened at that time, if I had been inadvertently involved in a road accident," he wrote in his book.[54]

The following day he appeared as a witness for the prosecution. As had been agreed, Tel asked him only a few routine questions, such as his name and age, and then immediately handed him over to Tamir for cross-examination. A day after Tamir's provocative statement, it was as if Tel were publicly declaring: "Here is that same Brand that everyone wants so much to

50 Ibid., pp. 132–133.
51 *Herut*, March 31, 1954.
52 Rosenfeld, *Criminal Case*, p. 47.
53 Kasztner's nickname, it was also a derogatory term for the 'apparatchiks' of Mapai.
54 Brand, *Satan and the Soul*, p. 136.

silence [...] here is that same Brand whose life is being threatened [...] We are not afraid of his testimony. On the contrary, let him say what he has to say [...]"[55] "His testimony contained all the ingredients the audience was waiting for," Hanzi Brand said, describing her husband's testimony, "the dramatic adventure of a man who went on a mission to rescue millions, and failed. His testimony had nothing whatsoever to do with Kasztner's activities in Budapest, but Tamir used it as a good move with which to shift the spotlight from the Gruenwald-Kasztner dispute to broader arenas."[56] Why did Tel summon him as a witness for the prosecution? Brand was in a very bad way; he had no work nor any chances of finding decent employment. Under these circumstances, he was neither prepared to nor capable of foregoing the opportunity to stand at center stage and utter his *J'accuse*. "And if Tel hadn't summoned him as a witness," Hanzi Brand said, "Tamir would have, and everyone would have given that a damaging interpretation."[57]

Brand's version of the circumstances that prevented his return to Istanbul differed from Bader's—in both his testimony and his book. When it turned out that Shertok was unable to get to Istanbul, he was told—so he testified—that he had to travel to the Syrian-Turkish border for several days to meet and speak with him there, "and that a few days later I would return to Istanbul. I told Barlas that I didn't want to go, that instead I wanted to turn to the Germans and return to Budapest. I had a fierce quarrel with him and one of my arguments was that I already had a temporary agreement and I asked him to let me return.[58] Barlas told me that I had no cause for concern, that I would be there two or three days and then I'd go back."[59] Avriel and Bader supported Barlas' view, and finally Brand accepted their position, although he argued that it was opposed to his own. Why did he do so? "The representatives of the *halutzim* (pioneers), Bader, Avriel and Barlas, were for me the supreme authority. They were the Palestinian representatives and of course I listened to them." The fast train that he took from Istanbul to the Turkish-Syrian border stopped briefly in Ankara. At the station two men were waiting for him: Yosef Klarman, representative of the Revisionists in the Yishuv's delegation, and Yaacov Griffel, the delegation's Agudat-Israel

55 Rosenfeld, *Criminal Case*, p. 47.
56 Brand, *Satan and the Soul*, p. 134.
57 Ibid., p. 135.
58 Trial transcript, p. 152.
59 When it turned out that there was no possibility of arriving at the signature of a real agreement, the members of the committee, together with Brand, decided to prepare a fictitious document, with which they hoped to dupe Eichmann and earn some time.

(the Orthodox religious party) representative. The two cautioned him against continuing the journey. The British are laying a trap for you, they said; they want to ensnare you and once you are in their hands, they'll arrest you. Brand was frightened by their warning, but continued on his way nevertheless. When they arrived in Aleppo, on the Syrian border, he was arrested. "Avriel got off to see to the luggage, and while he was there, outside, they took me from the compartment […]"[60] Before leaving the train, Avriel told him that if he were arrested, he should agree to be interrogated only in the presence of Jewish Agency representatives. "The British will unquestionably accept that demand," he told Brand. Brand also took this advice, and the British did accede to his demand. He was taken to the home of a British officer, where Moshe Shertok was waiting and greeted him, saying: "I have been waiting for you here for a day or two […]"

Thus unemployed, bitter, desperate and seeking revenge, Brand confirmed Tamir's version that the Jewish Agency had turned him over to the British after persuading him, against his will, to go to meet Shertok. They knew that the British were laying a trap and that without their cooperation Brand would not fall into it. And at this point, the court adjourned for a two-month recess.

VIII

Throughout the six weeks of the trial, both the political system and the government took a great deal of interest in it. They realized that here was not merely a marginal libel suit but rather a trial that could have far-reaching implications. One of those who took a special interest in the case was Prime Minister Moshe Sharett (who had changed his name from Shertok), who devoted considerable time to questions related to the trial. On February 27, in the midst of his cross-examination, Kasztner came to Sharett's home to ask his advice. As he wrote in his diary:

> Israel Kasztner has been testifying for days in the trial that is being held at the Prosecutor-General's instigation to defend him against libel owing to his role in the rescue efforts in Hungary, which involved negotiations with the Nazis. The libeler is a Revisionist and his lawyer is the greatly praised Shmuel Tamir. The problem is how to expand the public base of

---

60 Trial transcript, April 2, 1954.

the testimony to clearly prove that he is right. I suggested he ought to get Ehud [Avriel] involved, and agreed to invite him for a talk.[61]

Ten days later, on March 9, Sharett invited Avriel for a talk, during which he brought up the need to replace Tel. "It seems to me that the Attorney General has taken this explosive trial too lightly and appointed as prosecutor a spineless, ineffectual individual who has no understanding at all of the political and public issues involved, and is forever losing the constant battles against the ruthless defense counsel, Shmuel Tamir," Sharett wrote in his diary. "We have to get Haim Cohn to place someone quick-thinking and intelligent next to the prosecutor." Sharett spoke to Cohn that same day, "And I discussed the Kasztner trial with him. It turns out that he has already appointed an assistant to the prosecutor."[62] At the end of March, he wrote bitterly in his diary: "The Attorney General apparently had no idea of the public and political nature or the sensational repercussions of this trial. The prosecutor Tel is a total failure." The clear-cut conclusion he drew from this sad state of affairs was that "there's nothing for it but to demand that after the recess Haim Cohn himself take over the prosecution."[63]

In early April, immediately after Brand's testimony, Sharett spoke with spoke with the Attorney General again, and wrote in his diary that "It is highly likely that Tamir will demand that I appear in court. There's going to be a three-week recess in the trial now and we'll have time to get some advice."[64] At a meeting a few days later it was decided that Cohn, at Sharett's explicit request, would personally take on the task of prosecuting—a very unusual step considering the fact that the Attorney General generally does not appear in court. It was also decided that Sharett would not appear as a witness in the trial, instead of which, "I have resolved that I will hold a press conference after the trial, in which I will tell the whole truth about the Brand affair."[65]

The replacement of the prosecutor did not change Sharett's bad feeling about the trial and the Attorney General. When the trial reopened on June 1 he consulted Teddy Kollek and complained to him about the way Cohn was preparing the case. "The prosecutor was not replaced [Tel continued to

---

61 Moshe Sharett, *Personal Diary*, vol. 2, February 27, 1954, p. 376.
62 Ibid., April 3, 1954, p. 430.
63 Ibid., March 31, 1954, p. 425.
64 Ibid., April 3, 1954, p. 392.
65 Ibid., April 8, 1954, p. 443. Participating in the consultation were Haim Cohn, Amos Manor, Ehud Avriel and Teddy Kollek, then Director-General of the Prime Minister's Office.

work on the prosecution alongside Cohn, Y.W.]," he wrote in his diary. "Haim Cohn refuses to bring many witnesses for our side. I must speak to him again and exhort him to do more."[66]

IX

The Prime Minister was also troubled by the matter of Joel Brand. A day before Brand testified, when no one knew yet whether he would actually testify, and if so, for which side, Sharett described his dread of what Brand might say on the witness stand.[67] If he appeared in court, the situation was liable to get very complicated, because "during the period after the failure of his mission, he went wild, sending endless accusatory memos to heads of the Jewish Agency, blaming them for the corruption in Hungary, and now Shmuel Tamir will use all of those to condemn us." He was even more perturbed after Brand's testimony, when it transpired that he had confirmed Tamir's version of the facts, according to which Shertok was the one responsible for handing him over to the British and thwarting his mission. Ehud Avriel was the person who was supposed to prove that Brand's testimony was false and it was Sharett's intention to bring Venia Pomerantz back as well, to support his version of the events. "When the trial reopens, Ehud will appear as a prime witness," he wrote in his diary: "Teddy will find out if we can bring Vania Pomerantz to Israel from Paris." Within a few days, Pomerantz-Hadari arrived in Israel and "they [Venia and Ehud] are going over the material and constructing their testimony." Two days later the two met with the Prime Minister.[68]

Sharett took one further step. He engaged an attorney to advise and assist the parties and him personally in connection with the trial. The attorney was Meir Tuval (Weltman). Tuval (1905–1981) was born in Yugoslavia, immigrated to Palestine in 1939 and during World War II was a member of the Yishuv's delegation to Istanbul. During the latter half of the fifties, he was the Israeli minister in Budapest.

Tuval, who Sharett described in his diary as "a loyal member of Mapai," met the Prime Minister frequently to discuss the trial. Sharett also noted that he is "very closely informed on the progress of the Kasztner trial and has told me

---

66 Sharett, *Personal Diary*, vol. 2, June 1, 1954, p. 524.

67 Ibid., March 31, 1954, p. 425.

68 Ibid., April 8, 1954, p. 443; April 14, 1954, p. 458; April 16, 1954, p. 463.

The Israel legation, Prague: Ehud Avriel, Minister Plenipotentiary;
Mrs. Hanna Avriel; Joseph Ilan, 2nd Secy.; Mrs. Tamar Benshalom;
Mr. Rafi Benshalom, 1st Secy. and Dir. Consular
INPC, D750-052

much about what's happening behind the scenes."[69] Tuval's first task involved
the memoirs Brand was planning to publish. Before he testified, Avriel, Kollek
and Tuval had promised Brand that they would arrange a permanent job for
him in the "Shoham" shipping company—since throughout all his years in
Israel, he had not held down a steady job and had been unemployed for long
periods. Once the trial was over, the three were in no hurry to fulfill their
promise and Brand grew increasingly embittered.[70]

The Mapainiks changed their minds after seeing the first chapter of
Brand's book.[71] They apparently understood that the book would not show
them in a positive light, to put it mildly, and decided that Brand should
publish a book that presented a version of the events with which they would
feel more comfortable. To achieve this aim, Tuval involved Brand's friend,
Moshe Katznelson, an editor at the Mapai-affiliated Ayanot publishing house.
It was unthinkable, Tuval told Brand, that of all publishers, Ayanot should

69   Ibid., June 11, 1954, vol. 2, p. 545.
70   Brand, *Satan and the Soul*, p. 137.
71   Ibid., p. 140.

publish a book that leveled such grave accusations at Mapai. "If you want to write the truth," Katznelson told him, "we'll publish it. After all, all the time you were involved with the Rescue Committee, you were a member of our party. If you have any complaints about that period, and I know you do, it is your duty to present them to us."[72]

Yehuda Erez, Katznelson's colleague at Ayanot and another friend of Brand's, was also enlisted in an effort to cajole him. When the two promised to publish the manuscript word for word as he wrote it, he let them read what he had written so far. Once they had finished reading it, Katznelson got back to him and said: "Your book must be published by us. We won't change a single word […] the fact that some of the party's 'big shots' won't like it doesn't interest me or Yehuda in the least."[73]

Brand's publishing agreement with Ayanot was drafted by Tuval, who reported to the Prime Minister as soon as it was signed. Sharett wrote in his diary: "Joel Brand is writing a book describing the entire affair. At first, he contacted some shady publisher, a former IZL member, but under Meir's influence he has transferred the book to Ayanot."[74]

What position did David Ben-Gurion take on the matter? All during the trial, he was in Sede Boker, the kibbutz in the Israel's southern Negev region, where he settled after resigning from the government in 1953. Unlike Sharett, he showed no interest in the trial, although he may have met with Kasztner during that year. We know about that visit from a letter that Yehoshua, Kasztner's brother, sent to Ben-Gurion a few days after the Supreme Court handed down its verdict:

> My late brother, Dr. Israel Kasztner, of blessed memory, told me at the time about his last visit to you at Sede Boker and how understanding you were about the matter [the trial, Y.W.] and his mission. He told me about the great hopes he had pinned on you, and ended by saying: "You'll see, one day the Prime Minister will rise in the Knesset and express appreciation for all my work and that of my friends, and will publicly announce the real truth, to the whole world."[75]

72 Ibid.
73 Ibid.
74 Sharett, *Personal Diary*, vol. 2, June 11, 1954, p. 545.
75 January 19, 1958, ISA, 5432/1366C.

Elsewhere in his letter, Kasztner's brother asked Ben-Gurion "to give some expression to this wish of my late brother." In his reply,[76] Ben-Gurion wrote:

> I received your letter and I appreciate your concern for your late brother who was assassinated by despicable criminals and whose honor was trampled upon during his lifetime and after his death by villains who feigned to be the guardians of moral integrity. I am thoroughly familiar with the true nature of those "guardians of moral integrity" who slandered your brother, and I know about their abominable schemes. But my memory does not permit me to confirm or deny the words your late brother cited to you in my name.

In Ben-Gurion's 1954 diary, there is no mention either of the trial or of a meeting with Kasztner. However, Hanzi Brand claims that such a meeting did indeed take place.[77] According to her, the meeting was arranged by Dezső (David) Herman, and she had been supposed to accompany Kasztner, but in the end he had gone alone. When he returned from Sede Boker, he told her that Ben-Gurion had said to him: "Come to me when the whole affair is over." Later, Hanzi asked Yehuda Erez, the editor of Ben-Gurion's writings, to find some record of the conversation in his diary, but he found nothing.

X

In contrast to Mapai, the Herut Movement was in the enviable position of having its work carried out by others. At meetings of the movement's center, no reference was made to the trial. The party's only relationship with it was through the public committee for Gruenwald's defense that paid the expenses of his defense, most of whose members were also members of the Herut Movement. The headlines of articles reporting on the trial in the movement's newspaper, *Herut*, were mainly an expression of its solidarity with the defense, and through them, one could sense the party's joy at the prosecution's failure.[78] Only one editorial published in the daily related to the trial,[79] and that dealt

---

76 February 2, 1958, ISA.
77 Hanzi Brand, personal interview.
78 On this matter, see Yechiam Weitz, "The Herut Movement and the Kasztner Trial," *Holocaust and Genocide Studies*, vol. 8/3 (December, 1994), pp. 349–371.
79 J. Aviadi, "Joel Brand, the Forgotten Emissary," *Herut*, April 7, 1954; Aviadi is a pseudonym of the journalist Yehoshua Ophir.

with Joel Brand. Written several days after the massacre at Maʾaleh Akrabim,[80] it served as an introduction to the many articles that would be printed in the daily during the summer of 1955, after the verdict was published:

> For ten years, Joel Brand has been here in our midst, without anyone listening to his shocking story. With no one caring about him, he walked about in our midst like a long forgotten emissary. He saw how all the informers were rising to power, in the wake of the blood shed by the freedom fighters, those very traitors who with their own hands had turned him over to the enemy; he saw how the meanest of slaves had become the rulers in Israel, and not only that, but also had come to demand 'remuneration' for the spilled Jewish blood, as if they were owed the prize of reparations for the millions of slaughtered Jews. At that moment, he certainly must have thought of those hundreds of thousands who were slaughtered because of the failure of his mission, caused by those 'authors of the reparations' …And today when a person in Israel thinks about this clique leading the ship of Israel through the holocaust, on the road going up to Maʾaleh Akrabim, is it any wonder that his heart shudders with anxiety and trepidation?

To the right of Herut was an organization that showed a great deal of interest in the trial. The movement, known as Malchut Israel ("The Kingdom of Israel") was headed by Dr. Israel Eldad (Scheib), one of the leaders of Lehi and its paper, *Sullam* (Ladder), published the most outspoken, strident remarks about the trial. Like the Herut Movement, Malchut Israel viewed the trial as testimony to and a symbol of the treachery and weakness of the Israeli government, but it also regarded the Herut Movement itself as party to this weakness and immorality. The Herut Movement's willingness in principle to participate in the parliamentary democracy and to accept the rules of its game proved, as far as Malchut Israel was concerned, that it was an ally of the establishment, rather than one of the forces fighting it. To a large extent, Malchut Israel viewed itself as the successor to the underground and

---

80 On March 17, 1954, an Egged bus travelling northward from Eilat was ambushed and ten of its passengers were murdered. The public reacted strongly and the Herut movement accused the government of having failed to ensure the public's safety. An open letter published by *Herut* stated that "a government that has caused the death of innocent victims and is incapable of providing its citizens with security, has but one option—to resign!", *Herut*, March 19, 1954.

Herut as the successor to Ha-Zohar (the Revisionist Party). The underground movements themselves had organized a rebellion against the latter.

During the trial's recess, an article was printed in *Sullam*[81] commending Tamir for having exposed the link between Kasztner's collaboration with the Germans and the Jewish Agency's collaboration with the British in Palestine. "The deep-seated root is the very same," the article stated. "It was not for naught that Sharett's party and its newspaper supported the defense of the man accused of collaborating with Himmler's assistant and of freeing him." The article thanked Tamir for "removing the trial from the private realm of 'one who insulted and one who was insulted,' and raising it to the level of a national trial of the highest historical importance." According to it, Tamir had exposed the fact that "the leaders of the Jewish Agency and their agents [...] **are themselves war criminals**" [emphasis in the original]. It went on to say that this was significant not only because it afforded an understanding of the past but also because "these people who bear the guilt today hold the very highest positions, and if they have already died—they are adorned with garlands as the nation's heroes and its redeemers. This is an educational disaster and a national-political disaster, because this 'secret' of the leaders of the nation, who prevented or **consented** to the prevention of the rescue, is known to the heads of states throughout the world, and they draw the practical political conclusions today as well" [emphasis in the original].

XI

Another newspaper that showed a great interest in the trial was the weekly *Haolam Hazeh*. Founded in 1937, as a "photo-magazine for the whole family," its editor was the veteran journalist Uri Kesari. In 1946, its name was changed from *Tesha Ba'erev* to *Haolam Hazeh*, and in 1950 it was bought by Uri Avneri and Shalom Cohen. No longer a family magazine, the weekly became one of the key journals opposing the ruling Mapai party. In the fifties, the Mapai establishment loathed *Haolam Hazeh*, which it always referred to as "that particular weekly;" but it was also in awe of it. In his diary, Sharett called it a "filthy rag," "that obscene periodical" and "this vile, filthy weekly." At the same time, however, the Prime Minister held frequent meetings with the editors to discuss the weekly's write-ups, which he regarded as damaging.

81 S. Avinoam, "On the Kasztner Trial—An Interim Summary," *Sullam* 12 (Spring, 1954).

Not content with hurling criticism at the government and exposing its corruption, *Haolam Hazeh* also went to considerable lengths to depict it as a monster. Several people in the top ranks of the establishment—particularly its top level officials (not ministers)—were at the receiving end of the paper's special "treatment." The paper claimed that the main function of these officials was to carry out Ben-Gurion's dictatorial schemes. The term the "apparatus of darkness" coined by the weekly referred to the transfer of enormous powers into concealed apparatuses, while divesting the official, elected systems of government of all content.

The major figure in the apparatus of darkness, according to the weekly, was Attorney General Haim Cohn, and consequently it devoted many articles to him. In 1953, he was named "Man of the Year" and his photograph on the cover of the weekly's Rosh Hashanah issue was captioned "The apparatus against the individual." Under the headline, "The Year of the Crushing Apparatus" the write-up stated that Cohn embodied the process that during the year had been "conspicuously [...] in everyone's eyes, a terroristic monstrosity." What the process had mainly done was to:

> Break the vital spirit of man, for the glory of the soulless apparatus [...] crush the basic liberties, one after another [...] replace free will and the spirit of volunteerism with blind obedience to orders.

But beyond all these, the process reflected a salient change in the state of Israel that "was anchored in the heart of Hebrew youth and the simple man," and now was seeking "shelter in the arms of the reign of power."

This process was epitomized by Cohn not because he was an important or a brilliant man but because he was "a rather colorless man, with a less than fascinating biography." His main trait, "which paved the way to his rise, was simply this: his readiness to obey any order, without thinking too much about it, to find the legal, or quasi-legal basis for anything his masters sought." In the spirit in which the Nazi bureaucracy was later depicted, the paper wrote:

> Haim Herman Cohn is the perfect official, for whom officialdom has become almost a world view. He lives exactly opposite Ben-Gurion's home in the Rehavia quarter of Jerusalem. As befits an official, he does not stand out, either in his name, his appearance or his conduct. He rises every morning at the right time, waits at the right hour for the highly polished car that takes him to his office, on the third floor of the distinctly Colonial-style building next to the building of the Central Post Office

in Jerusalem. There, in an ordinary office, similar to hundreds of other offices, all during 1953, Haim Cohn supervised the gradual elimination of human rights in the Israeli legal system.

Hatred of Ben-Gurion and the demonization of the government were among the grounds for the relationship—which seems so odd in retrospect— between Shmuel Tamir, the patrician Sabra from Rehavia, a Jerusalem quarter inhabited by veteran Israelis and the elite, and Uri Avneri, who was born in Germany as Helmut Osterman and came to Israel as a refugee after the Nazi rise to power. They both saw the trial as an opportunity to demonstrate the decay and corruption in the government and its willingness to resort to any means to cover up its crimes. It also tied in with their shared self-image as representatives of the generation of fighters, natives of the land, who coming out of the trenches had seen how the rule of the country was being usurped by a clique of *galuti* (Diaspora-minded) politicians. The trial, they hoped, would enable them to prove that the route taken by these politicians was not only catastrophic but also criminal. As far as they were concerned, there was no difference between Kasztner in Budapest and Sharett in Jerusalem. The fact that Sharett, who had spent part of his childhood in Ein Seniya near Nablus and was a graduate of the first class at the Herzliya High School in Tel Aviv, was more a native of the land than Avneri, was of no importance. The stereotypical, polarized picture that the story of the trial produced was much stronger.

XII

The relationship between Avneri and Tamir was created during the libel suit in the matter of Yedidya Segal. In 1949, Paul Kollek, Teddy's brother, submitted a libel suit against the *Herut* newspaper. An article it printed had claimed that in the framework of the *"petite saison"* in 1947,[82] Kollek, a Haganah commander in Haifa, had been responsible for the murder of Yedidya Segal, a member of IZL. This was Tamir's first public trial and his media baptism of fire.[83] *Haolam Hazeh* took Tamir's side and supported him unequivocally then,

---

[82] An operation carried out by the Haganah to apprehend members of the IZL and hand them over to the British authorities. There were two such operations, the larger one in 1944, and the smaller one in 1947, known as the *"petite saison."*

[83] Ben Porat, *Conversations with Shmuel Tamir*; Uri Avneri, personal interview.

as well as in his other public trials. The fact that the Tzrifin Underground was put on trial before a military court was depicted as an attempt by the Attorney General to destroy the last stronghold of human rights in Israel—the civil court.[84]

In Avneri's eyes, the trial symbolized "Dov Joseph's squeaky voice and the bump on Haim Cohn's head,"[85] but his statement that "the trial would never have become more than a small libel suit against an old, eccentric Jerusalemite if *Haolam Hazeh* hadn't given it maximum publicity from the very first day,"[86] is an exaggeration. The first report on the trial appeared in the weekly only in early March—other newspapers had reported on it from the first day—and most of the write-ups were rather modest. Nonetheless, the weekly did play a unique role in covering the trial.

Alongside the modest write-up a few huge articles were placed in the centerfold of the paper and on its front page. One such was the March 4, 1954 issue that presented a special interview with Kasztner under the heading "Himmler wanted to see me." A week later, in the center of the March 11 issue, there was an article headed "Israel Rudolf Kasztner—A rescuer of Jews or a collaborator?" Another was the Rosh Hashanah issue (September 22, 1954) naming Kasztner "Man of the Year."

Haolam Hazeh became Tamir's home court. In 1980, Avneri stated that "A large proportion of our leading journalists' time was spent covering Tamir's actions." Innumerable articles praised him, some written by Tamir himself.[87] This was a marriage between a daring newspaper and a young, ambitious and publicity-seeking attorney.[88] His friend Shalom Rosenfeld had this to say about this last trait: "Tamir had an extraordinary sense of timing for public relations. He constructed his examinations of witnesses so that some of them would become headlines in the morning papers and some, in the afternoon papers."[89]

The trial's coverage in *Haolam Hazeh* was framed in terms of total confrontation. Although *Herut* also described it as a confrontation, from its

---

84 "The Year of the Annihilative Apparatus," *Haolam Hazeh*, eve of Rosh Hashanah, 1954.
85 Uri Avneri, personal interview.
86 Segev, *The Seventh Million*, p. 278.
87 Cited by Harel, *The Truth about Kasztner's Murder*, p. 332.
88 According to Avneri, Tamir's real talent lay in the area of public relations. He was naturally adept when it came to publicizing himself, and every legal step he took was taken with an eye towards the following day's headline. With time, for him "publicity became an end in itself and his mania for headlines was one of the main things that drove him." Uri Avneri, personal interview.
89 Rosenfeld, personal interview.

standpoint it was mainly a party confrontation and an historical reckoning with Mapai. In *Haolam Hazeh*, the drama became an apocalypse. In the fifties, most of the newspapers in Israel were partisan papers. The weekly, which was not affiliated with any political party, represented itself as the spokesman of the young state of Israel and the trial as the high point of a conflict between generations and cultures.

From the weekly's point of view, the trial stood as proof of the catastrophe inherent in the approach of the *galuti* Jew, who curries favor with the landowner or the civil authority, instead of insisting on his rights or taking a moral stand—"the affair proves how a collective that depends on this approach ends up." And how does it end up? "In the quarters of the landowner's servants."[90]

90 "Man of the Year—1954," *Haolam Hazeh*, September 22, 1954.

CHAPTER FOUR

A Trial in Jerusalem, 1954 (B)

I

The trial resumed on Tuesday, June 1, 1954. At this stage, it was clearly Kasztner who was on trial. Gruenwald, the formal defendant, had been hospitalized and was not even present during the proceedings. Several changes had been made by the time the trial resumed. The Attorney General himself now represented the prosecution. Tel sat next to Cohn and responsibility for the trial, "which probably should not have gone this far," was no longer his.

The first witness in this part of the trial was Ehud Avriel, who had held a series of key positions since the establishment of the state. His testimony was particularly important from the defense standpoint, not only because he had accompanied Joel Brand on his journey to the Syrian border, but because he was a consummate representative of "Ben-Gurion's boys" and of his "apparatus of darkness." His testimony would, therefore, enable the defense to turn it into a trial of the Mapai leadership.

During his testimony, Avriel stressed the point that Sharett had not come to Istanbul because the British were not interested in his obtaining a Turkish visa.[1] In addition, there was the difficult problem of Brand's visa: "Almost daily, we had to extend our permit to stay in Turkey."[2] Brand left for Palestine because he could no longer remain in Turkey and didn't want to return to Hungary.

Avriel didn't know in advance that Brand would be arrested, but he knew that such a possibility existed and had even warned Brand. Brand decided to go in any case, especially because of his disturbed mental state. In Avriel's estimation, Brand was a broken man who was not really capable of taking

---

1   Trial transcript, June 1, 1954, p. 170.
2   Ibid.

rational, well thought out decisions. It was because of Brand's state of mind that the committee had decided to send Avriel with him.

Consequently, Avriel's testimony was completely different from Brand's version of the events. According to Avriel, the reason Brand was handed over to the British and subsequently arrested had everything to do with the precarious circumstances and his disturbed mental state and nothing to do with the Jewish Agency. Avriel was no easy prey for Tamir. He tried to attack him "with all the weapons of cross-examination: once, taking him by surprise by revealing a sensational fact; once, laying a trap by asking a seemingly innocent question; another time by making a pathos-filled political declaration; and another, by nettling him with a stinging comment." But he met with no success—"the defense counsel was confronted by a man with many years of political and diplomatic experience [behind him]. A man with a keen mind and a strong character."[3]

In his attacks on Avriel, Tamir focused on depicting him as the man who had handed Brand in, along with the argument that his readiness to negotiate with the Germans was tantamount to collaborating with them. Tension in the courtroom was intense when Avriel submitted a memorandum Sharett had presented in London on June 27, 1944 to the Jewish Agency Executive. The memorandum was intended to prove that the British, not the Jewish Agency, had defeated Brand's mission. In it, Sharett described his contacts with the British in this regard. Tamir objected vigorously to the admission of this document, arguing that only Sharett could submit it, "[Otherwise] I cannot test the veracity of its contents in a cross-examination." However, beyond his formal argument, this provided Tamir with another opportunity to achieve the objective he had been aiming at for some time—a cross-examination of the Prime Minister that would incontrovertibly prove that the country's leadership was seated in the dock, and not a forgotten old man. As he did on almost all issues, the judge accepted Tamir's position in this instance as well, and ruled that only Sharett himself could confirm under oath that the document was authentic and true, and since he was not going to appear as a witness, the memorandum would not be admitted as evidence.

For Mapai and Sharett, this was a distressing setback—they had hoped the document would prove their basic argument that the British had foiled the plan. Now that they were not allowed to submit it as evidence, Avriel decided to publish it in a newspaper. He asked *Ma'ariv* to print it a few days later—on Sunday, the eve of the Shavuoth festival, June 6, 1954—and give it

3   Rosenfeld, *Criminal Case*, p. 59.

a prominent place.[4] The salient point in the memorandum was that Brand had agreed to travel to Aleppo, on the Turkish-Syrian border, only after the British had explicitly promised he would not be arrested on his arrival. The document also included the claim that the British were the ones who had prevented Brand from returning to Budapest.

After the event, Sharett approved the step Avriel had taken. "I first learned from Haim Cohn that the report I wrote in London about the Joel Brand affair would be published in full in the holiday edition of *Ma'ariv*," he wrote in his diary. "Ehud gave the document to the newspaper and its publication made an enormous impression."[5] Others were less enthusiastic. "It was hard to accept Sharett's words in *Ma'ariv* as a credible substitute for his testimony—under oath—on the witness stand," *Haolam Hazeh* wrote.[6] This action also enraged Halevi. On the first session following the publication, he stated, "this publication, after the court had decided not to accept the document as evidence, is contempt of court, a criminal offense."[7]

It therefore became necessary to find another platform from which Sharett could give his version of the facts. The possibility of his testifying was raised, but he was not prepared to fall into Tamir's hands, fully aware that being cross-examined by him was not usually a pleasant experience. The platform that was finally selected was a rally marking the tenth anniversary of Peretz Goldstein's death. The rally, at which the monument commemorating the paratroopers was to be unveiled, was scheduled for July 29 in Kibbutz Ma'agan on the shores of the Sea of Galilee. Sharett was to be guest of honor and the keynote speaker at the rally. He prepared his speech with great care, couching it in flowery, pathos-filled language.[8]

The rally itself was planned as a momentous event. Before the commemorative monument was unveiled, a Piper airplane was to drop a letter from the President of the state. But the occasion ended in a terrible disaster. The envelope containing the letter was caught up in the wheels of the small plane, and the pilot, trying to drop it a second time, flew too low and crashed straight into the festive crowd. Fifteen people were killed, and 26 wounded, two of them fatally. Among those who were killed were four of the parachutists who had been dropped into Europe during World War II.

4   "Sharett Describes Joel Brand's Rescue Mission," *Ma'ariv*, June 6, 1954.
5   Sharett, *Personal Diary*, vol. 2, June 9, 1954, p. 543.
6   "A Substitute for Testimony," *Haolam Hazeh*, June 10, 1954.
7   Trial transcript, June 13, 1954, p. C1.
8   Handwritten designation, CZA, A245-40III.

The Israeli public was stunned. The press gave wide coverage to the disaster and the mourning that followed it. The intensity of the shock is also evident in Sharett's brief, muddled entry in his diary: "The disaster, the victims? No panic, mute horror, wounded, weeping [...] how this great occasion came to an end." There were some who exploited the catastrophe to take a stab at their opponents. The real purpose of the rally, *Haolam Hazeh* asserted,[9] was to serve as a demonstration of the supreme solidarity of all those connected with the attempt to rescue Hungarian Jewry, in the face of the virulent attack on them by the defense in the Gruenwald-Kasztner case."

Deprived of his festive platform by the terrible disaster, Sharett found another way to give his version of the events. On August 5, a week after the accident, he spoke on *Kol Yisrael* (the Israel Broadcasting Service) in memory of its victims. A comparison between the eulogy he delivered on the radio and the speech he had planned to give at Ma'agan shows that he took that speech, added an opening in memory of the victims of the disaster and an ending that linked the seven parachutists killed in Europe and the four who died at Kibbutz Ma'agan, "whose glorious heroism now embraces all the other victims of the Ma'agan catastrophe," and delivered it as an "address to the nation."[10]

II

Following Avriel's testimony, three more witnesses who had testified previously were called to the stand: Kasztner and Palgi were brought at Tamir's request, and Brand was called by the judge.

All three testified on the same day, June 4. Kasztner's was the key testimony. As he took the stand, Kasztner appeared to have changed drastically. The last time he had testified, he had been smug and self-confident; on this occasion, according to a newspaper report, "he was pale, and looked as if he had just climbed out of bed after a long illness. He spoke in a soft, low voice."[11] He was questioned about a document that Tamir had discovered during the trial's recess. It was one of the affidavits Kasztner had given to Becher, stating that the latter deserved a great deal of appreciation. Even more important,

---

9   Sharett, *Personal Diary*, vol. 2, July 29, 1954, p. 562; "The Disaster at Ma'agan," *Haolam Hazeh*, August 5, 1954.

10 Designation of manuscript of speaker on the radio, CZA, A425-40III.

11 Description in *Herut*, June 6, 1954; "Trial of the Year," *Haolam Hazeh*, June 10, 1954.

Kasztner had given this affidavit not in his own name, but on behalf of the Jewish Agency and the World Jewish Congress. A debate ensued between the defense and the prosecution about the translation of the German words Kasztner had used in describing Becher. Tamir argued that Kasztner had used the term "the fullest measure of appreciation," while the prosecution claimed that Kasztner's wording was far less probative. As for the second point, Tamir repeatedly asked who had authorized Kasztner to make this statement on behalf of the Jewish Agency:[12]

> **Tamir:** Who authorized you not only to testify in the name of the [Jewish] Agency, but also to add an intervention, to intercede in the name of the Jewish Agency, the Congress, and the Jewish people?
>
> **Halevi:** Who gave you permission to give an affidavit in the name of the Jewish Agency?
>
> **Kasztner:** Dobkin and Barlas in the name of the Jewish Agency, and for the World Jewish Congress—Mr. Perlzweig, Director of its political department, and Mr. Rigner, its European representative.
>
> **Tamir:** You are saying that you were acting in their name; did they permit you to use these words [that appear in the document] and not merely to state the facts in their name?
>
> **Kasztner:** They did not see the affidavit.
>
> **Tamir:** Did they permit you to use these words and to make this interventional recommendation?
>
> **Kasztner:** There was no formal discussion; they did not see the wording.
>
> **Tamir:** Did they permit you to do more than state facts, and not to offer an opinion or to intervene?
>
> **Kasztner:** I understood from the conversations I had that I was authorized, and in this framework, that I was permitted to give the affidavit.
>
> **Tamir:** Explicitly in "their name?"
>
> **Kasztner:** In their name as well, in my name it was beyond any doubt.
>
> **Tamir:** When you said in this honorable court that you did not give any evidence or a sworn affidavit in Nuremberg—neither before the court nor before any of its servants—did you

---

12 Trial transcript, June 4, 1954, pp. 47–48.

knowingly lie in this courtroom? Evidence in the case of trials
brought before the Allies—did you knowingly lie?

Kasztner: I repudiate this. What you are doing is a national crime.

Tamir: To get back to a national crime—and this will be my last
question—when you said that any initiative, other than giving
evidence [...in relation to Kurt Becher] is a national crime,
you agreed with me. Do you agree with me that if you did so,
you are a national criminal?

Kasztner: That is your version.

Tamir: Precisely.

Kasztner had cited the name of Eliahu Dobkin to substantiate his version
of the facts. Thus, the defense called Dobkin who had been a member of
the Jewish Agency Executive during the nineteen forties and fifties, to the
witness stand. In an attempt to avoid having to testify, he sent a letter from a
convalescent home where he was staying, claiming that he was in poor health.
Finally, at the end of June, he did testify, but not in front of the court clerk,
who, instructed to do so by the President, had sent several telegrams to the
pension where he was staying, urging him to fulfill his civic duty.

Putting Dobkin on the stand was in itself a victory for the defense—"If
Dobkin's reply is in the affirmative, then Mapai and the Jewish Agency will
have brought disgrace upon themselves," *Haolam Hazeh* explained. "If his
reply is negative, then this will serve as the final blow to Kasztner from his
friends."[13]

In his testimony, Dobkin chose the second option. He completely denied
Kasztner's version. Not only had he not given Kasztner the authority to act in
the name of the Jewish Agency, he claimed, but also until Kurt Becher's name
had come up in the trial, he had never even heard of the man. The exchange
between Dobkin and Tamir shows how he played right into the hands of the
defense:[14]

Tamir: A claim has been made that you and Barlas agreed that
evidence be given in favor of the SS officer Kurt Becher, and
even agreed to a recommendation that he be given special
consideration for everything he did, in the name of the Jewish
Agency. Do you recall such a thing?

13　"A Trial—Every Reply is Bad," *Haolam Hazeh*, June 24, 1954.
14　Trial transcript, June 28, 1954, p. XI: 2–4.

Dobkin: No, I don't remember any such thing. After Mr. Tamir came to me to refresh my memory in this regard, I tried my best to remember, but I don't recall any such conversation.

Tamir: Anything similar?

Dobkin: What could be more similar than the conversation itself? I don't remember.

Tamir: And permission to Kasztner by the Jewish Agency to testify on his own behalf in Becher's favor or to give a recommendation for him?

Dobkin: I don't remember either a conversation like that or a subject like that.

Tamir: Did you know that Kasztner was going to testify at the Nuremberg trial?

Dobkin: No. In any case, I don't remember. It's possible that at the time someone or he himself told me, but I don't recall.

Tamir: Do you have any recollection at all of being faced with such a serious moral dilemma as giving permission in the Agency's name for anyone to testify on behalf of some Nazi? […] Do you remember such a dilemma facing you?

Dobkin: I don't recall.

Tamir: As head of the Jewish Agency's Organization Department, did you have the authority to give someone permission to testify in favor of an SS general or colonel on the Agency's behalf?

Dobkin: I had no authority whatsoever in such matters.

The Attorney General's cross-examination in no way changed the situation. Dobkin did not hesitate to say that his personal opinion of Kasztner was definitely positive, but he still had no recollection of Nuremberg or of Kurt Becher.

The story did not end with Dobkin's testimony. Kasztner, who probably felt he had nothing to lose, took a rather unusual step. About two weeks after Dobkin testified, he sent a letter to Judge Halevi claiming that Dobkin's version of the facts was not correct.[15] He began the letter by explaining why he had decided to send it:

Considering the fact that my testimony at the trial is over and I therefore have no possibility of pointing out several serious errors in the evidence

---

15 July 14, 1954, ISA, Kasztner trial containers, 512/B.

given by Mr. Eliahu Dobkin, a member of the Jewish Agency Executive, I am left no choice but to make my remarks about his testimony in this manner.

His main claim related to Dobkin's statement that he first heard Becher's name during the trial—**"This claim in Mr. Dobkin's testimony can only stem from a fatal defect in memory that has befallen him"** [emphasis in the original]. He asserted that Dobkin had heard about Becher as far back as 1944 and again in 1945. A report that Dobkin had to read, both as a member of the Jewish Agency Executive and in his position as a member of the Rescue Committee, contained four references to Becher's name. Moreover, during the 1946 22nd Zionist Congress, Dobkin would have come across Becher's name yet again.

Only towards the end of the letter, and then only briefly, does he touch upon his testimony in Nuremberg and the affidavit in favor of Becher. "In a conversation we had during the Congress," Kasztner wrote, "the problem also arose as to what, from the Jewish standpoint, should be the fate of those who helped us in our rescue operations. We spoke in particular about Becher's role in these operations. What we concluded was in the spirit of the testimony I gave to the honorable court during my second examination." In conclusion, Kasztner wrote:

> If it is possible that forgetfulness has had such a profound and fatal effect on Mr. E. Dobkin's memory that he does not recall the name Kurt Becher, which he heard innumerable times and saw in writing many times in reports relating to the rescue operations, I must assume that Mr. E. Dobkin suffers from loss of memory in relation to other relevant factual points as well.

When the judge, who received the letter in a sealed envelope, saw who the sender was, he handed it, unopened, to the attorneys for the two sides, Tamir and Cohn. According to *Haolam Hazeh*, this placed Cohn in an awkward position. After all, he himself had stated, at an early stage of the trial, "any attempt by one of the witnesses to approach the judge directly is tantamount to contempt of court." After reading the letter, "Tamir looked at Cohn as if to ask: 'What are you going to do?' Cohn didn't reply. He didn't know what to do."[16]

16 "Kasztner Affair," *Haolam Hazeh*, July 22, 1954.

The letter reveals Kasztner's feeling that those who had been his comrades in his rescue operations and were now his fellow party members were deserting him. He chose to accentuate those points he was sure about, while others he chose to play down. So he stressed Dobkin's claim that he had never heard of Becher, but brushed over a crucial point—whether he had given an affidavit in Becher's favor of his own accord or had really been authorized by the Jewish Agency to testify on Becher's behalf. Here again, Kasztner fell into a trap he had set through his own arrogance and conceit. He had obviously conferred on himself various titles, including some he had no right to flaunt, in order to inflate his own importance. During the trial, this trait, combined with his friends' tendency to walk out on him, had fatal consequences.

III

It was Brand's turn to testify a second time. First, he was cross-examined by Tel, who was now Cohn's assistant. The brief examination focused on the position taken by people at the Jewish Agency and on the Istanbul delegation in connection with Brand's trip to Syria and his arrest. Brand believed they had had no knowledge of his arrest and were enraged by it:

> I told Mr. Tamir that there is no truth in the allegation that this was a deliberate crime, and I cautioned him not to ask me this question because it is not true. **I told him explicitly that no one deliberately committed a crime**. I told him that what happened led to a disaster bordering on a crime. But I explicitly said that no one deliberately committed a crime, but rather that some big mistakes were made [...] And I am convinced that no one deceived me—that's completely out of the question [emphasis added].[17]

Brand's words not only contradicted Tamir's, but were the opposite of things he himself had said at various times. For example, in 1961, at the time of the Eichmann trial, Brand had given a long interview to a periodical called *Etgar*.[18]

---

17 Trial transcript, June 1, 1954, p. 168.
18 "Eichmann slaughtered, Weizmann kept silent," *Etgar*'s conversation with Joel Brand, *Etgar*, June 1, 1961; this periodical was published in the first half of the 1960s; its founder and editor was Nathan Yellin-Mor, one of the commanders of the Stern Gang. Brand was interviewed by Yellin-Mor, Uri Avneri and Boaz Evron, formerly a member of the Stern Gang.

During it, Nathan Yellin-Mor asked him whether, in his view, his arrest in 1944 "proved that the Jewish leadership and the Agency were completely subjugated to the will of the British." Brand's reply was, "Undoubtedly, undoubtedly."

Three days later, on June 4, Brand took the witness stand again, this time at Halevi's demand. Brand claimed that on the evening before he was to testify, Meir Tuval tried to convince him to state that Avriel had had nothing to do with his being handed over to the British. This pressure confronted Brand with an awkward dilemma. He finally decided not to concede to Tuval's request, because he feared that "this out-and-out lie would place me in Meir Weltman and Ehud Avriel's hands." [19]

Halevi questioned him at length about the circumstances surrounding his arrest and at one point asked him, "Was the jeep [in which he was driven to jail, Y.W.] standing on the same side where you had seen Avriel before, or not?" The jeep, Brand replied, was on the side where Avriel had alighted. Nevertheless, he did not retract what he had said three days earlier: "I spoke out against Avriel, saying that the overall policy of the Agency and towards me as a rescue worker, cost the Jewish people a great deal of blood," he said, "but I never accused him of being a willing agent of the British and handing me over to them."

Brand's refusal to confirm that Avriel had "collaborated" with the British infuriated Tamir—his numerous efforts to get him on the witness stand had been fruitless. His reaction to Brand's testimony was that because of the strong pressure applied to him—particularly by his wife Hanzi and by Kasztner—Brand had given a version of the events that he himself did not believe in. When Tamir argued that he himself had said, "The subject of this trial is the greatest crime ever committed in the history of the Jewish people," Brand countered, "It is a crime, Counselor, when someone tries to exploit this trial in favor of the Revisionists." These words enraged the Revisionist camp. [20]

After the judge finished questioning Brand, Tamir asked to question him again: "I want to question this man, the witness standing here, who has broken under the pressure of his wife, of Dr. Kasztner and of the Jewish Agency." [21] The re-examination, which the judge allowed despite the Attorney General's vigorous objection, was conducted in loud tones, but all of Tamir's

19 Alex Weissberg, *Advocate for the Dead—The Story of Joel Brand* (London: A. Deutsch, 1958), pp. 134–137; Brand, *Satan and the Soul*, p. 142–143.
20 Trial transcript, June 4, 1954, pp. 12v and 20b.
21 Ibid., p. 21b.

efforts to get Brand to explicitly admit that actions were maliciously taken to impede the rescue of Hungarian Jewry were futile. Brand, Tamir asserted, was denying things they had specifically agreed on prior to his testimony.[22]

Tamir: I expressly asked you: "What if I ask about the circumstances of your arrest, and ask if you had been turned in?" You replied: "My answer will be true, in the technical, physical sense—no; in actual fact—yes." You said that on the steps of my home [...] It's true that I wanted a fuller answer. And you replied: "That's the truth, and that's all I'll say."

Brand: It was the other way around. I told you that it wasn't true that I was turned in physically. And I said to you explicitly that I would not allow this trial to be turned into a trial against Jewry. The fact that I was arrested in Aleppo, and as a result of that and of other facts, tens of thousands of Jews that could have been rescued were not saved—that is a crime in Jewish history. But I will not permit things to be slanted in such a way as to insinuate that this was done knowingly or deliberately.

Tamir: You answered me by saying: "Avriel and Sharett are not complete idiots; if they made this gross error that even a child could not miss seeing—it is clear that they knew what would happen." These were your very words.

Brand: Mr. Tamir, I cannot recall saying these words. I may have once used some strong language, but it was never my position—in this conversation or in others—that criminals knowingly betrayed me. My position has always been that a great crime was committed in Jewish history, but not in the sense that you are telling me.

This is a good example of the "conspiracy claim," a key tool in Tamir's tactics: whoever did not wholly accept his arguments was necessarily collaborating with the ruling party or submitting to its pressures. This also came up in Yoel Palgi's examination, on June 4. Palgi was called to answer some questions about the discrepancy between his first testimony in court and the things he had written in an article entitled "The Hollow of a Sling," which appeared in the book *The Hidden Shield*, about the heroic mission of the Jewish parachutists in Europe. It related to the circumstances of Palgi's arrest: Who had arrested

---

22 Ibid., p. 26b.

him, the Hungarians or the Germans? How did they know his address? Was he arrested because he had reported to the Gestapo? Tamir was interested in exposing the contradictions, even after the witness' credibility had been irremediably damaged in his first testimony, if only in order to prove that the Mapai establishment had something to conceal.

When he gave evidence for the first time, Palgi had said that detectives of the Hungarian espionage service had arrested him, but in *The Hidden Shield* he wrote "a Hungarian officer and a Gestapo officer entered the apartment." In his reply, Palgi blamed Zerubavel Gilad, the editor of his book, for this inconsistency. He claimed that since one of the officers spoke German, "and for many people, every German is the Gestapo," Gilad had mistakenly assumed that it was a Gestapo officer. Tamir didn't waste any time in calling Gilad to testify.

Tamir:	Mr. Zerubavel Gilad, were you the editor of the book *The Hidden Shield*?
Gilad:	Yes.
Tamir:	There is an article here by Yoel Palgi called "In the Hollow of a Sling." Are you familiar with it?
Gilad:	Yes.
Tamir:	Whom did you get this article from?
Gilad:	Either from the Jewish Agency or from the Mossad Le'aliyah.
Tamir:	Who checked the material for accuracy?
Gilad:	Reuven Zaslani, now Reuven Shiloah, checked the accuracy of the facts. He was my advisor as to the accuracy of the facts.
Tamir:	Did you change anything relating to the facts in this article?
Gilad:	I was faithful to the facts I received.
Tamir:	In connection with this article, did you receive any corrections from Yoel Palgi?
Gilad:	No.
Tamir:	Did you meet with him to discuss this article?
Gilad:	No.
Tamir:	Other than Yoel Palgi, did you have anyone else, any other source of information about what happened in Budapest?
Gilad:	I had no information […] other than this article, I didn't receive any information.[23]

---

23 Rosenfeld, *Criminal Case*, pp. 134–135.

After he was once again shown to be prevaricating, Palgi was subjected to a double cross-examination—by both the judge and the defense counsel, who forced him to decide which of the two versions he confirmed. During his questioning, Tamir tried to argue that Palgi, who until he testified had been regarded as a national hero, had fallen into Kasztner's net and had in fact become a collaborator. This is how things went towards the end of this long, embarrassing testimony:[24]

> **Tamir:** I am telling you, Mr. Palgi and I invite you not to defend Kasztner, but just this once to tell the court the truth. You were an idealistic fellow, who left the country to save Jews and to serve in the Allied armies, and you risked your life. But when you arrived in Budapest, and the situation there was very bad, you decided, under Kasztner's influence and pressure, and the pressure of circumstances, to collaborate with the Gestapo, to save your own life. And that's why you remained alive. He led you astray. And that's why Peretz stayed behind, Hannah stayed behind and you returned, because you had accepted Kasztner's way.
>
> **Palgi:** Your Honor, must I answer? I am asking the Honorable President, out of respect for this court, that I not be compelled to reply.
>
> **Halevi:** First of all answer yes or no.
>
> **Palgi:** No.

Although he had replied in the negative, his testimony still made a very poor impression. After giving his evidence, he returned to Tel Aviv with Joel Brand who wrote, "Yoel Palgi was very dejected following a fierce cross-examination by Defense Counsel Tamir, who had forced him to admit that he had lied many times in his book and in his report on his mission as a parachutist in Hungary."[25]

---

24 Trial transcript, June 4, 1954, p. 89b.
25 Brand, *Satan and the Soul*, p. 143.

IV

Palgi was the last witness called by the prosecution; after him the defense witnesses testified. Before the procession of witnesses began, the words of a man, who, from the legal standpoint hardly existed any longer, were heard. The official defendant, Malkiel Gruenwald, made a statement but refused to be cross-examined. When he spoke, it was already obvious which way the wind was blowing in this trial, so he blatantly repeated all the things he had written in the newsletter that had led to the libel suit.

He opened his statement[26] by enumerating the reasons that had moved him to compose the newsletter, the first and main one being the murder of his family in the Holocaust: "Fifty-two members of my family were exterminated in the gas chambers of Majdanek and Auschwitz. From that time, Mr. President, I have known no rest [...] The man the Nazis used [in order] to carry out the vilest historical crime was, based on my investigation and as I became convinced, Rudolf Kasztner."

He described the publication of the newsletter as an act of self-sacrifice, intended to inform the public of the truth about the horrible episodes, such as the story of the parachutists' mission and the annihilation of the Jews of Cluj. The fact that these affairs were exposed only through the libel suit is "a mark of dishonor for our state [...] but a mark of honor for me." He claimed that the government "in striving to save a member of its Mapai party at any price is being dragged down with him."

After Gruenwald, Tamir rose to speak. In the first part of the trial, before the recess, there was already a sense that the defense had the upper hand. During her cross-examination by Tamir, Hanzi Brand, a witness for the prosecution, complained that although "I am sitting here as a witness, I feel as if I were the accused."[27] Now, at this stage of the trial, Tamir was even more confident. Completely sure of his victory, he shook his finger: the testimony given by the prosecution's witnesses up to this stage of the trial, covering hundreds of pages of transcript, were sufficient not only to acquit Gruenwald but to **convict** Kasztner under the Nazis and Nazi Collaborators (Punishment) Law. Not only to put him on trial—but to convict him.

The scales tipped even further during the testimonies of the witnesses for the defense. Scores of witnesses were called; some of them left a strong impression on the court. Katerina Szenes, Hannah's mother, testified on

---

26 Gruenwald's statement, Trial transcript, June 13, 1954, p. 1c–21c.
27 Ibid., April 1, 1954, p. 251.

June 14. She lived in Haifa and was employed as the manager of the clothing warehouse at a childcare center. She had learned enough Hebrew so that "when the time came, she could appear in the Jerusalem District Court, in the well-known trial, to give evidence that she wished to avoid, that was causing [her] great suffering."[28]

This was not the first time she was giving evidence on the horrors in Budapest. Shortly after the end of the war, on September 10, 1945, she submitted a report on her efforts to rescue her daughter that began with her release from the Kistarcsa concentration camp on September 26, 1944.[29] In the report, she stated that she had met with Moshe Krausz, Director of the Palestine Office in Budapest. She accused him of having washed his hands of the affair, claiming that he did not deal with such matters. Instead, she said, he had referred her to Shuny Groszmann, a member of Hashomer Hatza'ir. It was Groszmann who had mentioned to her Kasztner's many contacts and the fact that he was in the habit of visiting prisoners in jail. With great restraint, she described her abortive attempts to meet with Kasztner and to enlist his help:

> After a long search, I found Kasztner's address but once there I was received by a young woman who told me that Kasztner was going to visit Hannah the following day. I asked if I could be allowed to send her a food package. I was told to give the package to Lili Ungar, Kasztner's secretary, at the office of the Red Cross. I did so—although I had to wait for hours until the secretary received me, but she told me Kasztner was ill and couldn't go to the prison, and that I should come again the next day. This went on for several days until finally the secretary told me that from then on Kasztner could only deal with important and urgent matters.

Szenes' testimony was dramatic and very moving. At first, she described the very unexpected June 17, 1944 meeting in the prison in Budapest. Although she knew nothing about Hannah having been parachuted into Hungary, she was arrested that morning by a Hungarian detective and taken in for questioning. During her interrogation, she was asked again and again what she knew about her daughter's fate. Her reply was that her daughter was in a

28 David Lazar, Katerina Szenes, or "So Close to You and Yet So Far," in *Leading Figures in Israel* (Hebrew) (Tel Aviv: Amichi, 1954), pp. 101–102.

29 Designation, CZA, S25-8993.

kibbutz near Haifa whose name she doesn't know. The interrogator did not relent: "But still, what do you think, where is she now?" And without waiting for an answer, told her: "If you don't know where she is, I'll tell you. She's in the next room. I'll call her and you persuade her to tell us everything she knows. If not, this will be the last time you'll ever see her."[30]

As soon as he finished talking the door opened and into the room came Hannah, whose mother had firmly believed was living in absolute safety on the golden coast of the Mediterranean, far from the terrors of occupied Budapest. The meeting between the two was one of those powerful moments that defy description, however dramatic. The daughter, no less surprised than her mother, ran to her and embraced her wordlessly. She then said only: "Forgive me, Mother." The stunned mother did not reply—she looked into her daughter's face and could hardly recognize her. She could tell she had experienced some dreadful things. The Hungarians, who had arrested Katrina to get her to pressure her daughter into telling them all she knew, left the two alone. A few minutes later, the door opened and the mother was released, after being warned not to mention a word about the meeting to anyone.

She was arrested again later, for a longer time, and subsequently released on the eve of Yom Kippur (September 27, 1944). Now she tried to make use of the painfully meager means at her disposal to save her daughter's life. She met with a young lawyer called Dr. Nenoye, who told her he had already met with the other two parachutists and made clear to her the danger facing her daughter. Her situation is dangerous, but not hopeless, he said and explained that it depends largely on the political circumstances that prevail when she comes to trial. Katerina also tried to make contact with the Zionist circles—and that is how she got to Groszmann. In contrast to the evidence she provided after the war, this time she did not mention that she had come to him after Krausz had given her the cold shoulder. Tamir was conducting the cross-examination, and he intended to call Krausz as one of his key witnesses. Groszmann told her that there was no need for an attorney—Hannah was about to be released, perhaps the following day or the day after; maybe even that same day. "Go home," he advised her. "Maybe you'll find Hannah there."

Katerina Szenes did go home, where she of course did not find her daughter. She continued to call Groszmann every day, until some of her friends told her he was just a young man without any real connections and advised her to appeal to Kasztner. He's got the right connections, they said. He has a

---

30 "Hannah Szenes' Mother Gives her Testimony at the Trial," *Al HaMishmar*, June 15, 1954.

permit to enter every prison and he can help you. He can also deliver packages to Hannah.

Thus Katerina embarked upon the Sisyphean task of seeking Kasztner's help. She obtained his address and came to his home very early in the morning, in the hope of finding him there. When she got to the address, it turned out he no longer lived there, but neighbors gave her his new address. She hurried there and rang the bell. No one opened the door, but a woman's head appeared at a small peephole. She refused to open the door, and just asked what Katerina wanted. In a trembling voice, Katerina replied that it was a very urgent matter connected with Zionist activity. The door opened, and once she was inside, she explained to the woman, whom she did not know, what it was all about. Kasztner is aware of the problem, the woman replied, and although he has a very busy schedule, he is planning to visit Hannah in jail very soon, that day or the day after, and so she should hurry, prepare a package for her daughter and give it to Kasztner's secretary at an office whose address she gave her. Only later did Katerina learn that the woman she had spoken to was Hanzi Brand.

Katerina rushed to the office where she was met by a secretary who firmly refused to allow her to meet Kasztner or to give him the package. This is how the examination proceeded on this point:

Tamir: Did you speak to Kasztner's secretary, Lily Ungar?

Szenes: Yes. I told her I had heard that on that very day Dr. Kasztner was planning to go to the prison and I wanted to talk to him because I had a package to give him. Then she said: "No; definitely not today. He has such important things to do." I asked: "Then when?" and she replied "Perhaps tomorrow." I asked if I should give her the package and she said: "No, take the package and bring it tomorrow."

Tamir: And did you take the package and bring it the next day?

Szenes: Yes. I came there a second time.

Tamir: That same day [the first day] how many times [did you go to] Dr. Kasztner's office?

Szenes: I was there three times. I went there very early and the secretary wasn't there. I came again and she wasn't there and the third time I found her and then I said what I said.

Katerina Szenes chased Kasztner for three or four days. Each time, the secretary informed her that he was not in the office or that he was busy. On

October 12, she came there for the final time. As on the previous occasions, this time too, the secretary told her: "He's not here yet. Take a seat and wait. Maybe he'll come." As on the previous occasions, this time too she refused to take the package. Szenes, despairing, understood that she would never manage to meet Kasztner, and went to see Ottó Komoly who received her at once. Komoly, who knew the Szenes family well, was very surprised to hear that Hannah had parachuted into Hungary. Although he knew about the parachutists, it had never occurred to him that Hannah was one of them. When he heard that Groszmann had advised her against retaining a lawyer, he said: I promise you we'll do everything we can, but in the meantime do get a lawyer, today, at once."

Several days later, on October 15, 1944, the Arrow Cross party staged a coup, and its leader, Ferenc Szálasi, seized power. Hannah Szenes' trial was held at the end of that month. She was sentenced to death, refused to ask for clemency, and on November 7, 1944 was executed.

Tamir: Mrs. Szenes, so until the end did you ever meet Dr. Kasztner?
Szenes: No. Things were already so bad. No, no, never.
Tamir: You never met him?
Szenes: No. I never managed to.

After the war, when Katerina came to Israel and was living in Kibbutz Ma'agan, she was asked whether she'd like to meet Kasztner, to better understand what had happened then when her daughter's fate was sealed. She refused. There, in Hungary, she said, it was a question of life and death for me, here such a meeting would be meaningless and would only cause me needless agitation. Nonetheless, fate did bring them together—not in Budapest, but in the Palace Hotel—a colonial-style building in Jerusalem, which housed the offices of the Ministry of Commerce and Industry. She came there in connection with her work at the childcare center. When Kasztner, who was then the Ministry's spokesman, heard she was coming, he asked to meet her. Their conversation was an unpleasant one. He tried to explain to her what had happened during those awful days in Budapest. She responded by saying it was no longer important. It was their only meeting.

The testimony of Hannah Szenes' mother was one of the high points of the trial. The heightened emotions in the courtroom were reflected in the press reports. These were the words used by Shalom Rosenfeld to describe Szenes' testimony:

Throughout [...] this lengthy, important court case, there have been no hours of sanctity [or] of stillness as those during the testimony of this [Jewish] **mother**, who has known so much suffering. The figure of this woman and the lofty nature of the things she said reflected such greatness, such a pure soul, that beyond the evidential-legal aspect of her testimony, they were engraved on the hearts of all those present as an immensely moving experience [emphasis in original].[31]

V

It doesn't take much imagination to understand why Katerina's testimony so powerfully affected all those present in the courtroom. Beyond the emotions evoked by her dramatic story, her testimony had helped to create a polarized picture: at one end, here was Israel Kasztner, the very embodiment of obsequiousness and collaboration; while on the other, there is Hannah Szenes, symbol of dedication, self-sacrifice and heroism. On this point—to be more precise, on this point, too—the defense had scored a complete success. While Yoel Palgi, the parachutist called by the prosecution to place Kasztner at the "heroic" pole, had failed to fulfill that role and had actually contributed to the collapse of the prosecution's case, the parachutist's mother called by the defense filled her role to the utmost.

In 1950s Israel, one monopolistic and stereotypical approach was dominant. It depicted the millions of Jews who died in the Holocaust as having gone to their deaths like "lambs to the slaughter" and all members of the Judenrat as collaborators. Within this approach, these Jews were totally antithetical to the uprising and the members of the underground who died the deaths of heroes. But at the time, the best-known heroes of the Holocaust in Israel were not the leaders of the pioneering youth movements that led the rebellions, but the parachutists sent from the Yishuv in Palestine to carry out an extraordinarily dangerous rescue mission.

In 1954, the tenth anniversary of the parachutists' mission to Europe, this point was thrown into sharper focus as an occasion marked in various ways, not only in the tragic rally at Ma'agan. No flowery phrases were spared in numerous speeches and articles to lavishly glorify the parachutists' heroism. In particular, much was written on the subject in the publications of Hakibbutz Hameuchad (United Kibbutz Movement) and Hakibbutz Ha'artzi

---

31 Rosenfeld, *Criminal Case*, p. 150.

Movement, with special focus on the parachutists who were members of these movements. The words spoken by a member of Kibbutz Na'an, Moshe Braslavsky (Breslevi) at a memorial service on the tenth anniversary of Hannah Szenes' death, in her own kibbutz, Sdot Yam, were typically replete with pathos:[32]

> One thing we know: Hannah's image will not be touched by the ravages of time nor will it ever be forgotten. It will grow, prosper and increase in the life of our people. It is made of that same lofty material that a nation preserves in its archives. Tales will be told about her, poems written, and legends embroidered, to be passed down from father to son.

VI

A day before Katerina Szenes' testimony, André György, better known as Bandi Grosz, who had lived in Israel since 1950, took the witness stand. Later, in the early seventies, studies were published pointing to the importance of his mission, which as far as the Germans were concerned had been a cover for Brand's mission.[33] Towards the end of the decade, Yehuda Bauer published the results of his research, which stated explicitly that the Germans had attributed much importance to Grosz's mission,[34] but things looked different in the 1950s.

Two days before Grosz testified, *Ma'ariv* published a long article about him.[35] It described the abject circumstances of his life: a rented room in an apartment in the center of Tel Aviv, the rent for which he could hardly afford, and a "diet" of coffee at the Bitan coffee house:

> He has no money for even the most basic needs, but he does have some credit at the Bitan coffee house. So he sits there from morning to night, *kibbitzing* the card players and twice a day drinking coffee on the cuff [...] sometimes he also lives on a "bread diet," when he doesn't have enough credit to drink his daily dose of coffee.

---

32 "A Voice Called, and I Went" (Hebrew), *Bakibbutz* 279 (November 17, 1954).

33 On this matter, see for example, Bella Vago, "The Intelligence Aspects of the Joel Brand Mission," *Yad Vashem Studies*, vol. 10 (1974), pp. 11–128.

34 Yehuda Bauer, "Joel Brand's Mission" (Hebrew), *Yalkut Moreshet* 26 (November 1978), pp. 23–60.

35 David Giladi, "Please Meet the Third Man—Bandi Grosz," *Ma'ariv*, June 11, 1954.

This man, the article goes on to say, claims he played an important role in World War II. He was sent by anti-Hitler circles in the German leadership to bring the Allies a proposal to sign a separate peace agreement. According to him, if his mission had been properly evaluated, hundreds of thousands of Jews could have been saved. Grosz's version of the facts was given in full although the author of the article was very skeptical about its veracity. He stated that "as long as his story has not been disproved, we have no choice but to take the risk and to enter his castle in the air [...]."

He was received with a similar attitude in the courtroom. As he took the witness stand, all everyone saw was a man who was hard to take seriously. He was described as "a bundle of nerves, lean and haggard [...] a few gold teeth glinting in his mouth."[36] As soon as he began to tell his story, the skepticism gave way to astonishment. When he told how he had been sent by the SS to make a separate peace with the West, the audience was convinced that the man in the witness box had lost his ability to distinguish between truth and falsehood, between reality and fantasy.

Grosz's testimony was replete with conflicts—in particular, clashes with Attorney General Cohn, who throughout his cross-examination tried to undercut his credibility and to present him as a shyster who never spoke a word of truth. This is how the exchange between them went:

Cohn: Did the Germans pay you? Yes or no?
Grosz: I never heard that the Germans would pay Jews [...]
Cohn: Yes or no?
Grosz: No! No! No!
Cohn: As far as the Jews, the Jewish Agency, was concerned, you were supposedly working only for them; as far the Germans were concerned, you were supposedly working only for them; and as for the Hungarians, it was as if you were working only for them, and from all three you got money.
Grosz: I risked my life, and now you are saying I was a corrupt cheat.
Cohn: You were always a *gaunef*, a thief.[37]

Hearing these words, the witness leaped up, waved his clenched fist at the prosecutor and burst into hysterical sobs, all the while muttering: "God will

36 Rosenfeld, *Criminal Case*, p. 76.
37 Trial transcript, June 13, 1954, pp. 87C-90C.

punish you! This is the gratitude you give me!" Then he collapsed, slumped over into his chair. When the judge asked what had happened to him, he replied in a tear-choked voice: "Hunger and suffering have worn out my heart."[38]

Later in his testimony, he clung tenaciously to his claim that Brand had been only a cover for the truly important mission—his own. He also reasserted that he had been opposed to Brand's plan because he regarded it as "camouflage and a bluff." Grosz tried to commit suicide two weeks after he testified, by swallowing a large quantity of sleeping pills.

Counsel for the defense Tamir tried to use Grosz to show that Kasztner had led a raucous, immoral life in Budapest, and that the Jewish Agency had something to hide. In this context, he had argued during Avriel's cross-examination that the Jewish Agency had paid Grosz money and made sure he would not be put on trial for fear that he would "open his mouth." "He already has opened his mouth," Avriel retorted scornfully. "In Israel everyone has the right to say whatever they want."

It was the prosecution that missed an opportunity here. By destroying Grosz' credibility, it lost the chance to prove how complex the whole affair that formed the subject of the trial was and how simple and one-dimensional the defense's interpretation of it was. But by then no one believed Grosz. One newspaper wrote that some of Grosz's replies were greeted by loud guffaws from the spectators, and Rosenfeld's descriptions were full of sentences implying his total mistrust of the man and his story.[39] Therefore, this was far more than a missed opportunity; it was actually a tragedy and one that was almost inevitable.

VII

A succession of witnesses from Cluj, Kasztner's city, served as an important weapon in the defense's arsenal. Their testimony was intended to show how they had been lulled into complacency and, until they actually arrived in Auschwitz, had not realized what awaited them. The defense maintained that Kasztner was responsible for their failure to choose the one alternative that would have saved many of them—armed rebellion. These witnesses played a key role in demonizing Kasztner. He was depicted as a cynical, opportunistic

---

38 The description is from Rosenfeld, *Criminal Case*, p. 85.
39 Rosenfeld, *Criminal Case*, p. 80.

man, prominent in the community, who instead of protecting the lives of his "flock," had abandoned them to their death for the sake of a handful of privileged relatives and friends.

The first witness in this group was Yehiel Shmueli, a clerk in the Cluj community committee.

Tamir: Did the Judenrat officials [...] warn you [...] that you were being taken to Auschwitz?

Shmueli: No.

Tamir: Did you hear anything at all from them about Auschwitz, about the danger of extermination?

Shmueli: Not a word.

Tamir: Did it ever occur to you then that you and your family were being taken to be killed?

Shmueli: No.

Tamir: What possibilities of being saved did you know about, if you had known you were being led to your death?

Shmueli: I knew nothing about extermination. I only saw that people were being beaten to make them tell where their belongings were. Then I suggested to friends that we break out of the ghetto and cross the border to Romania, which was 15 kilometers from the city, and if they kill us [...] it's better to be killed than to be beaten to death, and we'd burn the city. But they didn't listen to me.

Tamir: How was the Cluj ghetto guarded? By how many people?

Shmueli: About 20 guards.

Tamir: How many people were there in the community?

Shmueli: About 10 to 20 thousand.

Tamir: They were all in the ghetto.

Shmueli: They were all in the ghetto.

Tamir: When you boarded the train did you show any resistance?

Shmueli: No. We boarded as usual.

Tamir: Why did you get on as usual?

Shmueli: Because we were told we were being taken to Kenyermezo.[40] And Dr. Endre Balazs, a Jew, was in charge of the ghetto, and he said: Brothers, the Hungarian government has decided

---

40 The name of an imaginary place, which, according to rumors, was supposedly where the Jews of the city were being taken.

to empty the city of Kenyermezo of all its inhabitants, and
to concentrate all the Jews of Hungary there until the end of
the war. Accept that calmly; you and your families will live
together.[41]

The Attorney General barely examined the witness—he made no effort to
construct a different picture to the one Tamir had drawn. The only question
he asked came back at him like a boomerang. He asked the witness what
had happened to Dr. Endre Balazs, whether he was also sent to Auschwitz.
He replied that Dr. Balazs did not arrive in Auschwitz, but went to
Switzerland—with the other favored individuals on the rescue train. This
further strengthened the impression that a few, to save their own lives, had
abandoned all those other Jews to their fate.

Irma Hirsch, who testified immediately after Szenes, was one of this
group.[42] A broken, wretched woman, she had lost her husband and only son in
Auschwitz. She spoke in a barely audible voice, her eyes filling with tears from
the moment she took the witness stand.[43] Her testimony showed that both armed
resistance and rescue were nothing but totally hypothetical possibilities.

The rescue train also figured in her testimony. Had she heard in Cluj
about the transport to Palestine? Tamir asked. I heard, she replied. Although
I didn't know it was going to Palestine, we knew that the fate of its passengers
would be better than ours. Did you try to send anyone of your family on the
transport? He asked. Her husband had tried to arrange a place on the train for
their son, she replied, "Then they asked if he has any money, and they knew
we didn't have money. They said if there's no money, then the answer is no."
Despite the incriminating things this witness had said, the Attorney General
did not question her either.

Another witness in this series was David Rozner, a metal laminating
worker and a member of Mapai.[44] He was asked about the attitude in Cluj
towards Kasztner after the liberation. "Feelings ran high against Kasztner in
Cluj," he replied. "If he had returned home, he would have been killed in the
street." He repeated this point when Judge Halevi questioned him.

Halevi: When did you return to Cluj?
Rozner: In 1945, on June 18.

---

41 Trial transcript, June 13, 1954, pp. 37C-38C.
42 Hirsch's testimony, trial transcript, June 14, 1954, pp. 41D-47D.
43 Rosenfeld, *Criminal Case*, p. 96.
44 Rozner's testimony, trial transcript, June 18, 1954, pp. 20F-30F.

Halevi:	Why would Kasztner have been killed there?
Rozner:	Because he had deceived the Jews.
Halevi:	How do you know that?
Rozner:	[I learned that] from the Jewish community.
Halevi:	That was the prevailing opinion there?
Rozner:	Yes.
Halevi:	Why Kasztner in particular, and not the Jewish Council?
Rozner:	They always blamed the man at the top.

This point did not come up at all in the Attorney General's cross-examination of this witness. He merely questioned him on an entirely different matter.

One after the other, the witnesses from Cluj took the stand, all doing a fine job as far as the defense was concerned. Paul Gross claimed in his testimony that had they known where they were being taken, they would have resisted the gendarmes—"We were young, healthy people, and there were no more than twenty gendarmes. We could have attacked and killed them […]" Joseph Katz, who was not from Cluj but from a small town only 4 kilometers away from the Romanian border, said that the men in the town knew how to use weapons and that from Cluj, they could easily have crossed the border. However, since they believed they were not being taken to their death, but to that same Kenyermezo, they did next to nothing.

The idea of calling this succession of witnesses, all of them survivors from Cluj or nearby towns, was of great help to the defense. They were all simple, hardworking people, who had lost many relatives—some had lost their entire families—in the Holocaust. Everything they said sounded authentic and reliable and the picture they painted was vivid and moving. The press, particularly those papers interested in seeing the defense win, pounced on these testimonies as if they were a rare treasure. For example, after Yosef Gross' testimony, the *Herut* headline on June 22, 1954 blared: "We could have killed the Hungarian police if we had known we were being taken to Auschwitz for extermination." And, in response to Irma Hirsch's testimony, the headline read: "We could have fled if the true situation had not been concealed from us."

These defense witnesses left an impression diametrically opposite to the one made by the witnesses for the prosecution, most of who were respected, well-known people who failed dismally to fulfill the objective for which they had been called to the witness stand. Here too, the prosecution demonstrated its ineptitude, even though it was no longer being conducted by a junior attorney from the Jerusalem district court, but by none other than the Attorney General himself.

He seemed to be standing there sheepishly in the face of these unbearably appalling life stories, unwilling or unable to ask these witnesses probing questions. Although their stories were dramatic, the categorical statements they presented were not devoid of inconsistencies and disputable points, which the prosecution could have explored. It would be no exaggeration, therefore, to say that the "parade of Cluj witnesses" scored several points in favor of the defense.

VIII

After the Cluj witnesses, the first to take the stand was Moshe Krausz, the ousted director of the Palestine Office, who was in fact the defense counsel's "key witness." To a large extent, his testimony supplemented Katerina Szenes'—if her words were the "heart," his were the "brain." As the counsel for the prosecution put it: "If Gruenwald is the knife in the case, then Krausz is the hand." *Haolam Hazeh* wrote, "The ten days of his testimony were ten days of the most serious indictment of Israel Kasztner."

His associates characterized Krausz as a distant, introverted person, whose relationships were cold and formal—as if he were a cut above everyone else. Until the end of his life, he felt that his role in saving Hungary's Jews had never been fully acknowledged. According to him, Raoul Wallenberg, a pretentious man, concerned mainly with rescuing the rich, became such an imposing legend for only one reason—he was not a Jew. Jews who had been much more instrumental in the rescue, Krausz bitterly asserted, had not achieved even a smidgen of the fame that the Swedish gentile was accorded.

His testimony began on June 25, and after a recess, lasted the entire first week of July (from the 2nd to the 9th). For many long hours, he was subjected to an unrelenting, exhausting cross-examination by both the judge and the Attorney General and, on more than one occasion, he clashed sharply with the prosecution, which did its utmost to shake his confidence and undermine his credibility. In the course of those days, he settled accounts with everyone—with Kasztner, with Mapai, with the Jewish Agency and its immigration (*aliya*) department and with many others. In his merciless attacks, Cohn failed to emulate Tamir's successes with Kasztner and Palgi, namely to utterly shatter Krausz's testimony and to expose him for what he was—a nonentity.[45]

---

45 Prat, *The Great Trial*, pp. 148 and 150; Rosenfeld, *Criminal Case*, pp. 164 and 177; interview with Menahem Zvi Kaddari, Bar-Ilan University, July 22, 1993.

Krausz's testimony prompted huge headlines in all the newspapers, particularly those vigorously opposed to Kasztner. *Herut*'s headline that day was, "If Kasztner hadn't collaborated with the Nazis, tens of thousands of Jews could have been saved." That paper's headline on the first day of Krausz's testimony read, "Through its contacts with the German rulers, Kasztner's committee gained control over the lives of Hungary's Jews."

Krausz put forth two main arguments. One, that Kasztner's intentions had at first been good, but since he was motivated by his own personal ambition to become the major power in the Jewish community, he became a collaborator with the Nazis. The second, that when he was still in Budapest he had been opposed to the rescue train, regarding it as a devious, dangerous German plot to mislead Hungary's Jews, to blind them to the truth and lull them into complacency. Not only was the train of no benefit in saving Hungary's Jews, it was actually injurious to them. The leaders and the main activists were taken out of the community, leaving it bereft of leadership; the tragic, frantic competition for the few places available on the train led to demoralization and mutual hatred; the survivors themselves became hostages in the hands of the Germans; the Jews were so deluded that they were blind to the horrors of reality and therefore never coped with them. He also claimed that, thanks to its contacts with the Germans and the enormous sums of money it received— in particular from the Yishuv's delegation in Istanbul, the Aid and Rescue Committee, which had never been an official body recognized by the Zionist institutions in Hungary, succeeded in gaining control over the lives of the Jews there. The whole affair also had a distinctly partisan aspect—owing to its contacts and money, the Ihud Haolami, the smallest faction in the Zionist Federation, succeeded in dominating Jewish life.[46] Tamir emphasized this party aspect by asking leading questions, in an attempt to depict Mapai as an organization that gained its power and influence through immoral means, such as corruption and collaboration:

Tamir: How did you then understand how it transpired that the key people on this committee, which later amassed so much power, were all from the Ichud [Haolami], the smallest group in the Jewish community?

Krausz: Because all the money was in their hands.

46 In the elections to the Zionist Federation, prior to the 21st Zionist Congress, in August 1939, the Mizrachi party achieved 41% of the vote; Hashomer Hatza'ir – 29%, the General Zionists – 17%, and the Ihud – 13%.

Tamir: Money they obtained from whom?

Krausz: From the Rescue Committee in Istanbul.

Tamir: Are you saying that the committee was expanded at certain times? [Shulem] Offenbach, [Arno] Szilágyi, and later [Andor] Biss. How were they added to it?

Krausz: Kasztner called them.

Tamir: In other words, he added them [to the committee].

Krausz: Yes. We later saw they were also helping Kasztner.

Tamir: How do you explain the fact that these three men were from the Ihud? Later on, the committee gained a great deal of power and authority in Hungarian Jewry. Yes or no?

Krausz: These men weren't recognized among the Jews, but they were recognized among the Zionists.

Tamir: But [where did] the power to decide things [come from]?

Krausz: In 1944, everyone recognized them and knew about their activity and wanted to be connected to them.

Tamir: I am asking [you], if as a result [of this] they had power on the internal scene.

Krausz: They did.

Tamir: What was the source of this power, only the money?

Krausz: In part the money. In addition, everyone knew they had connections with the Germans.[47]

Krausz had focused his rescue efforts on his contacts with the consulates of neutral countries in Hungary, particularly the Swiss legation. He wanted to turn these legations into rescue centers and through them to bring pressure to bear on the Hungarian authorities that opposed what the Germans were doing. He claimed that the information, which he had helped to provide the Swiss legation with regard to events in Auschwitz, led to a flow of international appeals to the regent, Admiral Horthy, which, according to him, caused the deportations to cease in the first week of July. In contrast, Kasztner's efforts did not help rescue the Hungarian Jews; rather they deluded and deceived them and made their situation far worse for them. Kasztner negotiated with the Germans over the rescue train, despite the fact that from the time of Brand's flight to Istanbul and until the train left, hundreds of thousands of Jews were being deported from Hungary. He continued these negotiations even after

---

47 This claim is inaccurate. Zvi (Arno) Szilágyi was a member of Hashomer Hatza'ir and its representative in the Palestine Office.

Horthy decided to stop the deportations although he had no information about the fate of the passengers on the train or of their whereabouts. Because of his powerful desire to collaborate with and to appease the Germans, Kasztner actually thwarted rescue efforts on several occasions. And most important of all—he continued using his "German channel" at a time when any sensible person would have realized that the only reliable body to deal with was the Hungarian government.

According to Krausz, the rupture between him and Kasztner began shortly after the Germans entered Budapest. At a meeting of the Zionist leaders, Kasztner raised a proposal he had received from the Germans: to get the Jews out of Hungary via the Danube to Vienna, and from there—through France, Spain, and North Africa—to Palestine. The Germans, Kasztner claimed, had demanded that he keep the plan completely secret, like a "secret of the Reich," because they didn't want the Hungarians to get wind of it. Why? Because since the Hungarians wanted to deport all the Jews, "the Germans cannot show the Hungarian government that they, the infamous antisemites, are helping the Jews escape to Palestine." That was why the "Germans could not allow the Jews to cross Romania, in order to get to Palestine," and were suggesting a strange, circuitous route so the Hungarians would think they were being deported.

It was at this point that Krausz's suspicions had been aroused. He testified to having told Kasztner that "the new Hungarian government has already officially agreed to allow the Jews to emigrate [to Palestine] and has already sent a letter to the German legation saying they do not want any deportations, but will allow emigration." When Kasztner continued to claim that the Germans were sticking to their demand, Krausz stopped believing in the plan: "Such activity would have been tantamount to assisting the deportations, we would have been showing the Hungarian government that it is all right to deport Jews," he said. He later added, "in any case no one was mentioning deportation yet,"[48] during those days immediately following the occupation.

Krausz, who broke off relations with the rescue committee, no longer attended the meetings at which Kasztner and Brand reported on their negotiations with the Germans. Instead, he sought alternative ways for saving Jews.

In June his strained relationship with Kasztner worsened, when he learned that preparations were being made for a train to transfer a number of

48 Trial transcript, June 25, 1954, p. 56.

favored individuals to safety. From the very first, he regarded the whole idea as a German ruse, not a rescue plan. He was particularly perturbed by the Germans' willingness to allow people to board the train without certificates, so long as they were in the possession of some document, especially if it was of a foreign power—"the organizers of the journey will bear all responsibility"— while people who had no papers were forced to "descend to the level of mere numbers; they were no longer human beings." Since for Krausz, the certificates served as the source of his power, he was incapable of conceiving the idea that anyone could somehow manage without them.

Over and over, Tamir grilled Krausz as to the basis of his grave accusations against Kasztner. One answer related to the man's personality. Krausz said that while Kasztner was a man of many talents and had keen political instincts, his obsessive desire to always take center stage totally clouded his moral judgment:[49]

> Even before [...] I had known him as a megalomaniac, someone with delusions of grandeur [...]. Aside from that, when it came to his interest in achieving [...] results, he is [...] immoral. He has no conscience and no consideration for others.

In Krausz's mind, the very idea of negotiations with the Germans was catastrophic, a view that Tamir led him to repeat again and again.

Throughout his testimony, Krausz repeatedly asserted that, in marked contrast to his own efforts, which culminated in the rescue of thousands of Jews, Kasztner was 'locked in' on an approach that changed him from a Zionist leader into a lackey of the Nazis. His testimony supplemented, to a certain degree, the claims put forth by Bandi Grosz. Just as no one accepted Grosz's claim that the Germans were serious in the negotiations they conducted with the Jews, and even found the idea ridiculous, everyone did take seriously Krausz's claim that as far as the Germans were concerned, the whole affair was a machination—an admixture of satanic cynicism and cynical Satanism. Needless to say, for Kasztner, who Krausz had depicted as a man whose arrogance had led him into the trap the Nazis had laid, the cumulative effect of these two witnesses was ruinous.

---

49 Ibid., July 1954, p. 21M.

IX

Having presented his point of view in the direct examination conducted by Tamir, Krausz was then subjected to a lengthy cross-examination by the Attorney General. Whereas Cohn had either only briefly questioned the other witnesses, or refrained from questioning them altogether, he kept Krausz on the witness stand for two whole days (July 4 and 5), cross-examining him aggressively and in great detail. One newspaper wrote that Cohn "who until that week [appeared to be] withdrawing, hardly examining the witnesses for the defense, decided to halt Tamir's attack at this point."[50] In order to shatter the witness's credibility and the reliability of his testimony, Cohn tried to show that Krausz's motives had been impure and that even in such desperate times, he had been motivated by his personal feelings rather than the cause for which he was supposedly working.

One of Cohn's tactics was to try to prove that Krausz's "Hungarian option" was no better than Kasztner's "German option" and that in any event anyone spurning negotiations with the Germans while he himself was negotiating with the Hungarians was like the pot calling the kettle black. There was a personal aspect involved here. Krausz had established contact with the commander of the Hungarian gendarmerie, Colonel László Ferenczy, who was in charge of deporting Jews from the outlying cities. It was said about him and his close assistant, Leo Lullay, "in all of Hungary there was no one who directly served the German murder machine more than they did."[51] With Becher and Eichmann it's wrong to establish a contact—Cohn pointed out—and with Ferenczy it's right? On this point, the following exchange took place:

Cohn: Do you agree with me that the deportations were actually carried out by the Hungarians?

Krausz: Do you mean under German orders?

Cohn: In practice, the Hungarians carried it out?

Krausz: Yes.

Cohn: And we have already heard that Ferenczy was the chief executor?

Krausz: Correct.

---

50 Prat, *The Great Trial*, pp. 149–150.
51 Cohen, *The Halutz Resistance*, p. 186.

Cohn: And if Eichmann is infamous as a 'bloodhound', then I am telling you that Ferenczy was no less of a bloodhound.

Krausz: Correct.[52]

In this way, Cohn tried to depict Krausz as a man in a glass house, throwing stones in every direction. He raised the allegation that Krausz had disappeared for a certain period of time following the German occupation and asked him repeatedly to confirm that he had panicked at the time of the occupation. He asked questions such as: "But weren't you gripped by panic?" "Were you in a panic too?" "Were your nerves always steady?" "Didn't your nerves let you down, too?" In an effort to destroy the witness' credibility, he hammered at the subject of Krausz's dismissal from the Palestine Office and his strained relations with the Zionist pioneer youth movements (*halutzim*). Krausz was a hard nut to crack and the volley of questions put by Cohn did not lead him to change his story. Towards the end of the lengthy examination, Cohn leveled some truly grave accusations at him, but Krausz did not budge from his original position:

Cohn: Isn't it true Mr. Krausz that a violent argument broke out between you and the *halutzim* over the Romanian passports?

Krausz: Never.

Cohn: They were furious with you because you had handed out these passports and received money for them, without even notifying them?

Krausz: Never.

Cohn: And isn't it also true that in February 1944 a large meeting was held in Budapest at which people demanded that an investigation be conducted in the Palestine Office because matters were not being handled properly there?

Krausz: No. There was no such meeting.

Despite all his efforts, Cohn did not succeed in crushing Krausz. Joel Brand later claimed that one reason was the ineffectual way in which he handled the cross-examination. "I prepared a list of over a hundred questions for him," he wrote in his book, "but he didn't use them." These questions related to the way Krausz functioned during the occupation—the fact that he closed the doors of the Palestine Office on that day, fled to a house that enjoyed the protection

---

52 Rosenfeld, *Criminal Case*, p. 174.

of the Swiss legation, and other grave issues. However, "the Attorney General asked different questions and Moshe Krausz was a lucky fellow. He got off easily."

In response to a question by Tamir, Krausz confirmed a claim that caused uproar. He stated that two men had been sent to him in an effort to dissuade him from testifying. From the beginning, Tamir tried to show how frightened the establishment was by the trial and the lengths it was going to in its attempts to sabotage its orderly course. The two men whose names he mentioned were members of Hapoel Hamizrachi—Mihai Solomon, who headed the movement in Hungary, and Yehuda Spiegel, the Deputy Director-General of the Ministry of Religious Affairs, then under the minister, Moshe Shapira, the party's leader. Spiegel was deeply wounded by this accusation. He had known Krausz for years and their relationship was good, albeit overshadowed by a particular episode. Early in 1944, Spiegel had obtained permits for his parents to immigrate to Palestine. He sent them to Krausz, who, according to Spiegel, gave them to a relative of his own who was not even a Zionist, while Spiegel's parents were sent to Auschwitz to die. The two met several times at the trial where Spiegel sensed that Krausz had become a tool in Tamir's hands, and that the defense counsel was almost cynically exploiting his rage and bitterness. When Krausz alleged that Spiegel had tried to influence and change his testimony—a claim, which, according to Spiegel, did not contain an iota of truth—relations between the two were finally severed. After the trial, Krausz sent emissaries to him who claimed that the entire story was Tamir's invention—but Spiegel refused to accept their explanation.

Tamir's allegation that Israel's frightened and corrupt establishment was doing its utmost to interfere with the course of the trial took a number of forms. For example, he claimed that the chairman of the Jewish Agency Executive, Berl Locker, had ignored his request to make available to him all files relating to Kasztner, Brand and Becher. And, in his re-examination of Krausz, he tried to insinuate that Krausz's dismissal from the Palestine office was a Mapai scheme devised by Eliyahu Dobkin.

His "conspiracy claim" also related to the letter that Ottó Komoly's widow sent to Judge Halevi, in which she had denied the allegation made by Krausz in his testimony—that her late husband had acted at Kasztner's behest and not of his own volition. Krausz's claim that her husband had been Kasztner's "flunky" was a "lie and an insult": my late husband, she wrote, devoted his entire life to the Zionist ideal and was a victim of his own sense of duty and responsibility. Throughout his life—in that tragic period of our people's history as well—he knew exactly what he was doing and why, and he never did anything or took part in any action that was not in keeping with his Zionist conscience and his profound sense of honor.[53] In his re-examination of Krausz, Tamir asked: "How old is Mrs. Komoly now?" "I don't know," Krausz replied. Later he asked, "Do you know if she is receiving any [financial] support from the Agency?" "She is," was the reply.

These claims of Krausz's were the final chords of his long, stormy testimony, which eminently served the aims of the defense. His testimony revealed the highly charged and hostile relationship between two of the key figures engaged in trying to rescue Hungarian Jewry. This is how Rosenfeld summed it up in his book: "Through the transparent walls of the 'glass house,' the murky picture of an abysmal schism between Jews in the very throes of the Holocaust was brought to light."[54]

X

The battle in the courtroom continued to engage the attention of the political system and the press. The subject was raised at a Cabinet meeting, when Moshe Shapira, the Minister of Welfare and Religion, submitted a question to Pinhas Rosen, the Minister of Justice, about the way the trial was being conducted. The matter was also discussed at a meeting of the Knesset's House Committee, when Member of Knesset Meir Vilner (Communist party) appealed the Speaker's decision to reject a parliamentary question submitted to the Minister of Justice regarding the failure to institute criminal proceedings against Bandy Grosz.[55] Prime Minister Sharett did not deal with the question again. After his memorandum in connection with Joel Brand was printed in *Ma'ariv*, he gave the affair only one rather obscure mention in his diary.[56]

---

53 The letter was sent from Tel Aviv on July 7, 1954, i.e., during Krausz's testimony. It is marked Exhibit 1 of the District Court, ISA, Kasztner trial container, 512/B.

54 Rosenfeld, *Criminal Case*, p. 183.

55 Vilner's argument was that since the question related to a witness in a trial and not a defendant, it could not be rejected on the basis of sub judice. The chairman of the House Committee, M.K. David Bar-Rav-Hai, replied, "In his verdict the judge will evaluate this witness and then the Attorney General can decide whether or not to put him on trial." Meeting of House Committee, July 13, 1954, ISA, 66/20.

56 Immediately after the disaster at Ma'agan, Sharett wrote in his diary: "Haim Cohn on [M.K. Israel Shlomo] Rosenberg—Kasztner—[M.K. Shlomo] Lavie," Sharett, *Personal Diary*, vol. 2, August 1, 1954, p. 563.

Press coverage of the trial was limited because it was still sub judice. The editorials, not very numerous in the summer of 1954, were all against Kasztner and all appeared in newspapers that were marginal in terms of their influence and circulation. Nonetheless, there were already some signs of a turn of events that would become all too clear in the summer of 1955, when Kasztner's opponents would dominate the press and use the trial to hurl abuse at the ruling party and its leaders.

One editorial, already mentioned, appeared when the trial resumed in the *Tevel* weekly.[57] The opening lines said it all: "In effect, those sitting in the dock today are the Jewish Agency and the heads of the national institutions of that time, namely, today's leaders of the country. Moshe Sharett, Prime Minister and Minister of Foreign Affairs, Ehud Avriel, former Director-General of the Prime Minister's Office, and others who now hold similar positions, but whose names have not been explicitly mentioned, have been publicly accused in the Jerusalem district courtroom of preventing the rescue of a million European Jews during the Holocaust." The editorial itself reviewed the trial from a standpoint consistent with the defense position—with emphasis on the 'crimes' of the Agency and its efforts to conceal them.

> Sharett ended his conversation [with Brand] by informing him that he could return to Budapest. Brand was taken to Cairo, imprisoned for five months, and several months before the end of the war, brought to Palestine. Brand asked for a meeting with the late Dr. Chaim Weizmann, who notified him that he had no time [for such a meeting]. (The original document was stolen. A photocopy was submitted to the court as an exhibit.)

Another journal that related to the trial was the weekly *Smol*,[58] the organ of the Socialist Left Party. In a series of three unsigned articles, the weekly reviewed the trial's three main testimonies—here, too, from a stance that was in keeping with the defense. In the sub-heading of the first article Tamir was quoted: "Kasztner—part of a Jewish Agency and JDC (American Joint Distribution Committee) trend to downplay the Holocaust, prevent any resistance and aid the Germans, albeit unwittingly, in their program of extermination." The

---

57 Ari Dagon, "The Filthiest Trial in the Country," *Tevel* (June 2, 1954).

58 "What did the Testimonies in the Kasztner Trial Reveal?" *Smol*, July 22, July 29 and August 5, 1954; M.K. Moshe Sneh, head of the Socialist Party, left Mapam in 1953 and joined the Communist Party a year later. The second representative of the faction in the Knesset was M.K. Avraham (Adolf) Berman, one of the leaders of the Warsaw ghetto revolt.

final editorial emphasized boldly that it was not an individual who was to blame, but the very flesh and blood of the Zionist establishment: "All those who today are covering up for and identifying with Kasztner and his actions, are the self same people who backed his actions and cooperated with him [before]!" On a subdued but insinuating note, the three-part series came to an end. The case was still sub judice, but maintaining its anti-Kasztner stance the final article promised that:

> Further witnesses will be called to testify [...] who will certainly reveal additional facts. However, based on the vast amount of incriminating material [... we have seen] the true face of certain leaders who have crowned themselves [...] patriots. [... Moreover] we have the answer to the question, what was revealed in the testimony provided by the Kasztner trial? The answer lies in the evidence itself.

XI

Many years after the trial, I learned from conversations with some of the witnesses for the prosecution that they still harbor strong feelings of anger and bitterness towards the prosecutors Tel and Cohn. Perhaps their words should be taken with a pinch of salt, but I believe it is only fair to give them a hearing and to show the divide that separated the prosecution from its witnesses. Peretz Révész was a member of Kibbutz Kfar Hamaccabi, a former leader of Young Maccabi in Slovakia and Hungary who organized aid for Kasztner after the trial.[59] During a break on March 30, the day of his testimony, Tamir stepped over and struck up a conversation with him. "They must have told you I have horns," he said. "I come from a family of lawyers," Révész replied. "My father was a lawyer and my brother is also a lawyer; you don't scare me." Tamir went on, "I know that you and your friends are decent people and I have all the respect in the world for what you are doing, but I am struggling to keep Kasztner, this ambitious careerist, from going down in history." Révész countered with a question: "If you knew that we were speaking the truth, why didn't you come to us?" But before Tamir could answer, Tel grabbed Révész' arm, pulled him away, and rebuked him in front of Tamir: "What are you doing talking to that liar?"

---

59 Peretz Révész, personal interview, Kfar Hamaccabi, March 12, 1992.

Those people whose testimony for the prosecution had been rejected fared no better. Levi Argov kept a close eye on the events surrounding Krausz's dismissal. He had wanted to testify on Kasztner's behalf and even made a special trip to Jerusalem to meet with Cohn to that end. He told me that Cohn barely listened to what he had to say and rudely declined his offer to testify.[60] Baruch Tzahor's story is even more disturbing;[61] he had wanted to tell the court that Kasztner had saved his life, even though he was just an "ordinary Jew," who had no connections and no money. He spoke to Kasztner, who arranged for him to meet with Tel. Their meeting was brief; Tel heard his story, asked him no questions and told him he would call him to the witness stand at once; in other words, the following day. When three days had gone by and he still hadn't been called, Tzahor notified Tel that he couldn't wait any longer. If an opportunity should present itself, Tel told him, he'd send him an immediate telegram. When they spoke afterwards, Tel told him that he was completely disheartened by the fact that the case had turned into an all-out political trial. Thus, Tel lost an opportunity to call a witness whose testimony was politically important, since Tzahor was also a member of the Achdut Ha'avoda movement. When he returned home, he said to his wife: "Hannah, it's a lost cause, [Kasztner's] lawyer is an idiot."

My impression from the statements of Kasztner's friends and close associates was that although he was doing his best to come to terms with his hopeless situation, he gradually collapsed under the strain. Tzahor, who met Kasztner on his way from Jerusalem to his home in Tzofit (in the Sharon region), saw a broken man. "Rezsö," he said to him, "you are in a bad way. Tamir is pulling Halevi by the nose and although you're a lawyer yourself, you seem to be indifferent." Drained and exhausted, Kasztner barely answered. He was unable to interfere, he said, the action hadn't been brought by him, but by the state.

Professor Rivka Bar-Yosef[62] told me that she had already sensed in the course of the trial that Kasztner was his own worst enemy because of his personality, the good traits as well as the bad. He was forever trying to prove himself, still unwilling to relinquish his role of key player; it was a role that promised him certain defeat. He had not grasped the world of concepts and norms that shaped Israeli reality during the early 1950s or Israeli society's ambivalent attitude toward the Holocaust. Nor did he understand that things

---

60 Levi Argov, personal interview.
61 Personal interview with Baruch Tzahor, at Tzofit, August 24, 1993.
62 Rivka Bar-Yosef, personal interview.

that were acceptable abroad were not so in Israel. Bar-Yosef was very worried when she heard that Kasztner was preparing a big speech for the trial, as were many of his other friends who were familiar with the intricacies of Israeli life. According to Bar-Yosef, Kasztner's wife didn't make things any easier for him either. The daughter of a wealthy, well-known family, she found it hard to function in a reality that had changed so radically. Moreover, instead of trying to soften his relations with his enemies and neutralizing some of them, she had internalized and adopted all her husband's hates and quarrels.

Hanzi Brand was the person closest to Kasztner during those trying times. She told me that Kasztner had managed to keep a grip on himself until the matter of his Becher affidavit was presented in court, notwithstanding "many problems, financial and others." But once that affair was raised, he utterly lost his self-confidence. He even began to fear, not for his life but for his livelihood and self-respect. "After all," she told me, almost diffidently, "we were used to our lives being in danger." His greatest fear was insult and derision and she saw him cringe in gas stations, when people refused to sell him gasoline.[63]

XII

One of the witnesses called by the court was Hillel Danzig, a survivor of the rescue train. He and Kasztner had a lot in common—they were the same age and were both born in Cluj, together they had been active in the Ichud Haolami. In Israel, Danzig worked as a journalist for *Davar*. His name had been mentioned in the trial even before he was called to testify. Yaacov Freifeld, one of Tamir's "parade of Cluj witnesses," stated that Danzig had strongly advised him to go to Kenyermezo, where he would find some peace. Because of his advice, Freifeld had boarded the train that took him to Auschwitz. When asked by the defense if Danzig had taken the train with him to Auschwitz, Freifeld replied: "Heaven forbid, how was that possible? After all, he was a member of the Judenrat. [As] leader of the clique [...] he stayed together with what was known as the 'Swiss group;' he stayed with the leaders." Thus Danzig was portrayed as a cut above ordinary folk, a man who abandoned his flock in order to save his own neck. Tamir had introduced Freifeld as a "foundry worker and Histadrut (General Labor Federation)

---

63 Hanzi Brand.

member;" in other words, a simple laborer, who belonged to the same camp as Danzig and Kasztner.[64]

In a letter to Judge Halevi two days after Freifeld's testimony, Danzig categorically denied the former's version of the events. It was this letter that brought him to the witness stand.

In his strident examination of Danzig, Tamir once again raised a long list of episodes already discussed in the course of the trial—the witness's meeting with Peretz Goldstein at the Columbus camp; the rescue committee members in Cluj, who made sure to save themselves first etc., including information Kasztner had given him when he visited Cluj regarding the Germans' extermination of the Jews:

> **Tamir:** Kasztner's meeting with you in no way, then, enhanced your knowledge of Germany's intentions as far as the danger facing you [the Jews of Cluj] was concerned?
>
> **Danzig:** I can neither deny nor confirm that assumption.
>
> **Tamir:** That's a formulation for the Foreign Ministry, not for a witness.
>
> **Danzig:** It was a time when there was a crisis in the negotiations and Kasztner had no concrete information about the Germans' intentions. That's how I remember that moment.
>
> **Tamir:** What you are prepared to say is that he had no compelling, grave information to give you that left any lasting impression on you or from which you could draw any conclusions.
>
> **Danzig:** No, there was none.

When he testified again, at Tamir's request, Kasztner denied Danzig's statement. He asserted that he had transferred all the information he could during his two visits to Cluj and had warned everyone he met that their lives were in danger. When Tamir asked him what kind of information he had transferred to Cluj once the trains had begun leaving for Auschwitz, he said: "By then I had no contact with Cluj, [but] I spoke on the phone with my father-in-law and transmitted to him whatever I could by phone. I also told him that the situation was very bad, and he knew what that meant. We had discussed the possibility of deportation and extermination."[65] To the question of whether

---

64 Trial transcript, June 28, 1954, pp. 49K-56K.
65 Tel Aviv, June 30, 1954, ISA, Kasztner trial containers, 514/B.

he had explicitly told the Jews of Cluj that the danger was deportation to Auschwitz, he replied:

> On neither visit did I say to all the people I spoke with, "Jews, you'll be going to Auschwitz for extermination." I didn't know that. What I said was: "Jews, your lives are in danger, there is a danger of deportation and deportation means extermination, you must escape; you must hide."

Not only had he warned them of the danger, Kasztner asserted, but he had also begged many of them to try to do something—to escape or to hide—but they wouldn't listen.

Which of these two versions was right? Which of them spoke the truth? We have no way of knowing exactly what was said, exactly what was heard and internalized during Kasztner's visits to Cluj—the occupied city whose Jews were fed by all manner of rumors. But it's easy to see that when Danzig, supposedly one of Kasztner's defenders, had an opportunity to help him, he chose to present a version intended to protect his own skin, even at the price of abandoning the man who had saved his life.

Another of the train's survivors who was asked to help Kasztner was Rabbi Yoel Teitelbaum, the Hasidic rabbi of Szatmar. Dezső (David) Herman, who took care of the rabbi when the survivors of the train were in Bergen-Belsen, was the one who appealed to him. A few weeks later, he received an evasive reply, signed not by the rabbi himself but by one of his secretaries. The rabbi refused to stand up for the man to whom he owed his life.[66]

XIII

Tamir constantly dwelt on the question of the identity of the train's passengers and the way in which they were selected. It was on this point, which was included in Gruenwald's libelous newsletter, that Tamir pinned his claim that the Germans had given Kasztner the possibility of saving his own family, his close associates and his friends, in return for lulling hundreds of thousands of Hungarian Jews into a false sense of security and it was this that made him an accomplice in their extermination.

The subject came up at the very beginning of the trial, when Kasztner first took the stand. He denied Gruenwald's allegation that 52 members from

---

66 "The Rabbi Refused to Help," *Ha'aretz*, June 16, 1994.

the "Kasztner-Fischer family" were among the rescue train's passengers and argued that the number did not exceed 19 and that most of his and his wife's families had perished in Auschwitz.

This arose again after several days of intense, exhausting cross-examination, by which time Kasztner was on the verge of collapse. Tamir did not ease off and raised the issue of the "Cluj favorites"—388 people from that city who were added to the train's passenger list. When everything was lost anyway, Kasztner stated, his action saved those 388 Jews, who would otherwise have perished at Auschwitz. Tamir countered with the allegation that it was a German ploy to soothe the ghetto Jews into complacency, and lead them like lambs to the slaughter. Rumors about the list of favored people had a demoralizing effect on the ghetto, which helped the Germans carry out their program of extermination.[67]

Various witnesses were heard on this point. According to David Herman, the Cluj people who were included on the train were generally deserving public figures and included several "non-Zionist public figures, but deserving nonetheless." Also included in this category was the vehemently anti-Zionist Satmar Rabbi Yoel Teitelbaum, who coincidentally, was staying in the Cluj ghetto at that time. Again, according to David Herman, the passenger list for the rescue train was in no way based on wealth, "the only consideration was their Zionist background." He added that that the survivors were full of admiration for Kasztner and were aware that they owed their lives to him. It was in this context that he described the party they had arranged in his honor in the spring of 1945, when he came to visit them at the camp in Switzerland where they were waiting to immigrate to Israel:

> We learned of his visit a week or two earlier and prepared a reception, organized a celebration, there was great excitement. An evening of high spirits [...] tears etc [...] we prepared a testimonial for him [...], which Dr. Kasztner did not of course extort from the refugees. He wasn't even in the camp when we prepared it. [It's] libel [to say so]. We all felt it was a great privilege to just touch Dr. Kasztner's coat. That evening I heard the longest applause in my life; for over twenty minutes Kasztner couldn't take the floor I had given him.[68]

---

67 On this matter, see "The Facts Underlying the Dispute," *Haolam Hazeh*, March 11, 1954.
68 Trial transcript, March 11, 1954, pp. 82–83.

Tamir attacked Herman in his cross-examination, trying hard to show that the passenger list had been compiled in a morally objectionable way. He asked whether the list of people from Cluj included converts; he wanted to know who had selected them; whether the Judenrat was involved in the committee that selected the passengers; and did anyone have the moral right to choose and rescue those particular 388 Jews, whereas a train was leaving Cluj every few days headed for Auschwitz; and how involved was Yosef Fischer in preparing the list. Herman was fairly successful in fielding Tamir's attacks. He claimed that four, men unconnected with the Judenrat had compiled the list—as a member of the Judenrat, he himself was not among them. He denied that a group of Revisionists included in the list, led by IZL member Yaakov Weiss, who was later hung [by the British]), boarded it against their will.

Herman tried to describe the dreadful predicament created by the whole issue in the ghetto, whose inhabitants lived in a state of increasing uncertainty, constantly fed by rumors. They were aware of the danger they were in when the idea of the train arose, but not of imminent extermination. Although they knew about Auschwitz being an extermination camp, "the idea of deportation [...] never crossed our minds, we were conscious of the danger [to Hungary's Jews, but] we never thought in terms extermination or crematoria, we thought of work squads. Therefore, in our minds, the train was not linked with rescue, but rather with immigration [...] immigration to Palestine via Spain."

Although unaware of the imminent danger of extermination, many were enthusiastic about the idea of going to Palestine, "the possibility of immigrating in those days was of course very attractive, in view of the dreadful conditions we were in." Under such circumstances, the list would have been extremely hard to compile, because any list "was too narrow to satisfy us." To Tamir's question about "the moral right to choose 388 people from among 18,000," Herman replied unequivocally that "perhaps there was no **moral** right to choose, but there was a moral duty."[69]

The thorny dilemmas confronting the besieged Jews of Cluj over the list were also the subject of Herman's second testimony, when he spoke of the heavy pressure brought to bear on the four men composing the list. He referred to the tragic situation created by the departure of 388 Jews and the bitter reaction of those who were left off the list. Tamir made full use of the feelings and frustrations created by the tragic circumstances by calling witnesses from Cluj who were not included on the train to provide him with

69 Ibid., pp. 86–87; Rosenfeld, *Criminal Case*, pp. 109–11.

the ammunition he needed. One of these, Yosef Krausz, was asked whether one of the things, among others, that Kasztner was accused of after the war, besides having "failed to inform the people that the transports were being taken to Auschwitz [...] was connected with the train carrying 300 Jews to Bergen-Belsen." To which he replied, "The opinion in Cluj was that this [the transport to Bergen-Belsen] was reward for the people's submissive behavior when they were herded into the ghetto."[70]

By questioning these witnesses, Tamir was able to create the picture he was seeking—demonization of the rescue train. He depicted it not as a desperate attempt at rescue based on the verse: "Whoever saves the life of one Jew it is as if he had preserved the whole world," but rather an arrogant, patronizing attempt to place greater value on one Jewish life than another during the most harrowing period of Jewish history.

XIV

Tamir continued to dwell on the question of Kasztner's financial situation and the profits he supposedly amassed through his connections with the Nazis, especially with Becher. At the beginning of the trial, David Herman had testified that Kasztner was impoverished and unable to provide his family with the most basic necessities. In Switzerland he had a furnished room in a *pension*, which was "definitely not luxurious" and as for his financial situation during the trial, he said: "Kasztner is a man who lives from hand to mouth. Sometimes he has 20, 30 or 40 pounds that he gets from his friends." He described Kasztner's housing problems when first arriving in Israel and that he had lived in a one-room apartment on Tel Aviv's Alexander Yanai Street:

> With the landlady's unbearable pressure and conditions [in the room] unbearable, friends who were in Bergen-Belsen [i.e., survivors of the train, Y.W.] decided it was unthinkable [to live under] such conditions. We collected money and rented a two-and-a-half room apartment on Amsterdam Street in north Tel Aviv. We signed the lease, and gave it to him as a gift from us on one of the memorial days. One of the rooms wasn't properly furnished.

---

70 Ibid., June 17, 1954, pp. 57–60.

The subject of Kasztner's finances also came up in Hanzi Brand's testimony according to which she, together with the committee's treasurer, Shalom (Shulem) Offenbach, had been responsible for handing over valuables to the Germans in exchange for the train. It was they who packed the valuables and the money in suitcases and transferred them to SS headquarters in Budapest. Kasztner had had nothing to do with it.

Tamir did not let up, despite witnesses who provided a concise account of the impossible situation in Budapest and Kasztner's woeful state. He hammered away at the subject for two reasons: first, because it was mentioned in Gruenwald's newsletter, and second because he needed to demonize Kasztner, by proving that he had amassed a fortune from his shady deals with the Nazis. He claimed that Kasztner knew what had happened to 'Becher's treasure' and why the discrepancy between the sum people claimed Becher had given to Schweiger and the sum that was finally found was so large. This came up when Schweiger testified for the prosecution on March 22. At the end of his cross-examination, Tamir declared that he intended to prove that a large sum of money was missing from the hoard of money, gold and jewelry that Schweiger received from Becher and, he said, since the witness is known to be an honest man, he concludes, by way of elimination that it was not he who had taken any of this money.[71]

Tamir honed his argument later in the trial. In July, when witnesses involved with the 'Becher treasure' were being heard, Tamir argued that Schweiger had been a victim of Becher and Kasztner jointly, and that the two had used him to cover up their mutual scheme to rob Hungary's Jews. That's why Becher pretended he was turning over to the Jewish Agency the entire two million dollars he had extorted, via Kasztner, from Hungary's Jews. In actual fact, he only returned about $50,000 and most of this was in counterfeit bills. That amount was returned through Schweiger, not through Kasztner, and the intention was clear. Basing his claim on Schweiger's words that "at the time, my mental and physical condition was such that I would have done anything," Tamir alleged, with unbridled cynicism, that the two took advantage of him to ensure that he would be held responsible for the loss or theft of the money. In that way, Kasztner and Becher would be left with most of the money, but the blame for its loss would fall on the pathetic Schweiger. And why did Schweiger, who never took one penny of the stolen treasure, agree to take part in this scheme? He had no choice. As the price

---

71 "Former Haganah Head in Hungary Testifies on Becher's Deeds," *Al HaMishmar*, March 22, 1954.

for his release from Mauthausen, he was forced to lie and to say that all the money had been delivered to him. When the judge interrupted Tamir to say he didn't exactly understand all the details of this infamous deal, Tamir replied that it's no wonder, that he realizes "that it's not easy for a decent man to grasp all the intricacies of the nefarious intentions and wrongdoings of these two criminals [Kasztner and Becher]."[72]

XV

Kasztner's testimony lasted only ten minutes when he took the stand for the third time, as the last witness in the trial. This time the courtroom was empty, as no one knew he was going to testify. When he finished, the judge turned to him and gave him another opportunity to give his version of the facts, "say what you have to say." Kasztner took full advantage of this opportunity. His hands joined, like those of a monk at prayer, he again tried to present his "credo" and to improve, even slightly, his tarnished image.[73]

His main point was that "we did our best within our limited possibilities." However, "compared with the dimensions of the catastrophe, that was very little." Among other reasons, the battle over the fate of Hungarian Jewry was decided not in 1944 but in the years that preceded it, "when we failed to prepare [...] for underground actions that would have enabled us to properly warn the Jews of Hungary and perhaps also to carry out acts of resistance." Despite this somewhat apologetic comment, he vehemently denied the allegation according to which he had prevented defensive actions that could have saved the lives of many more Jews. "The claim made here—that if we hadn't objected, the Hungarians would have come to our aid—is simply libelous," he said. The negotiations with the Germans, he asserted in his reply to Krausz, was not a principle as far as he was concerned, but a tactic and his attitude toward the Hungarians was also instrumental; "we took that route when we thought it would be of some benefit, and we were in close contact with the Hungarian opposition."

Tamir was silent throughout Kasztner's speech. At one point only, when Kasztner lashed out at him, did he arise and, full of righteous arrogance, say said that since Kasztner was the real defendant in this case, he had the right

---

72 The description is from "The Defense Counsel: Becher and Kasztner Split Monies Extorted from the 'Rescue Train'," *Herut*, July 13, 1954.
73 "The Kasztner Affair—The Defense Counsel's Turn," *Haolam Hazeh*, September 22, 1954.

to have the last word before the verdict was passed. "I don't want anyone [...] to claim that he was not given an opportunity to say his piece," said Tamir, "but he has no right to exploit the opportunity to insult me." At that moment, Tamir felt himself the victor. On one occasion, when Tel broke out in inexplicable laughter, Tamir silenced him, saying he had many reasons to cry, but none to laugh.

When Kasztner reached the end of his statement, he began speaking slowly, emphasizing each word, including punctuation marks. Using the last words at his disposal to convince his audience that a dreadful mistake had occurred in the trial, he declaimed loudly:

> I only hope that one day we shall have the opportunity to evaluate this whole tragic epoch outside the confines of a courtroom. We merely wanted to do our duty under conditions that were completely unprecedented. Neither my comrades nor I have anything to hide in this matter and need not regret that we followed the dictates of our conscience, in spite of all that has been said against us during this trial.[74]

After Kasztner, it was the turn of counsels for the defense and the prosecution to sum up. The Attorney General spoke for an entire day (September 19) while the defense attorney spoke for five days (he began on September 22 and continued, although not consecutively, until October 3). The Jewish high holidays fell during this period, and the holiday edition of *Haolam Hazeh*[75] was published on the eve of Rosh Hashanah, with a considerable portion devoted to the trial. The weekly named Kasztner "Man of the Year," and printed a photograph of him on the front page, surrounded with illustrations of barbed wire fences and parachutists dropping to the ground, and an engraving of the SS emblem. A huge, three-page write-up was devoted entirely to Kasztner, describing him as a colorless nonentity, an unimportant little official in the Rationing Ministry who had, completely by chance, been transformed into a man "whose name had become almost a new concept in the Hebrew language, who had made the headlines almost every day, whose every word became a subject of stormy debate in the streets and of legal deliberation in the courtroom."

Not only was the man himself dragged into the limelight, but a spotlight was also turned on the recent past of the Jewish people, from which everyone

---

74 The descriptions are from Rosenfeld, *Criminal Case*, pp. 266–267.
75 The issue was published on September 29, 1954.

had been fleeing as from a forest fire. The curtain of forgetting, behind which both the traitors and the rescuers, both the saints and the sinners had been hiding, was torn; "someone rudely moved it aside, almost inadvertently. The Attorney General, who had no understanding of the public mood, was handed a knife. A brilliant young lawyer took the knife and tore the fabric to shreds." And what was exposed behind the shreds of the curtain was beyond all imagination. Before the eyes of the astonished spectators, "who sat mesmerized in the courtroom, a horrifying picture unfolded, a plot that might have been taken from the work of a perverted author who belonged in a mental asylum." This, in the weekly's view, was the sum and substance of the "Kasztner affair."

Historically the trial was not important; it was significant mainly because of its bearing on current events. The struggle between Kasztner and Tamir focused on the future of the state of Israel, and the direction it would take. Kasztner, like Mapai and the Jewish Agency heads, who became the leaders of the state, represented the world-view and orientation of the Diaspora. The archetype that expressed their essence was Mordechai the Jew, "the hero of the biblical book, born in Persia," who fought against the evil decrees of the powers that be not by rebellion or by taking a stand, but by fawning and deviousness and "thanks to a Jewish maiden who found favor in the eyes of the landowner and melted his heart when he was merry with wine." Kasztner, as a man and a phenomenon, thus symbolized the past.

The antithesis of Kasztner—and of Mordechai—is Judas Maccabaeus, "the man who rebelled, fought and liberated." The obsequious Jews of the ghetto were the complete opposite of the "heroes of the Book of Joshua, Samuel and the Judges—the heroes and statesmen of a free people." The successors of the biblical heroes are the young Hebrews who, with their bodies and their blood remedied the errors of the weak *galuti* leadership, prodding them, almost against their will, to fight a war of independence." They were the ones who handed the people a state on a silver platter. But since those awesome days, when "it seemed as though a new page had been turned in the history of the land [...] the state went back to the well-paved road of the Jew Mordechai." This road led it "to scurry through the offices of the American government, currying favor," so that the security of the state, and in fact its very existence, were at the mercy of foreigners. Therefore, more than any historical lesson, what we can learn from this affair is the fate of a collective that relies on this servile, spineless approach, so typical of the *galuti* Jew." It illustrates the two diametrically opposed approaches, between which Israeli society must choose: "Servile deference towards hidden foreign rule, which still exists in this country, or for a sovereign people to try to take their fate in their hands, to fight their war of survival on their own."

In this way, *Haolam Hazeh* and its editor tried to turn the trial into a symbol of the all-out struggle between "the Hebrew land" and the "Jewish Diaspora," the victory of one side deciding the fate of the young state for years, even for generations. The main symbol of the Diaspora is not Kasztner the man, but 'Kasztnerism' as a phenomenon, in other words, the entire leadership of the State.[76]

XVI

The prosecutor's summation lasted for seven hours, almost without a break. Everyone in the crowded courtroom listened attentively, at times with bated breath. The two main witnesses were also present—Krausz, for the defense, and Kasztner, who had come with his wife and sat throughout the summation, tense, pale and motionless, for the prosecution.[77] Cohn's closing arguments were widely covered in the press. Nearly all the newspapers devoted a considerable part of their front page to them. For example, the headline in *Hatzofeh* read: "The Attorney General: It has been proven beyond doubt that Dr. Kasztner's object was to serve his people."

Cohn, the man responsible for opening the Pandora's box that was the Kasztner trial, formally known as Criminal Case 124/53, opened his summation in a stentorian tone. First, he explained why he was going to be unsparingly condemnatory "as I have never before been in a courtroom." The reason was the grave nature of the accusations Gruenwald had leveled at Kasztner, "alleging he had collaborated with the Nazis and shared with them the booty he had stolen from the Jews." This accusation is so monstrous; "because if it were true that Kasztner had collaborated with the Nazis as a quisling, in the full sense of the word, and shared with them booty stolen from the Jews, **then his sentence must be death** [emphasis added]. Therefore, I would add that if Gruenwald's allegations are not the truth, then he deserves to die at the hands of God."

---

76 In this regard, see Yechiam Weitz, "Changing Conceptions of the Holocaust: the Kasztner Case," *Studies in Contemporary Jewry*, vol. 10 (1994), pp. 211–230.

77 The description is from Prat, *The Great Trial*, pp. 164–165.

After Judge Halevi handed down his verdict, no one remembered the final words of Cohn's opening statement, but the first words came back at him like a boomerang, and all the more so, at Kasztner.

He then presented his closing arguments. The first was it had been conclusively proven in the trial that "from the first moment to the last, throughout all of his activity, Dr. Kasztner had but one sole aim in mind: to serve his people." The second argument was one of principle:

> For no man among us—including the honorable judge—has the right to criticize those who stood at the brink of the yawning abyss of extermination, a situation none of us can even conceive.

Cohn divided his speech into ten sections, according to the topics that arose during the lengthy trial: Kasztner's contacts with the Germans, his behavior in Budapest, the Cluj ghetto, Brand's mission, the parachutists, 'Becher's treasure', etc. By relating to these points, not all of which had been covered in Gruenwald's newsletter, Cohn was continuing the switch in roles that had characterized the entire trial. Rather than being a de jure prosecutor, the Attorney General had turned into a de facto defender, whose job it was to defend Kasztner—who from a witness had been turned into an accused— defending himself against the serious charges leveled against him.

The first section Cohn addressed was Brand's mission, an affair that had not been raised by the defendant Gruenwald, but that had become a focal point in the case, making it a trial of the ruling political party. Consequently, on this point, Cohn was primarily defending not Kasztner, but the Yishuv's institutions and leadership. "Just as the accused's slander of Dr. Kasztner is groundless, there is also no basis for the defense counsel's slander of the Jewish Agency, merely slander for the sake of slander," he said. He presented several arguments to substantiate this emphatic statement. First, he asserted, "cooperation with the British, who were fighting the Nazis, is not a shameful act, but rather a cause for pride and honor." Second, there is not even a shred of evidence that the institutions of the Yishuv were responsible for handing Brand over to the British. Here he relied on the Avriel's testimony that he had received an explicit promise from the consular official in the British consulate in Istanbul that Brand would not be arrested and would be allowed to enter Palestine. The defense did not even attempt to disclaim this evidence, Cohn argued. Another argument related to an internal contradiction in the defense's position, since it castigated Kasztner for having entered into negotiations with Eichmann that culminated in the mission and yet criticized the heads of the

Yishuv for not having given the mission the serious consideration it deserved. On this matter, he remarked sarcastically:

> I do not know what the defense is thinking. Whichever way you look at it—if it also believes Brand's mission from the outset was preposterous, what's so bad about his being arrested, spending a few weeks in a villa in Cairo and then going to Palestine? And what is so terrible if the Yishuv institutions defeated this mission by 'sitting on their hands'? But if, on the other hand, the defense believes the mission was truly a mission and the plan was a plan and Eichmann's offer was an offer—what flaw did they find in Kasztner and Brand who negotiated with the Germans, and who believed Eichmann?

Cohn found another contradiction in the defense's charges that related to the Germans' attitude towards Kasztner and Brand. Counsel for the defense had argued that the fact that Kasztner was not made to wear a yellow Star of David, that he moved freely around Budapest, and traveled throughout occupied Europe in the company of SS officers, was proof of his treachery, that he had crossed the lines and was one of them. On the other hand, the fact that Brand was given an 'Aryan' passport and sent to Istanbul in a German army plane did not make him a traitor, because in the defense's view, he was on a sacred mission.

By presenting this contradiction, Cohn began grappling with one of the most highly charged issues of the trial—the negotiations. Responding to Tamir's claim that "at the outset, the contact [between Kasztner and the Germans] had been legitimate, and that afterwards Kasztner began a downhill slide, and became a collaborator," Cohn asked when he had crossed the line between a legitimate contact and collaboration. To clarify this point, he referred to Krausz's assertion that the contact became collaboration at the end of June, after the 'Bergen-Belsen train' had set off. Then, "it was possible to see that the Germans had not kept their promise and therefore, Kasztner should have terminated the connection." First, Cohn argued, "actually, by allowing the train to leave, the Germans were fulfilling their promise;" second, "this claim sounds [...] strange and ridiculous coming from a man who thought that the address for collaboration was Ferenczy."

On this point, he raised a question that went straight to the heart of the matter: after half a million Jews had been deported to extermination camps, wasn't it necessary to insist that the train should leave? Wasn't it "right to try to free a group of people when the great majority of the Jews were being taken to extermination?" His reply was on two levels—the practical and the ethical, and on both it was categorical. On the practical level, he stated that the real choice was not 1,600 rescued Jews instead of half a million, but half a million exterminated without the rescue of the 1,600. On the ethical level, he argued not only was it permissible to allow the train to depart, it was in fact a moral obligation. In this context, he cited a comment by the defense witness, Philipp von Freudiger, about a Jewish law that states: "One life may not be taken to save another," and added:

> I submit that when Kasztner had an opportunity to send even one Jew, anywhere at all, to a relatively safe place, **he was obliged to do so under Jewish law** [...] if Kasztner had in that situation decided differently—by doing so, he would not have rescued half a million Jews from Auschwitz, but the 1,600 also would not have been saved [emphasis added].

Another highly charged issue involved the Cluj ghetto. On this issue, he began in an ironic tone, enumerating the list of Kasztner's "countless venial sins and wrongdoings," to the living and to the dead: that he had discriminated against the ghetto in favor of the train ("while from all the other ghettos, there were but a few, from Cluj he got 388 onto that train"); that among those who boarded the train were his friends and relatives, including his father-in-law Yosef Fischer, who Cohn called "that distinguished leader;" and that he did not warn the people of Cluj that they would be taken to Auschwitz for extermination.

By drawing this comparison, Cohn again played straight into the hands of the other side. In Israel of 1954, when the poet Nathan Alterman found himself in isolation he tried to find some justification for the behavior of the Judenrats, a comparison of this sort could only have one result—it reinforced the negative, passive, treacherous, *galuti*—stereotype of the case the prosecutor was trying to defend.

As for the parachutists' episode, Cohn argued that in all three cases—inducing Palgi to report to the Gestapo, turning Goldstein over [to the Gestapo], and dodging any attempt to help Hannah Szenes—"[Kasztner] had acted with the best intentions, honestly and courageously, to serve the Jewish cause [in general] and the good of the parachutists in particular."

Even if it could be proven that Kasztner had induced Palgi to report to the Gestapo, he argued, that still does not prove he was a traitor:

> Assuming that Kasztner's judgment [...] was thoroughly mistaken, and very dangerous. What does that prove? Was Kasztner forbidden to err? Is

he not flesh and blood? Does that prove him a traitor? [...] Based on this evidence, would the honorable judge convict him in a criminal court?

With regard to Hannah Szenes, he raised a similar argument. Let us assume that Dr. Kasztner was so preoccupied with his efforts to save tens of thousands of Jews, "that he did not make the same effort—whether because he did not find the time or forgot to do so—for one Jewish woman from Palestine. Does that make him a traitor? A collaborator with the Germans?"

The prosecution's use of this line of reasoning did not have the desired effect. While the defense counsel was describing the affair in the most lurid terms, placing Kasztner squarely at the darkest, most traitorous end of the spectrum, the prosecutor was taking a neutral tone. Even if he had been able to persuade the court that Kasztner was not guilty of treason, his arguments could not counterbalance the dark, demonic picture drawn by the defense counsel who constantly played on the most highly charged emotions.

Another charge that involved the affidavit Kasztner had given in Becher's favor presented the prosecution with a thorny problem. On this point, Cohn's line of reasoning was: Is the question of whether giving an affidavit in favor of a Nazi a 'national duty' or a 'national crime' a legal issue or an issue between a man and his conscience?

The question whether Kasztner had the authority to testify on behalf of the Jewish Agency and the Jewish Congress remained open. Eliahu Dobkin's testimony was contradicted by Kasztner's, and "the defense did not call Mr. Barlas, who is in Jerusalem, to testify, and a conclusion can be drawn from that."

The things Kasztner wrote in his letter to Kaplan ought not to be taken at face value, but understood as a reflection of his character:

I am prepared to allow that Kasztner was boasting here, as is his wont, because he likes to portray himself as someone who is at the top of the pile—but what does that prove? How does his boasting make him a traitor [...]?

Cohn ended his summation with a dramatic gesture. He quoted excerpts from a letter from a man whose name had come up more than once during the trial: "That same saintly man, Rabbi Weissmandl from Bratislava whom the defendant would probably even today hold in esteem." Among other things, he wrote in his letter: "My Jewish brethren, have you gone mad? Don't you know what kind of hell we are living in? [...] Who has given you permission to ask him for a reckoning?" After he finished reading this quote, Cohn paused for a moment, turned to Judge Halevi and in a loud voice asked him: "Have we gone mad, Your Honor? Who are they who have come here to heap their obscenities upon people who have given their blood?" A deathly silence fell upon the courtroom. But before taking his seat again, he turned to Halevi and added a sentence: "I ask Your Honor to convict the accused of the offense with which he is charged."

XVII

After the prosecutor's summation, Tamir delivered his own. He was given the last word because officially he was counsel for the defense. As a result, he enjoyed the best of both worlds: a de facto prosecutor who enjoyed the privileges of the defense counsel. After he was through, Halevi declared a recess in the trial until he pronounced his verdict and the sentence.

Tamir was even more trenchant and relentless than Cohn. He did not pose any rhetorical questions nor did he deal with hypothetical issues. He defended Gruenwald, or to be more precise, he accused Kasztner, with unparalleled ferocity. There were no doubts, quandaries or question marks in his words, nothing that could be variously understood or interpreted.

Tamir took full advantage of the fact that he was speaking after Cohn, and he related to the prosecutor's arguments one by one. "Not a single word uttered by the Attorney General remained unanswered. Every one of Cohn's hits called forth a counter-blow," *Haolam Hazeh* wrote.

The courtroom was jammed when Tamir gave his summation, and a crush of people crowded at the doorway hoping to push their way inside. Those who did manage to get in did not leave the courtroom, not even during the recess. One seat remained empty—the prosecutor's. At the end of his speech, Cohn declared that to his regret he was unable to stay, "to hear the summation of my learned friend." He left behind a rearguard in the form of his assistant, Tel, who towards the end of the trial found himself in the very same position he had been at its beginning—alone. The one who regretted Cohn's absence was Tamir. He declared that he did not like to attack a man in his absence, but he overcame his dislike and attacked him, again and again, with a vengeance.

The dramatic tenor of his summation made headlines, especially in those newspapers sympathetic to the defense. For example, the editorial in *Kol Ha'am*, the journal of the Communist party, on the first day of Tamir's speech (October 23, 1954) carried the headline "Kasztner must be tried under the Nazis and Nazi Collaborators (Punishment) Law.

Tamir's summation was devoted to a harsh attack on the wartime leaders of the Jewish Agency, who just happened to be the leaders of Mapai, some of whom also held key positions in the young state. Tamir appended a rather unusual document to his speech, entitled "A List of the Lies of the Prosecution Witnesses." According to it, in his testimony, Kasztner had lied 63 times, Menachem Bader—27 [times], Ehud Avriel—10 [times] and "Palgi's lies I couldn't even count."

Unlike Cohn, Tamir did not open his speech with the "Brand affair," saving that juicy story and the chance it gave him to deal with the big fish in Jerusalem, rather than the small fry in Budapest, for the third day. Instead, he opened with the Cluj ghetto episode, but before presenting a detailed account of his accusations, he went straight to the "bottom line" of his arguments. To do so, he quoted the Attorney General's statement "either death to Kasztner or death to Gruenwald at God's hands." He declared that although he was not saying "death to Kasztner," his aim was to show how a man "who was not a criminal from birth, a man who is not all bad" became "a man very dangerous to the fate of European Jewry;" how a "young Zionist, a member of a movement who believed in its ideology [...] a man afflicted with some serious weaknesses, and yet blessed with talents and fine qualities," had sunk so low as to become "a trusted intimate of Nazi leaders in Europe in 1944–1945."

Ostensibly Tamir did all this to achieve the formal goal of the trial—to clear his client, Malkiel Gruenwald, of the charge of libel. But his sights were set on far more important goals. One was to denounce Kasztner, he wanted to show that Kasztner "had knowingly lied in this court of law" and that he and his colleagues "had entered into a conspiracy to hide the facts from the court and to keep the court and the world from learning the historical truth, by appearing here and willfully giving false testimony." He also recommended "this Dr. Kasztner be placed on trial by the state of Israel under the Nazi and Nazi Collaborators (Punishment) Law."

His second goal was an historical one—to rip the mantle of falsehood, forgetfulness and silence that covered the Holocaust of Europe's Jews. From the time of the war and the mass extermination, "a kind of idyll of forgetfulness, of dissimulation, has prevailed," as if the horrible Holocaust had never been. As a result:

> The great majority of the assassins were set free and became the leaders of a great power; collaborators of all kinds infiltrated and returned to the

bosom of society; the sacred blood is gone, replaced by ransom money; and the memory of a great, spirited, vibrant nation is material for sites of commemoration.

However, Tamir went on, "that raging blood is not becalmed" and hence it is no accident that one drop of it "permeated and burst forth [...] up to the courtroom in Jerusalem and has forced us all to open the book of the Holocaust, to change its annals and to learn a lesson [from it]." The motif of "ripping the mantle of deceit" that he employed enabled him to divert his accusations from Kasztner to the Zionist establishment as a whole and Mapai in particular. In his view, it was this establishment that had created the "mantle of deceit and silence," and had covered up for Kasztner for years, and probably what he had to hide.

Using the motif of cover-up and camouflage, he turned Gruenwald, and in fact himself, into David, as a man who had defeated Goliath, the hydra-headed apparatus that had created the conspiracy of silence. Thus, he transformed Kasztner and the heads of the Jewish Agency—no longer men confused, stunned and despairing in the face of the extermination of Europe's Jews, they were now calculating demons that had planned everything down to the last detail. The Attorney General was not the only one defending Kasztner, he argued, many others—persons and institutions—had preceded him. They covered up for him at the Zionist Congress in Basel in 1946; they covered up for him at the 'Haganah' trial that same year; Minister Dov Joseph covered up for him in 1952:

> They all covered up! And when the Congress covers up, and the largest faction at the Congress covers up [...] when the 'Haganah' covers up, and when Minister Dov Joseph covers up, along comes a private individual, an old man; he reveals [the truth] and it was his duty to do so.

Tamir is not the father of the "conspiracy theory" but he elevated it into an art. It originated during the war years, when the Revisionist movement, then at the sidelines of the political stage and public consciousness, fiercely attacked the heads of the Jewish Agency, 'the Rehavia nobility', as they were referred to. The movement had accused the heads of the Jewish Agency of obscuring news about the Holocaust because they were indifferent to the plight of Europe's Jews and had turned a deaf ear to their cries for help[78].

---

78 See: Yechiam Weitz, "Revisionist Criticism of the Yishuv Leadership During the Holocaust," *Yad Vashem Studies*, vol. 13 (1993), pp. 369–396.

Tamir's line of argumentation can, therefore, be viewed as a polished, perfected version of the approach adopted by the Revisionist movement a decade earlier. The essence of that approach—during both the forties and the fifties—was to exploit the hard feelings aroused by any confrontation with the Holocaust, in order to delegitimize the ruling party, to undermine its status and to depict it as a monster.

XVIII

After his general introduction, Tamir discussed in detail several of the episodes covered in the trial. The first was the lamentable case of the Cluj ghetto. His argument was unequivocal:

> A community of about 20,000 Jews, one of the finest in Hungary, many of whose inhabitants could have been saved, was knowingly abandoned in order to rescue 380 of Kasztner's friends and close associates […] these 380 persons, all of whom are of course happy to have remained alive, were not an **achievement**; they were a **price** paid for the abandonment of thousands [emphasis in the original].

Tamir used this affair to show how that man "who is not a criminal by birth, not all bad, and you can't say he's just bloodthirsty," sank to the depths of moral depravity. To do so, he drew a distinction between a 'collaborator' and a 'traitor.' Treason, he explained, is a one-time act; a man receives some form of remuneration and in exchange he "betrays a regiment or provides some information and that's the end of his function." For this reason, in the Europe of 1944, "the traitor is not an effective tool […] in the hands of the enemy." Who, then, constitutes an 'effective tool'?" The collaborator. According to Tamir, this concept is underpinned by an idea that is amazing in its diabolic efficacy.

> Take someone from your adversary's camp, and begin playing a game with him, a game in which he continues to head his nation, he remains its leader. He can show his people achievements; he can point to successes, to changes. **But to pay for these successes, he smashes their skulls** [emphasis added].

The classic collaborators of World War II were Vidkun Quisling in Norway and Henri Petain and Pierre Laval in France. These were people who could not be bought for money. The enemy gives them a "subjective, psychological way out. Quisling saved Norway from destruction. Petain saved Paris; he saved all of southern France from ruin and destruction. He succeeded in saving hundreds of thousands of lives. But he relinquished France's freedom."

After the war, these collaborators became symbols of national shame, treachery and infamy. But Kasztner puts generals and prime ministers, men who were famous even before the occupation, in the shade. Kasztner, the godforsaken functionary from a godforsaken committee in Budapest. Compared to him, they are practically the most righteous of men. Why?

Because Kasztner's kind of collaboration was not one that relinquished merely freedom and honor, but a collaboration that was part of a process of biological extermination, of genocide, after which nothing remains. This is a collaboration that one cannot even justify with a platitude like: times will change and things will be different.

Only one single motif, Tamir asserted, lay behind Kasztner's reprehensible actions: his morbid, deranged ambition. When Eichmann offered him the train, "the little journalist from Cluj who had never been fussy about the means he used and was being driven over the edge by his morbid ambition and thirst for power 'came to terms' with his conscience." The whole process began rolling forward from this point in his agreement, "He was caught in the cogwheels and then the mill began grinding him up too."

Thus, Tamir explained Kasztner's acts; he fell into a diabolical, well-planned trap laid for him by the Nazis, whose aim it was to entice him into it with the use of bait and then to make him a key element in the extermination process. This was clear from his conversation with Eichmann, who said, "All is lost. Your damned Jews will go to their death. There's nothing you can do about it, in any case you will all be exterminated. But I can still save something, and in return, you'll help me."

It was this satanic alliance that sealed the fate of the Jews of Cluj, and caused them to go like lambs to the slaughter. Tamir presented his argument with ironclad logic: If the fate of the entire Jewish community of Cluj had been of paramount importance to Kasztner, rather than the fate of those 388 favorites, then he would not have withheld [...] information about the cruel fate that awaited them. Those desperate masses would then not have been deprived of the only remaining weapon at their disposal: "Knowledge of the facts and despair." Their fate could have been different; "Knowledge of the facts would have led to despair, and despair might have led to some action." The information that Kasztner, in his folly and malevolence, withheld from the Jews of Cluj was, therefore, the one thing that kept the ghetto from rising up and resisting the Nazis.

Tamir then went on to what he regarded as the crucial issue—the reaction of the Zionist institutions, namely the Mapai leadership, to the extermination of European Jewry, a topic that was never mentioned in the now-forgotten indictment. Continuing with his integrative approach, which left no room for coincidence and in which everything was interconnected, Tamir joined Kasztner to the Mapai leaders. "It is impossible to understand Kasztner and the crisis he experienced without taking a realistic look at the relationship between the besieged and annihilated Diaspora of Europe and the Jewish communities of the free world; first and foremost—the Jewish community in Palestine," he said.

However, he asserted, this is not the reason this subject was introduced in the trial. It was introduced because "from a public and historical standpoint, this is the crux of the matter," despite the psychological anguish "that, by its very nature, it must be causing everyone in this courtroom."

> On this point, the defense is asking the Court to wrest itself of the environment in which it lives, to rise to a higher plane, to be prepared to pass sentence on an entire public, on the leadership of a public within which it lives and in whom it has faith. Psychologically this is an immensely difficult thing to do [...] and, even though this may be too heavy a burden for a single man to bear, the defense is inviting the Court to pronounce its verdict in light of the facts alone, and they are incontestable.

After this learned introduction, Tamir went back to hurling grave accusations. He defined his main charges against the leadership of the Yishuv in the following words:

> We submit that here in Israel, the official institutions yielded to the British authorities. They were not prepared to take any risks. They were in the grip of their own narrow-mindedness and their reluctance to relinquish internal power. And the result of all this was the deed I am compelled to call "the abandonment of European Jewry at its most bitter hour."

Tamir went on to ask some searching questions in order to stress the *galuti* behavior, the spinelessness and readiness of the Yishuv leaders to collaborate during the Holocaust: Why did the heads of the community suppress the news of the Holocaust? Why did they desert European Jewry? To this question, too, he had a ready answer. Cooperation with British foreign rule was more important to them than the fate of Europe's Jews. Here again, collaboration and the thirst for power led to silence that in turn led to inaction. A different, more heroic, manlier, national leadership would have done something to reduce the dimensions of the extermination.

Tamir's attitude towards Brand's mission was predictable. Since the Yishuv leadership regarded collaboration as a supreme value, it had to defend it at any cost. Therefore, Brand was turned over to the British; a step that Tamir claimed was taken willfully and deliberately. He also argued that Brand's failure to return to Budapest—which he defined as a "real catastrophe"—was the result of nefarious, irresponsible behavior. His return, he asserted, would have immediately put the German offers to the test.

He connected another matter with the Brand affair—Prime Minister Sharett's unwillingness to testify. I invited him to come here and present his evidence, Tamir contended, I gave Sharett, "who knows more about this affair than any other person," an opportunity to tell the whole truth and to make a laughing-stock of me, to prove that "I'm a blabbermouth who talks nonsense," but he refrained from doing so. Why did he refrain—Tamir tossed a rhetorical question into the air of the courtroom—out of disinterest, out of insolence? On the contrary, he replied, and advanced his "suppression and concealment theory" for the umpteenth time. "The only explanation for the Prime Minister's failure to appear here is his fear that the truth might surface while he is under cross-examination." Afterwards, he asked the court "to draw the obvious conclusion from the absence of a very important witness who did not appear, when he could and should have appeared."

Tamir was aware of a certain contradiction between the way he presented the Kasztner affair and the way he presented Brand's mission. For if the German offers were merely a trap intended to make their extermination program more efficient by preventing Budapest from becoming a "second Warsaw," why should Brand's mission have been considered seriously? But even if collaborating was the wrong thing to do, he stated, "If a man receives such an offer even from the devil himself, he has to pass it on." In this way, Tamir held on to both ends of the stick: anyone who agrees to the devil's offer is a traitor and a collaborator, as much as someone who rejects it.

XIX

Later in his summation, Tamir spoke about other events and episodes that came up in the trial, such as the parachutist and, particularly, Hannah Szenes and Becher. In discussing these topics, Tamir did not add a new dimension; he continued to adhere to his overall approach, which connected with precise planning and evil intent.

As for Szenes, he alleged that Kasztner did nothing to help her, not because of any bureaucratic reasons or his heavy workload. He deserted her cruelly because any contact with her might have sabotaged his collaboration. Szenes represented resistance and rebellion—the very opposite of everything he represented—hence he sacrificed her cold-bloodedly, to avoid impairing the cooperation between him and the Germans.

Then Tamir moved on to the matter of Becher, which provided him with the ultimate proof of Kasztner's treachery and consummated the process of his demonization—Kasztner saved Becher, "one of the exterminators of European Jewry, and Himmler's right-hand man," from the punishment he deserved, thus "leaving an indelible stain on the entire Jewish people." He did that although he had no authority to do so, and his aim was two-fold: "to save himself by preventing any discovery of the crimes he had committed together with Becher, and because he had joined with Becher in robbing the Jews of Hungary."

Despite the evidence on Kasztner's dire financial situation, Tamir depicted him as the man who, together with an SS officer, had stolen hundreds of thousands of dollars from the tortured and butchered Jews of Hungary. Mixing assumption and fact, fact and conclusion, he said:

> But it's a fact that Kasztner gave Becher more than two million dollars in Budapest. Becher handed over to Schweiger $50,000, part of it in counterfeit notes, pretending he had returned the entire sum, in order to secure an alibi. Kasztner helped him cover up the theft of one million nine hundred thousand dollars. He also helped him create the circumstances that made this cover-up possible. And **he did that only because he received his share of the loot** [emphasis added]

This was too much even for Judge Halevi. Where was the money? He asked Tamir—if he shared about two million dollars with Becher, he would have had one million for himself; where is this money? Without batting an eyelid,

Tamir replied that there is no connection between Kasztner's present lifestyle and the fabulous fortune he was hiding away somewhere. While it is true that he "lives like any other government official" and that no evidence was offered to show his current financial state, "his very demeanor proves that he is capable of keeping money in Switzerland."

After turning Kasztner into a thief, Tamir began to sum up. He was obviously under great tension. Pale and agitated, on the verge of exhaustion, he closed the circle by again presenting the two points with which he had begun his speech. One was the request to acquit the accused and, "through him, the defense and, with all due respect, the Court as well:"

> To broach for the first time after ten years, from this lofty podium, the subject of the Holocaust [of] our people, to reveal the truth to its very core, without any bias and with no ax to grind—personal, factional or partisan—but rather out of a sacred sense of our indebtedness, of the great debt we owe to those who are no longer with us, who were not privileged to come to the state, and to those who lived and did come [to make their homes] here.

The second point was the appeal to the Court "to add honor to the state of Israel, by acceding to his request and recommending that an investigation of the truth be conducted in a legal setting and by a public commission of inquiry," because the truth must emerge and a judgment must be handed down. If the request is accepted, he said, the "exalted court will rise [...] above any consideration of prestige or interest" and will consider "nothing but truth, conscience and the obligation to the past, the present and the future."

Haolam Hazeh used superlatives to describe Tamir's speech:

> One of the most brilliant speeches ever heard in an Israeli courtroom. Tamir was scathing, laudatory, moralistic and abusive, he passed through all the points on the rhetorical scale, he once even donned a yarmulke to quote to Judge Halevi [who always wears one] verses from the Bible and the Talmud.

Tel's complaint that Tamir was speaking to a jury, not to a judge, was correct, in the weekly's view, "Tamir spoke not only to the judge, but to the Israeli public at large."[79]

---

79 "The Kasztner Affair—the Last Word," *Haolam Hazeh*, October 5, 1954.

When he ended his summation, the curtain fell on the trial that had begun on a weak and subdued note and quickly turned into an event that shook the very foundations of Israeli life. Nine months later, on the longest day of the summer of 1955, the curtain rose again.

CHAPTER FIVE

The Verdict

I

With Tamir's summation completed, the court adjourned and Judge Halevi secluded himself at home to write his verdict. The trial was taken off the public agenda and people's attention shifted to more urgent matters. In 1955, Israel was preparing for a series of election campaigns, a general election for the Third Knesset and local municipal elections, both scheduled for the end of July—the height of summer. Tensions rose as the date approached. Prime Minister Sharett's moderate policy of appeasement was the object of much criticism; there was friction within the coalition between the Mapai party and its senior partner, the General Zionists. Also, the Herut Movement was encouraged by the thought that the bitterness of many thousands of new immigrants could be converted into the kind of political capital that might just help it overcome its painful defeat in the previous elections to the Second Knesset, when it had lost almost half its 14 Knesset seats. And, having broken away from Mapam and forming an opposition to the left of the Prime Minister's line the radical Achdut Ha'avoda movement was running on a separate ticket.

In the foreground of such highly charged events, the Kasztner/Gruenwald trial was pushed to the fringes of public interest. However, although it had effectively been shoved aside, it did not go away. Following the attorneys' summations in the District Court, *Haolam Hazeh* continued to print news items connected with the trial. For example, a mere two days after Tamir completed his speech, *Haolam Hazeh* reported the government's intention to appoint Attorney General Cohn to the position of Israel's permanent delegate to the United Nations, thus giving him an appointment that would "honorably remove him from his [present] position."[1]

---

1   "Observation," *Haolam Hazeh*, October 5, 1954.

From early 1955, attention was focused on the question of why Halevi was taking so long to pronounce his verdict. On March 15, 1955 the issue was raised in the Knesset plenary when Communist Party M.K. Meir Vilner submitted a question about "the date when the verdict in the Gruenwald-Kasztner trial would be published."[2] The question contained four points: Is there any truth in the rumor that government circles are prevaricating over the publication of the verdict? If so, who are the people that make up these government circles? If not, what is causing the delay? When will it finally be published? Not unexpectedly, the Minister of Justice claimed that the rumor was baseless, that "the pronouncement of the verdict has not been delayed; it is still simply not ready," that it depends solely on the court, and he has reason to believe that "the verdict will be published at the end of May." Thus, the decision, which depended entirely on the President of the District Court, became part of the putative conspiracy aimed at sweeping the whole embarrassing affair under the carpet. After the verdict, it would become evident that the ruling party, whose adversaries believed was simultaneously omnipotent and terrified, had totally lost control of a great many things.

Tamir, in the meantime, was not resting on his laurels and continued circulating his interpretation of the events outside the court transcript. When he learned that Rosenfeld, with whom he was friendly, was writing a book on the subject, he hastened to arrange a meeting with him, immediately after which he sent him a letter.[3] "Although I have great respect for your work and your writing skills," he wrote, "I felt very despondent when I left your home on Friday [… because of the] feeling that historical falsehoods are likely to be perpetuated through your book." He would not have been so concerned, had he not attributed so much national importance to these matters, and "had I not known that because you are the writer, these things would carry some degree of authority. [People will say] 'Even Rosenfeld saw it in that light.'" As for the concrete reasons for his uneasy feeling, he wrote:

> If, in your book, the main version of the facts, for example the Cluj matter, comes from Kasztner, Herman and Danzig, the truth can surface only if emphasis is laid on the 'minor details' that I tried to point out to you, and which you brushed aside. When all is said and done, all of these people reached their high positions—despite their past—largely

2   Knesset records, vol. 18, p. 1384.
3   Tel Aviv, December 12, 1954. I am deeply grateful to Shalom Rosenfeld for giving me the letter.

because of their ability to find devious formulations for dark deeds. For that reason, for truth's sake, the **facts** are crucially important, more than their interpretation of the facts [emphasis in the original]

After apologizing for the fact that his comments "are apt to be taken as petty, narrow-minded faultfinding," Tamir goes on to ask Rosenfeld to restore an omitted excerpt to the text, because that excerpt "can somewhat offset Kasztner's declamation. Whereas it appears to merely shorten the text, in fact, it changes the entire picture, and gives disproportional weight to Kasztner's false statements, without presenting an opposing view." In a sharper tone, he wrote "I am not demanding any privileges, but I will be frank, as I usually am: I am terribly worried. Believe it or not, first and foremost, it's the facts I am anxious about and I am concerned that the awful clarity with which they were exposed may be dimmed. And for all our friendship, [I believe] there is cause for my fears."

Throughout May, over six months after the end of the legal proceedings, rumors were spreading that the verdict was imminent. The rumor was first published in Mapai's evening newspaper, *Hador*[4], and it evoked a flurry of intense activity. Scores of journalists contacted the District Court secretary, Moshe Atzor, who insisted the information was groundless and did not come from court sources. When the journalists persisted, the secretary picked up the phone and, with obvious reluctance, called Judge Halevi at home. He knew that the judge, who no longer appeared at the court, "was secluded in his home in order to complete his work on the most difficult verdict in the judicial history of the state of Israel. He also knew that the judge was enraged by anything that reminded him of journalists, or of the date on which the verdict was to be announced."

When the judge answered the phone and heard the question, he reacted with obvious exasperation, advising the reporters to ask their colleagues at *Hador* for the source of their information and asked them to wait for an official announcement regarding the verdict. Malkiel Gruenwald, who also heard the rumors, had only one concern—that any fine imposed on him by the judge should be in excess of five pounds, the minimum sum that would enable him to submit an appeal.[5]

4 "The Verdict in the Gruenwald Case—Next Week," *Hador*, May 11, 1955; among other things, the article stated, "the verdict is ready and [according to our information] contains more than 200 pages."

5 "The Kasztner Affair—A False Alarm," *Haolam Hazeh*, May 19, 1955.

II

The country was gripped by election fever and the date for submitting the candidate lists had been set for early June. This time the question was, who would be representing the Hungarian *landsmanshaft* on the party slate— would it be Kasztner, who had been nominated to the First and Second Knessets, or would the honor, which ensured a place on the slate but not necessarily a Knesset seat, go to someone else? The verdict in the trial had not yet been passed, but it was already clear that Kasztner was not about to emerge from it a victor or a national hero.

A fierce struggle took place over the 'Hungarian seat,' " even though it was not a sure thing. *Ma'ariv* reported on May 21 that the Hungarian contingent in Mapai had chosen Kasztner, "although, he was amicably requested at the same time to relinquish his candidacy." Kasztner acceded to this request and his announcement that he had withdrawn his candidacy "was received with accolades and a show of friendship." The fear was that "[Kasztner's] candidacy might provide a target for the barbs of the rival slates." All the other candidates—Dezső (David) Herman, Hillel Danzig and Eliezer Walter—were associated with the Kasztner affair. Danzig was placed in the 53rd slot on the slate for the Third Knesset, in place of Kasztner.[6]

At around the same time, Kasztner's job at the *Kol Israel* radio station was discontinued. The reason was that the studios broadcasting in Romanian and Hungarian were being moved from Tel Aviv to Jerusalem and Kasztner was unable to relocate there with his family. "It is with much regret that I am forced to inform you of the discontinuation of your work in the broadcasting service as of April 30, 1955," Zvi Zinder, the acting manager of the broadcasting service, informed him in a letter.[7] We have no way of knowing whether or not this was simply an elegant pretext to get rid of him, but one thing is certain: his dismissal must have exacerbated his feeling that everything was closing in on him.

Early June saw increasing rumors of an imminent verdict. "The veil will be removed in another fifteen days," wrote *Haolam Hazeh*.[8] On June 21, the news was out that Judge Halevi would begin reading his verdict the following

6   "Danzig Selected in Place of Kasztner," *Ma'ariv*, May 22, 1955.
7   On this matter, see his letter to Kasztner, Jerusalem, April 3, 1955, as well as a letter from Gedaliyahu Yaari, Acting Deputy Director-General of the Prime Minister's Office, Jerusalem, May 31, 1955, Suzi Kasztner-Michael's collection.
8   "The Kasztner Affair—Smoke without Fire," *Haolam Hazeh*, June 4, 1955.

day, Wednesday, in hall number two of the Supreme Court building. The secretariat of the court geared itself for the event by preparing 120 stenciled copies of the verdict so that every journalist could purchase one for two Israeli pounds. It also announced that the judge would not read out the entire verdict but only excerpts from it, and only after he decided which parts he would read publicly, would he decide when the journalists would get copies. The police also prepared for the event and stationed a special guard in the courtroom to maintain order.[9]

III

Halevi entered the packed courtroom and everyone present tried to guess by his expression what his verdict would be. But his face was inscrutable. Only his pallor revealed the heavy toll—physical and psychological—that writing the verdict had taken on him. Many of the heroes of the drama were present in the courtroom, first and foremost, the accused Malkiel Gruenwald, who was seated opposite the judge. He was in high spirits. "Why the hurry?" he said to his daughter Rina, who was rushing him along to get to the court early, "our seats have been reserved." To his right sat his defense attorney, Shmuel Tamir, and to his left, the lawyer for the prosecution, Tel. On this occasion, too, the Attorney General, who had not come to hear Tamir's summation, was absent.

Several of Kasztner's associates were in the courtroom, including the attorney Dezső Herman and Shmuel Springman, as well as Hanzi Brand, whose entrance was greeted by murmurs from the crowd. The man most conspicuous by his absence was Israel Kasztner, himself. That morning he had traveled to Jerusalem with Hanzi and closeted himself in the Moriah rooming house, waiting tensely for the outcome. Unlike the cheerful Gruenwald, Kasztner had been pessimistic and gloomy during the days leading to the verdict. All attempts by Hanzi and other friends to raise his spirits were of no avail. Nonetheless, he adamantly rejected her suggestion that he leave the country. "I must remain here, where my honor has been sullied, in order to fight to restore it," he told her.[10]

---

9 On this matter see, for example, "The Verdict in the Kasztner Trial Today," *Kol Ha'am*, June 22, 1955.
10 Prat, *The Great Trial*, pp. 219–220; Brand, *Satan and the Soul*, pp. 157–158.

The reading of the verdict began at 8 a.m. and continued until late in the evening. Halevi read the verdict in a soft voice. The verdict, which consisted of over 200 pages, was divided into several sections. The first, "The Holocaust in the Provincial Towns," dealt with the painful case of the deportation and annihilation of the Jews of Cluj. After comparing the defense testimonies with others—especially those by Herman and Danzig, the judge reached conclusions wholly compatible with the version presented by Tamir in his summation:

> The Jews of Cluj had boarded the deportation trains "not knowing the true destination of their journey and believing the false information [they had been given] that they were being transferred to a work camp in Hungary (Kenyermezo)." The Nazis had been successful in tricking the Jews because "they spread their devious rumors through Jewish channels. The Jews of the ghetto would not have trusted Nazi or Hungarian rulers, but they believed their Jewish leaders."
>
> Since the Jews of Cluj were unaware that they were going to be exterminated, they did not take advantage of the opportunity to flee the ghetto and cross the border safely into Romania. The same Jews who spread the false rumors in the ghetto did not warn their own people, organized no resistance to the deportations, and did not join their community on their journey to Auschwitz. Most of them were among the passengers of the rescue train instead."[11]

The next section dealt with Kasztner's agreement with the SS concerning a rescue train for a select number of individuals. On this point, Halevi's conclusion was unequivocal: as far as the Nazis were concerned, their negotiations in Hungary had a single purpose—"to obtain the collaboration of the Jewish leaders in Budapest and the provincial towns [...]" Since they never did anything for nothing, they "allowed a small number of Jews to be saved, in order to seize the others more easily." The Nazis were prepared to lend a hand to these rescue operations because of "their diligence [...] in preventing any resistance to or any interference with the implementation of their plan."

---

11 *The Verdict in the Trial of the Attorney General vs. Malkiel Gruenwald* (Hebrew) (Tel Aviv: Karni Publishing House, 1955), pp. 22–24. The verdict was also published in book form by Karni publishing house, which specializes in books connected with the history of the IZL and the Revisionist movement.

Halevi related to the train not as the rescue of a few from a sea of annihilation, but rather as the rescue of privileged individuals **at the expense** of attempted action to reduce the dimensions of the annihilation. On this crucial point, therefore, the judge adopted the defense counsel's position.

His words were razor sharp: Kasztner had been given an opportunity not only to save a group of Jews, but to choose which of them would be saved: "If he wished—his relatives; if he wished—his friends; if he wished—members of his movement, and if he wished—the prominent Jews of Hungary." He perceived the possibility of saving this group as "a great success, both personally and for Zionism. It was a success that would also justify his conduct—his political negotiations with Nazis, his 'takeover' of the political contact with the ruling power, the exhausting negotiations, and the Nazi patronage of his committee." To figuratively describe the trap into which Kasztner had fallen, he said:

> But *timeo Danaos et dona ferentes* ('beware of Greeks bearing gifts'). By accepting this gift Kasztner had sold his soul to the devil.

IV

Even years later, when the details of the trial had been largely lost from memory, it was impossible to forget this phrase—"sold his soul to the devil." It was not an everyday occurrence for a judge to deviate from "deliberately complicated, colorless legal terminology and to retrieve an expression from the vocabulary of the religious inquisition."[12] In the Jerusalem courtroom, these words fell like a bomb. Hanzi Brand could not believe her ears—she thought her senses were deceiving her. Afterwards, she rose demonstratively from her seat and made her way outside. "I saw no point in sitting there any longer," she wrote. The first to leave had been Dezső Herman. The two went to the hotel, to tell Kasztner how grave the verdict was.

No longer than half an hour had passed since the judge began reading his verdict, and it was already clear to one and all what the verdict would be. "People were no longer thinking about the judgment. It was psychologically impossible to reflect on it. All the tension was concentrated on the logical,

---

12 Uri Avneri, "The Moderate Fanatic," *Haolam Hazeh*, July 24, 1974.

incisive words issuing from the judge's mouth."[13] "Kasztner sold his soul to the devil," blared the headline in *Ma'ariv*.

Halevi realized in time that he had made a grave mistake, that the expression had been too loaded and that in the verdict of a trial that aroused such strong emotions, it would have been wiser to employ under-, rather than overstatement. As he told *Ma'ariv* after his resignation from the Supreme Court:

> This sentence was misinterpreted. In the context of what I said in the verdict, the reference was to the first 600 emigration permits that Krumey gave Kasztner to bind him to him and make him dependent on Eichmann and the Gestapo. I explained how very tempting Eichmann's 'gift' was [...] this figurative expression came immediately after the heading [...] as I said, it was misunderstood, and if I had foreseen how this expression would be interpreted, I would not have used it. It was not crucial.[14]

V

Halevi continued reading the verdict and arrived at the matter of the parachutists, Goldstein and Palgi. Here too his conclusions were decisive: Kasztner applied very heavy moral pressure on the two parachutists, compelling them to relinquish their mission; by prompting them to turn themselves over to the Gestapo, he was endangering their lives. Not content to merely state his conclusions regarding Kasztner's behavior, the judge also tried to examine his motives:

> The arrival of the parachutists placed Kasztner in a dilemma that touched the roots of his loyalty. On the one hand, he was called upon to provide shelter and assistance to two Haganah members; on the other hand, he had in fact long before undertaken to give his loyalty to the Nazi regime; not from love of the Nazis, heaven forbid, but, under the

---

13 Brand, *Satan and the Soul*, p. 158; Rosenfeld, *Criminal Case*, p. 406; Prat, *The Great Trial*, p.122.

14 From an interview with Raphael Bashan, *Ma'ariv*, October 3, 1969; in an article on Halevi, Shlomo Nakdimon wrote, "Apparently, he himself now believes the sentence may have been too harsh." ("From the Supreme Court Bench—to the Back Benches of the Knesset," *Yedioth Ahronoth*, March 14, 1975.)

circumstances, as a prerequisite and basis for his joint endeavor with the Nazis, which depended on their mercy. His most vital interests—the rescue project, the fate of the survivors, the fate of his relatives, and his own safety—compelled Kasztner to be totally loyal to the ruler. The totalitarian regime did not suffer 'dual loyalty.'

Halevi said something similar with regard to the tragic case of Hannah Szenes. This was not a disastrous coincidence, stemming primarily from the unbearable, inhuman tension Kasztner was subjected to, but yet another aspect of the 'method.' Release of the parachutist, who represented a set of norms and values antithetical to that which Kasztner represented, might have impaired his contacts with the Nazis.

On the question of what Kasztner knew about the Nazis' intentions and what he did with the information he possessed, the judge concluded that owing to his position, Kasztner knew a great deal about the bitter fate awaiting the hundreds of thousands of Jews. "From the early days of Nazi occupation, he did not delude himself as to the true objective of Eichmann and his gang in Hungary. He knew that the appearance of the 'Jew Commando' in Hungary, after more than five million Jews from all the previously occupied areas had been annihilated and after the horrors of Auschwitz, could mean only one thing—that [...] Auschwitz [was] ready for the large Jewish community of Hungary."

What did Kasztner do with this information? He did not distribute it among the Jews of Hungary, nor did he warn them of the bitter fate awaiting them. He did not do so because the only thing that truly interested him was the rescue train, and he was ready to give up everything for it:

One of the most shocking facts in this trial is that despite all the information possessed by the head of the rescue committee in Budapest, the masses of Jews in the provincial towns, about half a million men, women and children, unknowingly boarded the trains that carried them to Auschwitz, as victims of a malicious deception. The brutal truth is that the head of the Jewish rescue committee abandoned the large majority of Hungary's Jews to a fate that was known to him in advance, in order to save the few 'favored' individuals.

Kasztner, therefore, kept his agreement (with the Nazis) secret. Had it been disclosed, the masses of Jews would have understood that one fate awaited them while another awaited the favored ones. They would then have taken their fate into their own hands and rebelled. Here too, Halevi concurred with Tamir's position that Kasztner stood between the Jews of Hungary and the acts of resistance that would have reduced the dimensions of the annihilation. The prosecutor's claim that the rescue of the passengers on the train did not come instead of the rescue of hundreds of thousands was rejected.

When it came to Moshe Krausz's testimony, the judge once again accepted the defense's position, in other words, the witness' version. Totally ignoring the deep-seated antagonism between the two men, he viewed Krausz as Kasztner's direct opposite. Unlike Kasztner, Krausz had fulfilled his duty and had facilitated the rescue of thousands of Jews. Unlike Kasztner, who concealed essential information in his possession, Krausz created "good relations with the neutral legations and frequently provided them with precise information about the concentration of Hungary's Jews in ghettos and about the process of total deportation." Unlike Kasztner, who discriminated between one Jew and another, Krausz was a man "whose emigration certificates saved the lives of thousands of Jews under persecution by the Sztójay regime." Kasztner did nothing to help "and in some instances even hampered Krausz's activities and tried to abort his efforts." Why did he behave in this way? The judge's general, one-dimensional and sweeping explanation of Kasztner's deeds and failures applied to this instance as well:

> Taking note of Kasztner's subjugation to the SS throughout the lengthy period beginning with the holocaust in the provincial towns, I accept his explanation […] that Kasztner interfered with Krausz as a result of his collaboration with the Nazis, who had forbidden him to negotiate with anyone else and also, through him, sabotaged other people's independent rescue actions.

From this conclusion, the judge drew another: The whole affair of Brand's mission and subsequent arrest, with all it implied about the behavior of the Jewish Agency, was not relevant to the trial. Therefore, "the Court is obliged to refrain from making any findings in regard to this controversy."

Towards the end of the verdict, the judge related to Kasztner's relations with Becher, which the defense viewed as the ultimate proof of Kasztner's collaboration.

First, he stated, Kurt Becher "was a war criminal as defined in the main verdict of the international tribunal in Nuremberg and the verdicts handed down based on it. On the basis of those proofs, I am convinced that Kasztner knew that Becher was a war criminal."

A great deal of weight was given to Kasztner's affidavit in Becher's favor:

> It is clear that Kasztner's favorable affidavit, stating that Becher had courageously saved thousands of Jews, contradicting Hitler's aims of exterminating [Jews], [that he gave] in the name of the representative institutions of the Jewish people, was of decisive importance for Becher. Kasztner did not exaggerate when he said, in his letter to the late E. Kaplan, that Becher was released thanks to his personal intervention.

In his testimony in court, Kasztner knowingly perjured himself when he denied he had interceded on Becher's behalf. Moreover, he concealed the important fact that he interceded for Becher in the name of the Jewish Agency and the World Jewish Congress. As for the question of whether Kasztner had been authorized to do so by these institutions, Halevi stated:

> I do not believe that Mr. Dobkin gave Kasztner permission to give his affidavit in the name of the Jewish Agency. In all the above-mentioned circumstances, I am convinced that Kasztner used the name of the Jewish Agency without permission.

One after another, Halevi enumerated the six "concrete results" of the negotiations between Kasztner and Becher, and concluded that there were no grounds for the contents of the affidavit. He stated that the Bergen-Belsen train was "not a result of negotiations between Kasztner and Becher, but rather of negotiations between Kasztner and Eichmann"; "nor is there any proof that 85,000 Jews of the Budapest ghetto were saved as a result of Becher's intervention in the Hungarian puppet government's extermination plan." As for Becher's role in handing over concentration camps to the Allies, the verdict states:

> Kasztner knew very well that these actions were not "concrete results" of the negotiations between him and Becher, and that his role at Bergen-Belsen was merely to serve as an alibi witness. In this affidavit of his at Nuremberg, Kasztner gave Becher the alibi for which he had been summoned from the outset.

And the final conclusion was:

> The said affidavit in favor of Becher was willfully false [and] given in favor of a war criminal to save him from trial and punishment in

Nuremberg. Therefore, the defendant, Malkiel Gruenwald, has proven the truth of his accusation.

Only on page 204 of the 207-page long verdict, after leveling a long series of grave charges at the prosecution, did the judge find one accusation that remained unproven. Referring to clause 118 of the indictment, the judge stated, "the [third] count—collaboration in a robbery between Kasztner and Becher—has not been proved." Although Kasztner had been party to some serious discrepancies in relation to the "Becher treasure these […] cannot be viewed […] as proof that he shared the ransom money with Becher." Kasztner's behavior "in covering up for Becher from [the time] immediately after the war, trying to exonerate him in the eyes of the Jewish Agency and even saving him from a trial and from being punished for war crimes at Nuremberg, does indeed suggest strong and extraordinary motives, but it is not necessary to seek an explanation for them in the financial realm, as the defendant assumed in his newsletter." So what is the explanation? "Kasztner needed to exonerate and justify Becher in order to justify his own actions."

It was ten o'clock in the evening by the time the judge finished reading his verdict; time to pronounce his ruling. In less than one page the judge ruled that Malkiel Gruenwald was guilty of libel against Kasztner on the third charge (collaboration in a robbery), but he did not attribute much importance to that. Had this charge stood alone, he stated, "There would have been grounds for sentencing the defendant to real punishment" but, in light of his acquittal on all the other, far weightier, charges of libel, it would be unjust to levy more than a symbolic punishment." The defendant was fined "one Israeli pound for the offense he was found guilty of." The very next day, Gruenwald hastened to pay the fine.

VI

Halevi's verdict made all the headlines, several of which maintained a more neutral tone. The Progressive Party daily paper, *Zemanim*, wrote laconically, "A verdict has been handed down in the Kasztner-Gruenwald trial." The *Jerusalem Post* also ran a fairly noncommittal headline, according to which, "the Court found that Kasztner collaborated to 'rescue a few.'"

Other papers, with an obvious anti-Kasztner stance, had been anxiously waiting to pounce. *Lamerchav*, the daily newspaper affiliated with the Achdut Ha'avoda movement that was struggling to place itself on the political map, ran this headline: "The parachutists have been exonerated, Kasztner is indirectly guilty of murder; he served as a Gestapo tool to strangle Jewish resistance." This reflected the movement's activist image and its ambition to represent and express Jewish heroism in the Holocaust.

All the editorials over the next couple of days were devoted to the verdict. *Kol Ha'am* bore the particularly virulent headline, "The blood reckoning," and went on to announce that anyone whose relatives were slaughtered in Hungary, and not only in Hungary, "now knows **that Jews, who worked in the service of Jewish reactionaries, were party to a mass murder that was unprecedented in the history of the Jewish people**" [emphasis in the original]. The writer then went on to settle accounts with Mapai and, indeed, with the entire Zionist movement. Asking the question, "Who was that fellow who sold his soul to the devil and whose collaboration with the Nazis was criminal in every sense of the word?" the article replied, again in bold letters, **"Kasztner, one of the leaders of Mapai"** [emphasis in the original]. The editorial concluded by saying that the court's verdict did not constitute the end of the affair. First of all, Kasztner and his associates should now be arrested immediately and tried under the Nazis and Nazi Collaborators (Punishment) Law. And further investigations should be conducted to unearth others guilty of these crimes and to bring them all to justice, **"no matter who they are"** [emphasis in the original].

The Agudat Israel party's paper, *Hamodi'a*, on the other hand, regarded the verdict as proof that the religious Jew is superior to the secular Jew; Kasztner's failure is the failure of secular Zionism and the verdict is clear proof of that:

> Love of the Jewish people and rescue of the Jewish people go hand in hand with the love of and faith in the God of Israel. And the work of rescue, when it is guided by profound religious feeling and conducted according to the rules of the Torah and tradition, is much more effective and beneficial. It can avoid those things that are carried out rashly and carelessly.[15]

In *Hatzofeh*, the paper of religious Zionism, the headline was worded in a similar vein and went on to insist that it would be unthinkable for a devout

---

15 "The Echo of the Day," *Hamodi'a*, June 24, 1955.

Jew, who observed all the commandments, to be seduced into the trap of collaboration.[16]

VII

Only two national newspapers, the centrist Mapai party's *Davar* and *Ha'aretz*, avoided taking a firm stand on such a complex and highly charged issue. *Davar* was particularly cautious, writing that in his verdict "[the judge] undertook an enormous historical responsibility, assigning responsibility to those people who lived, acted and died under circumstances [...], which, hard as we try [...] we shall never be able to comprehend." Anyone in 1955 Jerusalem attempting to define "the way in which community leaders involved in rescue operations should have behaved and how [...] Jews should have behaved ten or fifteen years ago in the countries [in which] extermination [took place]" is undertaking an unbearable responsibility. Therefore, **the courage of [this] single judge [who took on such a responsibility] can only be wondered at.**" The article went on, "Previously, after thorough and prudent deliberation, the Supreme Court has, at times, overturned the verdicts of judges, **including some by the judge who gave this verdict**." This case, therefore, should not be considered closed [emphases added].[17]

In *Ha'aretz*, the editorial was more hesitant and more detailed: Halevi took upon himself a task that was beyond his ability, authority and responsibility. To arrive at the definitive truth in such a highly charged affair, on the basis of "the contradictory and incomplete testimonies of people who have never, nor ever will, recover from the shock of the upheaval that shook their lives in the troubled months eleven years ago [... is] a task too enormous for one man to undertake."

A cautious verdict, one that "left room for some doubt and reservations," would have been more just, the paper argued, "than this verdict, that sees but two colors, black and white." Although the judge did examine and weigh every detail, "it is this very thoroughness that gave rise to the superficiality of the verdict. For some reason, he was unable to see that together these trees form a forest—and what a forest! A forest full of poisonous trees, in which the air is so compressed as to render it hard to breathe, in which there are no paths and where no one can take a step without getting lost."

16 "On the Edges of the Verdict," *Hatzofeh*, June 23, 1955.
17 "Word of the Day," *Davar*, June 23, 1955. This article and others referred to the prosecution's decision to file an appeal against Halevi's verdict.

The article then posed some brusque, piercing questions. For example: "How could the judge ignore the extraordinary circumstances that prevailed in Hungary in 1944? How, in the peaceful Israel of 1955, did he presume to know "how these people, and Dr. Kasztner in particular, should have acted during those months?"

It is true, the article concluded, that "we are a long way from turning Dr. Kasztner into a national hero," but he had "no experience [...] in dealing with those beasts of prey that walked about in the guise of men." Hence, the verdict, "couched in a language [...] that is often more fitting to a defense counsel's speech than to a judge's considered opinion, is not only unproven, but erroneous and unjust."

It was the opinion of many that a solitary judge should not have undertaken a task of this kind, nor to reach such far-reaching conclusions. Even the anti-Kasztner *Lamerchav* wrote, "There is doubt as to whether the matter was given serious consideration and whether it was a responsible act on the part of the nation to burden a solitary judge with such an enormous task."

VIII

Coming in the midst of a ferocious election campaign, Halevi's verdict struck the political system like a bolt of lightning. Most of all, it harmed the ruling party. On the day it was given, Sharett wrote in his diary:[18] "A note [from Yael Vered, his personal secretary] about [the verdict in the Kasztner trial] [...] a new blow [...] a nightmare—dreadful, what did the judge take upon himself! A stranglehold on the party, running riot." From that day on, the man who served as both Prime Minister and Foreign Minister devoted many hours of his busy schedule to deal with the various implications of the verdict, beginning with a consultation with Teddy Kollek and Haim Barlas. On the same evening he discussed with Justice Minister Pinhas Rosen the possibility of an appeal. The following day, he discussed the issue again; a day later he had a long talk about it with Avriel and briefed *Ha'aretz* journalist Moshe Keren, who wrote a series of articles on the subject. On Sunday, June 26, he met once again with Avriel (in his diary, he wrote: "with Ehud on the train").[19]

---

18 "From Day to Day—Reading the Verdict," *Ha'aretz*, June 24, 1955.
19 "With Astonishment and Bewilderment," *Lamerchav*, June 23, 1955.

The subject also arose in the many election rallies that Sharett organized; the things he said at these rallies were sober and cautious—it was, after all, the verdict of a respected judge.

However, in a speech at a closed forum,[20] Sharett was more outspoken in mentioning the testimony of "our fellow party member Hillel Danzig," who, when asked by the judge: "What would you have done if they were going to take you and your wife to the death train?" had replied: "I don't know." When the judge continued to press him, the witness said that it was very hard, in 1955 Jerusalem, to say what he would have done in 1944 Cluj. When the flabbergasted judge asked, "What does that mean, don't you remember what was happening there at the time?" Danzig replied, "I remember very well what was happening at the time, I remember very well that the situation was so different from the situation now that I am completely unable to say how I would have behaved then."

Sharett pointed out scornfully that these words of Danzig's had led the judge to conclude that the witness was evading the question. With thinly veiled irony, he related to this conclusion:

> In my opinion, [these words] show something totally different. I said some important things about the judge that I do not retract. I said that he is honest; I said that he is courageous and that he is a good jurist. I **did not say a fourth thing. I think that the testimony of our fellow party member Hillel Danzig is not only the height of honesty, but also the epitome of reason** [emphasis added].

Sharett related to the trial in another, very unexpected and very undesirable context, as well. In a letter, Recha Freier, a founder of Aliyat Hanoar (Youth Aliyah), had advised a change of name for the Leo Baeck School in Haifa. Sharett was shocked to hear that the reason "incredible as it may sound [was] that this rabbi had been responsible for the death of several Polish Jews in 1939." At first, Sharett felt it would be best to leave the wording of the reply to his office manager, but Vered felt he ought to write it himself. "I have conducted a brief survey among some people who know Dr. Leo Baeck, about [Recha Freier's] accusations, and am left confused," she wrote in a note she handed Sharett. "Because the issue is so sensitive and so close in time to the Kasztner affair, it would be best if you answered the lady yourself."[21]

20 His address at a symposium for activists of the Jerusalem branch of Mapai, July 5, 1955, CZA, A245-36.

21 Ibid., Freier's letter to Sharett has not been found. The handwritten note was dated July 8, 1955 and marked CZA, A245/75I.

Sharett began his detailed letter thus: "I was very troubled by your June 14, 1955 letter." He gave various reasons why her request bordered on the absurd, and among other things, wrote that he "sees no justification for changing the name based only on your request, especially since the matter would undoubtedly arouse a wave of protest." Towards the end of his letter, he argued that no court in the state is authorized to deal with people's behavior during and before the Holocaust, and the legal proceeding in the Kasztner case only proved that it is impossible to establish such a court of law. Employing understatement, he wrote, "I doubt whether a partial and segmented hearing before an Israeli court in a widely publicized case involving such an issue has led to a thorough clarification of the matter."

Gabriel Sheffer, the author of Sharett's biography, wrote about Sharett's sad position during the trial:

During the trial, Sharett had instructed [...] Haim Cohn as to the strategy which eventually led to the failure in the district court. In a series of interviews in the Israeli press as soon as the verdict against Kasztner was issued, Sharett tried to explain his own attempts to persuade the British government to negotiate with the Nazis to rescue Hungary's Jews, but the Israeli public was so incensed upon hearing Halevi's harsh conclusion [vis-à-vis Kasztner] that Sharett realized he must take immediate action to prevent its implications from hurting his and his party's political position in the [upcoming] elections.[22]

Ben-Gurion, who now served as Minister of Defense, had shown little interest in the case, nor was he overly concerned with the verdict. But his few references to it shed light on his attitude to the affair. For example, in the only letter he wrote on the subject,[23] in reply to one from the *Davar* journalist A. Z. Stein, Ben-Gurion claimed, "Regarding Kasztner, I know hardly anything because I did not follow the trial or read the verdict, except for a few sentences in the headlines." But those few sentences that he did read, "amazed me by appearing in a judge's verdict, and I do not believe this issue (the conduct of various Jews in the countries of the Nazi inferno) is a subject for a judicial hearing." Later, he expressed his disgust at the "filth, the hypocrisy, and the unrestrained vulgarity" of the articles that appeared in *Haboker, Lamerchav*

22 Gabriel Sheffer, *Moshe Sharett—Biography of a Political Moderate* (Oxford: Clarendon Press, 1996), p. 814.
23 August 17, 1955; Correspondence, BGRCA.

and *Herut*, "fanning the flames ignited by the trial." He also asserted that he would never have undertaken "to judge any Jew who was **there**, while I was **here**" [emphasis in the original].

He later expanded the scope of his comments:

> The affair of the Judenrat (and perhaps also of the Kasztner case) should, in my view, be left to the tribunal of history in the generation to come. The Jews who were safe and secure during the Hitler era ought not to presume to judge their brethren who were burned and slaughtered, nor the few who survived. I saw some of the survivors in the German concentration camps immediately after the end of the war, I heard from them about some of the atrocities and I also saw some ugly behavior among some of them. **But I did not consider that I had the right to judge or rebuke them, after having learned what they had been through** [emphasis added].

Ben-Gurion ended his letter on a personal note, one of the rare occasions on which he revealed an aspect of his own life in relation to the extermination of Europe's Jewry:

> This is an abysmal tragedy, and those of our generation who did not experience this hell would do best (in my view) to remain silent in humility and grief. My niece, her husband and her two children were burned alive. Can one speak about that?

IX

The Mapai party's intense preoccupation with this case was focused mainly on the fear that the affair, especially the fact that Kasztner was a party member, would adversely affect its show at the polls. A look at the daily schedule of M.K. Yona Kesse, one of the two party secretaries, shows that from the day of the verdict he was constantly involved with this issue.[24] It also came up in

---

24 The archival marking of the agenda: Labor Party archives, section 2, Secretary-General's Office, file 32-16-9; during July, Kesse met several times with Kasztner, as well as with Danzig, Avriel and Weltman. He also arranged and participated in consultations dealing with the subject (e.g., on Monday, June 27, 1955, he met with Avriel, Danzig and Palgi, and on July 15, he attended a consultation at the Prime Minister's Office, attended, among others, by Avriel, Weltman, Kollek, and M.K. Yaakov-Shimshon Shapira—members of the party committee that were following the affair).

speeches delivered at election rallies organized by Mapai at the end of that stormy week. Two of the speakers attracted special interest, one because of his speech, and the other because of who he was. The first, M.K. Meir Argov, Chairman of the Knesset Foreign Affairs and Defense Committee, drew attention because of his harsh attack on Judge Halevi. At a Tel Aviv rally, Argov said, "Only a judge with no conscience would pronounce such a verdict." According to *Yedioth Ahronoth*, which devoted its main headline to the speech and the reactions to it, Argov's words infuriated many judges, who were considering "an organized response to the unprecedented harsh attack on Judge Dr. Benjamin Halevi." Argov retracted his words in the wake of these reactions, claiming he had not intended to offend Judge Halevi, but rather to present a general argument that no judge or court of law could pronounce a verdict on those who had been there.[25] But his words reflected Mapai's difficult dilemma. Any attempts to attack the verdict were not perceived as a legitimate opinion but rather as a blow to the prestige and autonomy of the legal system and an attempt by the ruling party to trample upon fundamental values for the sake of factional and partisan interests.

The second speech, delivered by Yoel Palgi, was covered on the front page of many newspapers.[26] Palgi spoke about the trial's effect on Kasztner, the man, and on the party; [27] and its content reveals how difficult it was for Palgi to free himself of his complex attitude toward Kasztner. Even if Kasztner did commit a criminal act, he argued, he should not be accused of murder but only of manslaughter, because "Kasztner did what he did out of good intentions, out of pure intentions." Hence, even if he is guilty under the law, "society, as does the judge, has to consider the fact that in preventing a catastrophe, he caused a catastrophe. So even if he is not acquitted in court, he should at least be shown some leniency."

In contrast to Palgi's tortuously worded statement about the man, what he had to say about the party was crystal clear—whether the man is guilty or innocent, his trial is his own private affair and is not connected with the party or the hard-fought electoral battle it is waging. For, "our movement has nothing to be ashamed of. The balance sheet is positive and lustrous,

---

25 "The Judges are Considering an Organized Reaction to the Attack on B. Halevi— Resentment of Argov's Comments," *Yedioth Ahronoth*, June 26, 1955; "M. Argov Issues a Denial," *Lamerchav*, June 28, 1955.

26 See for example, "Palgi, Kasztner's Intentions were Pure," *Zemanim*, June 26, 1955; "Y. Palgi on the Verdict," *Davar*, June 26, 1955.

27 I am very grateful to Dr. Ilana Kaufman-Palgi, Palgi's daughter, who gave me the full text of the speech.

full of glory and splendor." And this heartwarming balance sheet will not be impaired "even if it turns out that in our long list of deeds, there is one who slipped up, erred or even transgressed." No, the speaker emphasized, such a man will not detract "from the splendor of the balance sheet we are presenting to history." Palgi ended his speech with a sentence that might have been spoken by an inquisitor:

> We have the strength to denounce and punish if there is a reason for denunciation and punishment—our strength and readiness to do so will only add power and glory to our movement.

X

The former members of the Hungarian Halutz Underground, who lived in kibbutzim belonging to the Mapai-affiliated Ihud Hakvutzot Vehakibbutzim movement, mostly Ma'agan and Kfar Hachoresh, had adopted an entirely different attitude towards Kasztner. On the day of the verdict, members of the two kibbutzim assembled and (separately) composed public letters of support for Kasztner, which were then printed prominently in *Davar*.[28] Many of the members of Kfar Hachoresh spoke at a spontaneous and stormy meeting immediately after receiving news of the disastrous verdict. Some of them could barely contain their tumultuous emotions—a mixture of insult and rage. Two resolutions were adopted at the end of the meeting; one was to offer Israel Kasztner and his family membership in the kibbutz; the other was to establish an action committee "to organize additional steps and to collect the necessary material to controvert the mistakes of the court in an appeal to the Supreme Court."

One of the organizers and main speakers of the meeting was Alexander Barzel, who after completing a term as secretary of Hanoar Haoved youth movement was now employed as the kibbutz 'yard keeper.' He later became a professor of humanistic studies at the Haifa Technion. In a newspaper interview, Barzel asserted that some facts described in the verdict were so absurd as to be comparable to claiming, "a cow lays eggs." When asked whether the kibbutz's invitation to Kasztner was meant merely as a show of support,

---

28 "Members of Kfar Hachoresh and Ma'agan Protest against the Kasztner Verdict," *Davar*, June 26, 1955.

he replied: "Definitely not, if he accepts it, I'll put him straight to work in the yard."[29]

One wet winter's day I talked to him about the sentiments in the kibbutz and his own personal feelings about Halevi's verdict.[30] Barzel owed his life to Kasztner—he was one of the survivors of the train—and yet he didn't like him. "Kasztner wasn't my cup of tea," he said. "He wasn't my friend and I didn't want him as a friend. He was arrogant, patronizing and aggressive. I certainly wouldn't regard him as a 'knight of the Maltese order.'" Why then did you defend him so staunchly?" I asked. "For several reasons," he replied. "First, I realized that it was actually because of his character that he was capable of doing great things during the Nazi occupation. At that time, a 'knight of the Maltese order' wouldn't have stood a chance. To take any action under the conditions of the German inferno, you needed to have a very special personality, leadership and decision-making ability and especially, plenty of chutzpah. And Kasztner had all that, in large measure. Second, I realized that the verdict was a terrible injustice—to him personally and in fact, to us all."

"Moreover," Barzel went on, "as far as we were concerned, the verdict was like a bomb, like an earthquake. We were dumbfounded by the fact that the judge, who had failed dismally to understand the Hungarian situation, had taken upon himself the role of an historian, and we thought his verdict was nonsensical and evil-minded."

Another speaker at that rally was Yosef Shefer, a former leader in the Young Maccabee movement in Hungary and Ottó Komoly's personal secretary; some years later he was a professor of sociology at Haifa University. In the course of a long interview with the *Davar* correspondent in the Jezreel Valley, Shefer was very agitated. The verdict, he claimed, convicted and besmirched not Kasztner, but "all of us, all the members of the Halutz Underground in Hungary. If Israel [Kasztner] was guilty of wrongdoing," he said, "then we all were, hundreds of members of the underground, who operated under the cruelest conditions. And by no means does anyone have the right to complacently judge our actions or to besmirch the reputation and honor of those rescuers who did their work with great sacrifice and devotion." When asked why he had not testified at the trial, he replied that he had wanted to be

---

29 I found the letter (excerpts of which I quoted) in the Kfar Hachoresh archives (the documents in the archive are unmarked); Shaul Ben-Haim, "The Kibbutz that Invited Kasztner," *Ma'ariv*, June 26, 1955.
30 Interview with Professor Alexander Barzel, Kfar Hachoresh, February 13, 1992.

called as a witness, but the Attorney General, "who certainly never imagined that the judge would arrive at such bizarre, totally baseless conclusions," saw no need to summon him.

The members of Kibbutz Ma'agan took more constrained steps, since they did not all share the same opinion on the verdict. Some had expected Kasztner to be reprimanded, but no one had expected such a grave, disastrous verdict. The same day, on which the verdict was published, a group of Ma'agan members met to discuss their feelings "of bitterness and shock at the judge's verdict regarding the tragic events of the holocaust of Hungarian Jews." In their view, some serious mistakes had been made even in relation to something so elementary as the geographical description of the city of Cluj, let alone in the description of the situation that had prevailed there.

XI

Items and articles printed in the Mapai-affiliated press attest to the party's grave dilemma in the wake of Halevi's verdict. These papers published news items intended to discredit the other side—Tamir, but mainly Gruenwald, who was an easier target. This task fell mainly to *Hador*, Mapai's evening tabloid, which in terms of that period was the worst kind of gutter press. *Hador* published an item under the headline "Gruenwald steals documents and plans to sue" (July 7, 1955), with news that Gruenwald "who, in addition to submitting notices to the press and arranging wild parties," has begun legal proceedings against Kasztner, and "has admitted to the *Daily Express* that he organized the theft of documents from the Jewish Agency files."

It was argued that, "we should not judge what happened **there**"—we have no right to try them because we were not in their place. It was an argument that made it possible to sit on the fence—neither to attack Kasztner, not to adopt an unequivocal stance in his defense. An example of this outlook is an editorial in *Hapoel Hatza'ir*.[31] A look at the plethora of material connected with the trial, "gives one a feeling [...] that none of this happened in our world, but on some far-off planet." Halevi "undertook a task that no flesh and blood human being could possibly carry out" and consequently produced a verdict "totally opposed to the public's moral senses."

As soon as the verdict was pronounced, the Mapai-affiliated press chose not to sit on the fence, but to publish articles proposing an alternative theory

---

31 "From Contemporary Chapters—Around the Verdict," *Hapoel Hatza'ir*, June 28, 1955.

to the one presented by the Court. The people who wrote these articles were not key figures in the establishment and the entire issue was part of the intense and uncompromising political struggle that surrounded the trial; nonetheless the articles reflected the beginning of a different attitude not only towards the trial or Kasztner, but also towards the Holocaust. Nathan Eck[32] wrote one such article, challenging Halevi's claim that had their leaders forewarned the Jews of Hungary, they would have resisted. "No! I do not believe they would have risen up," he wrote. "It would have been impossible for reasons that were both objective and subjective." What were these reasons? First, any defensive action "would have required weeks and months of organization and preparation. Such preparation was never carried out, because the catastrophe of extermination came upon them so suddenly." Second, "They did not see the slightest chance of altering the course of events in their favor by resisting or risking their lives." Third, "They did not all know for sure [...] that they were being led to annihilation." Fourth, even those who did know believed in their hearts that there was some chance of rescue, and "even those who realized how desperate the situation was clung to this hope." And fifth, the alternative of "Let me die with the Philistines," in the words of the biblical Samson, was relevant only for a few, not for the masses—"women and children, the old and the sick." This leads the writer to conclude that no grounds existed for the judge's opinion that under some circumstances mass resistance was a realistic alternative for the majority of Hungary's Jews.

The members of the Halutz Underground movement in Hungary made the most serious attempts to deal with concepts presented by Halevi's verdict. To them the verdict was an irreversible blow not only to Kasztner but also to the honor of those who had risked their lives in Nazi-occupied Budapest.[33] Alexander Barzel made an intense attempt to defend the lost honor of the Hungarian underground by publishing a series of articles in one of the internal organs of the Ichud Hakvutzot Vehakibbutzim movement. There were more: articles by Moshe Keren in *Ha'aretz* and by Yitzhak Artzi, secretary of the Progressive Party and formerly a leader of the Noar Hatzioni (Young Zionists) movement in Romania, in *Zemanim*.[34] But Barzel's articles were undoubtedly

---

32 Nathan Eck, "On the Margins of the Verdict," *Davar*, July 15, 1955.
33 On this matter, see Yechiam Weitz, "Between Warsaw and Budapest: Regarding the Term 'Resistance' in the Kasztner Trial" (Hebrew), *Dapim Lecheker Tekufat Hashoa* (Pages in Holocaust Research), 12 (1995), pp. 309–330.
34 The articles were printed in the Ihud "Member's Newsletter," Number 186–189, between July 7–27, 1955 under the heading "Following the Gruenwald-Kasztner Trial." On Keren's articles, see: Moshe Keren, *Passing and Permanent Problems* (Hebrew) (Jerusalem: 1978),

the most serious attempt made in any Mapai-affiliated framework to contend with Halevi's claims, with no hint of apologetics and completely unrelated to the election campaign.

First, Barzel argued, **the situation of Polish Jewry** cannot be compared to that of **Hungarian Jewry**. Prior to the occupation, he wrote, most of Hungary's Jews were callously indifferent to the suffering of the Jews who were coming there seeking refuge, and flatly refused "to see that the plight of today's refugees was what awaited them tomorrow." Members of the *halutz* youth movements who tried to help the refugees worked alone and sometimes even met with open hostility on the part of the local Jews. Moreover, ghettos in Poland existed over a period of several years, providing "a permanent way of life for thousands of Jews [...] with institutions [and] well-established daily routines, whereas there were no ghettos in Hungary, except those designated as **round-up areas** [for the Jews], **before they were sent** [to their death] [emphasis in the original]." These existed for days or at the most for weeks, which made it impossible to organize any underground activity in them.

Barzel firmly addressed the question of why Hungarian Jews had not fled or rebelled, since anyone "capable of admitting to him/herself, or had taken in the warnings, knew all too well the **significance of deportation**" [emphasis in the original]. His assertion was that there had been virtually no contact with the overwhelming majority of the many Jewish communities throughout the country, nor had the slightest attempt been made to organize any *halutz* activity. Moreover, it was extremely dangerous for Jews to escape to Romania or Yugoslavia and many who tried were killed. Even when members of the *halutzim* movements tried to escape across the border, "[if they] were caught, [further] attempts were discontinued for a while."

Barzel devoted the final chapters of his series to criticism of the trial itself, which he felt was characterized by "the typical Jewish trait of self-hatred and the tendency to [...] place the blame for disasters on the closest and most vulnerable target—another Jew." The survivors' pain at having survived while others had gone to their deaths intensified this tendency of self-hatred and caused them to seek revenge for the death of their loved ones. Ironically this was "not from the predatory assassins, but from those who tried to stand

pp. 185–238; Segev, *The Seventh Million*, pp. 286–287; "Why was There No Mass Revolt and Escape?" the first in a series of articles by Yitzhak Artzi, "Rescue during the Holocaust," published on July 1, 1955.

between the victim and the beast." He also pointed out that the judge, swayed by the defense counsel, "turned the trial into an historical trial of the **past** with **current political intent**" [emphasis in the original], hence the proceedings were diverted to "a course that had nothing to do with either Gruenwald or Kasztner."

Barzel sharply criticized the fact that the proceedings had been turned into the 'Cluj trial.' "The Cluj ghetto **was extremely atypical** of Hungarian Jewry in general and this trial in particular." Except for the capital of Transylvania there was nowhere else where such a large number of Jewish functionaries—both Zionists and non-Zionists—were concentrated; it was therefore the "**only** ghetto in which Kasztner's **name** had any tangible meaning" [emphasis in the original]. Outside the boundaries of Cluj, Kasztner was totally anonymous, and among the hundreds of thousands of Hungarian Jews, probably no more than a thousand had heard of him. Cluj was the only place where the way the survivors were selected "could have induced strong emotions on a **personal** basis and, over time, personal bitterness and a suppressed sense of vindictiveness. If anyone from any other ghetto had testified, he would not have taken so personal a tone." His criticism of the witnesses from Cluj was no gentler. For example, he cited one of them, who testified, "that he had been told about the Hungarian government's plans to vacate the 'city' of Kenyermezo and to concentrate **all** the Jews of Hungary there." That man, who was a travelling salesman, must have been quite familiar with that not very large country and ought to have known that the reference was to a tiny farm, which could never have housed hundreds of thousands of people. About the comment of the witness who said to the Jews of the ghetto "that we must break out and flee, and if we don't succeed, we must burn the city of Cluj!," Barzel wrote: "How naive! And the city is like Petah Tikvah, times four."

At the end of his article, Barzel suggested a motif that would become a key theme in the articles he published over the years on this subject, which consumed his every waking thought. He wrote:

> We must know that the man, Kasztner, and those who stood **behind him** in the planning and **with him** in the implementation, as well as the **affair** itself, were pure and sincere. The **period** was as violated and tragic as Hitler and his bestial henchmen shaped it. And [it is] **they** we shall not forgive unto the final generation. That is the lesson to be learned [emphasis in the original].

XII

The struggle waged by Mapai did not focus only on the press. When the attacks grew more virulent, Party Secretary Kesse called a special meeting of the Mapai secretariat.[35] This meeting, the only party debate on the subject of which we have the complete transcript, was attended by many of the main protagonists of the affair—Ehud Avriel, Hillel Danzig, Meir Weltman, Yoel Palgi, Peretz Révész, Moshe Schweiger and others. It was a confused, turbulent meeting. No real plans were proposed, as one might have expected of an operative body belonging to the ruling party. This mood was set by Kesse's opening speech, in which he stressed the need to sweep this embarrassing affair under the carpet until things calmed down. "It would be best if this whole affair were taken off our agenda until [after] the elections," he said.

Ehud Avriel, who was next to speak, said he was not interested in the legal aspect but rather in the public aspect and the harm the trial was causing to the party and its inalienable assets and also because "of the way the Attorney General has been handling the affair." To minimize the damage and also because "this episode has been magnified out of all proportion [...]," Avriel proposed inviting an important and distinguished historian, whom he stressed should be from abroad, and who would be "provided with the necessary means to conduct an investigation into this case, the results of which would subsequently be published, so that the masses may read about it, both in Israel and abroad." However, Avriel added, it is important that this be presented "for its own sake, and [not for any] political gain."

He also proposed holding "a convention of former Hungarian underground members in one of the kibbutzim that had been settled by immigrants from Hungary." In contrast, Schweiger wanted to concentrate on the legal aspect of the struggle, in the belief that this was the way to decide the fate of the public campaign: "If it is possible to emerge victorious in this matter, it can only happen in the courtroom!" Therefore, while the 'other side' is persistently and enthusiastically collecting more material with the purpose of sharpening its 'case,' we must do likewise. And since "our primary task is to save the situation, anyone prepared to be of service in this regard ought to begin collecting material." Danzig warned, "We are deluding ourselves if we think this matter is no longer harming our interests in the elections," and suggested removing their kid gloves and instead of contenting themselves

---

35 Meeting of the Mapai secretariat, July 12, 1955, Labor Party Archives 23/55.

with merely "disseminating positive, historical information," they should expose the true face and true motives of some of the key players in the affair.

Weltman, the best informed of all the speakers, spoke after Danzig and provided up-to-date relevant information. To win the appeal, he said, we cannot make do with the status quo; the work has to be done "in a well-planned, concentrated manner by the best lawyers in the country," and not by Mapai, he stressed. The appeal would be submitted in coordination with lawyers "loyal to us," and "the groundwork has already been laid with the Minister of Justice and the Attorney General, because cooperation in this area is very important." Kasztner himself, Weltman added, has spoken to Minister Rosen, who "confirmed that there are such intentions." A special committee had also been set up to collect material, to be headed by none other than Shula Arlozoroff, oldest daughter of the hero of a highly charged affair, which was also on the public agenda at that time. The committee would inquire into questions like "what did Krausz do and how was the shipment organized?" This subject was given much consideration mainly because of the assessment that "The objective of the appeal is a difficult one to achieve, the verdict has to be overturned."

Several other members spoke as well, but most of the attention was turned to Yoel Palgi, who on this occasion, too, was unable to curb his hostility towards Kasztner. He suggested that the party adopt no less than "what the Attorney General said, namely that if Kasztner were guilty 'he should be condemned to death,' emphasizing the fact that we are appealing since the verdict is faulty from start to finish." With everyone present reacting harshly to his words, Palgi tried to give them a pragmatic twist:

> Someone should say it outright: if Kasztner were to be found guilty of collaborating with the Nazis, he should be condemned to die. **In my view, such a statement would give the party several seats in the Knesset** [emphasis added].

He later softened his position somewhat, "Since we believe that Kasztner is not guilty, my suggestion means only one thing—that the party does not cover up for criminals. These days, saying that carries some public importance."

This animated meeting also produced some practical results. One was the appointment of a lawyer for Kasztner, who until this stage had no real legal defense. The law firm retained was one of the largest, most important in the country—the partnership of Micha Caspi and Haim Zadok, the latter in the 48th slot on the Mapai list for the Third Knesset. They were contacted immediately after the verdict was pronounced, in July 1955, by two lawyers who were also party members—Meir Weltman and M.K. Yaakov-Shimshon Shapira, who had served as Attorney General between 1948–1950 and was Justice Minister from 1966–1973, as well as serving on the party's internal committee that followed the course of the trial. The two were also responsible for the financial negotiations with the law firm and for paying its fees.[36]

XIII

What happened to the protagonists of the affair during the turmoil aroused by the verdict? A day after delivering his verdict, Judge Halevi closeted himself in his home and did not appear in court. Callers were told that the judge "is exhausted by the intensive efforts he invested in writing the verdict," and the District Court secretariat stated that no trials were scheduled for Halevi for the coming two weeks since he was taking a vacation. The defense, on the other hand, was in a celebratory mood. The day after the trial, *Herut* printed an announcement by the National Labor Federation (Histadrut Ha'ovdim Haleumit) and the Tel Aviv Workers' Council congratulating Shmuel Tamir for "the victory of truth over lies." Gruenwald was celebrating too. He received hundreds of telegrams from Israel and abroad and, although he was exhausted by the tensions of the trial, he opened his home to the many visitors who came to congratulate him. These visitors were served tea and cake and Gruenwald shook their hands warmly and enthusiastically.

Needless to say, Kasztner, the reluctant hero of the verdict, was in a totally different mood. He had stayed at the Moriah while the verdict was being read—a small, but quite elegant hotel in the Talbieh quarter near Salameh square in the heart of Jerusalem (not to be confused with the present-day Moriah hotel). Some of his friends, Hanzi Brand in particular, had dissuaded him from coming to court, so he heard the news of the disastrous verdict from Hanzi. Arriving at the hotel, she had found Kasztner sitting, pale and tense, in an armchair. Several of his close associates were there with him: Dezső (David) Herman, who had also come from the courtroom, agitated and enraged, Shmuel Bentzur, and his brother-in-law Pesach Rudik.

---

36 On this matter, see for example, the letter from the Caspi-Zadok law firm to Yaakov-Shimshon Shapira, dated November 15, 1955, regarding payment of legal fees for July-November 1955, Micha Caspi's archives.

Kasztner rushed to meet Hanzi when she walked into the room, scrutinizing her face for the answer to the question that for months had caused him sleepless nights. Flustered, Brand did not know exactly how to tell Kasztner that the verdict had exceeded their worst nightmares. Finally, after a brief hesitation that seemed to Kasztner like an eternity, she said, "If the judge had found anything wrong in any of the things you did, it might have been possible to respect his verdict. But the words he used in condemning you were so scurrilous as to have lost all meaning. I am sure this day will be recorded as a black day in the history of Israeli jurisprudence." This only served to exacerbate Kasztner's tension. He looked at her and, almost in a shout, asked, "What happened, Hanzi? What happened?" Only then did Hanzi dare tell him exactly what the judge had said: "He said you'd sold your soul to the devil." Kasztner was silent. His face was implacable. Pesach Rudik accompanied his friend back to Tel Aviv. All his attempts to put on a brave face were futile. At home, he said to his wife, "The judge delivered an incredibly harsh verdict. Tamir never expected such a verdict, even in his wildest dreams."[37]

The following day, Kasztner and Hanzi Brand met again to see what could be done and if anything could be salvaged—almost as they had in Budapest eleven years earlier. This time, Kasztner permitted himself to give vent to the sorrow he had not expressed upon hearing the verdict. Brand, who had been with Kasztner during the most difficult times in occupied Budapest, now saw something in his eyes she had never seen before—tears. Again and again he asked her: "You know me well. Tell me, whom did I sin against? Who did I wrong? What crime did I commit for which I've been so badly beaten?" She didn't reply. It was a situation in which words no longer had meaning. Kasztner's world was totally shattered. For years, Hanzi wrote, his activity in Budapest had been a source of pride for him—he regarded it as a testament of his worth and a certificate of merit. And now, "the halo of glory had turned into the most despicable badge of shame that could become the lot of a Jew."

His friends watched Kasztner marshal all his strength into coming to terms with this badge of shame. According to Brand, the atmosphere surrounding Kasztner in wake of the verdict "was one of open hostility on the part of strangers, and cautious forbearance from his friends, which was no less painful."[38] He now had to withstand a test that was even more serious than the one he had faced in occupied Budapest—he needed vast, almost superhuman reserves of strength simply to get up in the morning, to leave

---

37 "An Appeal to be Filed on the Kasztner Verdict," *Ma'ariv*, June 23, 1955.
38 Brand, *Satan and the Soul*, pp. 158–159 and 168–169.

the house and to walk about the city streets as if nothing had happened and all was well. Zvi Herman, who met him on several occasions at the home of his brother Dezső (David), saw a very despondent man, convinced that he was the victim of an unbearable injustice—a man who still viewed himself as a national hero, now publicly denounced as if he were the devil's own helper. Yosef (Tommy) Lapid, who was in touch with him almost daily, saw a man languishing, gradually withdrawing into himself. His pride, arrogance and self-confidence were replaced by suspicion and anxiety; at a certain stage, Kasztner began to realize that in the struggle, not only his honor was at stake, but his very life.

Although he tried to put on a brave face, Kasztner was unable to conceal his tension. Sometimes his eyes would fill with tears; he spoke in a whisper and he chain-smoked—lighting one cigarette from the stub of another. He no longer went to cafes or movies; in fact he hardly ventured out of the house. "I don't want to see people and I sense that they no longer want to see me," he said. Nor did the many sympathetic phone calls he received do anything to raise his spirits. "I live in total solitude," he once said, "Alone with my conscience. No one can understand this kind of solitude. It is blacker than night; it is as black as hell."[39]

His family shared his misfortune. His wife said that in the grocery store she was treated with effusive politeness, as if she had some terminal disease, while his nine-and-a-half year old daughter, Suzi, said the children ran after her in school, shouting "Kasztner trial, Kasztner trial."

To Kasztner the most painful aspect of the whole affair was having to witness the suffering of his only daughter, Suzi, as she became the target of incessant harassment and abuse in school. Many years would pass before Suzi was able to discuss the subject. In 1982, following the screening of Yehuda Kaveh's TV series on the trial, she gave several interviews in which she described her childhood in the shadow of the verdict. It took a quarter of a century after the event for her to be able to speak about the nightmares that kept her awake at night, and how she told her mother that her classmates ran after her shouting, "You're the daughter of a murderer, the daughter of a Nazi!"[40]

---

39 "'I Live in Unbearable Solitude,' Kasztner says," *Ma'ariv*, July 7, 1955; personal interviews with Zvi Herman (Haifa, July 3, 1992), Yosef Lapid (Tel Aviv, December 17, 1991).

40 "Chaya Yosef, Childhood in the Shadow of the Murderer," *Ma'ariv Supplement*, March 11, 1987.

Even as the trial was in progress, she was already aware of the tensions at home. Eight years old at the time, she couldn't understand why neighbors, teachers and even her classmates had changed their attitude toward her, becoming aggressive and hostile. One of her teachers, Yosef Roth, treated her in a particularly outrageous manner:

> He treated me as if my father had already been convicted; and as if I, the child, was to blame for the horrors of the Holocaust. He said nothing explicit, but his behavior [toward me] and his attitude toward the children who were practically condemning me to [...] a lynching was worse than a physical beating. I began to be frightened! I didn't know what was actually happening.

The situation deteriorated after the verdict. Her anxieties multiplied; she felt lonely and abandoned, almost ostracized. The situation at home was unbearable—the front of their apartment building was covered with abusive graffiti—"Kasztner's a murderer" being the least offensive. Sometimes, the local grocer refused to sell to them. A fourth-floor neighbor incited all the neighbors against the Kasztner family, threw garbage on to their balcony and called Kasztner a "Nazi!"

Suzi's mother, who was under terrible strain, did not discuss the trial with her daughter and Suzi in turn, did not share with her mother her own problems at school and on the street. The children in the street called her a "murderess," and, worst of all, they nicknamed her "Kasztnerit," a name she would never forget. Her friends shunned her and with her only remaining friend, she never discussed her fears, or anything connected with the trial—afraid of losing her, too.

In desperation, she wrote a brief letter to the prime minister. I found the frayed sheet of paper on which it was written in Moshe Sharett's personal archive.

> To Mr. Moshe Sharett, the Prime Minister!
> I thank you for your kind treatment of my father, Dr. I. Kasztner.
> I hope you will not change your attitude toward my poor father.
> Mr. Moshe Sharett, I see that you are on my father's side.
> Respectfully yours,
> Shoshana Kasztner[41]

41 The letter, sent on July 8, 1955, was marked as CZA, A245-65II.

Was it the nine-year-old girl's idea to write this letter? Among the material Suzi Michaeli gave me, there was a draft of the letter that ended with the words, "but that is not enough." Someone deleted these words and they do not appear in the copy sent to the Prime Minister. All my attempts to find Sharett's reply to the young girl were unsuccessful.

XIV

But Kasztner, tired, withdrawn and despondent, never gave up despite the disastrous verdict, as I learned from Naphtali Lau-Lavie, then a young journalist and night editor at *Zemanim*. The paper, housed in an old building near the Tel Aviv Central Bus Station, shared its offices and printing press with the Hungarian language daily, *Uj Kelet*. That's how he met Kasztner, an acquaintance that developed during the late hours of the night, when the two went together, after work, to the nearby T'nuva dairy restaurant, to eat and to talk. According to Lau, Kasztner was a cold, introverted man. But he was also sharp and witty, and he enjoyed conversing with him. Kasztner was smart, cultured, and well informed about public and political affairs. His feeling of being the victim of a terrible injustice was expressed mainly in his adamant refusal to talk about the affair that bore his name. From the few sentences he uttered on the rare occasions the subject came up, his anguish was quite palpable. Almost every word he uttered revealed the torment he was trying so hard to conceal and deny.[42]

Zeev Ben-Shlomo, a member of the *Zemanim* editorial board, met Kasztner, who, despite his despair, was determined to put up a fight to clear his name.[43] At their meeting Ben-Shlomo saw a man, "who looked anxious, tired and apathetic," still, from time to time, his sharp features tensed in an expression of anger and obstinacy." His speech "alternated between the muddled and the lucid. His sentences, at first clumsy and vague, gradually became extraordinarily clear and orderly." Kasztner spoke primarily of Halevi's verdict. By the time the interview was over, Kasztner seemed to have completely regained his composure and self-assurance. When they parted, he

---

42 Interview with Naphtali Lau-Lavi (Jerusalem, June 24, 1993). See also: Naphtali Lau-Lavi, *Nation Like a Lion* (Hebrew) (Tel Aviv: Ma'ariv Press, 1993), pp. 209–210.

43 Zeev Ben-Shlomo, "Kasztner, No Historian will Judge Me Like That," *Zemanim*, June 25, 1955.

smiled at his interviewer, who wrote in an amazed tone, "Despite everything, he has strong nerves [...]."

Kasztner also gave interviews to the foreign press. He told a British journalist that all he had wanted was to save more and more Jews, and when he and his friends realized they couldn't save all the Jews of Hungary, they had to decide quickly whether they wanted to abandon their efforts or to rescue at least some. "For me," Kasztner stated emphatically, "the answer was absolutely clear."[44]

He was prepared to fight. His refusal to leave the country, even for a brief period, was unwavering. "Rezsö," Brand said to him, "there is nothing for you here! Leave!" "This is where I was vilified," he replied, "and here I will be vindicated." Rudik also advised him to leave the country until the storm blew over and things calmed down, but he refused to listen.[45] Not only did he refuse to leave Israel, he was not even prepared to move away from Tel Aviv. In reply to the invitation from the members of Kibbutz Kfar Hachoresh, he sent a cable saying he hoped in the near future to be free of the concerns involved with the trial and able to accept their offer; unfortunately, at that moment it was impossible. He feared that if he went to the kibbutz it "might be interpreted as an attempt to run away."

Endeavoring to clear his name, he issued a statement on the day of the verdict. The brief statement, every word of which was carefully weighed, was published in all the newspapers.[46] Although it was restrained and sober—or perhaps for that very reason—it is easy to sense how deep was his feeling that he was the victim of a terrible injustice:

> When Dreyfus, innocent of the crime he was charged with, fell victim to a terrible injustice, the danger of contempt of court precluded an immediate mass protest. His reputation and honor were restored only years later, following the efforts of Emile Zola. I do not need Zola to clear my name. History and all those who know what really happened during those woeful times will testify on my behalf. Now that those dreadful years have passed, during which I tried, not without success, to serve my people and to rescue at least some of my brethren who were

44 "Kasztner Speaks," *Jewish Observer and Middle East Review*, July 22, 1955.
45 Hanzi Brand; Pesach Rudik.
46 "Tamir Applies to Police Chief—Rumors about Kasztner's Meeting with Becher," *Yedioth Ahronoth*, August 24, 1955; Kasztner's letter, written the same day, is in Micha Caspi's archives; on his statement, see, for example, "Kasztner's Statement," *Lamerchav*; "Kasztner: Even Dreyfus was Acquitted Eventually," *Haboker*, June 23, 1955.

condemned to death by the Nazis, I will do everything in my power to clear my name and regain my honor.

This statement evoked a counter-statement by Tamir, who claimed he was not surprised by what Kasztner had written. Anyone closely following the trial, he claimed, "realized that thinly disguised cynicism and the assumption of a martyr's role were basic characteristics of his nefarious behavior."

The fact that some people gave him their support and expressed their disgust at the verdict helped Kasztner retain a certain measure of stability and sanity. After the verdict was pronounced he received scores of letters and telegrams of support.[47] "As people who went through the Holocaust in Budapest," members of Moshav Ben-Ami in the Western Galilee wrote, they were expressing their consternation at the "dreadful verdict of the Jerusalem District Court," and their total identification "with you and the actions of the Budapest Rescue Committee." Most of the writers, former Hungarians, were affiliated with *halutz* youth movements, who felt that their honor and reputations had also been trampled. Israel Sabo, a member of Kfar Maccabee, wrote, in his own name and that of Peretz Révész, that he was shocked by the miscarriage of justice, "perpetrated, to our shame, by a judge in Israel." Indignantly protesting in the name of the entire Halutz Underground in Hungary, Sabo wrote:

> You were not alone to be convicted; along with you are all those who did their best, in those dismal times, to devotedly serve their people with a Jewish conscience. Who ever dreamt that we would be so regarded by a Hebrew court in the city of Jerusalem? The only epopoeia of the Holocaust period in Hungary has been sullied and with it the entire Zionist movement has also been sullied.

The only member of his party's leadership to write to Kasztner was Gershon Agron, editor of the *Jerusalem Post* and later mayor of Jerusalem. His letter was written before the verdict was given, on the eve of Yom Kippur, 1954, in other words, after Tamir's summation. His words were extremely rancorous:

> On more than one occasion, I was grievously appalled by the behavior of the 'defense,' the real murderers [of the soul] – 'by chance,' your

---

47 I am profoundly grateful to Suzi Kasztner-Michaeli for giving me these letters and telegrams.

murderers—people who have chosen wicked counsel in the evil
plots they devised. How a Jew can stoop to such heinous behavior as
Gruenwald's lawyer has, I shall never, never understand!

The unbridled campaign of incitement against Kasztner resulted in the
Security Services appointing two bodyguards to keep 24-hour surveillance on
him. This protection was maintained over a long period, and discontinued,
according to Amos Manor, due to budgetary constraints, shortly before
Kasztner was murdered. He said that Meir Novik, then head of the Special
Duties Office [the police intelligence unit, Y.W.] nagged him about it for a
long time and the subject was also raised in a discussion with Yehezkel Sahar,
the Police Commissioner. Finally, Manor was persuaded that Kasztner was
not in any real danger and that this really was an expense that could be cut.

XV

Also critical was the matter of submitting an appeal. On the day of the verdict,
Moshe Sharett spoke to Pinhas Rosen—"in contact with the Minister of Justice
about an appeal," he wrote in his diary. The following morning, he discussed
the subject again, but did not note in his diary with whom. He spoke to Rosen
again on Sunday, June 26, before the cabinet meeting and, on the 29th of that
month the subject was raised at a meeting of Mapai ministers.

In the Ministry of Justice, too, work began on an appeal. On the evening
of June 22, even before Halevi finished reading his verdict, the Director-
General of the Ministry, Yosef Kokia, who was replacing Attorney General
Cohn, frantically consulted with his assistants and the decision was taken to
file an appeal. Cohn himself was on vacation in Athens at the time. As soon
as he heard the verdict, he fired off a cable to Kokia instructing him to file an
appeal.[48]

The acting Attorney General assigned several Ministry employees the
task of wording the appeal and collecting the necessary material. One reason
for acting so quickly was to protect Kasztner. Until the case was heard in
the Supreme Court, it was impossible to bring charges against him, as many
had demanded after the verdict. The following day, the Government Press
Office hastened to announce that the purpose of the appeal was "to request

---

48 Sharett, *Personal Diary*, June 22 and 26, p. 1073; his appointment book marked as CZA,
    A245-72I; Haim Cohn; *Haboker*, June 24, 1955.

the Supreme Court to pass judgment on the conclusions reached by the President of the District Court based on the facts brought before him, since in the opinion of the Acting Attorney General these conclusions are not substantiated by legally admissible evidence." The statement also emphasized that Yosef Kokia had taken the decision; in other words, the professional echelon in the Ministry of Justice.

Not everyone took these words at face value. According to *Haolam Hazeh*, the Prime Minister backed the decision and exerted all his influence to ensure it was adopted. The weekly claimed that Sharett called Kokia, even before Halevi had finished reading the verdict, demanding an appeal. Kokia refused, asserting that he had no authority to act without explicit instructions from the Attorney General. Sharett did not give up. In the early hours of the morning, he phoned the Minister of Justice, who was staying at the Megiddo *pension* in Haifa, and instructed him to file an appeal. Rosen agreed, even though he had not read the verdict. *Ma'ariv* printed a similar story.

Nearly two months were spent on preparing the appeal, which was filed on August 21 and signed by the Attorney General. The notice of appeal was very concise—only four pages—but it took exception to all the points in Halevi's verdict. These were the main arguments:

First, Gruenwald was acquitted on the basis of assumptions, some not supported by the evidence and some based on false evidence, and the Court totally ignored "the psychological state of the Jews in general, and of the members of the Rescue Committee in particular, under the Nazi occupation of Hungary."

Second, the judge's conclusions were greatly influenced by the fact "that he was not favorably impressed by Kasztner's conduct when he took the witness stand, and by his contradictions of his own statements and those of other witnesses, including prosecution witnesses." The judge erred in choosing a faulty criterion to determine the reliability of the testimony he heard. This faulty criterion led to several lapses in the way he arrived at his assessments and conclusions. For example: he totally overlooked the limits of human memory, and hence "failed to exercise any caution in drawing hasty conclusions from contradictions in the testimony about events that had occurred more than ten years earlier." In all the judge's lapses the common denominator was his inflexible reading of the situation. He apparently failed to understand the impossibility of fully and conclusively applying the rigid criteria of accuracy and consistency to everything connected to those awful times.

Third, there are no grounds for the Court's conclusion that Kasztner's negotiations were tantamount to "criminal collaboration with the Nazis," and his conclusion that Kasztner was aware "of the role he played in the extermination of Jews, and willingly and knowingly fulfilled that role, is baseless and tantamount to a miscarriage of justice." In his statement, that by agreeing to accept the "rescue train of favored individuals '[Kasztner] sold his soul to the devil', "the learned judge was expressing a subjective view for which there are no grounds either in the evidentiary material or in objective reality."

Fourth, his conclusions and statements regarding various episodes are unsubstantiated. His conclusion that Kasztner's motive in failing to warn the Jews of Cluj was "to enable the extermination of the masses or to make it easier," is baseless and amounts to a miscarriage of justice. There is no explanation for his statement that Kasztner's behavior in the case of the parachutists "was the result of his alleged loyalty to the Nazi powers" other than his previous conclusions that Kasztner had already willingly entered into a criminal collaboration with the Nazis. The evidentiary material did not justify the judge's statement that Kasztner gave his affidavit in Becher's favor "in order to obstruct the prosecution of a war criminal and to save him from trial and punishment."

These were the reasons that moved the Attorney General to petition the Supreme Court to reverse Halevi's decision and to find Gruenwald guilty of "the offense he was charged with in the indictment and to impose punishment upon him to the full extent of the law."

XVI

In the highly charged atmosphere that followed the verdict, the notice of appeal ignited another debate, which focused mainly on the reason for filing the appeal. Was it a legitimate response by the State Attorney's Office, or was it intended to protect the ruling party and a Nazi war criminal? A crucial question was, who had decided to appeal the verdict—the political echelon, namely the Prime Minister and the Minister of Justice, or the professional echelon, namely the State Attorney's Office. Those newspapers that took exception to Halevi's verdict supported the decision. *Ha'aretz* claimed that the wisdom of bringing the whole affair before a court of law was questionable, "but after what has happened, there is no longer any choice but to give a higher court an opportunity to investigate the matter and arrive at a conclusion more rational and judicious than its predecessor." Ben-Gurion was clearly in favor of the decision to appeal. He stated, "In filing an appeal to the Supreme Court, the Minister of Justice and his advisors have fulfilled their duty to the state, to justice and to the protection of human rights."[49]

In contrast to the moderate tone of the newspapers that favored the decision, those opposed to it expressed blatantly extreme views. On June 26, *Herut* asked, "Why is Mapai defending Kasztner?" The paper contended that inside Mapai itself there were differing opinions, some of which demanded that all attempts to defend Kasztner be halted, insisting that "considerations of the impending elections had influenced the decision to file an appeal." This led the paper to conclude that Mapai was protecting "a collaborator despite the decision of a judge in Israel," because of its grave concern about "Kasztner and the secrets it shared with him." That same day, its editorial (entitled "Two Affairs that are One and the Same") suggested another motive: the purpose of the appeal was to prevent Kasztner from being put on trial, because if he were, he would "be the end of the thread that unravels the entire ball." Following him, other 'public figures' from Hungary would be likely candidates for a trial, and following them, 'public figures' in Israel, all of them members of Mapai, of course. The editorial concluded by stating, "The developments following the verdict show that justice and truth will prevail in the end—despite and actually perhaps because of the desperate attempts at a cover-up."

Unsurprisingly, the most caustic words were written in *Kol Ha'am* on June 24. According to the main news item about the appeal, "the government continues to stand by Kasztner, which proves that Kasztner carried out his serious offenses against Hungary's Jews under the direction of official circles." Under the highly charged headline "Jewish blood must not go unavenged," the editorial asserted that the refusal to put Kasztner on trial and "the evasion of a complete investigation into the responsibility of all those who worked with him, who devised and followed **Kasztnerist** methods," conclusively proves that "this is not an isolated case of collaboration with the Nazis and that Kasztner has accomplices in the top ranks of Mapai [his own] party, and in other satellite parties on the right and on the left" [emphasis in the original].

The decision to file the appeal was on the agenda of the government's weekly meeting on Sunday, June 26. It would not be proper for the government to appear again in public as a party interested in defending Kasztner, Israel Rokach, Minister of the Interior, argued. His party, the General Zionists,

49 "An Appeal will be Filed in the Kasztner-Gruenwald Trial," *Ha'aretz*, June 24, 1955; "For Whom the Phone Rang" *Haolam Hazeh*, July 7, 1955; "Sharett Initiated the Appeal Against the Verdict," *Ma'ariv*, June 26, 1955; "Notification and Reasons for the Appeal," Jerusalem, August 21, 1955, Micha Caspi's collection.

The ministers of Moshe Sharett's new cabinet
INPC, D667104

believed that the wording of the notice of appeal implied criticism of Judge Halevi and undermined the freedom of the Israeli judiciary. The ministers from the religious parties, who felt there were no grounds for any further government intervention in the legal proceedings, concurred in Rokach's view.[50]

Rokach stated his opposition to the State Attorney's decision and wondered why it was taken with such haste. A two-hour long debate then ensued about whether the government had the authority to discuss and decide on issues of a professional legal nature, namely whether it was authorized to discuss a decision by the State Attorney's Office. Finally, it was unanimously decided, without a vote, that, "the Ministry of Justice should be allowed to handle everything relating to the verdict of the President of the Jerusalem District Court in the matter of the Attorney General versus Malkiel Gruenwald." The Minister of Justice announced that the appeal would be filed as he and the acting Attorney General had agreed.

---

50 "Word of the Day," *Davar*, June 23, 1955; "From Day to Day—With the Reading of the Verdict," *Ha'aretz*, June 23, 1955; *Davar*, June 28, 1955.

Another matter for discussion was whether a public commission of inquiry should be established vis-à-vis the various issues raised in the verdict. This proposal was supported by only two ministers—Rokach and Yosef Sapir, the Minister of Transport (the other General Zionist representatives, Peretz Bernstein and Yosef Serlin, were not present at the meeting). The other ministers (with the abstention of Moshe Shapira and Yosef Burg of the National Religious Party) felt the public debate should be postponed "until after the verdict on the appeal." The government did not refer to the position it would take if the issue were raised in the Knesset plenum.

Several heated exchanges between ministers took place during the meeting. In a tone critical of Halevi's verdict, Defense Minister Ben-Gurion insisted that no further damage should be caused to Kasztner until the Supreme Court heard the appeal; he also blamed Dov Joseph for having urged the Attorney General to institute the proceedings in the first place. Joseph totally denied having done so. Sharett, who also spoke, analyzed some of the issues that were raised in the verdict and said he was sorry he hadn't been called to testify.

After the meeting, the government spokesman went out to speak to the journalists, one of whom asked, "Is there any truth in the information printed in *Maariv* yesterday that the Prime Minister initiated the appeal?" The spokesman categorically denied the allegation. The decision was taken solely by the acting Attorney General, he replied. However, he refrained from clearly replying to the question of whether Sharett had been consulted before the decision was taken. "Is it customary for a decision about filing an appeal to be brought to a government meeting for discussion?" another journalist asked. "No," the spokesman admitted, "it's an unusual step, which was taken due to the widespread public interest in the trial."[51]

Following the meeting, the Minister of Justice issued a statement to explain the motives underlying the State Attorney's Office decision to file the appeal. In making this statement, he was trying to quell the public's outrage, to defend the legal system in general and Judge Halevi in particular, and to absolve the Prime Minister of any responsibility for the decision:

> I am calling upon the public to exercise caution and to avoid being dragged into a polemic regarding the verdict of the Jerusalem District Court in the matter of the Attorney General vs. Malkiel ben Menahem

---

51 On this matter, see "Sharett Initiated the Appeal against the Verdict," *Maariv*, June 26, 1955.

Gruenwald. In particular, I wish to issue a warning against any direct or indirect injury to the respected, high-ranking figure of President Dr. Benjamin Halevi, before whom the case was heard [...] I have asked the acting Attorney General to announce his decision to file the appeal; moreover, this was done at the request of Dr. Kasztner himself.

However, not everyone was convinced by the Justice Minister's statement. A writer for *Lamerchav* argued, "Despite the denials and the attempts to gloss over the Prime Minister's role in the decision to file the appeal, well-informed circles still maintain that M. Sharett played a principal part in adopting the decision."

The General Zionists made the first move. On the day Minister Rokach raised the subject at a government meeting, the faction demanded a debate on Kokia's decision to file an appeal. He claimed that the government must try Kasztner on charges of collaboration with the Nazis. A fierce discussion ensued, in which Minister of Defense David Ben-Gurion, opposed Rokach's position, claiming that the appeal against Halevi's verdict would have to be considered later. According to Minister Moshe Shapira the question of Kasztner's guilt is not an issue for the government to decide, since it is not a political issue. The meeting ended with a government majority rejecting the General Zionists' proposal calling for a discussion of the General Attorney's decision on the appeal.[52]

Notwithstanding the government's decision, the General Zionists demanded that the Knesset presidium urgently place on the agenda Kokia's decision to file an appeal. M.K. Chaim Ariav cabled Knesset Speaker Joseph Sprinzak on the matter, a step that many Knesset members found puzzling. The General Zionists, after all, were members of the coalition, and the Minister of Health, Yosef Serlin, had presented a parliamentary question on the issue at the government meeting.

The General Zionists were not the only faction to understand that the eve of elections was a propitious time to raise this burning issue onto the Knesset podium. Mapam and the Communists joined in the fray by submitting urgent motions for the Knesset's agenda but the Knesset presidium rejected

---

52 On this matter, see: Minutes of 53/1955 government meeting on June 26, 1955 (ISA), as well as news items printed in the press on June 27 (e.g., "The Ministry of Justice will Handle the Appeal Against the Verdict," *Zemanim*; "The Gruenwald-Kasztner Case is Not Removed from the Agenda," *Al HaMishmar*; "The Government Decided to Approve the Appeal in the Kasztner Case," *Lamerchav*; *Ma'ariv* published an especially detailed report on the meeting ("Sharett Expresses Regret at Not Being Called to Testify").

the motions proposed by the General Zionists and Mapam because the case was *sub judice*. The Communist party's suggestion for a debate on "placing Kasztner on trial under the Nazis and Nazi Collaborators (Punishment) Law" was rejected by the presidium, because "this matter is a subject for the administrative, not the legislative authority."

When it became apparent that through this approach—urgent motions for the agenda—the matter could not be brought for discussion, the Herut Movement and the Communists proposed a vote of no-confidence. From Herut's standpoint, the motion had a clear political intent—to embarrass the General Zionists, who were competing with them for the same electoral segment and were attacking the government's position although they were members of the coalition.

The no-confidence motions were brought up on Tuesday, June 28.[53] The spokesmen for the factions that made the motions were Yohanan Bader of Herut and Esther Vilenska of the Communist party. Vilenska's comments were particularly strident. Once she had spoken, the debate was opened but hardly anything new was said. Prime Minister Sharett argued that the decision to appeal was in no way damaging to Judge Halevi "who has earned a reputation in the country for his consummate integrity, his peerless character and his superb professional skills." Israel Bar-Yehuda, from the Achdut Ha'avoda movement, claimed that all those who, instead of raising the banner of revolt, had tried "to outwit the devil, to obtain the lesser of two evils by compromising with him, were corrupted in the end, and knowingly or not, became pawns in the enemy's game."

Mapai's position was elucidated by M.K. Yaakov-Shimshon Shapira, who delivered a concise, resolute address. The verdict, he stated, created a total absurdity. A man had in effect been convicted in court without having been given any opportunity to defend himself, since he was not the defendant. "He had no lawyer, no defense counsel to voice his claims [...] hence he was convicted without having a chance to defend himself," he said. Moreover, the appeal is the very least that the state "can and should do for a man against whom such a fatal verdict has been pronounced."

Although the debate did not proceed very smoothly and a lot of heckling went on, the real storm broke out when the General Zionists' representative, Chaim Ariav, mounted the podium to make a consummately oppositional statement on behalf of his faction. He spoke about the hasty decision to file

---

53 "The General Zionists Demand a Debate in the Knesset about Kasztner," *Haboker*, June 26, 1955.

an appeal, which gave the clear impression that "people in the top ranks of Mapai in the government and the Jewish Agency [...] feel obliged to defend him apparently without carefully considering all the facts and true circumstances." He also asserted that the government, instead of prudently weighing its steps "was continuing to leave the clear impression that it is still covering up for Kasztner." This led him, he concluded, to decide, "Under the existing circumstances [...] our faction will abstain from voting."

When he stepped down, Mordechai Namir called out to him: "You should abstain from being in the government." The Prime Minister, whose face clearly reflected his outrage at Ariav's announcement, sent a note to Interior Minister Rokach, who sat next to him on the government's bench (about whom he wrote in his diary: he is "pitifully primitive"): "You are removing yourselves from the government." Rokach responded with a note of his own: "No. But you will resign." Although the two motions were soundly defeated, 50 to 9, against Herut's motion and 60 to 7 against the Communists', because of the General Zionists' abstention the issue continued to occupy the government.[54]

S. Z. Abramov, a General Zionist leader and for many years a member of Knesset, believes that the reason his faction abstained in the vote was to reap as many electoral gains as possible from the verdict. This motive was reflected in the party's unsuccessful bid to induce Tamir to accept a position of leadership in it.

It was Health Minister Yosef Serlin who pushed for opposition to an appeal. Rokach's attitude was ambivalent, while the ministers Bernstein and Sapir were opposed to this move. Since the rapid pace of events made it impossible to convene the party's directorate, the issue was brought to the Knesset faction for its decision, and Serlin managed to persuade the members to accept his view. But many members realized, after the party was ousted from Sharett's government, that the move had been a grave mistake and they had played right into the hands of the Herut Movement. This feeling grew after the elections to the Third Knesset, and was one of the reasons for the discord that later wracked the party.

Later that night the Mapai faction convened for an emergency meeting. According to press reports, a sense of open crisis prevailed at that meeting.[55]

---

54 Minutes of debate, Knesset records, June 28, 1955, vol. 18, pp. 2107–2119. The descriptions are from "Kasztner has Split the Government," *Yedioth Ahronoth*, June 29, 1955.

55 Sharett, *Personal Diary*, vol. 4, June 29, 1955, p. 1075; on this, see: "Kasztner Has Split the Government," *Yedioth Ahronoth*, June 29, 1955.

Although there was no discussion on the Kasztner issue, the unavoidable crisis in the government was discussed at length. Sharett, who opened the debate, said that the General Zionists had couched their statement in "their finest style, reflecting their chivalrous sentiments." But in his great naïveté, he had never imagined they would go so far as to abstain in the no-confidence vote. Now that they had abstained, he had no other choice but to resign and form a new government immediately. Otherwise, "we will turn ourselves into a laughingstock [...] and, most important of all—we will create the most malignant precedent for the future of every government and coalition in Israel."

When put to the vote, the Prime Minister's position was accepted unanimously and he immediately dissolved his government and formed a new one. The following afternoon, Wednesday, June 29, Sharett submitted his resignation to President Yitzhak Ben Zvi, and that same night presented his new government to the Knesset. It was based on a slim majority of 64 Knesset members and comprised only 12 ministers. No new ministers were appointed and the General Zionists' portfolios were assigned to the ministers of the outgoing government. In the debate on the government's resignation and the establishment of a new government,[56] many of the speakers related to Kasztner and his case. Overall, what they said merely repeated things already said. In the best Revisionist tradition, Begin argued that throughout the Holocaust, Mapai had suppressed the bitter news from Europe, because those were the days of El Alamein, and "it was decided not to trouble the Yishuv with information on the exterminations."[57]

M.K. Yosef Sapir, a senior member of the General Zionists and Minister of Transport in the outgoing government, was another to address the subject. He praised his party for choosing to follow the dictates of conscience and morality rather than considerations of procedure or political gain. He claimed that his party could not come to terms with the fact that the government had decided to defend a man accused of such grave crimes and for whom "there were numerous ways to try to acquit himself." Hence, the position taken by the General Zionists in the vote of no confidence was anchored in "human conscience." M.K. Pinhas Lavon reacted to these words in a witty, scorn-filled speech. Where was your conscience during the last two and a half years, from the time the Attorney General filed an indictment against Gruenwald, he asked. It's a very puzzling fact, considering that these "people

---

56 S.Z. Abramov, personal interview, Jerusalem, June 3, 1992; Minutes of meeting, Labor Party Archives, Section 2, 6-2-11; I am grateful to Tom Segev for giving them to me.
57 Minutes of debate, Knesset records, June 29, 1955, vol. 18, pp. 2146–2167.

have such a sensitive conscience, that their conscience was drowsy in 1953, totally dormant in 1954, and in a state of complete inactivity in 1955," then suddenly, in June 1955, that same conscience took on "great cogency and enormous force." What happened all of a sudden, Lavon inquired with sharp irony: perhaps it's the dry desert air that blows in our country in the month of June? Perhaps the climatic conditions caused their conscience to suddenly rouse from its slumber, as we have seen from "the 'conscience-ridden' speech of M.K. Ariav?" Then, in replying to his own question, Lavon's ironic tone changed to polemic. "Anyone who speaks of conscience," he said, "should at least show some respect and proper regard for this word. Conscience is after all a serious matter. Not every move made in political chess or in the game of elections can be garbed in a vestment of conscience. What is the connection between conscience and filing or not filing an appeal? One can argue that it is an erroneous move; one can argue that it is not an erroneous move; one can argue that the Attorney General was obligated to do this in view of the course that events took; one can argue that he was not so obligated. But is this a question of conscience for a serious political party? No, ladies and gentlemen, this is a contemptible trick that you devised when you made calculations— not serious ones—based on the elections, and on them alone. No reason of conscience underpins this behavior."

XVII

In the wake of the rapid and dramatic developments in the political arena, an intense argument broke out about what exactly had motivated the General Zionists, making it clear that within a very short time, less than a week after Halevi gave his verdict, the affair was no longer an attempt to grapple with the memory of the Holocaust, but another chapter in Israeli politics. As a result, the election campaign did not focus on the relevant issues, but revolved around issues that did not really deeply concern the Israeli voter. "The Dr. Kasztner affair, as it took shape on the speakers' podiums, succeeded in creating a troubled, oppressive atmosphere," *Ha'aretz* wrote. "In this atmosphere, the voter does not know what the party, asking for his vote, is offering him. In this atmosphere [he is confused as to] the vital problems facing the country. And will Dr. Kasztner resolve the issue of the sidewalk in front of his house or his lack of a home?"

The General Zionists never stopped patting themselves on the back for having chosen principles over the delights of power. Their paper, *Haboker*, and their election propaganda devoted a lot of space to this self-congratulatory line. One of their election slogans read, "Conscience is not coalitional!" And another poster claimed that, unlike Mapai, whose newspaper and speakers publicly criticized Halevi's verdict, thus strengthening the impression that "the government as a whole wants to cover up for Kasztner and clear his name," the General Zionists "were not prepared to join in an attempt to identify the Israeli government with a man accused of horrible offenses during the blackest chapter of Jewish history."

But their move boomeranged. The party was the object of heaps of abuse from nearly all parts of the political spectrum. A succinct expression of this can be found in an election poster published by the Progressive party.[58] "Why did the government fall apart?" it asked, and replied, "The government fell apart because the basic principle that breathes life into every government—the principle of collective responsibility—was violated." And why was this basic principle violated?

> Because, realizing they were on the decline, the General Zionists had such a strong desire to exploit the Kasztner-Gruenwald trial for their own purposes in the elections. Because a month before the elections, they found it convenient to appear once again in the opposition.

Nor was the press sparing in its criticism of the General Zionists. Shabtai Teveth wrote that the verdict in the Kasztner-Gruenwald trial seemed to have "come raining down on the General Zionists like manna from heaven." Why? Because until that moment, "this party had stood, empty-handed, gazing back in yearning at the 1951 elections, when it managed to squeeze every last drop from the regime of austerity and control."[59]

Despite the criticism, the General Zionists stuck to their guns. On July 6, a front-page headline in *Haboker* read, "Who silenced Ira Hirschman?" The news item stated that a representative of the War Refugee Board in Turkey during the war, on a visit to Israel, refused to be interviewed and told a journalist that official circles had asked him not to talk to anyone. The paper also quoted Hirschman's memoirs, according to which Lord Moyne had told him that, "Mr. Shertok [Sharett] has been invited to London for a meeting with Foreign

58 Shabtai Teveth, "The Kasztner Affair and the Election Campaign," *Ha'aretz*, July 15, 1955; "Report to the Voter by the General Zionists—The Center Party," *Haolam Hazeh*, July 7, 1955; "To the Citizens of Israel," *Zemanim*, July 6, 1955.
59 Shabtai Teveth, "The Kasztner Affair and the Election Campaign," *Ha'aretz*, July 15, 1955.

Minister [Anthony] Eden," at the time when he (Hirschman) had refused to meet him. "Why did Sharett nonetheless go to London to receive instructions from Eden?" *Haboker* asked, "Why did the British try to hide Brand from the American representative? And, why all the mystery surrounding this affair?" It is difficult to answer all these vexing questions, the paper stated, because, in his book, Hirschman left the mystery unresolved, while Sharett, "who did not appear as a witness in the Kasztner trial, did nothing to publicly clarify this affair, which touches on fundamental matters relating to the negotiations conducted with the Nazis in those dark days." A key question was posed toward the end of the item, which was actually the reason behind the entire item, "Why does Mr. Sharett prefer to remain silent?"

The news item was of no importance. Dozens like it were published at the time in the press in general and in *Herut* in particular, and it was clearly part of the General Zionists' failed attempt to turn themselves into 'Herut number two.' However, it became a public event—clearly illustrating that in the blazing July heat, everyone had lost all sense of proportion and the ability to separate the wheat from the chaff. Although it was just one more newspaper write-up, Sharett turned it into a public scandal. "*Haboker* is provoking me," he wrote. "Why am I remaining silent in the face of all the vilifying accusations regarding the holocaust of Hungary's Jews? Why did I fly to London [at the time] at Eden's invitation? Why did I follow his instructions? And other such lies and slander." This particular article may have aroused his anger, or it may have been the accumulation of articles published daily that so infuriated Sharett. In any case, two days before the news item appeared in *Haboker*, Sharett had arranged a special meeting with Isser Harel, head of the security services. In a cafe, with their wives present, Sharett asked Harel "to suggest an appropriate response to the monstrous accusations of both *Lamerchav* and *Haboker*, alleging that Mapai had tried to establish ties with Hitler during WWII in order to save the Yishuv from invasion." Of Harel it could be said that, "it takes one to know one." He suggested that *Davar* print an excerpt from something by his own people, written by Haganah leader Eliyahu Golomb, about "attempts by the Stern gang [Lehi] to establish contacts with Germany and Italy." The Prime Minister liked the idea.[60] The following day, Sharett invited Avriel to lunch and poured out his frustrations about the press being full of accusations vis-à-vis Brand and his mission, while he himself— the Prime Minister/Foreign Minister—is helpless and doesn't know what to do. Should he convene a special press conference at which he can relate all

---

60 Sharett, *Personal Diary*, vol. 4, July 6, 1955, p. 1083; Ibid., July 4, 1955, pp. 1080–1081.

the facts? Harel had been strongly opposed to that idea, and Avriel "tried to dissuade me from doing so because it might just add fuel to the fire." He was also fed up with Achdut Ha'avoda. What audacity they have, he complained to his guest, to present the parachutists' mission "as if the whole operation was theirs alone." Avriel agreed with him—not only was it not their sole operation, but also a lot of time had been lost in pointless discussions because of the superfluous obstacles raised by Hakibbutz Hameuchad movement about the cooperation with the British, and as a result, "the beginning of the action was delayed for no good reason." The ongoing preoccupation with the question "who gave the order" to file an appeal, infuriated Sharett. After yet another article on the matter was printed in *Haboker,* he wrote a flat denial, which he distributed through the Government Press Office.

After that, Sharett could no longer exercise restraint. On the evening of the day *Haboker* printed its news item, he appeared at an election rally in Netanya and wrote in his diary, "I made a scathing polemical speech […] I settled accounts with *Haboker* and *Lamerchav.*" But the story didn't end there. A few days later, *Haboker* attacked Sharett once again. The lengthy article was nothing but a variation on the worn-out motif of the 'conspiracy of silence': Shertok had allegedly met with Joel Brand in Aleppo on June 7, 1944; Brand recounted to him all the details of the deportation and extermination of Hungary's Jews, but Shertok "concealed all this information from the Yishuv and world Jewry." To emphasize and illustrate how grave this sin of deception was, the paper calculated that from May 18, 1944, the day Brand arrived in Istanbul, until mid-July, when the appalling news he had brought with him was published, more than 600,000 Jews had perished.

This time, Sharett's response was different. He composed a long reply and asked that it be printed in all the daily papers. "Isser is against the publication," he noted in his diary.[61] In a letter, accusing *Haboker* of "committing the sin of defaming him and distorting the historical truth on such a grave matter," Sharett presented his version of the events. According to him, the historical truth was the very reverse of the false picture depicted in *Haboker.* In early June, immediately after Brand's news reached Palestine, everything was done to publicize it, and the National Committee even issued an open letter entitled "A Call of Alarm to Rescue Those Remaining." Sharett concluded his letter, in

---

61 Ibid., July 5, 1955; "Who is Responsible for the Kasztner Appeal?" *Haboker,* June 30, 1955; Sharett, *Personal Diary,* vol. 4, July 6, 1955, p. 1085; "Why did Moshe Sharett Suppress Information about the Holocaust of Hungarian Jewry for Many Weeks?" *Haboker,* June 12, 1955; Sharett, *Personal Diary,* July 12, 1955, p. 1091; the letter was marked CZA, A245-36; it was published in various newspapers on July 14, 1955.

his usual high-flown language with, "This document merits republication in full now so that people in liberated Zion may know the truth and, at the same time, inhale the air of those terrible days."

The following day,[62] *Haboker* printed Sharett's letter along with an editorial comment to the effect that the material published by the newspaper was a summary of the arguments made by the defense, ten months earlier; "during all this time, Mr. Sharett did not see fit to react. He is only doing so now that *Haboker* has repeated the contents of the verdict." A day later, again riding on Tamir's coattails, the newspaper printed a long article comparing Sharett's letter to *Davar*'s headlines during the war to show how "the Yishuv's attention had been distracted from the extermination of Hungarian Jewry." A week later, *Haboker* printed a cable proving that the Hungarian Catholic church, not the Jewish Agency, had informed the world of the slaughter of Hungary's Jews.[63] This was the last publication in the series. A few days later, on July 26, the elections to the Third Knesset were held.

XVIII

The item in *Haboker* was one of a series published at the time about various episodes dredged up from the past. Every party in the debate exploited them in an attempt to prove how their behavior had complied with the code of heroism, while their rivals had violated this code. *Lamerchav,* which devoted much space to the subject, printed many declarations applauding the fighters and denouncing Kasztner. In a putative news item, worded more like an indictment, the paper reported that an emissary from Hungary, a member of 'Kasztner's circle,' had suggested to the leaders of the Halutz in Poland that they save their own lives. The six leaders, including Yitzhak Zuckerman ('Antek') and his wife, Zivia Lubetkin, had adamantly rejected the offer and refused to accept the money he had brought for them. They told the emissary in no uncertain terms that the problem was not saving six people but the lives of all of Polish Jewry, and we, they informed him, "will remain and fight to save the lives of the Jewish masses."

---

62 "What was Published on the Holocaust of Hungarian Jewry—and When?" *Haboker*, July 13, 1955.

63 "Who Announced the Massacre of Hungarian Jewry—and When?" *Haboker*, July 21, 1955.

General Moshe Carmel, the highly respected commander of the northern front in the War of Independence and Minister of Transport after the elections, was first to raise the issue. Carmel did so at two election rallies at the end of the week following the publication of the verdict, and his words were quoted in a huge headline on the front page of *Lamerchav*.[64] Carmel brought it up to illustrate the proper code of conduct, the very opposite of Kasztner's. As an example, he cited "the behavior of the Yishuv when the Nazis were about to invade the country." The Yishuv, he asserted, prepared itself to actively resist the invader: units of the Palmach, the elite strike force of the Haganah, were transferred to the south "to set up resistance to the Nazis there" and "overnight, dozens of training camps were set up throughout the country, where scores of men, young and old, were trained to be prepared to resist the invader."

Carmel compared the exemplary behavior of the Palmach with the defeatist attitude of several of the Yishuv's leaders, who argued "we ought to find some way to establish contact with the Germans, to 'prove' to them that they have nothing to gain from annihilating the Jewish community." These leaders believed that if they could prove to the Germans that the "Yishuv is a constructive community," whose production could be of interest to them, "it could serve as an important factory working for the Germans."

This issue was not a new one. Achdut Ha'avoda leader and Carmel's teacher and mentor, Yitzhak Tabenkin, had already raised it at the end of 1942, after El Alamein, when the threat of a German invasion had been lifted.[65] Carmel came back to it to show how Halevi's verdict had "lifted a veil [and] shed light on Jewish heroism on the one hand, and collaboration with the Nazis on the other. What took place during that time in the European Diaspora reveals not only the deep chasms of history, but our present-day existence as well. And it teaches us a lesson for the future."

Carmel wanted to convey a clear political message: his party, Achdut Ha'avoda, was identified with the heroic line, with the fighters in the ghettos of Europe and the Palmach in Palestine, while Mapai was identified with the defeatist line, with Kasztner in Europe and with those who wanted to negotiate with the Nazis during the days when El Alamein aroused fear and anxiety. His words were in complete harmony with his party's fundamental

64 Israel Galili, "A Jew Must Never Hand over His Brethren to Satan," *Lamerchav*, July 3, 1955; General Moshe Carmel, "An Emissary from Hungary Wanted to Save Zivia and Antek, but They Refused," *Lamerchav*, June 26, 1955.

65 On this matter, see: Yechiam Weitz, "The Yishuv's Self-Image and the Reality of the Holocaust," *Jerusalem Quarterly*, vol. 48 (Fall, 1988), pp. 73–88.

motto—We stand for Zionist socialist activism. One of the party's election ads also reflected this message under the heading, "Where were you during the War of Independence?" A map of the war was drawn, emphasizing those areas where Palmach units fought, in particular the area of Abu-Ageilah—El Arish, from which the IDF was forced to retreat in January 1949 under orders from Ben-Gurion. To underscore the connection between the Palmach and the new party, the names of its candidates to the Third Knesset, who had fought in the war, were printed at the bottom of the ad.[66]

Davar wasted no time in reacting. Under the headline, "Moshe Carmel's falsification of history,"[67] it wrote that the decision to send the emissary was taken by the leadership of the Kibbutz Hameuchad in Palestine, not by Kasztner in Hungary. The paper claimed that the decision was taken in September 1943 at a meeting in Kibbutz Shefayim, attended by three of the movement's leaders—Yitzhak Tabenkin, Israel Galili and Moshe Kliger (who headed the Diaspora department in the movement's secretariat). The man who dealt with the letter "was also a member of the Kibbutz Hameuchad, who was then posted in Istanbul for the purpose of rescuing the Jews of Europe." In light of this information, *Davar* addressed an "open question" to Tabenkin:

> Is he prepared to publish the true facts, since he himself was responsible for the decision, or does he choose, for purposes of election propaganda, to be a party to the malicious, false accusations made by one of his associates, Moshe Carmel?

Two days later, *Lamerchav* revealed the identity of the man who handled the transmission of the letter; it was Venia Pomerantz, whose letter was printed in a prominent place on the front page.[68] The letter, which the paper alleged had been sent to *Davar* but was never published, attests to the grotesqueness of the story. It consisted of two parts; the first was sent to the *Lamerchav* editorial office on June 26, but was not published. This letter in fact contained *Davar*'s claim regarding the source of the mission, and in it Pomerantz wrote that he was "utterly astonished" by Carmel's interpretation of his words. In the second half, which contradicts the first, Pomerantz claimed that after a

---

66 "In Your Hand," (a propaganda leaflet distributed by Achdut Ha-avoda), July 8, 1955; among the names mentioned in the ad were Israel Galili, Yigal Allon, Moshe Carmel and commanders of Palmach brigades Nahum Sarig, Mula Cohen and Yosefele Tabenkin.
67 *Davar*, June 29, 1955.
68 "A Former Emissary to Istanbul Confirms Carmel's Statement and Defends *Davar*," *Lamerchav*, July 1, 1955.

thorough investigation of the facts, he had learned that the emissary from Istanbul had never reached Poland and the emissary whose offer Antek and Zivia had rejected had come from Slovakia, not from Istanbul. Pomerantz concluded the letter with two paragraphs. In the first, he wrote, "I am now sticking precisely to the facts, after all, [our country is going through] a time of legal proceedings [...]." In the second part, which was printed in bold letters, he wrote that he was amazed by what *Davar* had published, "which I did not give to the newspaper—so it is not fair, neither from the public standpoint nor with regard to intentions." "The *Davar* writers," *Lamerchav* concluded, "have lost their heads. In connection with the Kasztner trial, someone feels the need to rewrite the history of the Holocaust and the resistance, to adapt it to his own current needs."

Then, wonder of wonders, that very same day, *Davar* also printed Pomerantz' letter. "We have never claimed that Pomerantz gave us the things we printed on June 29, 1955 for publication," the paper commented, going on to intimate that Pomerantz's fellow members in Hakibbutz Hameuchad had pressured him into publishing the last part of his letter. But this bizarre episode did not end there. The following day, *Davar* printed a statement vehemently attacking *Lamerchav*.[69] The paper had agreed to print Pomerantz's letter, the statement claimed, only after "he had agreed to add to the letter some inarticulate remarks, which do not contradict the main points of his original letter, and also agreed—under heavy pressure—to state that he was astonished by the publication in *Davar*." Moreover, the statement goes on to say, *Lamerchav* had depicted the conduct of the heads of the Halutz in Poland, who refused to save themselves, as an exemplary model, in contrast to the rescue train. If that is the case, why did members of Hakibbutz Hameuchad go to such lengths, desperately trying to save the poet Yitzhak Katznelson? And then, "why are you making such denunciatory allegations?" Avriel made his own contribution to the argument by asking, with palpable pain, his friends-adversaries in Hakibbutz Hameuchad, "Was it really necessary to drag this panoply of horrors, known as the Jewish Holocaust and the rescue attempts, into an arena of mockery?"

As far as *Lamerchav* was concerned, the polemic was closed in a long article written by Moshe Carmel, articulately expressing the polarized world-view, in which there is room only for 'heroes' and 'traitors'. Any attempt to cast doubt on this view and to "blur the lines between heroism and weakness,

---

69 "*Lamerchav* and Y. Tabenkin Deny," *Davar*, July 1, 1955; "*Lamerchav* Shows No Shame," *Davar*, July 2, 1955.

between self-sacrifice and egoism, between loyalty and treachery," was liable to be catastrophic. It was liable to "shake the very foundations of the generation, to destroy the most sacrosanct moral values, to sap the mind and soul of the *halutz*, of the zealous Hebrew fighter."

However, although it did engage in a heated polemic with Mapai, the Achdut Ha'avoda movement did not accept the sweeping criticism of Herut and the Communists. The claim that Kasztner had represented Mapai was joined by another, according to which he had in fact "betrayed those who had made him their agent—the Zionist institutions in Palestine." And Moshe Braslavsky, a member of Kibbutz Na'an, advised caution with regard to "the filth of the Communists and Herut [who are] trying to besmirch the Zionist emissaries and institutions" and whose newspapers "continue [...] to pollute the atmosphere."[70]

The aftermath of the verdict rekindled the debate about the 'two paths' that had raged a year earlier. In his column *Hatur Hashevi'i* (the seventh column), Nathan Alterman inveighed against *Lamerchav*'s categorical statement that a clear distinction could be drawn between heroism and submission, between resistance and collaboration:

> Let us not today compose speeches about that same arrogant, clear-cut division of methods and ways, which is characterized primarily by hindsight. We shall not plumb the depths and foundations of the period by trying to alter and distort its face.[71]

Alterman's arguments gave rise to immediate and sharp reactions. Carmel's article was largely a response to them, and journalist Meir Ben Gur, who wrote for the paper, argued that if we were to educate our children according to these views we would raise a confused generation that, instead of choosing one of these two paths, "would continue to stand at a crossroads."

Beyond the ideological argument, the issue had a distinctly political aspect. Alterman was a leading intellectual associated with the Mapai party and its leadership; and at the meeting of the Mapai secretariat that discussed

---

70 "Ehud [Avriel], "Those who Seek Warmth in the Light of the Conflagration," *Davar*, July 6, 1955; "Chasms at the Feet of the Generation," *Lamerchav*, July 8, 1955; "A Trial and its Significance," *Bakibbutz* 26 (July 13, 1955), p. 4.

71 "Around the Trial, the Seventh Column," *Davar*, July 1, 1955; about the argument on the 'Two Paths', see Nathan Alterman, *On The Two Paths—Pages from the Notebook* (Dan Laor edited, explicated, and added an afterword.) (Hebrew) (Tel Aviv: Hakibbutz Hameuchad Publishing House, 1989).

the trial, the party secretary, Kesse, ceremoniously announced that he had met with the poet, who told him he was drafting a reply to Carmel and Ben Gur that would be "the longest column he had ever written."[72]

Achdut Ha'avoda, too, gave the dispute a political cast; in its election campaign, it enlisted its biggest cannon—Antek Zuckerman, a member of Kibbutz Lochamei Hageta'ot, who did not usually involve himself in politics. He appeared at a select forum of activists at Efal and at a public meeting at the Esther cinema in Tel Aviv. At both meetings, he proposed the same argument, using nearly the same words: no contradiction exists between the path of resistance and the path of rescue; on the other hand, there is a profound contradiction between the path of rescue and the path taken by collaborators. *Lamerchav* covered the public meeting under the headline, "If the way of the Judenrat is right, the fighters should be put on trial." At the meeting, Zuckerman had stated, "only in the lines of Alterman's poem do the members of the Judenrat live in peace with the fighters." Afterwards, he asked a series of rhetorical questions:

> Did the Judenrat save anyone? Did the *galuti* approach save anyone? Who did rescue anyone? [Mordechai Chaim] Rumakowski in Lodz? Did [Moshe] Merin in Zaglembie? Did [Jacob] Ganz in Vilna? Did [Ephraim] Barash in Bialystok?

Not surprisingly, his response to all these questions was, "The only thing capable of rescuing anyone was the spirit of resistance. The only ones capable of saving anyone were those who preached non-submission, only those who preached refusal to obey German orders." Later, he said that he had no doubt that "were it not for the resistance and the anti-submission movement, even those few Jews who did flee from the oppressor would not have fled."[73]

---

72 Meir Ben Gur, "The Poet Natan A. and the 'Two Paths'," *Lamerchav*, July 7, 1955; meeting of Mapai secretariat, July 12, 1955, Labor Party Archives, 23/55; on the political aspect of Alterman's position, see: Yechiam Weitz, "Two Explanations for the 'Two Paths'," *Cathedra* 53 (October, 1989), pp. 53–61, and Dinah Porat, "There Were No 'Two Paths'," *Zionism* 15 (1990), pp. 223–235.

73 From his address at an Achdut Ha'avoda—Poalei Zion rally at the Esther cinema in Tel Aviv, on Friday evening, July 15, 1955; I was given the minutes of that meeting by Zvika Dror of Kibbutz Lochamei Hageta'ot, and I am grateful to him.

XIX

Another movement that referred incessantly to the trial in its election campaign was Herut. It regarded the verdict as supreme proof of Mapai's treacherous nature, and the people who wrote its election slogans echoed the arguments Tamir had made in court. It also made the man and his trial a symbol of all the ills of the government in power; a journalist jeered that as far as Herut was concerned it would take no more than hanging him [Kasztner] from a 100-foot tree, "to restore the Land of Israel to the borders of the Kingdom of David. Solel Boneh, Hamashbir, and Kupat Holim [companies owned by the Histadrut], like the other enemies of the Jewish people would collapse, crumbling into dust as soon as the nation wreaked revenge upon Dr. Kasztner." An example of the use the movement made of the trial can be found in a circular printed by its propaganda department. Under the heading "We were not the ones who said it," it read:

> **The Court stated:** that a man loyal to Mapai, a member of the rescue committee, and Knesset candidate—Israel Kasztner—sold his soul to the devil, became a quisling, knowingly collaborated with the Nazis and obstructed rescue and escape activities, prepared the ground for the extermination of Hungary's Jews, sent the rescue parachutists to their death, and saved Nazi war criminals from punishment.[74]

XX

In addition to all these attempts to use the trial as a vehicle for hurling all manner of accusations in order to reap political gains, efforts were also made to achieve some kind of understanding of the painful affair, regardless of its political aspects. *Haaretz* stood out in these attempts. Throughout July, the paper printed a series of articles by Dr. Moshe Keren, a senior journalist on its staff. From conversations with Kasztner's acquaintances, whom he claimed did not speak affectionately about Kasztner, Keren obtained a picture of a character "of mixed color, like all of us, consisting of many and varied shades [...] neither all black nor all white, neither a monster nor a saint." Keren portrayed him as "a man who found certain satisfaction from his close

---

74 Circular Number 69 of the Herut Movement's Central Publicity Department dated July 14, 1955, the Jabotinsky Institute in Israel.

association with the leaders of the world at that time, and from the measure of importance accorded him [...];" but he was also a courageous man, who could have, without a doubt, "made his own escape on many occasions, had he so wished, as many other Jewish leaders had done, without anyone blaming them for deserting the front."

Keren presented him as the victim of a tragedy, of the fate that "sent him and all his friends to the depths of the blazing inferno." He found himself dealing with problems of a fearful magnitude—at a murderous pace and deprived of any free choice. But the man did not break; marshalling all his strength he tried "not to lose his senses, not to become a helpless pawn in the game of the elements." At least for this he was worthy of just esteem, but his misfortune was that he emerged alive from the valley of death.[75]

Many of the letters to the editor were about the trial—especially in the wake of Keren's articles. One Baruch Shor from Haifa asserted that while Israel is a democracy and one of its basic principles demands freedom of speech and of the press, he does not believe that "venomous criticism bordering on contempt of court is permissible in the daily press." How does Keren dare," asked Asher Lazar of Jerusalem, "to cast aspersion on the verdict of a judge who sat in judgment, who listened and investigated the affair, as it was brought before him by the Attorney General and counsel for the defense."

The bulk of the letters expressed a different view, and not for formalistic reasons. Yehuda Talmi of Kfar Glickson, who in 1945 was sent on a mission to Hungary, wrote that throughout the period of his stay there he listened to the stories of hundreds of people and read hundreds of testimonies, but "never did I hear or read anywhere, on any occasion, the accusations that were leveled by the judge, Dr. Benjamin Halevi, against Israel Kasztner." He also claimed that the verdict totally ignored the dreadful problems involved in every rescue attempt in Hungary, and the indifference, even hostility, towards any Zionist activity. He concluded by saying "on hearing so categorical and unequivocal a verdict on the rescue efforts, every human heart should be horrified, [and have] doubt constantly nibbling away at it."[76]

However, it was in an article in the prestigious Jewish-American periodical, *Commentary*, that the harshest criticism was leveled against the judge and the trial.[77] Its author was journalist and historian Walter Laqueur,

75 Moshe Keren, "An Unconvincing Document," *Ha'aretz*, July 14, 1955.

76 On his mission to Hungary, see: *Mission to the Diaspora, 1945–1948* (Hebrew) (Efal: Yad Tabenkin, 1989), pp. 257–274.

77 W. Z. Laqueur, "The Kasztner Case—Aftermath of the Catastrophe," *Commentary* 20 (December, 1955).

who lived in Israel for many years and was very familiar with Israeli life. He put down on paper some sensitive, highly charged opinions, which hereto had only been whispered behind closed doors and could not be published in Israel: how Tamir had succeeded in gaining control of the trial and the judge and the things that made it possible for him to demonize Kasztner and the [leaders] of Mapai. Although admittedly Kasztner did not emerge squeaky clean, Laqueur wondered why the prosecution had called upon him in the first place, especially as its first witness. Still, Laqueur devotes the main part of the article to Tamir and his machinations and to Judge Halevi and asserts that Tamir began demonizing Kasztner after he discovered the affidavit he had given in Becher's favor. This discovery was the beginning of the end of the trial. From here on, it was easy for him to prove that:

> [...] A Jew willing to testify on behalf a high-ranking SS officer was capable of any infamy. And if Kasztner had intervened on Becher's behalf, it meant that there must have been good reason for it—that Kasztner had been in cahoots with Becher! How could anyone believe a man like Kasztner who had already proved himself a liar? Hadn't all his other statements been lies too?

In his demagogy, Tamir denounced the Jewish Agency for having done nothing to save the six million Jews that perished. His attempt to unload the blame for the catastrophe on the pre-state Jewish national organizations is reminiscent of the Weimar Republic's use of the "stab in the back" legends and the claims of McCarthy and others in the United States on the "betrayal of China." Since the extermination of one third of the Jewish nation was a far more traumatic event for the Jews than Germany's defeat in World War I was for the Germans or the Sovietization of China was for the United States, "Tamir did not find it hard to tempt willing ears to his own new 'stab in the back' legend. If not for men like Kasztner, he argued, everything would have been different. The Kasztners were at fault, **they were the real war criminals**" [emphasis added].

Tamir's tactics enabled him, to a great extent, to manage the course of the trial; he was thus able to extend the trial's framework to include matters that were totally irrelevant to the original indictment. About Tamir's tactics and the free hand he was given by Judge Halevi, Laqueur wrote:

> Tamir wanted to prove that Avriel and Bader were also liars and traitors and had sabotaged the rescue attempts. All this had little to do with the

Kasztner-Gruenwald case, but was aimed at discrediting the majority parties in Israel. Judge Halevi barely interfered. Shortly before the opening of the trial, he had resigned from the bench because he had been passed over when a new appointment was made to the Supreme Court; perhaps a member of a government party had been given preference over him? A few weeks later Halevi would withdraw his resignation.

Laqueur ended his article with a direct attack on Judge Halevi: It was Kasztner's misfortune that he had to face this particular judge. Although Halevi, in Laqueur's view, was a decent man and independent in his judgment, he was also:

> [...] narrow-minded, devoid of historical perspective, and lacked the capacity to put himself in another person's shoes—and these were extremely important requirements in delivering a verdict in this particular case. Had he possessed these qualities, he might have refused to be the sole judge of this [...] most tragic epoch in Jewish history. That he, a single individual, was ready to undertake to do so can be understood either as evidence of personal courage or of lack of imagination. It was probably a mixture of both.

Halevi's verdict included one fundamental that was almost absurd—his determination that it would all have been different had Kasztner not negotiated with the SS officers, because then the Jews of Hungary could have been forewarned and many of them would have been rescued. This, Laqueur wrote:

> [...] is a fantastic hypothesis that can only be entertained by a person who is completely ignorant of the conditions that prevailed in Europe at that time. It can be argued that the policy Kasztner and his colleagues pursued was wrong and ended in failure, but they cannot be accused in retrospect of not having followed a 'policy of strength' in Budapest in the summer of 1944. It may be said that a man who, like Kasztner, had been trapped in such a frightful dilemma ought never to hold public office again, but how can he be considered a criminal? Is it a crime to speak the truth even if it is about an officer of the SS?

No one in Israel would have dared raise Laqueur's third point, even if he or she was convinced of its truth. Laqueur suggested, albeit in a cautious and moderate tone, that it was no coincidence that Halevi had postponed delivering his verdict to the end of June 1955, the eve of the general elections; he chose that timing "to insure its reappearance in the headlines—but perhaps this is unfair, perhaps the trial meant more to him than the elections and their outcome. I don't know."

In reaction to Laqueur's critical remarks about the judge, the Minister of Justice sent a letter of protest to the editor of *Commentary*. This letter led Laqueur to publish an apology, in which he wrote that on further reflection, "there is no reason to assume that Judge Halevi in his choice of the date [to pronounce his verdict] was influenced by any extraneous motive."[78] But that did not put an end to the matter. M.K. Meir Vilner of the Communist party submitted a question to Minister Rosen: Laqueur, whom he represented— not by accident—as the political commentator of *Kol Israel*, had denigrated the judge in his article; does the Minister intend to "institute a legal action against [...] Laqueur under the Courts Ordinance or the Criminal Law Ordinance?" Rosen replied that Laqueur had apologized and that in any case, it was impossible to take legal steps against him, since the offense was not committed in Israel.[79]

78 "Second Thoughts on Kasztner," *Jewish Observer and Middle East Review*, 5 (August, 1955); *Commentary* (February, 1956), p. 184.
79 Knesset session on March 7, 1956; Knesset records, vol. 20, p. 1336.

CHAPTER SIX

From One Verdict to Another

I

The elections to the Third Knesset were held on July 26. Mapai took quite a beating, losing five of its previously held forty-five seats. The General Zionists, despite their "Kasztner ploy," or perhaps because of it, suffered an even harder blow—they won only thirteen seats as compared with the twenty they had won in the 1951 elections. In contrast, all the 'anti-Kasztner' parties grew in strength: Achdut Ha'avoda won ten seats, the Communists increased their number from five to six, and the greatest victory of all was Herut's. That party nearly doubled in strength winning fifteen seats, as compared with eight in the previous elections, making Herut the second-largest faction in the Knesset.

The Mapai central committee devoted a series of meetings to analyzing the election results; throughout these, Halevi's verdict was barely mentioned. Aryeh Bahir, who headed the election headquarters, was one of the few party members to bring it up and according to him, "To some extent the Kasztner trial and the Arlozoroff affair shook the public's confidence in some of the party's leadership."[1]

While it was gradually removed from the political agenda, the affair did not disappear, with most of the activity surrounding it being in the legal arena. The State Attorney's office was busy preparing the appeal, an event that some expected to be no less dramatic and stormy than the trial in the lower court. As in the past year, in the year to come, too, the Kasztner trial will constitute the country's "big issue," wrote *Haolam Hazeh* shortly before Rosh Hashanah, 5716 (1955); but unlike the "first round," in which the prosecution

---

1 Meeting of Mapai central committee, August 8, 1955, Labor Party Archives, 23/55; on this meeting see: Yechiam Weitz, *A Party Contends with its Failure—Mapai Faces the Elections to the Third Knesset* (Hebrew), *Cathedra* 77 (October, 1995), pp. 124–138.

was conspicuous in its weakness, this time "all the big guns will be pointed at Shmuel Tamir." And in this round, the paper promised, well-known people from abroad will be taking part and revealing some startling secrets from the past.

In Tel Aviv, the hearing of the 'real Kasztner trial' began. In this trial Kasztner was the official, rather than merely the de facto defendant. When the verdict was handed down in the district court, Tamir and Gruenwald agreed they were not satisfied and decided to institute another lawsuit. In early July, Tamir submitted a personal complaint against Kasztner on Gruenwald's behalf to the Tel Aviv Magistrate's Court. It related to Kasztner's testimony in the Jerusalem district court, on February 22, 1954, in which he denied having provided an affidavit in Becher's favor.

In light of Halevi's position in his verdict with regard to this testimony, Gruenwald asked the Tel Aviv Magistrate's Court to summon Kasztner to a preliminary investigation and to issue an injunction to place him on trial in the district court for the aforementioned crime. Gruenwald opted for this action because he was unable to achieve his desired aim—to bring Kasztner to trial under the Nazis and Nazi Collaborators Law, since only the relevant authorities were able to file an indictment under that law.

Gruenwald had been certain, he said, that after Halevi's judgment Kasztner would be placed on trial for perjury. In response to his appeal, Gruenwald claimed, the Attorney General had told him he would not deal with the matter until after the appeal was heard, and this could take a long time. Gruenwald added that if his complaint were heard prior to the Supreme Court appeal he "[would have] the opportunity to clarify at least part of the affair in light of the facts."[2] The complaint was heard in July by Tel Aviv magistrate Max Czernobilsky.

As one of the newspapers pointed out, this time Tamir and Gruenwald's task was ostensibly a very simple one. All they had to do was "submit two pages of the transcript, in which the fateful contradictions had been recorded in the previous trial." For this purpose, Miriam Bernstein, Halevi's assistant, was summoned to the court to bring the original transcript signed by the judge.

In actual fact, it was not that simple. This time, Kasztner appeared accompanied by his lawyer, Micha Caspi, who was described as "one of the most brilliant lawyers in Israel." When the hearing opened, Caspi argued that since the offense imputed to Kasztner was committed in a Jerusalem court,

---

2   "Grunewald Suing Kasztner," *Ma'ariv*, July 7, 1955; "Grunewald Submitted a Complaint Against Kasztner," *Ha'aretz*, July 8, 1955.

the only court competent to deal with it was one in that district, rather than in the defendant's place of residence. The judge accepted the argument, and the rest of the trial was postponed. According to one assessment, Caspi requested the transfer despite the inconvenience it involved, because the defense was interested in gaining time; maybe it even hoped to further put off the trial, if it were to take place just as the Supreme Court was hearing the appeal.[3]

The hearing, which was removed to the Magistrate's court of Jerusalem, opened at the beginning of February 1956, before the Chief Magistrate Judge, Moshe Peretz. On this occasion, too, many of the original players in the drama took the stage again, eight months later; although this time, their roles were reversed. Gruenwald had become the plaintiff and his defense counsel, Tamir, was now the prosecutor. Both arrived in court belligerent and convinced of their victory. In contrast, Kasztner was tense and morose. His hair had turned gray in the meanwhile and he took his place at the rear of the courtroom unobtrusively, "as if he were not himself; only his shadow."[4]

On the first day of the trial, each side presented its position. Tamir argued that in his testimony in the District Court, Kasztner had knowingly, deliberately and maliciously made a false statement, according to which he had not testified in Becher's favor and, by doing so, saving the German from facing trial at the international tribunal in Nuremberg. He did so, Tamir alleged, to conceal the truth from the District Court. To substantiate his claim, he inundated the judge with exhibits, including letters, documents, excerpts from the transcript of the trial, and more. Caspi's line of argument was that Kasztner had indeed provided an affidavit on Becher's behalf, but not to the international court in Nuremberg or to its institutions, but rather to the Denazification Court. In other words, he did give an affidavit, but did not lie in his testimony before the District Court.

Kasztner did not give his statement under oath, so that Tamir would have no opportunity to cross-examine him. His first argument was that his decision to give the affidavit for Becher was a matter between him and his own conscience "which was as clear then as it is now." He was "one of the few Jews to remain alive and to have the opportunity to see the Nazi beast from close up, to judge it and also to assess those—if there were any—who helped us, at various times and to various degrees, to save Jews [...] I was the only one to witness his actions from beginning to end."

3   "The Kasztner Affair—On One Bench," *Haolam Hazeh*, 4 August, 1955.
4   Shalom Rosenfeld, "The Kasztner Affair (Phase 2)," *Ma'ariv*, February 6, 1956; A. Avidan, "The Second Act of the Kasztner Trial Opens," *Herut*, February 7, 1956.

His second argument was that he was asked at the trial if he had testified in Becher's favor at the Nuremberg international tribunal "and, as a former lawyer, I had to answer the question in the negative." Another point he raised in this context was that during his direct examination, he was asked whether he had given an affidavit in regard to Becher to the Denazification Court. His reply to that question was affirmative, and he added afterwards that "it was only in this preliminary examination that I heard for the first time that this affidavit, which I had been asked to give for the German Denazification Court, was in Becher's file in Washington, according to what Tamir said."

In contrast to the proceedings in the District Court, when the stage was almost entirely Tamir's, this time he was faced by a no less formidable adversary. At the end of the first week, Caspi asked the court to adjourn for three weeks, until early March. The reason for his request was linked to the only two witnesses he had called. These were Dr. Robert Kempner, who had served as a prosecutor in the Nuremberg trials, and Benno Zelke, to whom Kasztner had given his affidavit; and they had both informed him they could not come to Israel in February. Tamir vigorously objected to Caspi's request, sarcastically arguing that while the two had stated they could not come in February, how could the court be sure they would arrive in March? This is an evasive trick, he charged, and it would be a crying injustice to grant Caspi's request. When Judge Peretz accepted Tamir's position, Caspi rose and in a move that astounded everyone present, announced he would petition the High Court of Justice to instruct the judge to adjourn the trial.

Another surprise was in store for everyone when Caspi questioned Tamir, who appeared at the trial not only as counsel for the plaintiff but also as witness for the prosecution, namely on his own behalf. The background for his appearance was his request for the trial to be adjourned until he could bring one Walter Rapp, head of the U.S. Department of Prosecution at the Nuremberg trials, to Israel. It was Rapp, Tamir alleged, who received Kasztner's affidavit for Becher and he was the one who decided not to put Becher on trial, on the basis of the affidavit. After the judge refused his request, Tamir announced that he would be forced to take the unusual step of placing himself in the witness box. And that is precisely what he did.

Tamir presented several documents during his testimony, all of which he claimed to have found in the archives of the American public prosecution at the Nuremberg trials. He presented the two most important of these documents, with barely concealed excitement. One was Kasztner's affidavit, given to and signed by Zelke and the second was Zelke's September 1947 request to change Becher's status from that of an accused to that of a witness.

With the help of these documents, as well as an undated document about Becher's release, Tamir tried to prove that:

> It was due to Kasztner's affidavit that the decision had been taken to release Becher from the status of a war criminal. And that the fact that Kasztner's affidavit was in the archives of the public prosecution in the Nuremberg trials proves that he gave his affidavit on behalf of the war criminals tribunal and not [on behalf of] the German Denazification Court, as he had claimed.

When Tamir was through presenting these documents, Caspi conducted an unrelenting cross-examination, during which Tamir admitted that all the correspondence between him and Robert Kempner, the American assistant public prosecutor at Nuremberg, had been forwarded to the Attorney General. "Kempner, it seems, is cleverer than Tamir," Caspi derisively stated; "it seems he is more of a conniver," Tamir responded angrily.[5]

Caspi dropped the real bombshell at the end of Tamir's testimony, when he demanded that the judge rule that Tamir could no longer serve as prosecutor in the case. To substantiate his demand, he cited a long list of precedents stating that an attorney who has given evidence in a case that he is conducting cannot continue to appear in that same trial as a prosecutor. The judge rejected Caspi's demand, but it was clear to all the spectators at the trial that Tamir was dealing with a fierce adversary who would not give in easily.

Three judges of the Supreme Court heard Caspi's request for an adjournment of the trial: Moshe Silberg, Zvi Berinson, and Alfred Witkon. The three issued an interim injunction postponing the continuation of the trial, after Caspi declared that if Kempner's testimony—he had agreed to come to testify—was not heard, his client would be liable to suffer a grave wrong, which would lead to a miscarriage of justice. He attached to his request a declaration under oath by Shmuel Barzel, a lawyer in his office, who handled the trial-related material.[6]

5   Aviezer Golan, "The Bomb That Never Went Off," *Yedioth Ahronoth*, February 8, 1956.
6   "An Interim Order to Postpone the Continuation of an Investigation of Kasztner," *Ha'aretz*, February 12, 1956.

II

Instead of confronting Tamir's accusations head on, *Ha'aretz* wrote,[7] Caspi offered two arguments; one was that Becher was never placed on trial before the international tribunal in Nuremberg, and the second was that Kasztner gave his affidavit before Zelke, an official in the American Defense Department, not at the international tribunal. If these arguments were accepted, that would disprove the prosecution's allegation that Kasztner had perjured himself when he testified in the District Court that he had never given evidence or an affidavit in Becher's favor to the international tribunal or one of its institutions. That might also make it possible to accept Kasztner's version of the facts, that he had provided an affidavit to the Denazification Court, not to the international tribunal.

This line of defense was put forward in a more detailed manner in an internal memo at the Caspi-Zadok law office. On this matter, Shmuel Barzel wrote to Haim Zadok:

> As you will certainly recall, our defense is based mainly on the fact that this affidavit was intended for the Denazification Court, not for the purposes of the international tribunal at Nuremberg. Although the affidavit was given before Zelke, who was employed at the international tribunal in Nuremberg, it was authenticated by him, not in that capacity, but rather as a public notary, before whom any person could draw up documents for any purpose whatsoever, without any connection to the international tribunal.[8]

According to Tamir, the memo went on to say, the affidavit in fact reached the files of the international tribunal. To substantiate this claim, Tamir had put on the witness stand a lawyer by the name of Ziegel. During the Gruenwald trial, Ziegel "had been asked by Tamir to search for various documents in Germany, and among other places, also went to the office of the international tribunal in Nuremberg where he received an authenticated copy of the German translation of Kasztner's affidavit, which at the time was submitted to Judge Halevi and was now being produced in the preliminary action." In Barzel's

---

7   Shlomo Goren, "Caspi's Tactics," *Yedioth Ahronoth*, February 29, 1956.
8   Tel Aviv, February 5, 1956, Micha Caspi's archives (based on its contents, the letter was written several days after the date noted in it). Haim Zadok (1913–2002) was Israel's Minister of Justice between 1974 and 1977.

estimation, Tamir was trying in this way "to prove that Kasztner's affidavit had in fact been given to the files of the international tribunal (contradicting Kasztner's claim that his testimony was given for the Denazification Court)."

When Caspi cross-examined Ziegel, it turned out that he didn't know "whether the office [he visited] in Nuremberg was in fact that of the international tribunal, because the place bore no sign attesting to the name of the international tribunal." The witness also was unable to provide any exact details about the file from which the document was removed or about other documents found in it. This testimony led Caspi to conclude that the said office was nonetheless the office of the Denazification Court, not of the international tribunal.

To confirm Caspi's conclusion, his law partner, Zadok, was asked to travel via Nuremberg on his way home from the United States, to find out "what that office is, what files are found in it, what file was Kasztner's affidavit in—so that you can give evidence about that in the preliminary examination." This was one of Caspi's reasons for requesting the adjournment.

Kempner also helped Caspi in formulating his position. Despite his promise, Kempner refused to come to Israel to testify, but in the lengthy correspondence between the two, he raised several key points. Tamir had distorted Walter Rapp's words—"insofar as Mr. Rapp is concerned," Kempner wrote, "I don't believe he would have stated that Mr. Becher was not placed on trial because of Kasztner, but would have admitted that even **without** Kasztner, Becher would not have been tried [emphasis in the original]."[9] Elsewhere, he wrote that "In Nuremberg he was already there as a witness, not as a defendant."[10]

Another point was even more significant. Kempner explicitly stated that Becher did try to save Jews and to stop the exterminations.

Throughout his correspondence with Caspi, Kempner did not try to conceal his intense animosity towards Tamir. One reason was the fact that Tamir had not called him to testify before the District Court. On August 19, 1954, he wrote to Tamir that if a person like himself, whose only interest was in getting to the truth, was not called to testify, Tamir must have had some other ax to grind in his conduct of the defense.[11]

Caspi's office tried to find out what Rapp's position really was. They contacted a New York lawyer by the name of Arthur Palmer to help them. He

---

9   Ibid., from his letter dated February 17, 1956.
10   Ibid., from his letter dated February 14, 1956.
11   Ibid., quoted in his letter to Caspi, dated February 17, 1956.

met with Rapp, who insisted that Kasztner's purpose in giving the affidavit was to clear Becher in the eyes of the American military authorities in Germany, and that he did indeed achieve that aim. He defined as "absurd" Kasztner's claim that his affidavit for Becher had no influence on the American authorities. Palmer found this position rather suspicious: When he asked Rapp how it was possible for Becher to have been a potential defendant in July 1947, when it had already been decided three months beforehand who would be put on trial; Rapp responded in general terms without referring to any dates.[12]

III

The hearing was resumed at the end of February and the judge gave his decision about three weeks later, on March 15. In his summation, Caspi reproached Tamir for having failed to provide the court with information that could have helped the defendant, asserting that consequently he had neglected his duties as a lawyer. He accused Tamir of having possessed the transcript of Becher's July 1947 interrogation, in which he had been explicitly told there was no intention of placing him on trial, but failing to bring it to the Court's attention. When Tamir replied that he had not been asked to inform the court, Caspi derisively remarked: "The complainant here is no longer Gruenwald, but Tamir, he is the witness, he is the one delivering a demagogic speech, and he is the one concealing documents from the court [...]" Beside himself with rage Tamir cried out: "That's a deliberate lie!"

The verdict was pronounced the following day. Judge Moshe Peretz decided that Gruenwald's request that Kasztner be tried for perjury was groundless, and hence there was no cause to place him on trial before the District Court. Peretz's verdict was brief—only five pages—and it took him no longer than half an hour to read it. When he'd finished, a disappointed Tamir announced that he was going to "seek justice" from the High Court of Justice, before which he would appeal the decision. Caspi, on the other hand, asked the judge to order Tamir and Gruenwald to pay the trial's legal expenses. Peretz declined to do so, stating that the proceedings had not been a trial, but a preliminary investigation.[13]

---

12 From his letter to attorney Haim Zadok, dated February 25, 1956, Micha Caspi's archives.
13 The description is taken from "Dr. Kasztner Acquitted of Perjury in the Matter of Becher," *Davar*, March 16, 1956.

In his brief and concise decision,[14] Judge Peretz cited the reasons for there being no grounds for placing Kasztner on trial. The first reason was that in July 1947, when Becher asked to meet with Kasztner, he had been told there was no intention to try him before the international tribunal. Why then did he ask to meet Kasztner? Because "although he had not been charged, he had already been under arrest for 26 months, and he hoped that Kasztner, by stating who Becher was, could help him get transferred quickly to the German court without having to be jailed again in a German concentration camp." The second reason related to the question of to whom Kasztner had given his affidavit—the international tribunal or one of its institutions, or to the German Denazification Court, which was also in session in Nuremberg. The judge concluded that the attorney for the plaintiff, namely Tamir, had not succeeded in proving his allegation that the fact that he had found a copy of Kasztner's affidavit in Alexandria, Virginia confirmed that the affidavit had been given before an institution connected with the international tribunal.

Another piece of evidence the judge rejected was Tamir's conversation with Rapp. "We have before us a clear case of hearsay," the judge wrote, "therefore, I am not taking this part of Mr. Tamir's testimony into account." These reasons and others led him to conclude that "sufficient and reliable evidence was not presented to me, and I am therefore dismissing the charges against Dr. Kasztner and releasing him."

This was a great victory for the defense, especially since everyone had estimated when the trial was resumed that its chances were not very good.

IV

Judge Peretz' decision stirred a wave of protest. According to Tamir "not only has a miracle occurred here, but a miscarriage of justice as well."[15] And on the day after the decision, *Herut* wrote, "the verdict of the judge Dr. M. Peretz has deeply confounded broad sectors of the public that have been following the trial."[16] This was mainly due to the fact that the judge had agreed to accept the defense counsel's line of argument, which had given up trying to "defend Kasztner's morality and had limited itself mainly to technicalities

---

14 The decision on the preliminary investigation 1011/15, before *Davar*. Moshe Peretz, Chief Magistrate Judge, as investigating judge, Micha Caspi's archives.
15 "Tamir Says Kasztner's Acquittal is a Miscarriage of Justice," *Kol Ha'am*, May 23, 1956.
16 "The Public Reaction: The Verdict Does Not Pass the Test of Criticism," *Herut*, March 16, 1956.

and formalities." After all, the "fact that Kasztner had testified in favor of an arch-murderer was not in question [...] and in the frenzy of the trial, everyone had forgotten that, from the public and moral standpoint, it makes no real difference before whom Kasztner gave his affidavit." The paper also asserted that Peretz had exceeded his authority as an investigating judge: "Many have pointed out that in his verdict the honorable judge weighed the evidence—which is definitely not within the competence of an investigating judge—while, at the same time, overlooked some important evidence." Other newspapers also published critical comments about the decision.

Haolam Hazeh[17] was also among the critics, "No other verdict has caused so much consternation among legal circles in Israel [as this one] [...] an extremely bizarre, amazing verdict." To prove its sweeping claim, *Haolam Hazeh* assigned its anonymous "legal commentator" the task of analyzing the verdict. The aim of this interpretation was ostensibly to "enable the reader who is not well-versed in legal matters and legal stratagems to arrive at his own opinion." Its real purpose, however, was to try to demolish the verdict. The paper was enraged by the judge's statement that at the time Kasztner gave his affidavit for Becher, it was clear, beyond any doubt, that there was no intention to put Becher on trial before the international tribunal at Nuremberg. One of the commentator's reservations was that even if the investigator had told Becher he was not one of the accused at Nuremberg, it meant nothing. Saying "speak up, you are not being accused," is, after all, one of the ways investigators routinely get the people they are questioning to talk. Moreover, "it's a fact that Becher himself didn't believe that, and claimed that despite the repeated promises he'd been given, he had already been in jail for 26 months, without being released." The anonymous commentator produced further arguments against this statement and other statements by the judge that underpinned the decision, which aroused serious concerns in legal circles. Most of this commentator's assertions were based on the arguments put forward by the prosecutor in his summation, which leads one to suspect that the "commentator" was none other than Shmuel Tamir himself.

However, the most blatant attack on the verdict and on the judge himself was not published in the media. Before the verdict was published, some of Kasztner's opponents must have gotten wind of the fact that the judge was going to acquit him. To whip up a barrage of criticism questioning the moral and legal fitness of the verdict and the judge, they distributed a handbill on March 15, 1956, just before the decision was to be published:

17   "Did Kasztner Lie?" *Haolam Hazeh*, March 22, 1956.

A disgraceful act has been committed in Israel—Kasztner is to be acquitted!

The Minister of Foreign Affairs, Moshe Sharett, met last week with Magistrate Judge Moshe Peretz and forced him to acquit Kasztner at his perjury trial in Jerusalem. Judge Peretz, a loyal member of Mapai, knuckled under and agreed to write a verdict exonerating Kasztner of the crime of perjury, against all law and judgment.

Citizens! A court in Israel has also been harnessed in the defense of war criminals!

Long live Sharett! Long live Krumey!

Long live Kasztner! Long live Himmler!

Long live Becher! Long live the SS![18]

Yaacov Heruti, who had been sentenced to ten years imprisonment in the Tzrifin Underground trial, conceived the idea of the handbill. Later his sentence was lightened, and after less than two years he was released from prison in April 1955. The job of printing the handbill was assigned to a young man by the name of Ze'ev Eckstein, who, two months earlier, in January 1956, had been ousted from the Security Services, where he had been employed for two years. The handbill was printed by Tel Aviv printer Zvi Stern, and was also distributed among Knesset members.

Heruti was tried in the Tel Aviv district court, which handed down its verdict on January 24, 1958, a few days after the Supreme Court gave its decision on the state's appeal of Halevi's verdict. In his decision, Judge Nathan Bar-Zakai, President of the District Court, stated that the calumny contained in the handbill "was clearly intended to engender suspicion that there had been a miscarriage of judgment and to show contempt for Judge Peretz and his decision—and with him—for the courts," and sentenced Heruti to 18 months in prison.[19]

A few months earlier, in August 1955, the Public Committee to Discover the Truth about the Extermination of European Jewry was established by Revisionist circles to assist Tamir in his public campaign. Most of its members came from Herut and its Secretary-General was Captain Yermiyahu Halperin, one of the founders of the movement and a leader of Betar. "Entire teams of agents are swarming throughout the country and in the Diaspora," Halperin claimed at a press conference the committee had called to mark its

---

18 Text of the handbill from Harel, *The Truth about Kasztner's Murder*, p. 106.
19 Ibid., pp. 205–211.

establishment, "whose duty is to prepare false witnesses and forged documents and to spy on every person who is prepared to discover the truth about the extermination of European Jewry."[20]

V

Caspi's law firm also was engaged in collecting evidence. It is not altogether clear to what end, perhaps in order to prepare the suit—which was never heard in court—that Kasztner filed against Gruenwald for the payment of 50,000 Israeli pounds in compensation for libel.[21] It is possible that in this matter, the firm was assisting the State Attorney's office. Testimony was also taken from some persons, like Yoel Palgi, who had already testified in the 'Gruenwald trial,' and others who had not testified there, like Zvi Goldfarb, a member of Kibbutz Farod, in the Upper Galilee, who had been a leader of the Dror movement in Hungary during the German occupation, and Israel Sabo, a member of Kibbutz Kfar Hamaccabi, who was at that time a member of the Young Maccabi movement in Hungary. Several points arose in these testimonies that would have made it possible to pursue a different line of argument from that used by Halevi in his verdict. Sabo discussed two subjects: the escape to Romania and the resistance to deportation. About the escape to Romania, he said:

> The Hungarian press contained frightening articles warning against escape, and those attempting to escape were sentenced to death. A mass flight from Hungary, as well as from Slovakia, was impossible. There were several requirements for escape and only people who wouldn't talk and could stand up to the test were eligible [...] and there were many other elements [...], the border was well guarded by Hungarians and Romanians.

About resistance to deportation, he drew a complex picture. It was true that:

> [...] I had already heard about Auschwitz in 1942. The ordinary Hungarian in the street knew about Auschwitz [...] 15,000 Jews

---

20 On the committee, see: Yechiam Weitz, "The Herut Movement and the Kasztner Trial," *Holocaust and Genocide Studies*, vol. 8/3 (December, 1994), pp. 360–1.

21 On this suit, see, for example, "Kasztner's 517 Replies to Gruenwald," *Haboker*, July 19, 1956.

crossed from Slovakia; they all knew what Auschwitz was [...] In 1942, a deportation was carried out from Carpathian Russia to Auschwitz. Some returned from there and told exactly [...].

But despite this knowledge, it was impossible to defy deportation. During the deportations of June 1944, the witness was in the town of Oradea-Mare.

I saw the deportation in Oradea-Mare. I knew they were being taken to Auschwitz. People I spoke with knew they were going to Auschwitz. But their earlier experiences caused them to show no resistance at all. [They had experienced] confiscation of their property, loss of their place of work, the yellow Star of David patch, being confined to their homes and in the ghetto, under inhuman conditions. At a certain point, a person becomes apathetic.

Elsewhere in his evidence, he claimed, "whoever believes that Hungarian Jewry could have organized any resistance [...] is making a fatal error. They knew about the danger but didn't want to believe it [...]. The majority believed that Horthy would protect them." The witness denied that there had been rumors suggesting that the deportations were to work camps and not to extermination: "If I had heard rumors that people were not being sent to extermination but to work camps, I would have warned them that it was a delusion [...] everywhere in the world people boarded [the deportation trains] because the Germans had their ways [of getting them to do so]. Nine million gentiles were exterminated as well."

Special importance was attributed to Hakibbutz Hameuchad (United Kibbutz Movement) member Goldfarb's testimony; no members of Hakibbutz Hameuchad had testified at the trial. The things he said were often totally opposed to the canonical line of his movement and his party, Achdut Ha'avoda.[22] Hungarian Jewry, he said, did not rebel, not because of its special character or because of anything Kasztner said or did not say:

Hungarian Jewry is not [the same as] Polish Jewry. They, ostensibly, lived as Hungarians of the Mosaic faith. When we came [Goldfarb arrived in Hungary from Slovakia in 1942, Y.W.] and told them [what was happening], they didn't believe us; they didn't want anything to do with us. Even at a later period, they didn't want to listen.

22 The testimonies taken on July 15 and September 1, 1955 are in Micha Caspi's archives.

The possibilities of fleeing to Romania were extremely limited: "It's hard for me to say, but about 600–700 escaped to Romania. To get more [people] across the border was very difficult." Moreover, the *halutz* youth movements were not opposed to the negotiations that Kasztner and the committee were conducting with the Germans. To the question "Were you opposed to the plan?" he replied, "No. We didn't think anything would come of it. We would go our own way and wouldn't miss taking any action because of these negotiations, but we weren't opposed to them. No one thought they would have the effect of weakening the resistance attempts of Hungarian Jewry." Nor were they opposed to the rescue train. "It was [meant] to earn some time. It was 1944 and the front was advancing. We had nothing to lose. It was a deposit on account."

He did not even see anything wrong with the fact that some people paid for their place on the train. "We knew that these places were being sold and that was justified. Every means was legitimate to save people, including bribery," he said.

In his testimony,[23] Palgi claimed that "with regard to the parachutists, Kasztner made a fatal error, but it was no more than an error." The error was that "he was too hasty in notifying the Germans within 12 hours after we disappeared," but not the notification itself, because "what wasn't clear to me when I testified in court is clear to me [now]—that when we went to report to the Germans, they already knew about me."

VI

Contrary to the pro-Kasztner activity, which involved many high echelon party and government members, there was only one man—Shmuel Tamir— who oversaw the counter-activity. Tamir's activity was fueled in part by a letter from Kasztner to Hermann Krumey, which he found in February 1956, i.e., even before Judge Peretz's decision.

At the end of the month, Tamir wrote to the Attorney General,[24] describing the letter as a "shocking revelation [...] Dr. Kasztner's declared willingness to do his utmost to obtain the release of one of the leading exterminators of millions of European Jews [...]. Now it is really impossible, from the standpoint of morality, justice and law, to avoid far-reaching

---

23 This testimony was taken on August 18, 1955.
24 Tel Aviv, February 29, 1956, Micha Caspi's archives.

conclusions about Dr. Kasztner's personality and actions." It was only a short leap from this conclusion to Tamir's request-demand. "With all due respect," he wrote to Cohn, "I believe that in view of this development it would be right and proper to reconsider whether there is any justification whatsoever in continuing the appeal against my client's acquittal in the Jerusalem District Court." We have no knowledge as to whether the Attorney General replied to this letter, and if so, what he said. In any case, he forwarded the letter to Kasztner, who replied six months later that the letter had in fact been bait with which he hoped to uncover Krumey's whereabouts. And indeed, he said, "as a result of this action of mine, Krumey was arrested and afterwards, I did what I could to make sure he would be [...] put on trial."[25] As a matter of fact, in the petition he filed in July 1962 for a new hearing of the Kasztner trial (not the Gruenwald trial; the Kasztner trial!), Tamir mentioned that "Kasztner's letter to Krumey was received by the attorney for the petitioner after the District Court's verdict and before the appeal was heard," but he did not suggest that as far as he was concerned, the letter was sufficient cause to request a dismissal of the appeal.[26]

Tamir also wrote to the Minister of Police, Bechor Shitrit. The content of this letter was similar to the one he sent to the Attorney General, but the demand he made was different. After listing all his findings, he stated that:

> In view of this development [the letter he discovered in relation to Krumey, Y.W.], it would be right to reconsider the police's position in regard to our request **to open an investigation against Dr. Kasztner**, with all that entails, under the Nazis and Nazi Collaborators [Punishment] Law [emphasis in the original].[27]

The reason for this demand was "the sacred duty that the state institutions have towards the exterminated millions." Tamir sent a copy of this letter to the Prime Minister and to the chairmen of two Knesset committees (Interior, and Constitution, Law and Justice). The reply to his letter was totally formal. On March 4, 1956, Yitzhak Navon, the Prime Minister's secretary, informed him in writing that "his letter had been received and would be forwarded

---

25 Tel Aviv, August 26, 1956, Micha Caspi's archives; it is not clear why there is a discrepancy between Tamir's letter and Kasztner's reply, but we also have a draft of the letter of reply, dated July 31, 1956. The draft is signed by the Caspi-Zadok law firm, while the reply itself is signed by Israel Kasztner.

26 *Request for Rehearing of the Kasztner Trial*, p. 24.

27 Kasztner/Prime Minister's Office files, February 29, 1956, ISA.

to the appropriate party" and two days later, news came from the official in charge of the Ministry of Police that "the matter is being handled, and I will get back to you."

When Tamir realized three months later that the government was in no rush to put Kasztner on trial, he wrote another letter, dated June 10, 1956, to Shitrit. In it, he asked the Minister to inform him "whether the police had investigated Dr. Kasztner in this matter" and "whether the Ministry of Police is planning to take some action against Dr. Kasztner." A few days later, he received a laconic reply from the official in charge of the Ministry:

> I am informed by police national headquarters that so long as the Supreme Court either hands down its decision on the appeal filed against the district court's verdict in this matter, or the appeal is dismissed, the police see no grounds at this stage for opening a police investigation.

"The delay in giving this reply," the official explained, "occurred due to my illness, and I apologize."

During those years, the complaint that Mapai, as the ruling party, was trying to harness the legal system to promote its own interests was heard repeatedly. A major mouthpiece voicing this complaint was *B'terem*, a magazine edited by Eliezer Livna, a member of the first and second Knesset who was so furious at not being included on Mapai's list of candidates for the third Knesset that he left the party in 1957.

A glance through *B'terem*'s 1955–1957 issues shows how often it harped on this issue.[28] The strongest words on the subject were those used by Professor Yeshayahu Leibowitz:

> The prosecution and the police in the state of Israel have lost their credibility as defenders of law and justice, since they are now subject to the government's instructions as to the opening and closing of criminal files, in accordance with the standing of the offenders within the party-government hierarchy or their relationship with the ruling oligarchy. Those close to the top ranks of government in Israel are above the law.[29]

---

28 For example: "The Government and the 'Ranks of Volunteers', From One Thing to Another," *B'terem*, January 1956, p. 5; Yitzhak Shalev, "Mr. So-and-So is Fighting Corruption," Ibid., February, 1957, pp. 4–5; Eliyakim Haetzni, "The Conclusion of the Braunstein Affair—A Trial or a Farce," Ibid., August, 1957, pp. 14–16.

29 "Signs of Cheka in the State of Israel," *B'terem*, January, 1956, pp. 10–11; The Minister of

Early in August of 1956, Leibowitz sent a letter to the editorial board of *Ha'aretz*, in which he alleged that Prime Minister Ben-Gurion had instructed Police Chief Yehezkel Sahar to desist from investigating suspicions raised against M.K. Yitzhak Raphael.[30] The day after the letter was printed, Ben-Gurion's sharp retaliation appeared in *Davar*: "The undersigned never heard that the Police Chief was about to open an investigation against Raphael, and in any case, gave no instruction in this matter. And in general, he has never given any instruction to close anyone's file," the letter ended. Then Tamir sent an urgent letter to Ben-Gurion, in which he wrote that in light of the Prime Minister's statement that he had never ordered any file to be closed and that he regarded the closing of a file as a serious act, he was once again drawing Ben-Gurion's attention to his demand regarding Kasztner and asking for his immediate intervention. In highly charged words, Tamir wrote:

> What this case involves is not smuggling or anything of that kind. This case involves the most heinous crime known to Israeli law and morality—collaboration on a hideous scale with the Nazi exterminator and shocking and nefarious support for arch-murderers to help them escape punishment. The discontinuation of all action on the said file by the Israeli Police, after much weighty testimony has been gathered and convincing documents have been received, is substantively and morally tantamount to the closing of a file.

A reply to Tamir's long, detailed letter was sent a month later. "Your letter of August 3, 1956, along with its attachments," Navon wrote, "has been referred to the Prime Minister."[31]

VII

The hearing of Criminal Appeal 232/55, filed by the state against Benjamin Halevi's verdict, opened in January 1957. Because the case was one of such importance, the President of the Supreme Court, Chief Justice Yitzhak Olshan, decided it would be heard before a panel of five judges. Tamir, too, was

---

Justice himself reacted to the article ("Protest Against an Article," *Beterem*, March, 1956, pp. 11–13).

30 "Professor Leibowitz Repeats his Accusations," *Ha'aretz*, August 1, 1956. Raphael was a leader of the religious-Zionist party.

31 Tel Aviv, August 3, 1956, ISA, Kasztner containers, Prime Minister's Office.

interested in the appeal being heard by an expanded panel. The most senior Supreme Court judges were selected to serve on the panel, which was headed by Olshan himself; sitting beside him were the permanent acting President, Shneur Zalman Cheshin and Justices Shimon Agranat, Moshe Silberg and David Goitein. Olshan insisted that the hearing be to the point and that the claims heard throughout should not deviate from the legal framework. In his memoirs he wrote—with hints of criticism in Halevi's direction—that he was determined "not to allow the appeal to be turned into another showcase trial." To ensure that the hearing adhere to the relevant facts, Olshan denied Tamir's request for a decision on an appeal lasting at least one month; instead he allocated two weeks. In fact it lasted 17 days, from January 19 to February 6, 1957.

The subject resurfaced briefly in the press—usually on the last page. Cohn was the first to address the bench. "An injustice was done to Kasztner," the headline in *Davar* read, while *Haboker* headed the same speech with, "I will not defend everything that Kasztner did." Cohn bluntly attacked Halevi's verdict in a strident tone, which led Justice Olshan to ask him several times to stop using "those expressions." On one occasion, when Cohn asserted that one of Halevi's statements "bordered on the absurd," Olshan interrupted him and said: "Do you not have a more appropriate word?"

Cohn opened his address by stating, "No court anywhere, neither in Israel nor abroad, has ever perpetrated so great an injustice as that done to Israel Kasztner." One of the arguments with which he supported this statement dealt with the issue of armed resistance. His arguments were a mixture of historical-factual proofs and matters of principle. Cohn unequivocally rejected Halevi's statement that Kasztner was faced with the choice of spreading the truth about Auschwitz and organizing escape and resistance operations, on the one hand, and rescuing Jews by negotiating with the Nazis, on the other; which meant relinquishing the first option. The situation, according to him, was that while Kasztner was trying to save Jews through negotiation, others were trying to organize resistance and rescue operations. On this point, Cohn raised an argument intended to shatter the claim that relations between Kasztner and the Halutz Movement were antagonistic:

> The *halutzim* received their funds from Kasztner and none of them thought Kasztner's negotiations with the Germans were inconsistent with the escape operations they were trying to organize. Kasztner conducted the negotiations with the Germans knowing full well that the

other avenues should not be neglected, and he did his utmost to assist in them.[32]

Next he attacked what Halevi had said from a different angle. While Kasztner and his associates had made superhuman efforts to rescue every single Jew, the judge in his verdict was dealing with imaginary reckonings of honor. Relating to the judge's statement that it was Kasztner's duty to join the underground "even though you don't know how many you can save in this way, but even if you save fewer people, it is a more honorable way," Cohn said, "it was better for Kasztner to think, with all due respect to the underground, that he was obliged to save every Jew that he was able to save through negotiations." Here, Cohn tried to substantiate his argument in principle with empirical proof. He argued that "there were hundreds and thousands of ghettos in Europe but there were revolts in only two or three of them," and even the Warsaw Ghetto Uprising was an exceptional event because of the actual act of rebellion and not because of any success it met with, and "out of six million Jews, 5,900,000 went to their death as did the Jews of Cluj."

The situation in Hungary was particularly desperate: there were very few possibilities of escape; there was no real chance of any rebellion, and despite the warnings they heard, the Jews of Hungary believed no ill would befall them. After all, Admiral Horthy was the supreme ruler of the country. To support this argument, Cohn quoted from a letter written by Krausz to Chaim Posner, the Agency's representative in Geneva during World War II, on June 19, 1944. All the Jews of Hungary without exception were doomed to die, he wrote, there is no possibility of fleeing to a neighboring country and the only choice left to the Jews is suicide or surrender to their fate. This letter was never mentioned in Halevi's verdict, Cohn said. It is true that Krausz had tried to alter its contents in his testimony, "but he, like the rest of us, is very wise in hindsight."[33] He also took another line of reasoning that touched on whether anyone had the right to judge those who had been there or what had happened there:

Where is the man who wasn't **there**, who has the right **today**, after the fact, to argue that that [i.e., escape and resistance] was the order of the

---

32 Ibid., Jerusalem, September 4, 1956.
33 "Never Before Has There Been Such a Miscarriage of Justice as in This Trial—Haim Cohn Asserts in his Appeal on the Kasztner Verdict," *Ha'aretz*, January 21, 1957; "The Rescue of the VIPs Was Not Opposed to Saving Everyone—The Attorney General Stated," *Lamerchav*, January 23, 1957.

day, rather than Kasztner's desperate attempt to save the few that could
be saved, "to fight for every Jewish life, even the life of only one Jew"—in
the face of the certainty of total extermination?

Cohn raised several other arguments. The Nazis had no need of Kasztner at
all, he claimed, in order to exterminate Hungary's Jews; they were interested
only in extorting money. He stated that "the rescue of a favored few in no
way contradicted the overall rescue attempts," and that in the painful episode
of the parachutists, Kasztner "acted in good faith, honestly and humanely."
He had the harshest things to say about Halevi's statement that Kasztner
had "sold his soul to the devil." This remark, he asserted, was not only unfair;
it constituted an injustice of unparalleled proportion. Kasztner did not
sell his soul to the devil, and his soul emerged from the dreadful negotiations
as pure as it had been before. Beyond that, he went on to say, Halevi might
have thought he was playing with words, but in truth he was playing with
fire.

In his forceful address, Cohn lashed out at Halevi, but also at Kasztner.
He was not Kasztner's attorney, he declared, and was not prepared to defend
everything he had said or done, "There are many things he did that I do
not understand and that no one here, including the Court, can understand
[…] the learned President [Halevi] was right in criticizing Kasztner for
his contradictions, inaccuracies and even lies in the District Court, as well
as several things he did during or after that period." With these words, he
wished to stress that although he was aware of Kasztner's weaknesses and
problems, "an abyss lies between that and stating that he sold his soul to the
devil and collaborated to exterminate the Jewish people." He had another aim
in making this attack—to challenge those statements of Halevi's on the basis
of what Kasztner had said. He argued that the fact that Halevi "was filled with
repulsion for the witness Kasztner," who indeed was a "very poor witness," led
him to "reach hasty and unfair conclusions about him." For example, Cohn
tried to refute the judge's statement that Kasztner had promised the Germans
"to keep secret from the Jewish public some of his actions;" this statement
was based on Kasztner's testimony, which simply cannot be trusted because
it originates from the "show-off" trait in his personality. "Kasztner only tried
to create the impression that he was keeping a secret from the Jews, out of his
desire to "show off," and that was his downfall," Cohn said.

The last days of the hearing were devoted to Tamir's summation. When
he failed to nullify the filing of the appeal, his main aim became to ensure that
the upper court would uphold the lower court's verdict. To achieve this aim,

he repeated the main arguments he had made in his summation in the District Court, all of which Halevi had adopted. His aim is not "to defend Gruenwald or to indict Kasztner," he asserted, but rather to "defend an historic verdict." Accordingly, he asked that the judges rely on:

> The findings of the lower court and decide that you too, had you been sitting in judgment, would not have been able to avoid the horrifying conclusion that a Jew actually collaborated with the Nazis in their extermination program and saved Himmler's right-hand man from the punishment he deserved.[34]

Like those of the Attorney General, Tamir's words were a mixture of factual arguments and ideological statements largely intended to invoke the concepts of heroism and 'honorable death' prevalent in the country in those days. Of the right that Dr. Kasztner assumed for himself, "to save the few and not to warn the many," Tamir said that if the court were to give it its stamp of approval, then "we are lost, because that means reconciling ourselves to the annihilation of the nation." He further argued that no one is entitled to deprive 800,000 Jews of knowledge about what awaits them "and the right to try to flee, to jump off the train or even to commit suicide honorably." He concluded his argument by asking the court to uphold Judge Halevi's verdict, as well as his client's acquittal on three of the four charges in the indictment.[35]

Tamir had asked the Court's permission to submit additional evidence to support his arguments. This came up on the very first day of the hearings, when President Olshan unexpectedly decided that the defense counsel's request to submit additional evidence would be heard at a later date. Walter Rapp, who had come especially from the United States in the hope of being allowed to testify, was present in the courtroom. Finally, the court denied Tamir's request to hear Rapp's testimony and to call Kasztner for a re-examination. When the hearing ended, Rapp returned to the United States without having been given the opportunity to testify.[36]

The way the hearing was being handled in the Supreme Court had a calming influence on Kasztner and boosted his self-confidence somewhat. He felt certain, he told his old friend Eliezer Barzilai, a colleague on the *Uj*

---

34 "Tamir Asks Court to Convict Kasztner," *Ma'ariv*, January 27, 1957.
35 "Kasztner Concealed from 800,000 Jews Knowledge of What Was Awaiting them," *Ha'aretz*, February 4, 1957; "Arguments in the Kasztner Case are at an End," Ibid., February 6, 1957.
36 "The Attorney General's Appeal Against Halevi's Verdict Concluded," *Davar*, February 8, 1957.

Kelet editorial board, that the Supreme Court would clear his name. "The hearing in the District Court was a sorry affair [...] the State Attorney's Office handled it wrongly. People I had recommended were never called to testify." Now, he was convinced, everything would be all right and the justices of the Supreme Court "will see from the evidence that I was not a mass murderer."[37]

VIII

Once the hearing was over, the matter was again dropped from the public agenda. As far as the Israeli public was concerned, that year February was too eventful. In February, Israel agreed to retreat, giving up control over the Tiran Straits and the Gaza Strip, which it had captured during the Sinai Campaign. Throughout the month, exhausting negotiations were conducted in Washington between the U.S. Secretary of State, John Foster Dulles, and Israeli Ambassador, Abba Eban, about the completion of the withdrawal.

Then, in the midst of the arguments and mutual accusations, the Kasztner affair was once again at the very heart of public consciousness. This time, in a way that was predictable and yet managed to surprise everyone. Haim Cohn's statement that Halevi "thought he was playing with words but in fact he was playing with fire," suddenly took on a palpable, terrible meaning. On the night between March 3 and 4, around 23:30, Kasztner finished his day's work as night editor of *Uj Kelet*, and drove to his home on 6 Emmanuel Boulevard. At seven minutes past midnight, he parked his old "Henry J" car in front of his apartment building. Even before he had a chance to switch off the engine, a short thin man, dressed in khaki, walked over to the car window, flashed a torch in his face and asked, "Are you Dr. Kasztner?" When Kasztner replied in the affirmative, the stranger drew a revolver, aimed it at his head and pulled the trigger. But no sound of a shot was heard. Kasztner instinctively pushed his assailant aside, got out of the car and ran towards the entrance. The stranger fired another shot, which hit the car door, then turned around and fired once more. This time the bullet hit Kasztner, who fell to the sidewalk near the building entrance and, lying in a pool of blood, he cried out with his remaining strength, "I've been shot! Call a doctor! Help! Call an ambulance! I'm going to die here!"

His desperate cries awoke the neighbors. On the top floor, Kasztner's neighbor opened the shutters and, realizing who it was, ran down to the

---

37 Eliezer Barzilai, "The Man Who Didn't Sell His Soul to Satan," *Davar*, April 30, 1957.

street, where he found an army major trying to help the injured man. The neighbor rushed back to his apartment and called the police and Magen David Adom (national emergency service). Another neighbor hurried to rouse Mrs. Kasztner, who went downstairs, but could hardly make her way through the crowd of curious onlookers who had, in the meantime, gathered around her wounded husband. Although she was shocked at the sight, she remained calm. She asked someone to bring her a pillow and a blanket, and a few minutes later, when the ambulance arrived, its siren wailing, she accompanied him to Hadassah Hospital. Suzi, who did not wake up, remained at home, alone.

Kasztner reached the hospital in a grave condition—the bullet had entered his left side, torn his spleen, penetrated his intestines and damaged internal organs near his chest. The finest surgeons, including Professor Marcus, were summoned to his beside and decided to operate immediately. Still fully conscious Kasztner recounted his version of the attack to a police officer from the Tel Aviv district before being taken to the operating theater. After the operation, which lasted three hours, the doctors declared that although his condition had improved somewhat, his life was still in danger. In the afternoon, the hospital issued a statement saying that his condition was still very serious. Kasztner's wife, Bodiya, sat stunned at the entrance to the operating theater, weeping bitterly.

Scores of telegrams and letters arrived at the hospital, expressing shock at the attempted murder and wishing Kasztner a complete recovery. His daughter Suzi sent him a childishly handwritten note: "To my daddy, a speedy recovery and warm kisses, your daughter, Shoshana." Yoel Palgi and his wife Phyllis sent him a bouquet of flowers with a note saying: "Wishing you a speedy recovery." But one telegram was totally unexpected: "Shocked by the inhuman act. Wishing you a complete recovery despite our fundamental disagreements." The telegram had been sent from Jerusalem on March 4, at 9:40 a.m. and was signed "Malkiel Gruenwald."[38]

Gruenwald was not alone. In a conversation with a *Ma'ariv* writer, his attorney also expressed "sorrow and disgust at this attempt on Dr. Kasztner's life." Later in the conversation, Tamir tried to gloss over any possible connection between him and the attack. "I don't know who was interested in interfering with the court's judgment," he said hinting at a new variation on the "conspiracy of silence" he was so fond of, but "there can be no act more

---

38 I was given the letters and telegrams by Suzi Kasztner-Michaeli.

repugnant to those who view Kasztner's activity in Hungary in light of what the defense revealed at the trial in Jerusalem."[39]

Years after their friendship had turned into bitter hostility, Uri Avneri testified with regard to Tamir's reaction and his fear that following the murder there might be some who would point an accusing finger at him. In 1980, during a Knesset debate on a survey by Justice Minister Shmuel Tamir regarding his Ministry's activities, Avneri, then a member of Knesset, said:

> I never saw Mr. Tamir so pale, so shaken and frightened as he was on the day that Rudolf Israel Kasztner was murdered. After all the terrible things that Tamir had said about Kasztner over the years, he was afraid that someone would try to hold him responsible for that act.[40]

IX

Most of the newspapers that less than two years earlier had brutally denounced Kasztner, now reacted with shock at the attack on his life. In a country where the fine, winding line between outspoken, inflammatory words and their translation into the squeeze of a trigger had hardly ever been crossed, the incident aroused strong emotions and intense discomfort. For several days, it was given prominent coverage on the front pages, alongside news about the withdrawal from Sinai. Editorials were worded in the most acrimonious language. For instance, *Ma'ariv* wrote, "The man who aimed his revolver at Dr. Kasztner tonight, aimed it at the heart of the entire nation." It went on to ask, "Who is this dangerous madman who has taken into his own hands the awful authority to pass judgment with the help of a revolver? Where did he suddenly appear from in the darkness of the night?"[41] This time, two newspapers, *Herut* and *Kol Ha'am* deliberately ignored the subject, reporting on it only briefly and devoting no editorials. In his report to the Middle East department of the Foreign Office in London, the counselor at the British Embassy in Tel Aviv wrote that although many Israelis believed Kasztner was indeed guilty of collaborating with the Nazis, the news of attempted murder aroused sympathy for the man and deep remorse for an incident that

---

39 "Tamir and Gruenwald Denounce the Murder," *Ma'ariv*, March 4, 1957.
40 Knesset records, June 9, 1980, vol. 88, p. 3247.
41 "The Fateful Moment," *Ma'ariv*, March 4, 1957; "Kasztner's Assassination," *Lamerchav*, March 5, 1957; "Acts of Terror Should be Uprooted," *Ha'aretz*, March 5, 1957.

many feared was in fact politically motivated. He also noted that it was the first incident of this kind since the murder of Count Folke Bernadotte, the Swedish diplomat appointed by the United Nations to mediate peace between Jews and Arabs during the early days of the state. (Bernadotte was murdered on 17 September 1948 in Jerusalem.)

Meanwhile, Kasztner was lying in an isolated room in Hadassah hospital, guarded by two policemen, with no one allowed to visit him other than his closest relatives. He was completely conscious, but spoke very little. His family members—who until the last, believed he would recover from the serious wound and regain his health—wanted to conserve his strength. While his brother-in-law, Pesach Rudik, was sitting with him, Kasztner constantly and laboriously repeated the same words: "Why did they do this to me?" Other than his immediate family, Hanzi Brand was the only other person to get to his bedside. Coming out of the room one day, Pesach Rudik and Bodiya met Hanzi in the corridor. She pleaded with them to tell the policemen to permit her to enter the room. Bodiya cut her completely, but Rudik spoke to the policemen, who allowed Hanzi into the room for a brief visit, which later turned out to be their last.[42]

It looked at first, as if Kasztner's condition was improving. But eight days after the attack, on Tuesday, March 12, it worsened:—"General condition poor" the medical report stated. The symptoms included suppuration of the wound, a very rapid pulse—more than 120 beats per minute—and an accumulation of phlegm in both lungs. The following day his condition deteriorated further and towards evening Kasztner was rushed to the operating room where the doctors reinforced the stitches to prevent further suppuration. But within two days his blood pressure had dropped to 60, he was covered with a cold sweat and gradually lost consciousness. On Friday, March 15, at 2 a.m., his heart and lungs began to fail and he died at 7:20 that morning. According to the medical report, the cause of death was heart failure.

The news of Kasztner's death came as no surprise to the Israeli public. Two days earlier, a newspaper had reported that because his temperature had risen so high, he was operated on immediately and after the surgery, was in critical condition.[43] But the news of his death aroused very strong emotions. Despite the political and ideological polarization that characterized Israeli

---

42 The report, written in Tel Aviv on March 8, 1957 was labeled P.R.O./F.O.-371/128087; Pesach Rudik.

43 The information is from a 'medical report' (*Ärtzlich Bescheinigung*) written by Joseph Kesar, the medical secretary of Hadassah Hospital, on December 26, 1963, Suzi Kasztner-Michaeli's collection; "Kasztner's Condition Deteriorates," *Ma'ariv*, March 13, 1957.

society and the previous pre-state society, it was not customary to settle conflicts with a gun. Kasztner's death made front-page headlines in all the newspapers except *Herut*, which relegated the news to its last page. *Davar* was the only newspaper in which obituaries appeared; one of these was placed by Mapai's central committee, "In mourning for our comrade, Israel Kasztner, who was murdered by heinous scoundrels." The passengers of the rescue train, who had failed to support Kasztner during the trial, now failed to publish an obituary for the man to whom they owed their lives.

Most of the newspapers reflected the sense of sorrow and astonishment evoked by Kasztner's untimely death. "No one thought the stormy affair that split public opinion in Israel would end like this," *Lamerchav* wrote on its front page. In an editorial, it stated, "this despicable murder is a warning to the Israeli public that evil lurks within it."[44] "Woe betide us if Satan has now entered our lives [not only] as a 'buyer of souls,' but also as a 'wreaker of vengeance,'" David Lazar wrote in *Ma'ariv*.[45] As to the identity of the perpetrator, the press provided two different versions. One was that the responsibility lay with those who for years had incited against Kasztner and had not shrunk from turning him into a Nazi criminal. Thus, according to *Hapoel Hatza'ir*:

> Of course we all recall the intense and murky atmosphere in which the Kasztner trial was conducted. The prosecution [the reference is to the defense, Tamir. Y.W.] did not show so much as a speck of decency towards the defendant. Certain political parties and newspapers also joined in the chorus of those who so stridently and recklessly slandered him. They permitted themselves to pass judgment on a Jew, an activist [on behalf of his community], who under the horrible conditions of the Nazi regime did his utmost to save whoever could be saved. They failed to take into account the fact that such unbridled slander might expose him to [...] an act of terrorism.[46]

Some people tried to pin responsibility for the murder on the government, which they believed had two reasons for getting rid of Kasztner. First, the man knew too much about the government's activity, its blunders and its misdemeanors; and second, by disposing of Kasztner the government could

---

44 "Israel Kasztner Died From His Wounds," *Lamerchav*, March 17, 1957; "Victim of Terror and Lawlessness," Ibid.
45 "Beside an Open Grave," *Ma'ariv*, March 17, 1957.
46 "The Despicable Murder," *Hapoel Hatza'ir*, March 12, 1957.

draw the public's attention away from its latest crime—Israel's withdrawal from the Sinai peninsula. This view originated in those circles most vehemently opposed to Kasztner, who hoped in this way to wash their hands of the affair while reinforcing the government's demonic image.

In an article entitled "The Black Hand," Uri Avneri addressed the first reason[47] "Why was this man murdered?" he asked, "[...] a man who knew more than any other about one of the blackest events in the lives of the leaders of the present government? Why was this man murdered [just] a few weeks before the verdict was pronounced in his trial, after which the Attorney General might have been forced, based on his explicit promise, to place him on trial under the Nazis and their Collaborators [Punishment] Law?" His very tentative reply to these questions was that the real power in the state of Israel is not in the hands of the elected government, "which is nothing but B.G.'s puppet theater," but is actually in the hands of a group of people "acting in the shadow of B.G.'s broad back." This group, which Avneri calls 'the black hand'—by which he is referring to the security services, "the apparatus of darkness," as he put it, was interested in the "heinous murder of Dr. Rudolf Israel Kasztner," in order to "prepare the ground for the introduction of new emergency laws, with the aim of finally shutting the mouths of the free press, to chop off the hands of the whistle blowers and to liquidate undesirable persons—legally or otherwise."

Menahem Begin addressed the second reason:[48]

Kasztner was shot, so people say, "just in time," when the status of the ruling party was in decline, and was rightly in decline, because of the government's insane act in ordering, against all its solemn undertakings, the withdrawal from Jewish Gaza. Is that so? No, my friends. It is mere conjecture. Someone in Mapai may be pleased that Kasztner was murdered at this particular time; someone in the ruling party may try in the wake of this murder to distract public opinion from its calamitous policy.

47   *Haolam Hazeh*, March 27, 1957.
48   *Herut*, March 22, 1957.

X

The bereaved family observed the *shiva*, the seven-day Jewish mourning period, in their Tel Aviv home. Eleven-year old Suzi, who had been taken to Kibbutz Ma'agan while her father was in critical condition, came home on the day he died. Moshe Sharett, who returned from a trip abroad the day after the funeral, came at once to pay a condolence call. "I found the tragedy quivering between the walls of this home," he wrote in his diary, and added:

> I heard a shocking description of the assassination, of what Rezsö went through after it, of hopes for his recovery being suddenly crushed. Mrs. Kasztner's brother-in-law [Pesach Rudik, Y.W.], a member of Haganah, who had lived in Israel for a long time, walked me out, showed me exactly where Rezsö had parked his car, where the man had been lurking in wait for him, how he approached him, fired and missed, then fired again and again until he hit him, and where the getaway jeep had been standing.[49]

As if the shock and the pain were not enough, Kasztner left his widow and only child bereft of any income. Several people in the top ranks of government were aware of the family's dire financial situation and tried to do something so that the widow and small child would not have to literally starve. Teddy Kollek and Zvi Herman, then Managing Director of the Zim maritime company, raised the issue. A month after Kasztner's death, Herman wrote to Dr. Nachum Goldmann, President of the World Zionist Organization that "the family is penniless and I think it is the fundamental duty of the Jewish Agency to deal with the matter." While Kasztner's activity may have aroused differences of opinion, he added, there can be no doubt that he acted in the name of the Zionist institutions and that "throughout his life he had been a veteran Zionist, dedicated and loyal." Specifically, Herman suggested that a "committee of veterans" of the Zionist Organization grant the widow a monthly allowance of 200 Israeli pounds. He concluded his letter by remarking, "By the way, in addition to her mental state, she is sick, which is easy enough to understand."[50] A while later, he sent an undated note in which he wrote, "Kasztner's widow is in a desperate state. Based on our conversation, I would suggest you send her a check for 1,000 pounds until the committee

---

49 Sharett, *Personal Diary*, vol. 7, March 19, 1957, p. 2046.
50 The archival label of this letter and the others on the subject: CZA, S66-80.

reaches some decision." On August 12, he wrote, "The situation is desperate [...] there is absolutely no need to have one more episode of suicide or some other act of desperation added to this affair." The following day, on August 13, Kollek wrote to him that:

> The Kasztner family has been left with no income. All [they] receive today is a monthly pension from the [Jewish] Agency amounting to a little over 50 pounds. Clearly, the family cannot live on this sum.

Kollek suggested the family be provided with a further source of income by "establishing an agency [for them] to sell theater and cinema tickets." An enterprise of this kind would involve an initial sum of around 20,000 Israeli pounds, of which Kollek asked Goldmann to raise a quarter. Three days later, on August 16, Goldmann suggested to the Agency treasurer, Dov Joseph, that he allocate the necessary sum from the reserve budget, "and, together with you, I'll take responsibility for this decision."

Eventually, Kasztner's widow was able to eke out a meager livelihood from a national lottery stall. About five years after Kasztner's death, the National Insurance authorities denied her request to recognize her husband's murder as a work accident. The court of the National Insurance institution ruled that although Kasztner was murdered on his way home from work, the murder itself was not connected to his job, and therefore his widow was not entitled to a widow's pension.

In the sixteen years that passed between her husband's murder and her own death, Elizabeth (Bodiya) Kasztner never came to terms with her loss. "I still shudder whenever anyone refers to me as 'the widow'," she said in an interview she gave on the tenth anniversary of Kasztner's murder, "I cannot reconcile myself to the thought that he was murdered."[51] But beyond the grief, over which she remained inconsolable, her desperate financial situation cast a gloomy, grotesque light on Tamir's claim that the man had hidden away vast sums of money.

Thirty days after Kasztner's death, the poet Nathan Alterman dedicated his weekly column to Kasztner's memory. It related mainly to Halevi's verdict and its connection to the fact that Kasztner was fair game for any would-be assassin. Only one stanza was more personal. It read:

---

51 "Appeal by Kasztner's Widow Rejected," *Davar*, July 5, 1962; Dan Oferi, "My Husband Told Only the Truth," *Yedioth Ahronoth*, March 17, 1967.

Thirty-day memorial service of Kasztner's murder (Moshe Sharett, third from left)
Courtesy of Suzi Kasztner-Michaeli

Because for only a few seconds
He ran, this man, and following him, the sin and darkness of fired bullets!
But day and night, moon after moon, we saw him running among us, alone
And after him, the righteousness of wise men, brave men and heroes!

Israel Eldad responded to these words in *Sullam*:

There's no cause for surprise
The poet's pity was aroused
For Kasztner, who struggled alone
On his side only Mapai
And the Israeli government
And *Ha'aretz* and *Davar*
He and they all alone together
Versus Tamir and *Sullam*.[52]

---

52 Nathan Alterman, "Thirty Days after Kasztner's Murder, The Seventh Column," *Davar*, April 25, 1957; [Israel] Eldad, "Nathan Alterman, Poet," *Sullam* (May, 1956), pp. 20–21.

XI

Several suspects had already been apprehended on the night of the attack. The police launched an investigation immediately upon hearing of the attempt on Kasztner's life, set up roadblocks and dispatched large numbers of mobile forces. After receiving a phone call from someone who said he had seen a jeep speeding away from the scene of the attack, the police located a gray Willis jeep, abandoned near the Tel Aviv Zoo, several minutes' drive from the Kasztner home. In the jeep's glove compartment they found a .38 revolver. The vehicle, which belonged to the Mekoroth water company, had been stolen that night from its regular parking place on the corner of Elharizi and King Solomon Streets.

Four men were arrested. The first was the owner of the jeep, 28-year-old Yosef Meyuchas, who lived on King Solomon Street. He was questioned and released after a few hours, when it turned out he had been asleep in his apartment and did not even know the jeep had been stolen. The police also arrested three other men who had been wandering around the streets under suspicious and unexplained circumstances. During the early morning hours, the police removed the road blocks it had set up at the entrances to the city, on the assumption that the assailant or assailants had made their way on foot after fleeing from the jeep and had had enough time to escape. The case was assigned top priority by the Tel Aviv district police. Officers and plainclothes detectives met to discuss it at district headquarters. Based on the nature of the crime the district commanders assumed that it had been committed by a group of youths who had undertaken the job.

The police acted swiftly, some thought with truly surprising speed. Two days after the attack, the police announced the arrest of seven young men who had been taken to jail for interrogation. The following day, they announced that arrest warrants had been issued against four young men suspected of belonging to a group that had devised a plan to kill Kasztner and had carried it out. Two of these men were 24-year-old Ze'ev Eckstein of Tel Aviv, and 30-year-old Yosef Menkes of Kfar Saba. The announcement also referred to a third arrest—a 28-year-old Tel Aviv resident.[53] Eckstein and

---

53 "Four Men Arrested after Kasztner's Murder," *Ma'ariv*, March 4, 1957; Uri Dan, "Three Shots at Midnight," Ibid.; "Kasztner's Murder under Police Investigation," *Kol Ha'am*, March 5, 1957; "Who Assassinated Kasztner?" *Haolam Hazeh*, March 6, 1957; "Further Arrests in Connection with Kasztner's Assassination," *Herut*, March 6, 1957; "Arrest Warrants Issued Against 4 Suspects in Kasztner's Assassination," Ibid., March 7, 1957.

Menkes were arrested on the night of the attack on Kasztner by order of the security services director, Isser Harel, after an examination of the files of men suspected of membership in right-wing nationalist underground movements. According to Harel, Eckstein was arrested even though neither the security service nor the police had any evidence linking him to the crime. But he broke down under interrogation, and after a short time admitted his guilt. Following his confession, Dan Shemer, who also confessed to his part in the crime, and Yosef Menkes were arrested, too. Menkes, a former member of the Stern Gang, who had been linked to the Tzrifin Underground but was never tried, was suspected of being the group's leader. A few days later another suspect was arrested, Attorney Yaacov Heruti. Soon after the wave of arrests, Heruti appeared as legal counsel for Eckstein and Menkes, but at about 3 a.m. one night, a week after the attack, two plainclothes policemen visited his home and arrested him under suspicion of membership in the group that had carried out the attack on Kasztner's life.

In the days that followed, it turned out that these were not individuals acting on their own, but rather an underground group that had amassed a large quantity of weapons and ammunition. In a search of Menkes' home in Kfar Shalem near Tel Aviv, the police found a revolver and bullets, and on the very day that Kasztner died, a store of weapons was found in Kfar Saba. It was discovered on the edge of the town, in a small, neglected farm that belonged to a man called Israel Teig. Police officers were astonished by the quantity of weapons in the arsenal: machine guns, grenades and ammunition. They were particularly shocked to find flame-throwers hidden under the chicken coop. An officer escorting a group of journalists on a tour of the arsenal said, "This time, this isn't just a group of adolescents with their heads in the clouds. This time we're dealing with a good-sized underground, with extensive branches and enough power to throw the whole country into chaos and anarchy." The officer, who did not give his name, added, "This underground organization had prepared many future operations. The attack on Dr. Kasztner was only the first [...] If we had allowed them to continue growing and gaining in power, they would have been capable of causing serious damage to the state and its citizens."[54]

---

54 Harel, *The Truth About Kasztner's Murder*, pp. 110–111; "Attorney Heruti Arrested as a Suspect in the Kasztner Case," *Herut*, March 11, 1957; "Kasztner's Condition Deteriorates," *Ma'ariv*, March 13, 1957; Shaul Ben-Haim, "The Chicken Coop Gave Up Weapons," *Ma'ariv*, March 17, 1957.

The police spared no effort in proving that the arsenal proved that this was not a marginal, short-lived phenomenon, but an extremely dangerous underground group. National Police HQ issued frequent statements on the case, and police spokesman Ya'acov Nash held a special press conference to announce that the police were convinced that at least three more such weapon stores were about to be discovered.

The police statements were aimed at proving that they had uncovered a hydra-headed monster, that while Kasztner was its first target, its true objective was to undermine the foundations of the young state's democracy. Kasztner's murder was merely the first shot in a revolt against the government. This is the version put forth by Isser Harel in his book, *The Truth About Kas[z]tner's Murder—Jewish Terror in the State of Israel*, and it was reflected in other things written at the time. According to Mapai's weekly, *Hapoel Hatza'ir*:

> Our impression, after taking all aspects into consideration, is that Kasztner was chosen as a symbol. If the underground had any political aims, it could not have restricted its action to a delayed protest against Kasztner's role in the rescue attempts in Hungary [...] the desire to harm and shock the government by murdering Kasztner may not have been linked to a naive belief by the underground that the shots fired in Emmanuel Boulevard would bring it the power it wants. But one thing is certain: this clique decided to inflict enormous damage and many casualties to achieve the initial shock. And perhaps also to publicly demonstrate that this way—via personal terror—is the only way and the only choice that opens the door to a change of government.[55]

This version of an anti-government plot was given top billing in *Rimmon*, a weekly published between 1956–1958 under the aegis of the security services, and intended to serve as a counterweight to *Haolam Hazeh*. It printed many articles relating to Kasztner's murder and the underground group that was allegedly behind it. As soon as the cache of arms was discovered in Kfar Saba, *Rimmon* printed a long article headlined "An underground in Israel." It purported to "expose once again, and with greater seriousness than ever before, the existence of underground groups that are organizing, training and secretly aspiring, sometimes even openly declaring their aim to stage a political and social revolution by force of arms:

55 Yona Yagol, "The Roots of the Terror," *Hapoel Hatza'ir*, March 26, 1957.

Menkes and Heruti know very well, just as does Tamir, that Kasztner's murder was only the signal and the opening shot for other assassinations. They know there was a plan to create such commotion as to plunge the entire country into grave danger. They know that the arrest of the main activists prevented further underground activity.[56]

XII

Another version claimed that the murder was provoked by the security services and poured scorn on police attempts to depict the underground as a powerful, threatening organization. *Haolam Hazeh* wrote that anyone reading statements issued by the police "could only assume that they are facing a hugely monstrous terror organization with hundreds of arms and thousands of heads, capable of committing robbery and murder, acquiring weapons and storing them in four different arsenals."

Haolam Hazeh's view was based on three premises. First, the link, which Isser Harel and Amos Manor did not deny, between Eckstein and the security services.[57] Under the headline "The Assassin: On the security services payroll," *Haolam Hazeh* wrote: "for a long time [Eckstein] was a salaried agent of the "apparatus of darkness", providing it with information about the underground." Second, the "apparatus of darkness" possessed details on the underground, including its arsenals," but nothing was done about it. This led to a third premise, albeit implied, that the "apparatus of darkness" was responsible for the murder and took the form of rhetorical questions, such as: "If all of this was known to the "apparatus of darkness", why weren't members of the underground arrested before the crime was committed?" The first answer scoffed that the heads of the security service are simply inefficient and that the top ranks of the service should be replaced at once before additional catastrophes occur through their fault. According to the second answer the loud public relations campaign conducted after the discovery of the arsenal in Kfar Saba had but one purpose—to divert the fire from those really responsible for the murder. Although this may have been only implied, it was very heavily implied. The reason for the campaign, it suggested, was probably

---

56 *Rimmon*, March 20, 1957; "The Bomb of Despair," Ibid., December 10, 1957.
57 In this regard, Harel wrote (p. 111) that Eckstein had offered to serve as an informant for the security services inside the underground, but was very soon caught in their net. When there was some suspicion that he was playing a double game, the security services severed all relations with him.

"the desperate need to distract [the public's] attention in order to cover up tracks that might lead to the Black Hand itself. In an unsuccessful attempt to hide his complicity the guilty party tried to shift the blame to someone else—and that person was someone who had long been infuriating him."

Thirty-five years after these events, Uri Avneri told me that a meeting with the security service heads had convinced him that they were not involved in any way in Kasztner's murder. In the summer of 1957, however, he felt differently about how satanic the "apparatus of darkness" was.

XIII

Over the first few days following the assassination, the police arrested dozens of suspects and interrogated hundreds. Most of them were linked in one way or another to the Tzrifin Underground, and some were former members of the Stern Gang. Most of those who were arrested were released shortly afterwards. Less than two weeks after the attack, the police announced that three men were to be placed on trial. Ze'ev Eckstein and Dan Shemer were accused of Kasztner's murder—Eckstein, according to the police, had fired the fatal shots and Shemer drove the getaway car; Yosef Menkes was accused of heading the underground responsible for the murder. The police also announced that it would request an extension of attorney Yaacov Heruti's detention, and his lawyer hastened to state that there was no cause for the extension.[58]

The trial opened in the Tel Aviv District Court in April 1957. The judge was Nathan Kennet, the relieving president of the District Court. The verdict was pronounced on January 7, 1958, only a few days before the Supreme Court handed down its decision on the state's appeal against Halevi's verdict. The three were convicted of murder and given life sentences. Eckstein, the court ruled, "is the one who shot the deceased on the night in question;" Shemer was convicted as an accomplice to the murder, while Menkes was convicted of having persuaded Eckstein to commit the murder and having assigned the mission to him. The three appealed to the Supreme Court and their appeal was heard before a panel of three justices: the President Olshan, and Justices Zussman and Landau. On December 17, 1958, the three judges

---

58 "Dr. Kasztner Died of His Wounds 12 Days after an Attempt on His Life," *Ma'ariv*, March 15, 1957.

rejected the appeal.[59] Heruti, who was accused of having led the underground, was acquitted after a long, exhausting trial.

But the three men did not serve the full term of their sentences. The battle over their pardon focused mainly on Menkes, who persistently claimed he was innocent and had been convicted only because the "provocateur Eckstein" had informed on him, and that he was being discriminated against in prison in comparison to Eckstein and Shemer. His wife, who from time to time went to Jerusalem to stage a sit-down strike in front of the presidential residence and the home of the Minister of Justice, also prevented the affair from being removed from the public agenda.

Isser Harel brought the issue of Menkes' pardon to Ben-Gurion's attention. About their meeting on November 26, 1962, Ben-Gurion wrote:

> Isser raised the problem of Eckstein, one of Kasztner's murderers, who is behaving well in prison [...Israel] Eldad and [M.K. Yohanan] Bader guarantee his good behavior if he is released. They have been in prison now for five years, and in Isser's view it would be right to pardon them. The third man as well. I asked for information about the Kasztner family. He has a fifteen-year-old daughter, who is enrolled in the [kibbutz movement] teachers college. [Kasztner's] widow would certainly be displeased by the parole. She is barely eking out a living.

Another attempt to obtain a pardon for the three was made by Yehoshua Cohen, of the Stern Gang, a member of Kibbutz Sede Boker and a close friend of Ben-Gurion. He raised the subject in a conversation with Ben-Gurion on November 29, 1962, in which he described Menkes' poor mental state and his family's desperate situation. "Yehoshua visited me," Ben-Gurion wrote in his diary, "[and told me that] Menkes is on the verge of insanity. His release may halt his mental deterioration." On the rest of the conversation, he wrote:

> I told him I had received an assessment of the situation from Amos [Manor], who suggests that maybe the punishment should be reduced from life imprisonment to 15 years. He said that Menkes' two friends are behaving properly and their sentence should be lightened, but that raises the matter of the Kasztner family. His daughter, who was devastated by the murder [classified], was abroad a lot, and has now returned. For Mrs. Kasztner too, their release would come as a terrible blow. On the other

---

59 Harel, *The Truth About Kasztner's Murder*, pp. 186–264.

hand, it seems to him that it's an injustice to Menkes' wife and family—what wrong did they do? And the problem is not a simple one. Manor suggests the sentence be reduced to fifteen years, which means they would be released after serving ten years, in another four years. Yehoshua believes that if Menkes stays in prison another four years he will go out of his mind, because he's already on the verge of insanity. I asked him if there's any reason to fear he may commit some crazy act if he gets out. He replied that it's possible, but that he and his friends will be on guard.

Two months later, on January 20, 1963, the subject came up again in a conversation between the prime minister and senior officials of the security services. Once again, he weighed the suffering of the Menkes family against that of the Kasztner family, and finally decided to meet with Kasztner's widow and daughter.

The meeting took place on February 22, 1963. According to Ben-Gurion, Suzi agreed unreservedly to Menkes' release; her mother did not object, but gave her consent with a heavy heart. "I was surprised by my daughter's position," Bodiya said, "but didn't want to try to influence her." She herself, however, was angered by the dilemma they had presented her with. She told Ben-Gurion, "Don't expect that from me. I know that in any case the murderers will be released. At the most, they'll sit in prison another few years. That won't bring me back my husband. But no one should expect this from me."

In reply to Ben-Gurion's question, the daughter said she felt no hate for Menkes, she didn't even know what he looked like, but she had read that he has three children, and they surely need him. Afterwards, she was silent for a moment, looked straight into the face of the tired old man sitting opposite her, and said to him: "My father will never return. At least their father can return to them." Ben-Gurion, visibly moved by the words of this 16-year-old girl, made a gesture not at all typical of him. He rose from his chair, went over to her and kissed her on the forehead.[60]

Three days later, on February 25, Ben-Gurion told Cohen about the conversation and, in his presence, called Justice Minister Dov Joseph to inform him of his intent to pardon Menkes. Joseph was not completely comfortable with this decision. In a diary entry dated February 25, 1963, Ben-Gurion wrote, "Joseph doesn't accept Manor's suggestion, he opposes the idea of a pardon. He

60 Oferi; Yosef Lapid, "People in the News" (Yiddish), *Letzte Neiyes*, November 10, 1963; "President Reduces Prison Sentences of Shtarks, Menkes, Shemer and Eckstein," *Ma'ariv*, May 23, 1963.

suggests sending Menkes for a psychiatric evaluation." But on April 5, Cohen told the Prime Minister that Joseph had recommended to President Yitzhak Ben-Zvi (who died shortly afterwards), that he commute Menkes' sentence, thus allowing his release after serving six years. Ben-Gurion promised to talk to Joseph about having Menkes released by Independence Day.

In the end, not only Menkes, but Shemer and Eckstein as well, were released from prison that same summer. On May 23, 1963, on his first day in office, Zalman Shazar, the new President of Israel, signed the pardon. Shemer was released the same day; the sentence of the other two was commuted to ten years, and thereafter reduced by a third, they were released on November 6, 1963—six years and eight months after they were arrested.

XIV

Less than one year after Kasztner's assassination, the curtain rose on the final act. It was a breathtaking drama, but no less than that, it was a nerve-wracking one. In January 1958, the Supreme Court handed down its decision on file 232/55—the appeal filed by the State against Halevi's verdict, file 124/53. Since Kasztner's murder was still so fresh, the police adopted very strict security measures. Dozens of officers and policemen were deployed in the corridors leading to the courtroom as well as in the room itself.

Five judgments were read out during the hearing. The first, by Justice Shimon Agranat, was read on January 15; it was over 130 pages long and very detailed. It was a complete antithesis to Judge Halevi's verdict and totally overturned it. It is not surprising, therefore, that Shalom Rosenfeld wrote:

> This is the day Kasztner was hoping for—but never lived to see. This is the day on which Supreme Court Justice S. Agranat not only fully and absolutely reversed the grave conclusions reached by the President of the District Court, Dr. B. Halevi, but also completely rehabilitated the name of Dr. Israel Kasztner, and enshrined him as the most dedicated rescue worker of his community. Where Dr. Halevi saw treason and malice, Dr. Agranat saw good faith and devotion[61].

> All the murk and darkness in the lower court's verdict turned into a dazzling white in the verdict of the higher court.

---

61 *Ma'ariv*, January 16, 1958.

Absolute acquittal versus absolute conviction.

Justice Agranat's main criticism of Halevi's verdict can be summed up as "knowledge gained from hindsight." He alleged that Judge Halevi examined Kasztner's actions and considerations based on what we now know about the sequence of events. He did so instead of examining the extent to which [Kasztner's] considerations were logical and reasonable under the circumstances prevailing in Budapest of 1944:

> In my view the main danger in attempting to objectively judge the behavior of "dramatis personae" from the past—including the not so distant past—is that one tends to fail to place oneself in their situation; to evaluate the problems that they faced as they had evaluated them; to sufficiently take account of the conditions of the time and the place in which they lived, and to understand those lives as they themselves understood them. Hence, anyone who undertakes such a task—whether he be an historical researcher or a judge—must make a concerted effort to set aside his previous views [...] and aspire to adopt a viewpoint that is independent of the events he is judging [...] And I am convinced that one of the weaknesses in the above-mentioned opinions of the learned judge is [...] that when reaching a conclusion about the motives that influenced the late [Dr. Kasztner] in certain stages of his negotiations with the Nazis—he was not always successful in evading that danger of making judgments based on "knowledge gained from hindsight."

Since he considered the matter from a different vantage point, Agranat's conclusions were in stark contrast to those reached by Halevi. Unlike Halevi, whose standpoint was absolute and abstract, Agranat tried to place himself in Kasztner's shoes to understand what had prompted him to act as he did—in real time and under the same circumstances. For example, on the question of whether Kasztner's failure to tell the heads of the community all he knew about what was in store for the Jews of Hungary, when he visited Cluj in the first week of May, really did show he had become a Nazi tool, he said:

> Kasztner was entitled to consider that disclosing the "news of Auschwitz" to the Jewish leaders in Cluj would not only fail to lead to any successful rescue attempt, but also that if, in the wake of this information, any such acts of resistance, interference or mass escape were tried—acts that also endangered the lives of the perpetrators—they would destroy any

remaining chance of the success of the said negotiations. As long as he believed that this line of action was the sole means likely to secure the lives of the majority of the Jews in the provinces—and not only of most of the Jews of Cluj—and that on May 3 the time had not yet come to abandon [that line], **then it was reasonable for him to act, during the above visit, as he acted** [emphasis added].[62]

Later, in addition to this general argument, Agranat raised a concrete question: "Was [Halevi] right in his basic assumption, that the immediate motive for Kasztner's conduct […] was to rescue the individuals he favored by means of the 'Bergen-Belsen plan'?" His reply was unequivocal:

> I have arrived at the opinion that [Halevi] was wrong in making this assumption, since the facts […] clearly show that Kasztner's effort were aimed, at all the important times, at rescue, and rescue on a large scale, of **all of** Hungary's Jews, and that the implementation of the 'Bergen-Belsen plan,' which was intended for only a small number of Jews, always remained but one part of this aim and never became his sole objective.[63]

Just as he rejected Judge Halevi's conclusions on these matters, he also reversed his ruling on others, including some highly charged and sensitive issues such as the degree to which Kasztner's "collaborative" conduct prevented widespread rescue attempts, and the parachutists' episode, including the Hannah Szenes' story. He also refuted those of Halevi's statements that were based on the testimony of "character witnesses," including Moshe Krausz. The only point on which Agranat accepted Halevi's position was on Kasztner's testimony in Kurt Becher's favor. "[Kasztner's] intervention on Becher's behalf," he wrote, "by means of the affidavit, played an important role in his [Becher's] release by the Allies." In summing up, Justice Agranat stated that the things Gruenwald wrote in his newsletter were not "fair criticism" but "words of libelous abuse which bear no resemblance whatsoever to the expression of criticism in the public interest." He also announced that he had accepted the appeal of the Attorney General and found the defendant guilty of four of the five counts in the indictment, adding, "the token sentence […] passed by the President of the District Court is [hereby] repealed."[64]

---

62 *Verdict of the Supreme Court*, p. 68.
63 Ibid., p. 39 and pp. 47–48.
64 Ibid., pp. 126–129.

XV

The President of the Supreme Court, Justice Yitzhak Olshan, wrote the second judgment. It was a brief judgment, in which Justice Olshan concurred with the conclusions reached by Justice Agranat. Olshan chose not to devote the greater part of his judgment to Halevi's verdict, but to the way in which he conducted the trial. His criticism was harsh, and coming from the man at the apex of the judicial pyramid, it carried special weight. He stated that Halevi had allowed irrelevant testimony and "lengthy examinations on trivial matters, which caused the trial to drag on far too long," had admitted hearsay evidence even from people no longer alive and intervened far too much in the cross-examination of the witnesses.[65]

Justice Moshe Silberg wrote the third judgment. It differed from the previous two, since it, on the whole, accepted Judge Halevi's verdict. The key question Silberg addressed was: "What interest [...] did Eichmann and Krumey anticipate and hope to gain from the agreement to rescue the [chosen passengers of the rescue train]?" After rejecting a few possible answers—for example, that [money] was the main incentive behind their offer—Silberg concluded:

> Since the Nazis and the 'bloodhound Eichmann'—as he called himself—at their head, desired with all their hearts and souls not to leave one Jew alive on the soil of Hungary; and since it was not [the money], or contact with the West, or bait [with which to catch] Brand that motivated them to save a few prominent [Jews], there is but one unavoidable conclusion—that the purpose of the rescue was extermination, and that by promising this minute rescue, they wished to facilitate total extermination; To make it easier, in what way? By misleading the victims and keeping them sedated until they were butchered.[66]

This conclusion led Silberg to another—the 'big' rescue plan never existed and at a time when Kasztner was so totally engrossed in it that he lost all sense of proportion toward the 'small' plan, to save a number of prominent Jews, it quickly turned out, and not merely from "knowledge gained in hindsight," that the Nazis were only mocking Kasztner and the victims and had never really taken the 'big' plan seriously. Based on a combination of

---

65 Shalom Rosenfeld, "The Vindication vs. The Conviction," *Ma'ariv*, January 17, 1958.
66 *Verdict of The Supreme Court*, pp. 135–137.

these conclusions, Silberg charged Kasztner with "having acted in accordance with the German line [and thus binding] himself, hand and foot, to his Nazi masters and knowingly, albeit unwillingly, helping them to expedite the extermination." However, although this judgment was consistent with Halevi's ruling, the two were still not completely analogous. Silberg took exception to Halevi's statement that Kasztner had "sold his soul to the devil," because even the 'learned President' "does not actually utter the **prima facie** accusation implied by that deadly statement, and does not say that Kasztner willingly assisted in the extermination of 600,000 Jews [emphasis in original]."[67]

Later, the relieving president of the Supreme Court, Shneur Z. Cheshin, read his judgment, in which he concurred with Justice Agranat.

Justice David Goitein, who vacillated, wrote the last judgment. On the one hand, he wrote, "it is clear that if [Kasztner] had been pressured by the thought that any means justified the aim of rescuing a small group of prominent Jews, then the learned President of the District Court was right in describing Dr. Kasztner as a Nazi collaborator." But, on the other hand, if his aim was to rescue whoever could be rescued, and hence was forced to submit to the deeds of the Nazis, then my learned colleague Justice Agranat is right in justifying his actions, and it is impossible to decide between the two." Despite his hesitation, Goitein finally decided to accept the Attorney General's appeal.

After the judgments were read, the five justices decided unanimously to reject the appeal of the Attorney General on the fourth charge, namely, Kasztner's testimony "to save the war criminal (Becher) from punishment after the war." In the matter of "collaboration with the Nazis," the Court decided to accept the appeal by a majority of four to one (Moshe Silberg). The justices then retired for a brief consultation, after which the defendant Malkiel Gruenwald was read his new sentence—a one-year prison term, suspended, and a fine of 200 liras.

XVI

For the Kasztner family, the Supreme Court's verdict was a sad victory that came too late. "With the verdict of the Supreme Court," his widow said, "my husband has been vindicated," and she saw in "the decision of the Supreme Court justices, the right, just and humane conclusions." Afterwards, she

---

67 Ibid., pp. 131–133.

added in a barely audible voice that she was very sorry that her husband had not lived to hear his name cleared, but nonetheless, after years of unbearable pain and suffering, the decision had caused her and her daughter a great deal of satisfaction.

After the verdict was handed down, hundreds of visitors came to the Kasztner home at 6 Emmanuel Boulevard to congratulate the family; the widow received them all, dressed in black. Dozens of flower bouquets were delivered to her home, including one from the Speaker of the Knesset, Joseph Sprinzak. Among the scores of letters and telegrams, one was particularly moving. On January 18, after the verdict had been pronounced, the Attorney General, Haim Cohn, wrote the following letter to Kasztner's widow:

> Dear Madam!
> Please allow me, too, to be among those who are congratulating you this day and to express my deep sorrow that the late Dr. Kasztner did not live to see his victory.
> May you and your daughter find consolation in the fact that the injustice done him has been remedied and that his name and memory have been honored.[68]

The family also tried to persuade the prime minister, David Ben-Gurion, to say a few words to clear Kasztner's name. With this aim in mind, Yehoshua Kasztner, Israel's brother, wrote asking him to issue an appropriate statement about "the triumph over the dark, destructive forces in the country and their plots." The request was made after he had written [to Ben-Gurion] that his brother had told him about "his last visit to you in Sede Boker and how understanding you had been with regard to the matter and about his mission."

Ben-Gurion's reply to this request was evasive and to some extent also surprising. After stating that he "was very familiar with the 'devotees of pure virtues' who slandered your brother, and knows their filthy plots," he wrote:

> Even at the time, I was not really familiar with the efforts to rescue the Jews of Nazi-occupied Europe, even though I was chairman of the Jewish Agency Executive during those years. My main activity was centered on mobilizing world Jewry to establish a Jewish state, and several members of the Jewish Agency Executive are far more knowledgeable than I am about

---

68 "Elizabeth Kasztner: The Judges' Conclusions are Correct, Just and Humane," *Davar*, January 19, 1958; I was given Cohn's letter by Suzi Kasztner-Michaeli.

what was being done then to rescue European Jewry. Therefore, I would be reluctant to take it upon myself to determine what the facts are.[69]

Unlike Ben-Gurion, Justice Minister Pinhas Rosen did react. In a personal letter addressed to "My dear Haim Cohn," he congratulated him, "upon the end of the nightmare, namely the trial [...] and on your great success." He went on to write:

> Even you yourself did not always rightly assess Kasztner, and were influenced by his shortcomings as a witness, which were surely a result of the confusing and lengthy examination. But in essence, Kasztner was a simple man, in whom there was more good than bad, a man whose honor you redeemed and whose name you cleared—a very great deed.[70]

XVII

Public reactions were mixed, even polarized. Those people who had objected to Halevi's verdict, or had been hurt by it, were overwhelmed with relief and joyfully welcomed the Supreme Court's decision. In a special editorial *Davar* wrote, "Kasztner did not sell his soul to the devil," rather, he "gave up his soul, his very life, to the devil in order to rescue one more Jew from his hands." Moreover, according to *Davar*, Kasztner was guided by one, and only one, objective: "to save as many Jews as possible, to stave off as far as possible the [hand] brandishing the murderous axe [and] to postpone as far as possible the implementation of the slaughter." Even *Lamerchav*, which three years earlier had spearheaded the attack against Kasztner, now wrote that although the issue of Kasztner's testimony on behalf of Becher was still in the realms of the obscure, "this in no way detracts from the value of Dr. Kasztner's exoneration."[71]

Yosef Shefer wrote some particularly emotional words in the Kfar Hachoresh newsletter.[72] The verdict came as no surprise to him or to his fellow kibbutz members, he wrote, because no one knew better than they that "such an injustice could not prevail in Israel" and that "it would be unthinkable

---

69 Kasztner's brother's letter, dated January 19, 1958 and the Prime Minister's reply, dated February 2, ISA, 1366/5432/C.

70 Tiberius, January 17, 1958, ISA.

71 "Word of the Day," *Davar*, January 19, 1958; editorial, *Lamerchav*, January 19, 1958.

72 From *Newsletters to Newsletters*, No. 76, January 25, 1958.

for an existing nation to denounce itself in such a way." And yet "it was profoundly satisfying to hear and read that [all that] was said and written by our representative as a spontaneous reaction to that worthless verdict, has been confirmed by men whose knowledge, character and experience have placed them at the very apex of the Israeli judicial system." Shefer went on to harshly criticize the "parade of Cluj witnesses" brought by Tamir. He claimed that even if they were not influenced "by the unavoidable discrimination they suffered then because of the cruel selection process of the rescue effort," in the state of Israel, where the Holocaust is viewed only through "the heroic splendor of the Warsaw ghetto uprising," it is very hard for a survivor to come right out and say that even if he had known what was going to happen to him, "I still would have gone to the gallows like a lamb to the slaughter."

> But to us, who did not go to be massacred, but stood together with Israel Kasztner in the very heat of our efforts in those difficult days when we fought for every Jewish soul, it is no thanks to these witnesses that we live. We remember the troubled times of the deportations when we did our utmost to warn and to persuade them: "Save yourselves, escape while you can!" We spoke to individuals, because we had no way of speaking to the masses. And what were their replies? "We don't believe you, you are spreading false rumors, how can you imagine that we will go underground in our own country" [...] the Jews refused to believe.

Those who had supported Halevi's verdict and benefited from it, attacked the new verdict and claimed that it did not in fact exonerate Kasztner at all. *Haolam Hazeh*, the Communists and the radical right articulated this approach. *Haolam Hazeh* attacked the verdict and insisted that it did not amount to an acquittal of Kasztner. An unsigned article[73] claimed that despite "the refrain played again this week under the baton of a supreme conductor," which repeatedly claimed, "Dr. Kasztner's name has been cleared!" there remains "one thing that all five Supreme Court justices agreed on unanimously, and [that is] that Israel Kasztner's name was not cleared." The article went on to say that if Kasztner were alive, then based on the judgments of Justices Silberg and Goitein, "it would have been mandatory to open an investigation against him, and to try him on the charge of having collaborated with the Nazis in expediting their extermination operation, as Justice Silberg noted." The article concluded by emphatically stating that [even after that verdict]:

---

73 "Was Kasztner Really Cleared?" *Haolam Hazeh*, January 22, 1958.

In the eyes of history, Kasztner will remain a leader of the murdered masses who after the war saved one of the greatest murderers from punishment, and his name will continue to symbolize one of the blackest deeds in our people's history: collaboration with the enemy.

Haolam Hazeh also attacked the verdict from another angle, claiming that beyond the legal aspect, Justice Agranat's basic decisions reflected the *galuti* set of norms that characterizes the "existing regime" in the state of Israel. The "astounding decision" of Justices Olshan, Cheshin and Agranat, Avneri wrote,[74] in effect also created both a distinction and a separation between the 'prominent Jews', "those apparatchiks of the ghetto, whose seats were reserved in the last train," and the "masses in the ghetto," who stayed behind, alone, to face the annihilator." This theory, Avneri went on to say, has a far-reaching topical significance, since a similar approach can also be taken vis-à-vis a different public in another place. After all, in Israel too, "there is no dearth of the kind of people [...] who believe that the masses are riffraff, who ought to be deprived of free thought and freedom of expression, whose lives should be organized in advance through emergency laws and with the help of "repressive state agencies."

Opposite these justices, who are incapable of freeing themselves of the system of concepts and values that prevail in the society in which they live, Avneri pitched Justice Silberg, who, according to him, had risen to such a high level of greatness as to enable him to free himself of the concepts of his society.

Kol Ha'am interpreted and attacked the verdict in a similar fashion. First, it placed its emphasis on Silberg's judgment and on the fact that the Supreme Court had rejected the state's appeal in connection with Kasztner's affidavit in Becher's favor. *Kol Ha'am's* headline regarding the verdict read: "Supreme Court affirms: Kasztner saved a Nazi war criminal," and went on to list the main points of Silberg's judgment.[75]

The Herut Movement's paper also gave prominence to Justice Silberg's judgment, devoting little space to Chief Justice Olshan's. *Herut* claimed that the verdict had in no sense exonerated Kasztner, and it underscored the fact that "five justices unanimously concluded that Kasztner had saved a notorious war criminal."[76]

---

74 Ibid., "Re: The Prominent Jews."
75 *Kol Ha'am*, January 19, 1958. Regarding the publication of Silberg's verdict, see, for example: "Despairing of the People—Aiding in the Extermination," Ibid., February 6, 1958; "Those who Profit from Forgetting the Holocaust," Ibid., February 10, 1958.
76 *Herut*, January 19, 1958, on this matter, see: Yechiam Weitz, "The Herut Movement and the

The movement also expressed its position in a series of six articles by Knesset Member, Yohanan Bader, a senior member of the Herut Movement's hierarchy. The purpose of the six articles was to incontrovertibly stress that the verdict had not removed the stigma of 'collaboration' from Kasztner's name. To prove this, Bader, interestingly enough, chose to relate to Justice Agranat's judgment:

> In any case, is not Kasztner's image, as depicted by the honorable judge, similar to that of Petain and Laval (to mention [...] the least heinous of the collaborators)? They also thought it was their duty to save their people in the 'maximal' way, they also thought their obligation was not towards individuals, each and every one, but towards the public at large. They also thought that by non-resistance to evil, for the time being, they would ultimately succeed in saving their homeland to a maximal degree—and they did not hurry to meet the dangers as did that adventurer De Gaulle. And for that, they were condemned. Is Kasztner any better than they?

Shmuel Tamir's reaction was published when the verdict was pronounced;[77] he must certainly have carefully weighed each and every word. First, he argued, the Supreme Court had neither cleared Kasztner nor acquitted him. A situation had been created in which Kasztner was convicted by three judges (Halevi, Silberg and Goitein) and all the judges, "without exception, found him guilty of the terrible charge of willfully saving a notorious war criminal from punishment." Hence, Tamir demanded a public committee of inquiry, comprised of "judges, historians, rabbis and a statesman [...] to thoroughly and comprehensively investigate the deeds and blunders of the Jewish leaders in Europe, in the free world, and in Palestine, during the Holocaust."

Tamir never let the matter drop but continued to raise it even when he was very ill, in fact until his dying days. First, he demanded a renewal of the legal proceedings on the subject—particularly after Adolf Eichmann had been captured and brought to Israel and subsequently placed on trial. In July 1960, Tamir raised the possibility of reopening the trial since Eichmann, a key witness in the events discussed in it, was now in custody in Israel, and "no

---

Kasztner Trial," *Holocaust and Genocide Studies*, vol. 8/3 (December, 1994), pp. 349–371 and 363–364.

77 "Attorney Tamir: A Committee of Inquiry on the Holocaust Must be Appointed," *Herut*, January 19, 1958.

matter what he states in his testimony—can there be a more important witness than he in a trial about collaboration between him and Kasztner?"[78] Two years later, in 1962, he submitted a detailed memorandum to the Attorney General, and "in the name of my client, Malkiel Gruenwald, of Jerusalem," requested a "retrial, under clause 9 of the 1957 Courts Law, of the case: the Attorney General vs. Malkiel Gruenwald, criminal case 124/53 in the Jerusalem District Court, and criminal appeal 232/55 in the Supreme Court in Jerusalem." The Attorney General at that time, Gideon Hausner, advised the President of the Supreme Court, Olshan, to refuse the request.[79]

Later, particularly during the 1980s, Tamir focused mainly on his argument that the Israeli legal system had never cleared Kasztner's name, and persisted in defending the views he had aired at the time, which in later years had become increasingly unpopular. At the end of April 1987, when he was already terminally ill and only two months before he died, Tamir still saw fit to comment on a radio play that portrayed Kasztner as a victim. In a letter to the broadcasting system, he wrote that the play "is a distorted description, and an ignoble attempt to broadcast to the public a play based on a misrepresentation of the historical truth for political gain."[80]

According to a British Embassy report, drafted in Tel Aviv in early 1958, the majority of the Israeli public was aware of the fact that the political right had taken advantage of the Kasztner/Gruenwald trial in order to undermine the reliability of Mapai. In 1958, the right was even prepared to admit that in the Nazi hellhole that was 1940s Europe, it was imperative and unavoidable for Jewish Agency leaders to conduct sickening negotiations in order to rescue even the fewest of Jews from destruction.[81]

78 Shmuel Tamir, "After Eichmann's Capture—Will the Kasztner Trial be Renewed?" *Ya'ad, Iton Chofshi*, July 6, 1960.

79 "Request for Re-hearing of the Kasztner Trial," Tel Aviv, July 22, 1962; "Hausner against Renewal of Gruenwald Trial," *Ma'ariv*, October 28, 1962.

80 "An Historical Distortion," *Koteret Rashit*, April 28, 1987; Shmuel Tamir died on June 29, 1987, at the age of 64.

81 Report of the Advisor to the British Embassy in Tel Aviv, January 23, 1958, P.R.O/F.O. 391/34268.

Epilogue

The Supreme Court verdict did not put an end to the Kasztner affair. On the contrary, the story of Israel Kasztner's trial and death was one of those events—like the murder of Chaim Arlozoroff or the Lavon affair—that gives us no respite, but remains as sensitive as an exposed nerve.

In 1960–1961, with the capture and trial of Adolf Eichmann, the subject resurfaced and held the public's attention with even more intensity than during the 1980s and 1990s. In 1982 Israeli TV screened a documentary series about Kasztner; the Cameri theater staged the play *Kasztner* in 1985; in 1993 a proposal was made to name a Tel Aviv street after Kasztner, and in 1994, Israeli Television's drama department produced the series, "The Kasztner Trial." On each of these occasions, the debate flared up again and it seemed as if the wounds would never heal. The issue was so highly inflammable as to appear to have occurred now, rather than decades ago.

In the 1980s and 1990s, a marked change took place in the perception of Kasztner and his activity during the German occupation of Hungary. Israeli society began casting off the stereotypes and images of the fifties, which had prevented the public from viewing Kasztner in a rational, relevant manner. At that time it had been almost impossible for people to understand how courageous and daring he had to be, that man whom the judge had so callously described as having "sold his soul to the devil." Within only one generation, the perspective had completely changed, and the Israeli public, now more mature and confident, was capable of understanding that there was no shame in conducting negotiations, no matter with whom, if the objective was to save lives.

Much of what was said and written during the later debates was not only in defense of Kasztner; it actually depicted him as a hero. The survivors too, whose silence during the trial was more damning than any words, finally dared open their mouths and stepped up to speak. "I owe my life to Israel Kasztner and thanks to him, the lives of my daughters and grandchildren as well," wrote the survivor Helena Gafni to one of the newspapers. Reacting to what Shmuel Tamir had said, she added:

Kasztner was not a leader of Hungarian Jewry. He was not at all well known and had no influence on the Jews of Hungary, on their fate, on the path they chose. He was not an independent man who could do whatever he wanted. He was, after all is said and done, in the hands of the Germans, and if he succeeded under the prevailing circumstances, to achieve something, then he really was a hero.[1]

David Giladi wrote "Israel Kasztner revealed his courage when a sharp sword was laid on the neck of the Jewish masses, while the elected community leadership was hiding in holes and tunnels, or using their gold to buy a seat on a plane to Spain or Bucharest."[2]

This change in attitude related not only to what had happened in Budapest in 1944, but also to what had taken place in Jerusalem a decade later. Thus, according to the author, Hanoch Bartov, who described the absurdity that was the very existence of the trial as:

Only seven years from the day Nazi Germany was defeated, only four years after the establishment of the state of Israel. The country is impoverished; immigrants are arriving in their hundreds of thousands. There is no housing for them, no jobs for them, and no food for them. There is a kind of terrible confusion—people speak in seventy languages, struggling for their very existence, torn between the nightmares of the recent past and fears for the present and the future. That is the reality into which Gruenwald's newsletter was circulated, which Tamir cynically exploited to smash the "regime" and the Sharett government.

But a distinction must be drawn between Kasztner's activity in saving Jews during the war and some aspects of his behavior after the war. The affidavits he wrote in favor of Kurt Becher and other SS officers were particularly disturbing and the matter resurfaced with great intensity early in 1995 after an embarrassing and completely uncalled-for interview Becher gave to Israeli Channel Two TV host Ilana Dayan. In the ensuing stormy debate, even Kasztner's staunchest supporters, including those who regarded him as the man who saved the largest number of Jews during the Holocaust, found it hard to come up with a reasonable explanation for his motives in providing the affidavits. Although allegations made by Shmuel Tamir's supporters, especially those of his relatives, that "Kasztner had saved Becher from the

---

1   "Kasztner was a Hero," Letters to the Editor, *Ha'aretz*, May 17, 1982.
2   "Let's Not Pick at our Wounds," *Ma'ariv*, May 26, 1982.

gallows," can be easily dismissed as cheap demagogy, this still does not make Kasztner's reasons any less perplexing.

As I see it, the entire episode of the affidavits at Nuremberg provides an acute expression of an outstanding feature of Kasztner's personality and of his inherent irregularity. He must have possessed some extraordinary traits to dare to enter the lion's den and to fraternize with SS officers, in particular when his hands were empty and he had nothing to offer in return for the Jews he wanted to save. To do this, Kasztner had to have courage and nerves of steel. But he also had to possess other, more problematic, traits—cunning and the ability to lie without batting an eyelid—traits, which are usually considered negative and harmful, but were absolutely vital in the hell that was Budapest.

In the postwar world, which had resumed normal life, these traits were a serious shortcoming. A man who assumed titles and honors he was not entitled to, obsessively tried to take center stage, and who, from time to time, also told lies, was perceived not as a hero, but as a deviant. For months on end during the war, Kasztner lived almost around the clock in the company of SS officers, ate with them, played cards with them and perhaps also shared women with them. This extraordinary experience raises the question—how did this period in his life affect Kasztner's character, his system of values, his worldview and his attitude to life? Did he regard it as a necessary evil, as part of his work to save the last survivors in the concentration camps, or as one of the glorious and most fascinating pages in his life story? It unquestionably had the effect of playing havoc with his world of norms and values.

His behavior during this period—the fact that he did not flee but after a trip to neutral, tranquil Switzerland, he returned to the Nazi hell, daring again and again to enter the office of the arch-murderer—shows he was able to draw on extraordinary strengths and inner resources. His biography is replete with expressions of his strength. In his short life, he had had to rebuild everything time after time, in new places within new cultures, new languages and unfamiliar rules of the game. That was the case in 1940, when he left the small, intimate town of Cluj where everyone knew him and moved to the large city of Budapest, where he was completely anonymous. That is how it was when the Germans occupied Budapest five years later, and then two years later, in 1947, when he left Europe and immigrated to Palestine, with its different, inhospitable climate. The fact that within a short time he managed to find a respectable position and connections in the top ranks of the government also shows his fortitude and his ability to survive and adapt. Even the last, cruelest test of all that he was forced to undergo did not succeed in breaking him. Even when he was accused of the most absurd and heinous crimes, withstood physical threats to his very existence and lost his self-confidence, he refused to give in. He did not leave the country and even rejected the tempting offer to move to a kibbutz until things calmed down. Those same nerves of steel that enabled him to carry out his activities in Budapest enabled him to endure the hell into which he was thrust in the sovereign state of the Jewish people.

In contrast to the attitude towards Kasztner, which over the years became more sympathetic, Shmuel Tamir lost much of his power and influence, and after the trial, his career was checkered. In 1964, he returned to the Herut movement and a year later was elected to the Sixth Knesset. In 1967, he left Herut again and founded a new political movement, called the Free Center. Following the Six Day War, he took his party to a position at the right end of the political map. In 1973, his party joined the newly founded Likud party, and left it in 1976, when, following the Yom Kippur War, Tamir suddenly showed signs of becoming moderate in his views. Then, when it seemed as if his political career was over, Tamir joined the Democratic Movement for Change and, in October 1977, was appointed Minister of Justice in Menahem Begin's cabinet. He filled this position successfully for three years, and in 1981, after his attempt to return to the Likud failed, he was forced to resign from political life and resumed work at his Tel Aviv law office. In 1987 he died following a prolonged illness at the age of 64.

During the last years of his life, he often referred to the Kasztner affair both in writing and in interviews. Despite the many years that had passed, the Israeli public's changed attitude to the Holocaust, and the fact that Kasztner himself had paid for the affair with his life, Tamir did not budge one inch from the position he held in the 1950s. He continued to view Kasztner as the "greatest Jewish Nazi-collaborator" and insisted that the sole significance of his negotiations [with the Nazis] was to assist in the annihilation of Hungarian Jewry. Reacting to the play *Kasztner*, he wrote:

> Kasztner chose life. He chose his own life and the life of the 'select group of privileged [Jews].' While nearly three-quarters of a million Hungarian Jews were being killed, the arch-annihilators—Eichmann, Becher, Krumey and Himmler—protected Kasztner from any harm and, towards the end of the war, brought him safe and sound to the Swiss border, so that the leader of the exterminated Jews would save them, the leaders of the extermination, from the gallows.[3]

---

3 "Trumpeldor or Kasztner?" *Ma'ariv*, May 26, 1982.

But this did not bring any closure to the connection between these two men. How ironic it was that while Tamir scathingly denounced Kasztner, turning him into a monster, he himself became a Kasztner. In his last public position he represented Minister of Defense Yitzhak Rabin in the negotiations for the release of Israeli prisoners of war captured in the Lebanon war. In May 1985, these negotiations culminated in the "Jibril deal"—the release of 1,100 terrorists in exchange for three Israeli soldiers. The fact that Tamir was one of the leading negotiators in brokering this problematic deal makes the comparison between him and Kasztner unavoidable. In the wake of the harsh criticism leveled against the deal, Nathan Donevitz suggested, "perhaps Tamir should consider some of the parallels between the Kasztner affair and the prisoner exchange agreement."[4] I first referred to the affair in an article entitled "Another Kasztnerian Dilemma,"[5] in which I argued that in discharging his duty, Tamir had found himself "in the center of a dilemma that to a great extent could be defined as a 'Kasztnerian dilemma.'" On one horn of that dilemma, there was the security of the country, its declared norms and the very core of its ethos, and on the other horn—a mother, who, according to his description, "suddenly faints on your desk."

In an article defending Kasztner's honor, Yosef Lapid, who knew and respected Kasztner, made the same comparison:

Shmuel Tamir, who knows exactly how Kasztner should have behaved towards little Eichmann, is the same Shmuel Tamir, who sold the great Jibril over a thousand terrorists in exchange for three [Israeli] prisoners of war. That Shmuel Tamir, who knows how Kasztner should have stood firm in the face of the extermination of hundreds of thousands of Hungarian Jews, is the same Shmuel Tamir, who described to us, in the editorial committee, the immense pressures brought to bear by the parents of the three prisoners—which he was unable to endure. I sat there, looking at Tamir's tormented face. He had not conducted the negotiations from a house in the Budapest ghetto in the midst of a horrible war, but from the calm fortress of the Ministry of Defense in Tel Aviv; not in a hotel belonging to the Gestapo, but in a deluxe hotel in Geneva; not out of fear and desolation confronting a powerful enemy, but out of a sense of power confronting a small group of terrorists. I saw the torments he was

4   "Arlozoroff, Kasztner and Lebanon," My Column, *Ha'aretz*, May 29, 1985.
5   *Chadashot*, June 11, 1985.

suffering, and I thought to myself: Now do you understand Kasztner? Now do you understand the injustice you did him?[6]

6   "Irrefutable Replies," *Ma'ariv*, October 11, 1985.

Sources and Bibiliography

Archival Sources

Ben-Gurion Research Center Archives (BGRCA)
Central Zionist Archives (CZA)
Israel State Archives (ISA)
The Jabotinsky Institute in Israel—Archive
Kibbutz Haogen Archive
Labor Archives
Labor Party Archives
Micha Caspi Archives
Public Record Office—London
United Kibbutz Movement Archives (UKMA)
Yad Vashem Photo Archive (YVPA)

Newspapers and Periodicals

Al HaMishmar (Hebrew)
Ashmoret—Journal of the Mapai Young Guard (Hebrew)
Bakibbutz (Hebrew)
Barkai (Hebrew)
Beterem (Hebrew)
Commentary
Davar (Hebrew)
Etgar (Hebrew)
Ha'aretz (Hebrew)
Haboker (Hebrew)
Hador (Hebrew)
Hamodi'a (Hebrew)
Haolam Hazeh (Hebrew)
Hapoel Hatza'ir (Hebrew)
Hatzofeh (Hebrew)

Herut (Hebrew)
Jewish Observer and Middle East Review
Kol Ha'am (Hebrew)
Koteret Rashit (Hebrew)
Lamerchav (Hebrew)
Letzte Neiyes (Yiddish)
Ma'ariv (Hebrew)
Mishmar (Hebrew)
Molad (Hebrew)
Newsletters to Newsletters
Panim el Panim (Hebrew)
The Jewish Chronicle
Rimon (Hebrew)
Smol (Hebrew)
Sullam (Hebrew)
Tevel (Hebrew)
Yedioth Ahronoth (Hebrew)
Zemanim (Hebrew)

Books and Articles

Ahimeir, Yosef, ed., *The Black Prince—Yosef Katznelson and the National Movement in the Thirties* (Hebrew), Tel Aviv: Jabotinsky Institute in Israel, 1983.

Alterman, Nathan, *On The Two Paths—Pages from the Notebook* (Dan Laor edited, explicated, and added an afterword.) (Hebrew), Tel Aviv: Hakibbutz Hameuchad Publishing House, 1989.

Aronson, Shlomo, *Hitler, the Allies, and the Jews*, Cambridge: Cambridge University Press, 2004.

Bader, Yohanan, *The Knesset and I* (Hebrew), Jerusalem: Edanim Publishing House, 1979.

Bauer, Yehuda, "Negotiations between Saly Mayer and Representatives of the SS from 1944–45," in Yisrael Gutman and Efraim Zuroff, eds., *Rescue Attempts During the Holocaust*, Jerusalem: Yad Vashem, 1977.

———, "Joel Brand's Mission" (Hebrew), *Yalkut Moreshet*, 26, November 1978.

———, *Jews for Sale? Nazi-Jewish Negotiations, 1933–1945*, New Haven and London: Yale University Press, 1994.

Ben-Gurion, David, *Toward the End of the Mandate—Memories (June 1946—March 1947)* (Hebrew), in Meir Avizohar, ed., Tel Aviv: Am Oved, 1993.

Benshalom, Rafi, *We Struggled for Life* (English translation by O. Cummings), Jerusalem: Gefen Publishing House, 2001.

Bondy, Ruth, *"Elder of the Jews": Jacob Edelstein of Theresienstadt*, New York: Grove Press, 1989.

———, *Felix—Pinhas Rosen and his Time* (Hebrew), Tel Aviv: Zmora, Bitan Publishing, 1990.

Braham, Randolph L., *The Politics of Genocide—The Holocaust in Hungary*, New York: Columbia University Press, 1981.

———, ed., *The Tragedy of Hungarian Jewry*, New York: The City University of New York Press, 1986.

——— and Katzburg, Netanel, *The History of the Holocaust— Hungary* (Hebrew), Jerusalem: Yad Vashem, 1991.

Brand, Hanzi and Joel, *Satan and the Soul* (Hebrew), Tel Aviv: Ladori Press, 1960.

Cohen, Asher, *The Halutz Resistance in Hungary 1942-1944*, New York: City University of New York Press, 1986.

Danzig, Hillel, "The Zionist Movement in Transylvania," *Encyclopedia of Jewish Communities in Romania* (Hebrew), vol. 2, Jerusalem: Yad Vashem, 1980.

Eldad, Israel, *The First Tithe* (Hebrew), Tel Aviv: The Veterans of Lehi Press, 2008.

Feurstein, Emil, "In His Nation's Service," Mordechai Arieli ed., *Natan Ottó Komoly: A Profile* (Hebrew), Kfar Glickson, 1970.

Gutman, Yechiel, *The Attorney General Versus the Government* (Hebrew), Jerusalem: Edanim Publishers, 1981.

Harel, Isser, *The Truth about Kasztner's Murder—Jewish Terrorism in the State of Israel* (Hebrew), Jerusalem: Edanim Publishers, 1985.

Heller, Yosef, *The Stern Gang—Ideology, Politics and Terror, 1940-1949*, London: Frank Cass, 1995.

Joseph, Dov, *The Dove and the Sword* (Hebrew), Ramat Gan: Massada Publishing House, 1975.

Kasztner, Israel, *Kasztner's Truth: Report of the Jewish Rescue Committee in Budapest, 1942-1945*, [no citation of place or date].

Keren, Moshe, *Passing and Permanent Problems* (Hebrew), Jerusalem, 1978.

Kolb, Eugen, "Bergen-Belsen Diary" (Hebrew), *Yalkut Moreshet*, 57, May 1994.

————, *Mission to the Diaspora, 1945–1948* (Hebrew), Efal: Yad Tabenkin, 1989.

Lau-Lavi, Naphtali, *Nation like a Lion* (Hebrew), Tel Aviv: Ma'ariv Press, 1993.

Lazar, David, *Leading Figures in Israel* (Hebrew), Tel Aviv: Amichi, 1954.

Olshan, Yitzhak, *Deliberations* (Hebrew), Jerusalem and Tel Aviv: Schocken Publishing House, 1978.

Palgi, Yoel, *A Great Wind a-Coming* (Hebrew), Tel Aviv: Am-Oved, 1977, second edition.

Prat, Immanuel, *The Great Trial—The Kasztner Affair* (Hebrew), Tel Aviv: Or Publishing, 1955.

————, *The Verdict in the Trial of the Attorney General vs. Malkiel Gruenwald* (Hebrew), Tel Aviv: Karni Publishing House, 1955.

Raphael, Yitzhak, *Not Easily Came the Light* (Hebrew), Jerusalem: Edanim Publishers, 1981.

Ronen, Avihu, *The Battle for Life—The Shomer Hatzair in Hungary 1944* (Hebrew), Givat Havivah, Yad Yaari, 1993.

Rosenfeld, Shalom, *Criminal File 124* (Hebrew), Tel Aviv: Karni Press, 1955.

Rotkirchen, Livia, "The Final Solution in its Final Stage," *Yad Vashem Studies*, vol. 8, 1971.

Segev, Tom, *The Seventh Million—The Israelis and the Holocaust*, New York: Henry Holt, 1991.

Sharett, Moshe, *Personal Diary* (Hebrew), Tel Aviv: Ma'ariv Press, 1978.

Shashar, Michael, *Haim Cohen, Supreme Court Judge* (Hebrew), Jerusalem: Keter Publishing House, 1989.

Sheffer, Gabriel, *Moshe Sharett—Biography of a Political Moderate*, Oxford: Clarendon Press, 1996.

Sofer, Sasson, *Begin—Anatomy of Leadership*, Oxford: Basil Blackwell, 1988.

Stauber, Ronny, "The Controversy in the Political Press Over the Kasztner Trial" (Hebrew), *Zionism*, 13, 1988.

Tamir, Shmuel, *Son of this Land* (Hebrew), Tel Aviv: Zmora, Bitan Publishing, 2002.

Vago, Bella, "The Intelligence Aspects of the Joel Brand Mission," *Yad Vashem Studies*, vol. 10, 1974.

Weissberg, Alex, *Advocate for the Dead—The Story of Joel Brand*, London: A. Deutsch, 1958.

Weitz, Yechiam, The Yishuv's Self-Image and the Reality of the Holocaust, *Jerusalem Quarterly*, vol. 48, Fall 1988.

————, Revisionist Criticism of the Yishuv Leadership During the Holocaust, *Yad Vashem Studies*, vol. 13, 1993.

————, "Changing Conceptions of the Holocaust: the Kasztner Case," *Studies in Contemporary Jewry*, vol. 10, 1994.

————, "The Herut Movement and the Kasztner Trial," *Holocaust and Genocide Studies*, vol. 8/3, December 1994.

————, "Between Warsaw and Budapest: Regarding the Term 'Resistance' in the Kasztner Trial" (Hebrew), *Dapim Lecheker Tekufat Hashoa* (Pages on Holocaust Research), 12, 1995.

————, *A Party Contends with its Failure—Mapai Faces the Elections to the Third Knesset* (Hebrew), *Cathedra*, 77, October 1995.

Weizmann, Chaim, *Trial and Error*, London: East and West Library, 1950.

Index